THE LAW'S CONSCIENCE

The Thornton H. Brooks
Series in American Law and Society

THE LAW'S CONSCIENCE

Equitable Constitutionalism in America

———

Peter Charles Hoffer

The University of North Carolina Press   *Chapel Hill and London*

Library of Congress Cataloging-in-Publication Data

Hoffer, Peter Charles, 1944–
   The law's conscience : equitable constitutionalism
in America / Peter Charles Hoffer.
      p.   cm.
   Includes bibliographical references.
   ISBN 0-8078-1919-0 (alk. paper).—
   ISBN 0-8078-4294-X (pbk. : alk. paper)
   1. Equity—United States—History.   2. United States—
Constitutional history.   I. Title.
KF399.H59   1990
342.73′029—dc20
[347.30229]   90-50016
                                                        CIP

The paper in this book meets the guidelines for perma-
nence and durability of the Committee on Production
Guidelines for Book Longevity of the Council on Library
Resources.
Manufactured in the United States of America
94   93   92   91   90   5   4   3   2   1
Portions of Chapter 2 have been published in somewhat
different form in the *Maryland Historical Magazine* 82
(1987) and in William Pencak and Wythe Holt, eds., *The
Law in America, 1607–1861* (New York, 1989).

For Abe Chayes,
who stands in the line of the great chancellors,
seeking justice for the oppressed by compelling
the conscience of the strong.

CONTENTS

PREFACE

Professionally written history cannot be objective in the manner of experimental science, but fair-minded history—a fair hearing to evidence and argument that opposes one's own tentative conclusions—is the hallmark of the scholar. In the language of the law, such fair-mindedness is the standard to which the rule of objectivity refers. I use the legal analogy because legal history has sometimes failed to sustain this standard of fairness. When professional lawyers use history in aid of their client's cause, they are wont to replace historical context with ellipses. Their profession's code of ethics requires acknowledgment of opposing arguments and citation of opposing authorities, but the whole point of a legal brief, including its historical materials, is to sustain a claim. Consequently, adversarial legal scholarship is often denigrated as "law-office history" by professional historians.[1]

Were this obloquy confined to the work product of practicing counsel, it would not be prejudicial to the enterprise of legal history. Unfortunately, on occasion historians, law professors, and judges working in the penumbras of law-office history also transgress the standard of fair-mindedness. Historians are regularly employed as expert witnesses, for example, in disputes over the discriminatory practices of great corporations. These scholars advance their side's case.[2] Constitutional writers more interested in providing evidence for a point of law than for scholarly exploration of that point also may violate the standard of fair-mindedness. Over the past three decades, the Fourteenth Amendment seems to have attracted a goodly portion of law-office history. Judges seeking to support an opinion already prepared have allowed outdated and questionable works to serve as citations.[3] There are valid controversies about the history of much of the Constitution; a fair-minded scholarship requires that the arguments of other scholars be given a full hearing and that refutation rely on thorough acquaintance with primary sources.

Admittedly, my censure of law-office history is overbroad. It ignores what legal scholars and counsel are trying to do with history. They use historical materials to further their professional endeavors. History as such has little independent value to them unless they decide to assign it some formal weight in their strategy of textual construction.[4] Lawyers, judges, and judge's clerks do not thus set out to misrepresent the past. When their historical research does not support a legal argument, they often forego the historical argument, sometimes conceding that their position cannot stand on historical ground.[5] Even when such historical research is requested by a judge of his or her law clerk in order to refute the legal history in another judge's draft opinion, that research can match the most exacting professional standards.

My indictment of law-office history must also be mitigated by the recognition of a distinct characteristic of legal and constitutional materials. The past actions of courts, the opinions and decrees that make up "precedent" or "common law," live on in ways unlike other historical sources. A modern court can and quite often will resuscitate old legal materials and breathe new life into past cases. Rarely is an old case as definitively discarded as *Plessy v. Ferguson*[6] was by *Brown v. Board of Education*.[7] Even the most disinterested disinterment of a line of cases, or, in this book, a way of thinking about a line of cases, thus goes beyond mere scholarship. It verges on a legitimating exercise, rationale, and defense. Given the sustained life of old cases, the appearance of some special pleading in a work of legal history may be inevitable.

In our own time, the Scylla and Charybdis of legal history seem to me to be too critical an appraisal of our predecessors on the one hand and too naive a faith in progress and enlightenment on the other.[8] The former exhibits itself in an all-encompassing cynicism about the racial attitudes, economic motives, and intellectual honesty of earlier American courts, counsel, and legal writers. The latter is merely a species of "Whig" celebratory history, whether its objects are the emergence of an energetic capitalism, an administrative welfare state, or a system of modern legal pleading. If there is much to censure in our legal past and much to regret in our present legal system, comment on these questions is as much the province of the historian as the jurist, the political scientist, and the law professor.

At the same time, the historian must not let commitment to a particular policy or its reform dictate a reading of past documents that distorts their sense or ignores their context.

Were this a treatise on the medieval English chancellor, the origin of the doctrine of "constructive trusts," or some other highly focused subject, I hardly would have burdened the reader with the foregoing remarks. Students of the Warren Court and its constitutional jurisprudence will concede that by any historical measure the Warren Court had greater impact on our constitutional law than any of its predecessors, save John Marshall's Court, and no previous Court had more influence on the way ordinary Americans lived. Warren Court rulings in civil rights, voter reapportionment, privacy, criminal law, and employment cases were not mere adumbrations of constitutional principles; they profoundly changed the way millions of Americans got an education, found a job, participated in politics, and enjoyed the benefits of the welfare state. For its intrusion into Americans' lives the Warren Court was both extolled and excoriated.

The first of its great cases, *Brown*, set that pattern. From the president of the United States to the demonstrators in the streets of Little Rock, more Americans came to know and respond to the work of the Supreme Court after 1954 than ever before. The fading "Impeach Earl Warren" billboards one still encounters on the back roads of South Carolina are a memento of that feeling. There were no comparable roadside signs calling for the impeachment of Chief Justice William Howard Taft, despite the widespread criticism of his Court's voiding of Progressive economic regulation. Even Roger Taney's tragic misreading of the Court's role in slavery cases, a major cause of the Civil War, did not bring him such ill-tempered notoriety in the North as Chief Justice Earl Warren's ringing denunciation of segregation brought in the Deep South. In the mid-1950s popular feeling ran ahead of scholarly criticism, but lawyers, policy analysts, journalists, and historians were quick to join in the controversy over *Brown*. Warren had intended to write an opinion any woman or man could understand, and he succeeded.[9]

Successive generations of constitutional scholars, riding new waves of interpretation, have flooded the libraries with books and articles on *Brown* and its progeny. Scholars routinely square their theories with the result in *Brown*, as do nominees for federal judicial office. One may say that making sense of *Brown* has become the central enterprise in modern American constitutional jurisprudence. Anyone writing a history of equity and the Constitution who focuses on *Brown* and the controversy surrounding it will find it impossible to escape all suspicion of law-office history.

During nearly a decade of research and writing, I have come to believe that *Brown* and its legacy may or may not be good constitutional law but they are very good constitutional equity. They rest on a long line of cases defining the province of equitable remedies and the legitimate discretion of chancellors in providing those remedies. What is more, that way of thinking about harms and remedies can be generalized to comprehend the development of an equitable approach to constitutional quarrels. The book that follows explores the roots and flowering of equitable constitutionalism—the law's conscience. Its core is six chapters of legal and constitutional history, tracing equity from early modern English courts through the civil rights cases of the 1950s, 1960s, 1970s, and 1980s. An epilogue applies the chapters to the affirmative action cases of our own day. These chapters are preceded by a prologue arguing that *Brown* was an equity suit as well as a constitutional one and by an introduction, "What Is Equity?"

In that same spirit of affirmative action and equity, and mindful of both my publisher's and my own commitment to gender neutrality, I have attempted to balance historical reality (in which chancellors are portrayed uniformly as male) with situational neutrality (in which individuals could be either male or female).

Throughout, this book tells two stories. The first soars in the ether of political and constitutional ideas, above civil wars and revolutions, in search of the ideal of public trusteeship, equal protection, and realistic justice. The second slogs the legal terrain, doggedly following the trail of equity practice through courtrooms, law schools, and legislative chambers. Each of these stories is important in its own right, but I join them here because, like the doubled helix that binds our genetic material into a whole, they appear to cross each other at critical points. In those historical moments when theories of mutual fairness spoke to working lawyers, and the authority of chancellors turned theory into reality, the law's conscience was the conscience of the people.

ACKNOWLEDGMENTS

Scholarly acknowledgments are the markers of debts we can never repay. We inflict our manuscripts upon our colleagues, borrowing their time and expertise. They read, comment, cajole, and share in our efforts for little recompense other than a word or two of thanks on the printed page. Many colleagues and friends have read parts of this manuscript. To John Arthur, Milner Ball, Mike Belknap, Les Benedict, Bob Bone, Bob Brugger, Abe Chayes, Terry Fisher, Owen Fiss, Dick Helmholtz, Wythe Holt, Harold Hyman, David Konig, Paul Kurtz, Ed Larson, Bill McFeely, Earl Maltz, Bill Nelson, Bob Pratt, Ed Purcell, Lew Sargentish, Steve Subrin, Bill Stueck, Jeff Tulis, and Ted White go my thanks for thoughtful and caring suggestions. Bob Bone, Owen Fiss, Paul Gewirtz, Bill LaPiana, Bill Nelson, Don Nieman, and Steve Subrin shared unpublished manuscripts with me. N. E. H. Hull and Mark Summers did extra duty, reading an early version of the entire manuscript and forcing me to confront my own preconceptions of the work. Stan Katz kept me on the straight and narrow throughout the many years of the project, insisting on and helping to arrange for my year at Harvard Law School as a Liberal Arts Fellow. I am grateful to him and to Lew Sargentish, director of the program, for the fellowship. At Harvard it was my great fortune to study with Morty Horwitz, Abe Chayes, Terry Fisher, Randy Kennedy, and Cass Sunstein over the course of a year I will always treasure. To the other students in "Experimental Section I," particularly Liz Koppelman, who accepted me and shared their experiences with me, I am equally grateful. Morris Cohen, librarian of the Yale Law School Library, offered a helping hand when it was greatly needed, and Mark Schultz, David Negus, and Williamjames Hoffer checked footnotes and chased down citations. Though all of these kind friends and colleagues had some part in the book that follows, none of them should be blamed for its errors. These are mine alone.

No historian can succeed without the aid and comfort of librarians and archivists. I am happy to have the chance to thank the staffs at the Library of Congress, Manuscripts Division; the Harvard Law School Library; the Sterling Library at Yale University; the University of Pennsylvania Archives; the Rutgers Law School Library—Camden; the library systems of the University of Georgia, the University of Pennsylvania, and Princeton University; the State Department of Archives and History of South Carolina in Columbia; the State Archives of North Carolina in Raleigh; the State Archives in Annapolis, Maryland; the State Library in Trenton, New Jersey; and the State Library in Albany, New York. I am grateful to Professor Paul Freund of Harvard Law School for permission to quote from the Felix Frankfurter Papers; to the Harvard Law School Library for permission to quote from the papers of Roscoe Pound, Austin Wakeman Scott, and Zechariah Chafee; to the Yale University Library for permission to quote from the Charles E. Clark Papers; and to the University of Pennsylvania Archives for permission to quote from the George Wharton Pepper Papers.

Support of a more material sort for this project came from the National Endowment for the Humanities, the Humanities Center of the University of Georgia, the Harvard Law School, and the departments of history at the University of Georgia and Princeton University. This book would not have been possible without the assistance of these kind benefactors.

Portions of the book were originally presented as papers at the New-York Historical Society conference on early American law, the Charles Warren Center, the New York University School of Law seminar in legal history, the Society for the History of the Early American Republic, and the University of Georgia Humanities Center. To the organizers of all these sessions, I am grateful.

Finally, my editor at the University of North Carolina Press, Lew Bateman, encouraged, counseled, underwrote, and understood my efforts from their inception nearly a decade ago. I have dedicated this book to another, but no one had more to do with its final form than Lew.

THE LAW'S CONSCIENCE

PROLOGUE *BROWN V. BOARD OF EDUCATION*, 1954

Yet it is a people plundered and despoiled:
All of them are trapped in holes,
Imprisoned in dungeons.
They are given over to plunder, with none to say, "give back."
If only you would listen to this,
Attend and give heed from now on.
—*Isaiah 43:22*

The opinion came down on May 17, 1954. Warned by one of their number, reporters hurried into the marble courtroom from the makeshift pressroom on the ground floor. Word had filtered as well to the law clerks laboring in the justices' chambers above. The clerks joined the densely packed audience. The justices were seated in their places when the chief, Earl Warren, began to read. Though dying from heart disease, Justice Robert Jackson had left his hospital bed to occupy his seat and visually reinforce the unanimity so strenuously won and so vital on this occasion. The Court's deliberation in the case had stretched over a year and a half; indeed, the history of the case reached back to the beginnings of the nation, echoed through the Civil War and the Reconstruction amendments to the Constitution,[1] and reverberated in the rise and ebb of Jim Crow before it came at last to the highest court.[2]

Brown v. Board of Education took two centuries to decide and ten minutes to read. Finding the history of the Fourteenth Amendment "inconclusive" and precedent inadequate on the question of segregation of elementary schools, the Court looked to the "effect of segregation itself on public education"—in effect, to factual demonstrations of real injury.[3] Among these were results of sociological experiments, but far more telling for the justices was their common sense that segregated schools marked their students with a sense of inferiority that lasted a lifetime. Evidence of inferior facilities and lower per capita expenditures for black schools proved bad faith on the part of local school boards supposedly operating under the separate-but-equal rule; but physical inequalities, at least in theory, could be remedied without altering that rule. The stigma of officially sponsored discrimination could not be erased by building better schoolhouses for black pupils.[4]

The opinion of the Court in Brown has an oracular tone, as though the nine judges reached up into the heavens and brought down justice. In fact, courts, even Supreme Courts, cannot speak unless there is a "case or controversy" brought before them.[5] The cases heard and determined in Brown had a history of their own, a human dimension, with litigants and litigators carrying the dispute before the highest tribunal. If there were no villains in that story, there surely were heroes. The petitioners themselves dared calumny to demand equality. The lawyers of the Legal Defense Fund (LDF) of the National Association for the Advancement of Colored People, led by the veteran litigator Thurgood Marshall and younger attorneys like Spottswood Robinson, Robert Carter, Louis Redding, Charles Black, Jr., and Jack Greenberg, represented the parents in all five suits against segregated public schools. They argued before the district federal courts, brought their clients' claims to the panels of the federal circuit courts, and stood at the bar of the Supreme Court to ask for immediate, practical relief. They were not dreamers or philosophers, but working counsel representing clients with slender resources and specific needs.[6] The Court, divided in mind, ordered reargument on a series of questions. The LDF reminded the Court that its petitioners wanted a declaration that all state-sponsored segregation was unlawful.[7] When linked to a case or controversy, such "declaratory" relief is permissible and often accompanies a plea for injunctive relief.[8] The Court did not issue a declaratory judgment; instead, the opinion in Brown delayed enforcement until the parties could return to Court and speak to the question of relief.

The two opinions in Brown v. Board of Education—the first, in 1954, finding that the state-enforced policy of separate but equal in elementary education was inherently unequal and violated the Fourteenth Amendment to the Constitution, and the second, in 1955, directing lower federal courts to implement desegregation with "all deliberate speed"[9]—now stand as a landmark in American constitutional history. The four cases joined under the title shifted not only the boundaries of federalism, pitting federal trial courts against local authorities in a war of nerves, they altered the ordinary American's perception of the power of courts.[10] More, Brown is part of our social history. The retreat of segregation may have seemed glacial at times, but, like a glacier, *Brown* and its progeny remade the face of everyday life in every hamlet in the country. In the words of Charles Black, "Before *Brown* there was, in a large section of the United States, a well-masoned Cyclopean wall of racial segregation by law, scribbled over with insult to millions of blacks, and shutting millions of whites away from the well of human kindness. The Southern segregation system no longer exists in *specie*; bits and pieces of it, some quite big, still lie about, but the system is gone."[11]

Black is now a law professor emeritus, but before *Brown* he was one of a handful of whites to join Marshall and the LDF in the assault on segregation in the schools. For a white Texan who grew up with segregation, the social revolution wrought by *Brown* and later desegregation decrees was deeply moving:

> About five years ago, and not so much more than twenty years after the *Brown* decision, I went down to Austin, Texas, to testify on a death-penalty bill pending before a state legislative committee. Between committee sessions I went to eat in a middle-sized cafe near the Capitol. A black family, parents and several children, came in, took a table, dealt with the children's disputes over seating, and started studying the menu. When I was young, a black family that tried this would have been lucky to escape without serious injury. I sat quietly, with that tingling feeling in the neck—the very feeling by which (I think it is Houseman who says) we recognize poetry that works. It may not mean much to sit down in that cafe. It meant a lot not to be allowed to sit down there with your children—generation after generation.[12]

The inability of Afro-Americans to shape their children's lives for generation after generation was the *gravamen*, the essential evil, of slavery.[13] It was also the crucial issue in *Brown*.

Historical greatness is never achieved without notoriety. For the 101 southern members of Congress who joined in the "Manifesto" of 1956 rejecting federally directed desegregation and denouncing the seemingly unlicensed discretion of the Supreme Court, *Brown* I and II seemed a rehearsal for another northern invasion of the South. White Citizens Councils sprung up in southern cities to organize massive resistance to desegregation.[14] Supportive scholars and lawyers rushed to the defense of the Court,[15] but other academics insisted that the decisions amounted to "disaster by decree."[16]

Critics of the decision accused the Court of misusing its discretion, reading liberal social ideas into the narrower and more disciplined language of the Fourteenth Amendment, but the justices disclaimed any discretion in their holding in *Brown*. The Constitution spoke; the Court merely listened. How then did the Court justify a series of critical moves during its deliberations and in its decision? First, in hearing a broad range of factual arguments, the Court seemed to be departing from its role as an appellate forum. Appeals courts accept the record from the lower court; they do not try to determine the evidence for themselves.[17] Nevertheless, the Supreme Court in *Brown* and its sister cases twice sent counsel back to the library and the field to gather more facts on the history of the Fourteenth Amendment and the effect that desegregation would have on localities. Second, the plaintiffs wanted immediate relief, a court injunction ending state-sponsored segregation.[18] The Court agreed that the plaintiffs had been wronged and merited relief but did not order that relief. Instead, the justices scheduled a rehearing on the implementation stage of their decision. Finally, the plaintiffs had asked for relief for themselves and all others similarly situated. Although the first successful civil rights cases of our era sought relief only for the "named plaintiff,"[19] the great cases that followed were "class actions" in effect if not in final form.[20] Before the Court was done with *Brown*, it would decertify the class action, leaving every victimized minority group in each school district to bring its own suit in the federal courts.

By what authority did the Court exercise such sweeping discretion? The answer to this puzzle, and to the critics' misunderstanding of discretion in *Brown*, was that the justices were acting as "chancellors." *Brown* was and remains the greatest "equity" suit in our country's history, perhaps in the history of equity. Though fully blended into the fabric of modern law, equity suits and equitable relief remain distinct in their cast—the chancellor is vitally concerned with the workability and fairness of his decrees. He will not be disobeyed, but he will not decree the impossible. He will do justice for all parties on the basis of good-faith compliance with his decrees. He will probe the reality behind the legal issues, prod, investigate, provoke, and, if all else fails, hold the erring parties in contempt.

The justices of the Supreme Court regarded the implementation question as part of the constitutional problem. How were they to write a decree that would be obeyed? As accounts based on memoirs, interviews, and manuscript research into the deliberations of the Supreme Court demonstrate, the justices took their roles as chancellors in these cases seriously; they worried incessantly about the enforceability of their decree. Justice Felix Frankfurter wanted the issue a little riper; Justice Robert Jackson hoped that Congress would intervene; Justices Stanley Reed and Hugo Black, on different grounds, predicted resistance; Chief Justice Fred Vinson, while he lived, opposed any decree; Chief Justice Warren, when he came aboard, searched for the correct formula to make an injunction palatable. The equitable question, the question of remedy in context, was on all of their minds.[21] On and off the bench, jurists and scholars feared that most frightening specter for judges and lawyers: willful noncompliance. In past years, the injunction remedy had been withheld or limited by federal judges' fears that white southerners would not obey civil rights decrees.[22] Faced with an intractable dilemma and warned away from precipitous action by more experienced members of the Court, Warren elected to delay the enforcement decision until the Court could hear testimony from those states with school systems that would be directly affected by the ruling. The discretion of the Court rested on its reading of equitable principles. The chancellor has always had the discretion to choose the manner in which to effectuate his decree. *Brown* called forth the greatest powers of creativity of American equity. So broad was its implication, so deep its thrust into the affairs of every locality, that any decision to honor the petitioners' rights must entail the greatest ingenuity.

Chief Justice Warren contributed to this technical exercise of conventional judicial authority his own sense of the high purpose of equitable intervention. Although Warren was a novice chancellor, unused to the tangled underbrush of federal equity rulings, relative inexperience did not cause him anxiety.[23] After his retirement, he spelled out a judicial philosophy that rested not on mincing caution but on firm grasp of principle: "Where there is injustice, we should correct it." While it was not always the job of the Court to provide the correction, discrimination by race was palpably unconstitutional and mandated the intervention of the Supreme Court.[24]

Whatever Warren's personal vision, a final opinion of the Court in any case, particularly in the segregation cases—when public acceptance and judicial unanimity were so vital—must rest on some body of principled, established legal opinion. In May 1954, Warren prepared a memorandum for the conference. The first draft appears in his private papers, written in his own hand. Three passages in the memorandum, changed somewhat in his published opinion for the Court, strike the eye. The first portrays the schools as trustees for children's lives and fortunes. "There are reciprocal rights and responsibilities between parents, pupils, and governments," and on the school's side lay more than the duty to build and teach; "no child can reasonably be expected to succeed in life today if he is deprived of the opportunity for an education." Second, as part of the terms of the trust (an implied trust, perceived by the chancellor in the nature of the legal and moral relationships between schools and students), students were entitled "to share equally with every other child in his state and community" this opportunity. Such equality was not just an abstract constitutional requirement, it was part of the trusteeship relationship. Third, a chancellor was obligated to penetrate to the reality of the social condition behind the legal duties of plaintiff and defendant. Warren was convinced that "To separate them [black children, or Oriental children, or Indian children] from others of their age in school solely because of their color puts the mark of inferiority not only upon their status in the community but also upon their little hearts and minds in a form that is unlikely ever to be erased."[25]

Upon what body of doctrine, what rules and authorities, could Warren found these three themes of trusteeship, equality, and reality? His draft memorandum for *Brown* found the principles of equitable relief at the very core of American constitutionalism, but did the history of equity, particularly applied to public questions, bear out Warren's vision? And if it did—the subject of the following chapters—did this vision also point a way to a constitutional program of genuine relief for the victims of discrimination? The delay in ordering enforcement of desegregation was fraught with much danger for the Court; redocketing the cases for further hearings was nothing more than a promise that some relief would be forthcoming, leaving the nation waiting while its highest court explored "equitable principles."[26]

1 WHAT IS EQUITY?

When Chief Justice Earl Warren invoked "equitable principles," his professional readers presumed he meant the black-letter rules for granting injunctions. These were outlined in the Federal Rules of Civil Procedure and detailed in the rules of practice in each of the judicial circuits, but Warren meant his opinion to touch the heart of the average American. To the ordinary citizen, Warren implied that equity was an approach to law, including constitutional law, based on doing justice for all concerned. He conveyed his sense that ideal equity is fairness, giving all their due. Such fairness is expansive and realistic, adjusting disputes and redressing hardships so all parties can live with each other; it does not end with barren recitals of impersonal rights but addresses real harms; it is mutual, multilateral, and reflexive, making the world whole again.

THE TWO EQUITIES

Imagine for a moment an ideal court whose magistrate is charged with such fair dealing. Let us call him a chancellor. He demands that parties litigating in the court act toward each other, and toward the court, with good faith—revealing the truth, making efforts to find some middle ground, and obeying the dictates of conscience (if not their own, then the magistrate's). The chancellor's insistence on good faith rests on his power to compel obedience from the parties, a jurisdiction over their persons. The parties may rely on his good conscience to act in the best interests of them all. He trusts them to carry out his decree; they trust him to order a fair solution to their dispute. There is no jury in his court to act as intermediary, finding facts or insisting on their vision of the law; his fairness requires mutual trust.

This chancellor has to regard all parties before him as equals and formally or informally redresses inequality in the legal capacities, the representation, and the adequacy of pleading of the parties. Again, in a larger sense, our imaginary court, under its first principles of fairness, treats the parties' claims equally. The poor farmer's or mill worker's land and labor are not subordinated to the great planter's or the manufacturer's will. Our chancellor protects the weak against the strong in the courtroom. Fairness elevates individual equality into a communal goal.

Above all, fairness in this court embraces a flexible and humane realism. The chancellor peers behind the formalities to seek the real extent of harm. He tries to induce parties to settle their differences, intruding himself and his appointees into the process, if necessary on a continuing basis, to oversee the settlement. His decree brings the parties back before him, and he retains jurisdiction over the suit until its resolution satisfies him.

Here doubt plucks at the prudent scholar's sleeve and warns against re-creating a Camelot inhabited by good chancellors and their courts. Nevertheless, something approaching this reverie, under the rubric of *epieikeia*—equity, has long been a dream of Western jurists. Indeed, when one thinks of equity, one does not first think of chancellors and their courts, but recaptures instead a philosophical ideal coeval with Western civilization. Its most famous and long-lived expression appears in Aristotle's *Nichomachean Ethics*. Equity offered a remedy where the law did injustice. "The reason for this is that law is always a general statement, yet there are cases which it is not possible to cover in a general statement."[1] In equity, the spirit of the law, the lawgiver's intention, is extended to cover a case not comprehended in the generality of the statute. Equity embodies the highest justice because it is flexible and gives priority to the actual situation of the petitioners.[2]

Two corollaries to Aristotle's theorem framed the later development of the idea of equity.[3] First, Aristotle derived equity from an analysis of remedy. His argument presumed a breakdown of law but did not focus on that breakdown. He gave no guide to the perplexed judge, only the instruction that where the law did an injustice through failing to provide a remedy where it should have, equity might enter. The second characteristic of Aristotle's formulation is that equity worked in the interstices of law. If the law gave a full remedy, there was no need for equity. If equity was a requirement of any legal system (for the laws could never be comprehensive enough to do justice in all cases), it only applied to particular cases of injustice (though these might involve a multitude of petitioners for redress). The theory of equity was universal, but the practice of equity confined itself to individual cases.

Roman jurisprudence accepted and extended this essential duality of universal justice and practical, individualized remedy at the heart of equity. Among the Romans, good faith and full disclosure were essential parts of any legal sale or contract for land. Cicero went further: "The civil law derived from nature condemns malice and deceit not only in the case of real estate transactions, of course. In the marketing of slaves, too, it forbids any fraud on the seller's part. The aediles [magistrates of the city of Rome] have decreed in their edict that sellers who are aware of a poor state of health, of a tendency to escape, or a record of theft have to report these traits."[4] As Romans found themselves dealing with foreigners, commercial transactions required constant equitable adjustment. There could be no *ius gentium*, a law for all the peoples in the empire, without *aequitas*. The rules of equity were firmed in the schools of the "jurisconsults," paid legal advisers, in the second century of the common era and made their way to the far reaches of the empire. This duality was an uneasy one. If the magistrates had discretion to adjust law to the expectations and claims of the petitioners, what control was there upon the lawgiver? Where could one look to know the rules? In Justinian's codification of the Roman law, philosophical generality again bowed to institutional rigidity; natural law became rule-bound.[5]

Both Aristotle and Cicero regarded remedial justice as external to custom and convention. Cicero in particular believed that equity derived its force from nature, "the source of law."[6] That refrain would periodically appear in legal texts thereafter. Medieval canonists, church lawyers, and lay professors of Roman law also associated equity with natural law. They then extended equity from private commercial dealings to embrace the proper relationship between rulers and peoples.[7] A short step forward enabled early modern exponents of natural law to find in equity a model for relations between nations. Grotius, for example, identified equity with both fair dealing and equal treatment in war and peace.[8] In trying to fuse Aristotle's two equities, Grotius produced a set of absolute rules, much like the *Institutes*. Such rules were at once inevitable and yet contrary to the individuation of Aristotelian equity.

Early modern English jurisprudents juggled the universal and the mundane in equity. Christopher St. German's *Doctor and Student* (1523–32) declared that equity "is a right wiseness that considereth all the particular circumstances of the deed, the which also is tempered with the sweetness of mercy. And such an equity must always be observed in every law of man, and in every general rule thereof," while at the same time equity comprised those remedies available from the English chancellor and nothing more.[9] Edward Hake's *Epieikeia* (1603) described equity as a "correction" built into every law, which, when expanded, meant that all law ought to be equitable, but that the equity "of the judge" was confined to particular cases under well-understood rules.[10] The bifurcation of equity was built into its very structure, according to Scotland's eighteenth-century jurist Henry Home, Lord Kames. A century and a half after Hake, Kames sounded the same two-part harmony of ideal justice and earthbound relief: "equity, in its proper sense, comprehends every matter of law that by the common law is left without remedy; and supposing the boundaries of the common law to be ascertained, there can no longer remain any difficulty about the powers of a court of equity. But as these boundaries are not ascertained by any natural rule, the jurisdiction of the common law must depend in a great measure upon accident and arbitrary practice; and, accordingly, the boundaries of common law and equity, vary in different countries, and at different times in the same country."[11] Kames's equity began with a commitment to natural law and ended with practical concession. His equity did not define itself but was a by-product of the indefiniteness of common law. If the latter was inevitable, it made equity a perpetual wanderer on the outer edge of settled law. Kames knew that no judge or chancellor would want to be a nomad on the rim of the legal world and devoted the rest of his treatise to rules for the equitable adjudication of specific cases.

Both aspiration and actual redress found expression in equity courts. It was for practicing solicitors and chancellors that Hake and Kames wrote. The most often cited summary for the rules of equity in these courts was Richard Francis's *Maxims of Equity* (1726). There was nothing brilliant about his short collection of cases; he was popular because he brought together the conventional wisdom of his day.[12] There were fourteen maxims, and all echoed the duality of equity—natural justice captioned as mechanical rules:

1. He that will have equity done to him, must do it to the same person; 2. he that hath committed inequity, shall not have equity; 3. equality is equity; 4. it is equity that should make satisfaction, [he] who received the benefit; 5. it is equity that should have satisfaction, [he] who sustained the loss; 6. equity suffers not a right to be without a remedy; 7. equity relieves against

accidents; 8. equity prevents mischief; 9. equity prevents multi-plicity of suits; 10. equity regards length of time; 11. equity will not suffer a double satisfaction to be taken; 12. equity suffers not advantage to be taken of a penalty or forfeiture, where compensations can be made; 13. equity regards not the circumstance, but the substance of the act; and 14. where the equity is equal, the law must prevail.[13]

These maxims, apparently reaching up to a higher sphere of human justice, were in reality chapter headings for densely packed epitomes from equity reports. Much of their substance, obscured for modern readers by their cryptic formulation, is part of equity today. For example, maxim number three merely means that the court will divide an estate equally if there are no other considerations dictating its apportionment. Maxim numbers four and five together are the doctrine of restitution, preventing unjust enrichment. Maxim number seven has nothing to do with automobile crashes; it provides that a contract accidentally misdrawn may be reformed or rescinded. Maxim number eight prevents a litigant or a trustee in a pending suit from wasting the assets of an estate. Maxim number nine allows the equity court to join together suits arising out of the same transactions, or suits against the same defendant by many petitioners, or different suits between the same petitioner and defendant. Maxim number ten warns petitioners not to sleep on their rights; they must petition the chancellor within a reasonable time. Maxim number twelve refers to the defaulting mortgagor's or debtor's right to pay the past due installments, interest, and court costs and thereby prevent foreclosure on the mortgage or penalty bond attached to the debt. These technical matters were familiar then and remain so to lawyers.

By the end of the eighteenth century, England's chancellors reasoned much the same way as its common-law judges. Analogy, precedent, and rule had largely replaced case-by-case flexibility. Francis's maxims of equity were categories, not abstract principles, mirroring the self-imposed restraint of contemporary chancellors. Nevertheless, William Blackstone, a conservative jurist whose influence on the interpretation of common law, statute, and equity was felt throughout the English-speaking world, recognized that the duality—the periodic recrudescence of higher principles of natural obligations—inherent in equity still rendered it a loose cannon on the ship of state. In his Vinerian lectures on the law, later published as *Commentaries on the Law of England* (1765–69), he insisted that equity was purely auxiliary to law. Narrowly reading Aristotle and emphasizing the technical side of English and Scottish equity treatises, he defined equity as "correction of that, wherein the law (by reason of it's universality) is deficient."[14] For Blackstone, there was but one equity, and it had nothing to do with universal principles of conscience or fairness. It merely was a set of rules, as Frederic William Maitland later put it, once used by chancellors in their courts.[15]

Much influenced by contemporary English jurisprudence, Joseph Story, the foremost equity commentator in the first century of the American republic, conceded that there were two equities. The first was marked by great discretion, based on the canon-law backgrounds of the first English chancellors, but Story found it suited only an infantile era of law and was wholly supplanted in his time by a controlled, constrained science of equity, ancillary to common law.[16] A similar view prevailed throughout the later years of the nineteenth century and has many exponents in law schools and on the bench today.[17] Story and his successors recognized that equity must be flexible but denied that the chancellor introduced new remedies. In favor of Story's analysis one must concede that by his own day equity had its own reporters, precedents, rules, and limitations. Indeed, early in its career, the United States Supreme Court attempted to limit the reach of federal equity to only those causes in which English chancellors had already used their powers.[18]

THE TOOL KIT OF THE CHANCELLOR

Blackstone and Story may have had political reasons for trying to curb the discretion of chancellors, but they quite sensibly balked at the prospect of different chancellors issuing widely disparate decrees in similar cases. Like Justinian and Grotius, Blackstone and Story demanded an equity on which suitors could rely. By the time Story published the first volume of his *Commentaries on Equity Jurisprudence* in 1836, precedents for chancellors were well developed. Though they changed much in the next 150 years, the outlines of modern equity can be traced back through Story and Blackstone to the first chancellors.

In the traditional formulation of his authority, the chancellor's jurisprudence followed his "conscience." That doctrine was built upon his power to compel the consciences of defendants. Without a court of equity in which the chancellor wielded his subpoena (literally "under power of") to compel defendants to come before him and answer his inquiries, the idea of equity would have remained a philosopher's dream. In fact, every legal system has and must have some avenue for appeal for the sweetness of mercy from its laws. Granting this proposition, one may regard the metamorphosis of the office of the English chancellor from royal confidante and secretary of state to foremost judge in the realm as historically inevitable. The kings of England were perambulatory princes with their eyes on their French and Norman dominions. They had little time or expertise to manage the flow of petitions to them for exceptions from unjustly applied laws and against corrupt local legal officials. By the end of the thirteenth century, the chancellor was commissioned to hear and deal with these petitions in the name of the king. His rules for proceeding with such cases would ultimately become English equity, and his court would rival the king's other central courts.

The procedural and substantive content of equity cannot be adequately summarized here, but an outline of the reach of equity will illustrate the power and obligations of the chancellor. The special powers of the chancellors are a product of the history of his court, a court of petition to the mercy of the king. As such, it relied on straightforward, factual complaints written in English rather than the formulary system of Latin writ pleading used in the common-law courts. The chancellor readily allowed amendment of both the complaint and the answer, rather than dismissing a suit for technical deficiencies in its form. The common law, under the formulary system, commanded literal compliance with the forms of pleading or the case could not go forward. Petitioners in equity claimed that they had been wronged, either through an abuse of power by a legal official, through some mischance or malfeasance of the defendant's conduct (a fraud, accident, mistake, or misconstruction of a contract, deed, promise, or exchange), or through a misapplication of a statute. Relief was not possible in the common-law courts, either because there happened to be no grounds for the suit (for example, a defrauded purchaser could not prevent the one who defrauded him from forcing payment of a penalty bond), or because the award in common law was not comparable to the loss itself (the value of performance of a promise, for example, might far outweigh the mere return of the contract price).

The chancellor used his power, drawn from the king's prerogative, to summon the defendant to reply to the claim. Refusal to obey the subpoena or any subsequent decree of the court was grounds for a contempt order against the defendant. Brought before him, parties were questioned by the chancellor or one of his masters in equity. If they could not come to court, depositions were taken from them. Many of the modern rules of evidence are taken directly from the procedures of equity. It alone could compel a defendant to produce account books, provide an inventory of an estate, give evidence about or from missing documents, and otherwise facilitate the "production" of evidence. The common-law courts would not aid the plaintiff with such matters. In modern federal procedure, these powers are given all judges under the rubric of "discovery."[19]

Though it dealt with individual injustices, the jurisdiction of equity was multiple rather than individual. The chancellor looked for justice on both sides of the suit and beyond. A formal expression of this concern for communal justice was his willingness to allow the combination of a multiplicity of suits, claims, and remedies when combination was the fairest way to sort out harms and remedy them. In common law, each suit had the form of A versus B. In equity, if A wished to sue B and B wished to sue A for different claims arising out of the same transaction, or many plaintiffs wished to sue a single defendant over the same matter, or a series of plaintiffs and defendants had claims, cross-claims, and counterclaims that arose when an issue was litigated between any two of them, or wished to allow one of their number to represent their community of interest in the court, the chancellor could combine some of these suits in the name of substantial justice to all parties (by preventing multiple suits) and efficiency for the courts (by eliminating rehearing of the same fact situation for each plaintiff's suit against each defendant). Modern mass tort suits—for example, the Agent Orange suits—are the descendants of such pleas for joinder, interpleader, and class action in early equity.[20]

The chancellor could also command litigants' personal conduct during or after a lawsuit. He could compel a defendant to perform or not perform an act, to convey property or fulfill a contract even when the property itself was not in the same jurisdiction as the court. The power of the court over the person of the suitor (so long as the suitor was in the court's jurisdiction) gave equity a longer reach than common law. When fine or imprisonment failed to move the conscience of the malefactor, the chancellor could order the sequestration of the assets in question and payment of the disputed amount out of them. He did not have the power to transfer title to property.

The most powerful (and today the most widely discussed) of his procedural tools was and remains the injunction. The injunction is a command by the chancellor to a party to do (mandatory or positive injunctions) or not to do (prohibitory or negative injunctions) an act.

The act had to be possible; equity did not demand the impossible. An injunction to integrate a school is mandatory; an injunction to stop polluting a river is prohibitory. If the plaintiff could prove to the court that the actions of the defendant posed an irreparable and immediate danger to the plaintiff's person or property, and that the plaintiff had a good chance of winning on the merits of the suit when it was fully heard, a court of equity could grant a temporary restraining order. Traditionally, this was *ex parte*, that is, without the participation of the defendant. Such powers are easily abused however they may be constrained by formal rules, and modern practice demands that every effort be made to bring the defendant into court to argue against the temporary restraining order. Preliminary injunctions, while not final adjudications of a suit, prevent parties from changing their situation until a final hearing. A preliminary injunction requires the participation of both parties. In modern complex litigation, injunctions often exhibit a mixed form.[21]

After the injunction is issued, the chancellor can maintain jurisdiction over the case to insure compliance, in effect becoming a manager of the solution to a claim. The court can name its own assistants in the management of these injunctions. Special masters, experts in the subject matter, may be asked to investigate the facts of a case, take testimony or examine accounts, or even do independent testing. They report to the court. Receivers act for the court as administrators of property during litigation, in a sense a living part of the equitable remedy. These court-appointed assistants also manage trusts, bankruptcies, and even police departments and prisons, if the court so orders within its discretion.[22]

Equity had a substantive side as well, which is now almost fully incorporated into the body of law.[23] Equity required good faith by parties to a contract. A court of equity had the power to order rescission or reformation for mistake, accident, duress, fraud, and other hard or sharp practices, although different courts of equity divided over the question of rescinding contracts that were patently unfair to one of the parties. Specific performance by one of the parties was another unique equitable remedy. Much of the early twentieth-century casebook material on equity was concerned with equitable reformation of contracts. The central concept in these works was the prevention of "unjust enrichment" by one party at the expense of another. Equity could order restitution of things or payment of a part of profits (for example, of royalties in copyright and patent cases).[24]

Although equity rarely interfered with criminal prosecutions (save when the penalty amounted to irreparable damage and the criminal court abused its powers or overreached its jurisdiction), equity regularly intervened in suits concerning civil wrongs. Such "torts" might include private nuisances and trespasses. The chancellor could order a defendant in such a suit to clean up a garbage dump, stop polluting the air, cease running a pigsty, reduce the hours of operation of a cracking plant, or stop digging under the petitioner's house. The chancellor might ask a court of law to determine whether there was a nuisance or a trespass, or simply handle the entire suit himself, from finding facts to overseeing compliance with his decree. The doctrine "equity loves justice, and not by halves" referred to this "clean-up" power of the chancellor.[25]

Equity also concerned itself with disputes over the use and ownership of property. Equitable easements, in which one party claimed the fruits of its improvement of property or its access across property established by long usage, were one example. Equity protected the rights of downstream owners against diminution of the natural flow of water and homeowners against loss of their access to light and air from the incursions of neighbors. By far the most compelling imposition of equity in property lay in the defense of the trust. A trust is a transfer of property to a party (the trustee) for the use of a third party (the beneficiary). Chapter 2 describes how a medieval knight's answer to the king's claims on infeudated land became a major concern of chancellors, and how equity transformed a formula for devising land into a property "interest" that could be itself bought and sold. Equity still takes parental pride in trusts, and it has long recognized that implied trusts (inherent in the intent of the testator if not in the precise language of a will) and constructive trusts (created by the court to force a defendant to act as a trustee and employed in a wide variety of disputes) must be protected with as much vigor as express trusts. Enforcement of trusteeship was the purest example of the way in which "the conscience of equity finds expression."[26]

Equity was also charged with the protection of the legally incapable—widows, orphans and other minors, the mentally ill, and foreigners. Chancellors would hear suits on behalf of all these individuals, protecting their rights through the special powers of equity. Other courts in England, notably the ecclesiastical courts and the orphans' court, joined the chancellor in exercising this jurisdiction.

THE PROBLEM OF DISCRETION

Judges sitting in equity cannot fill the gaps left by law without the exercise of discretion, but discretion may always be abused. Critics of equity have faulted its potential for variability. Does granting such discretion to judges run riot with suitors' expectations? Who could predict or, in the case of corrupt chancellors, constrain such judicial license? Uncontrolled individualism on the bench, extremes of flexibility, might lead to judicial tyranny or the abnegation of all standards.[27] Indeed, the chancellor's conduct seems far from common notions of the role of a law judge. Conventionally, the judge acts as an impartial arbiter of suits brought to her court.[28] She speaks the law and, whether aided or not by a jury of fact finders, applies the law to the case before her. Her opinion is final, save for appeal to a higher court, itself acting as another neutral dispenser of legal reasoning.[29] Fairness per se is not an issue. Legal rights contested by the litigators are the struts of the case. The factual dispute is its walls and roof. The judge has no discretion to adjust the outcome to aid both sides, even when she personally wishes to maximize the total good. She is bound by strict rules—precedent, statute, administrative regulations—which she may reshape into standards but not ignore.

But the chancellor—who could tell what he would do? John Selden's puckish witicism is still quoted: "Equity is A Roguish thing, for Law wee have a measure known what to trust too. Equity is according to the conscience of him that is Chancellor, and as it is larger or narrower so is equity. Tis all one as if they should make the Standard for the measure wee call A foot, to be the Chancellors foot; what an uncertain measure would this be; one Chancellor has a long foot another A short foot a third an indifferent foot; tis the same thing in the Chancellors Conscience." Selden's satire had a bitter flavor—he was no friend of the Crown or its special courts. Nevertheless, an able and well-connected seventeenth-century common lawyer, he knew that the uncertain discretion of chancellors worried working lawyers.[30] In the 1600s, the incoming chancellor established his own rules of court; there were no official reports of his decrees or their rationale, and he viewed each case anew, unhindered by precedent when he wished. By the eighteenth century, Blackstone, with great confidence, could insist that "the system of our courts of equity is a laboured connected system, governed by established rules, and bound down by precedents, from which they do not depart, although the reason of some of them may perhaps be liable to objection."[31] As his final disclaimer hinted, Blackstone was a diehard opponent of equitable discretion, for he feared that nothing he had said could prevent some future chancellor from abusing his discretion. Lord Eldon, the most cited of the nineteenth-century English chancellors, agreed with Blackstone on this point at least. Selden's accusation still rankled Eldon: "I cannot agree that the doctrines of this court are to be changed with every succeeding judge. Nothing would inflict on me greater pain, in quitting this place, than the recollection that I had done anything to justify the reproach that the equity of this Court varies like the Chancellor's foot."[32]

Modern rules of equity and books of equity precedent in England and America would seem to put an end to Eldon's nightmare. And, indeed, all judges must have some discretion or they could not adjudicate cases. Mechanical application of constitutional rules, statutory provisions, or prior cases may suffice in most disputes, but hard cases resist easy determination. Even common-law judges face a multiplicity of cases falling outside of precedent or the exact terminology of statutes. What are they to do? The "gremlin" of interpretation pokes a sharp nose into hard cases all the time.[33] The common-law judge follows the example of the chancellor on such occasions, inquiring into the spirit of the legislation, the "equity of the statute," to apply it to the individual case. There are rules for such an inquiry, similar to the rules for determining the meaning of a will or a contract.[34] The chancellor's or judge's discretion is confined as well by community standards and craft expectations.[35]

A second area of potential abuse of equitable discretion lay in conflict between common-law courts and courts of equity. This quarrel marked Tudor and Stuart English courts; it surfaced occasionally in early American jurisdictions, but it does not seem to have persisted far into the nineteenth century. If there was competition in the coexistence of the two systems, it expressed itself in a theoretical rather than a practical rivalry. Law and equity represented different ways of thinking about the rules of adjudication. By the end of the nineteenth century, common-law orthodoxy had organized legal claims into categories, each proceeding from a handful of inviolable principles that, properly applied, decided every case in that category.[36] Even though this formalism came under fire in the early twentieth century under successive assaults of Progressive and then Realist legal scholarship, the common law continued to rely on precedent or custom for its guiding rules.[37] Despite the growing body of equity rules, equity retained greater flexibility than common law.

Discretion remained its hallmark. Although many trial judges seem comfortable with the merger of law and equity in the Federal Rules of Civil Procedure written in 1938 and amended periodically thereafter,[38] a number of law professors recently have expressed sharp criticism of judicial discretion under the rules of civil procedure. The targets variously include the drafters of the Federal Rules, the judges operating under the Rules, and the philosophy underlying the Rules. In effect, these academic critics maintain that legal and equitable ways of thinking are fundamentally distinct, and that merging them only subordinates known rules and safeguards to misguided faith in the omniscience of judges.[39]

There is another, far more insidious form of abuse of equitable discretion. Discretion may be corrupt. If not open, personal, and self-serving (accepting the family goose in payment for a favorable decision, unless the other party brings along the family silver), corruption may be ideological. This is the charge laid against the Warren Court and lower federal courts acting under its direction by opponents of desegregation, busing, reapportionment, prison and mental health reform by court order, and affirmative action. The critics are not always political conservatives, but they share an aversion to sweeping equitable remedies.[40] Three generations ago an equally pointed attack on the abuse of equitable discretion came from political liberals. In an era when federal courts were hostile to social and economic reform, equitable discretion appeared to be a threat to democracy. Federal judges antipathetic to organized labor used their equitable discretion to issue very broad injunctions against unions.[41] In the same era, some chancellors refused to aid petitioners seeking relief from racial injustice and industrial nuisances. The chancellor has always had the discretion to tailor the remedy to the harm or to refuse a remedy when a suitor has acted inequitably, there is no way to administer the remedy, or there is an adequate and complete remedy at law. The refusal to give injunctive relief to black voters suing the state of Alabama under the Fifteenth Amendment fell under this heading; Justice Oliver Wendell Holmes, Jr., writing for the Court, knew that the Court could not enforce an order to the local electoral authorities.[42] In similar fashion, chancellors would not enjoin industrial polluters if the polluters could convince the court—as most did—that their property interest was more substantial than the damage suffered by the victims of the pollution.[43] Even modern scholars who approve of the new substantive due process of the Warren Court have voiced fear that its discretion was unconstrained. Litigants at the bar and those affected by the outcome of the suit have a right to expect that judges will play by the rules. The potential for abuse of discretion is always there.

The fact is that the chancellor always has been constrained by internal rules not necessarily visible to the lay observer. Even when they are deciding the hard cases—the 2 percent of cases that do not fit comfortably under the many rules and precedents that have grown up in equity—chancellors and judges have a professional audience that they strive to satisfy. Their peers on the bench, their clerks, counsel, law professors, and politicians in the other branches of government all scrutinize decrees of chancellors. Important cases have a gestation period when chancellors take the measure of this community of learned discourse. Chancellors are sensitive to currents of professional opinion. Such unwritten but strongly understood rules enabled the greatest of chancellors to reach deeply into the harms and gains behind the pleading. The principles of equity, not the whims of chancellors, offered a petitioner the chance to introduce a bigger piece of social reality into a lawsuit. In effect, this is just what a bill for discovery of missing documents or accounts, a petition to join parties, or a request for a setoff of debts and credits did in an ongoing lawsuit. So, too, equitable doctrines like restitution and trusteeship ordered the chancellor to surmount legal obstacles to full justice.

EQUITABLE CONSTITUTIONALISM

There is a fine line between the chancellor who exercises the full scope of his powers to do justice and one who combines ideological perversity with tyrannical license. Drawing such a line without a clear sense of the historical development of equity would be incautious. One discovers in the historical record that the terminology in the maxims and the case law chancellors reported was part of a language whose application did not stop with technical legal exchanges. In the hands of skilled advocates, all such public languages take on or shed meaning when shifted from one context to another.[44] When counsel or chancellors talked about conscience dictating a result in a particular case, they might well be resting their argument on precedent settled in court, but the effect, the historical impact of their words, was not confined to the four walls of the courtroom. The community of discourse widened dramatically in times of political controversy. The same language, without its technical trappings or institutional authority but with all of its moral force, was available to political reformers, propagandists, and even revolutionaries as they compiled a vocabulary of modern constitutional analysis.[45] In this lexicon the two equities infused one another with energy drawn from different sources—the philosophical yearning for a fairer world with more equal distribution of power and wealth, and the authority of a real-world court to force men and women to act in good faith toward one another. One can thus speak of two equities in the chancellor's court: a series of technical remedies and substantive provisions and an equitable approach to law, making the world whole.

There is thus an equitable way to read and apply fundamental law. Rooted in our legal and constitutional history, applied in lawyers' briefs and judicial decrees, equitable constitutionalism is part of our intellectual heritage. The performance of the actors in this constitutional discourse did not always distinguish between equity *in* constitutions—allowance for courts of equity, for example—and equity *and* constitutions—a more diffuse concept of mutual fairness. The slurring was often deliberate, an appeal by counsel to the conscience of the judge, sitting in equity, and an opportunity for the chancellor to exercise his own conscience. The call for an accountable government in the eighteenth century, the experiment in public trusteeship called the Freedmen's Bureau in the nineteenth century, and the overthrow of Jim Crow in the twentieth century all involved the fusion of the two equities.

PART ONE TRUSTEESHIP

There are two stories in Part One. The first is about the chancellor and his court, about the mechanics of equity, the other about the emergence of a theory of constitutional governance in England and its North American colonies resting on a higher equity. They are often told, but hitherto they were regarded as distinct from one another. In truth, they came together for two extended "moments" in times of crisis for the courts and the Constitution.[1] Such moments sometimes open a door to great creativity of thought and liberty of action, when new groups of people are drawn into the political process, old ideas are recaptured and refashioned in altered contexts, and novel paradigms of political legitimacy are assayed. In both the English Civil War and the American Revolution, the fusion of the two equities enabled a handful of men to portray government as an equitable trusteeship for the benefit of the governed, with removal from office the penalty for misuse of power.

In England, this moment came near the end of a century of strife. In America, it came at the beginning of a sudden upheaval. In England, its crowning achievement was a brilliant treatise whose call for constitutional accountability rang throughout a century but went unfulfilled. In America, its result was a confederation of trusteeship republics pledging themselves to the proposition that governors were the servants of the people.

2 THE TRUST AND ENDS OF GOVERNMENT

England's medieval kings were warrior princes whose courts and councils were in constant motion. With military and dynastic interests straddling the English Channel, these monarchs had little time to hear and dispose of pleas for exemption from the rigors of royal law or petitions against the corruption of local officials.[1] Edward I found a solution to the vexation of personal dispensation of justice; he commissioned his secretary, his chancellor, to act in his stead. The chancellor did not distinguish between this dispensing power and his other administrative business. There was no "equity" per se, only mechanical responses to formalistic pleas; but as more and more petitioners were directed to the chancellor in his own person, rather than as the administrative arm of the king and his Council, the chancellor's quasi-judicial function began to coalesce into a recognizable court of justice.[2] At first, much of his judicial business came from his colleagues on the king's Council. As time passed, more of it came from farmers trying to maintain their rights to their copyholds against the will of their noble landlords, widows scrapping to hold on to their dower rights, ordinary purchasers defrauded by unscrupulous merchants, and inheritors cheated out of property devised them by their fathers.[3]

THE CHANCELLOR

Bit by bit, a jurisprudence began to emerge in the chancellor's court based on the personal training and predilections of the chancellor himself and on the mission he was to perform. There was a "gap" in the remedies available in common law, which petitioners asked the chancellor to fill.[4] Chancellors were not only efficient public secretaries and loyal political assistants, they were men of education and understanding. Until the troubled stewardship of Thomas More, a trained lawyer, the chancellors were clerics, educated in canon (church) law. Although that body of precepts drew its form from Roman law, in which equity played a major role, the equity of the English chancellor was not mere formulae borrowed from the Roman. It rested instead on a very active, personal concept of "conscience."[5] On a case-by-case basis, after hearing evidence from both sides, the chancellor exercised his personal jurisdiction over the parties to convince them to act in good conscience toward one another.

Gradually, as the jurisdiction of the equity court crystallized, the "conscience" of the court became less the disputants' and more the chancellor's. It is not clear when this transformation began to occur, nor did it ever prevent chancellors from prodding litigants to reach a settlement on their own. In Christopher St. German's early sixteenth-century treatise, *Doctor and Student*, both defendant's and chancellor's consciences were essential to the work of the court. The chancellor coaxed the conscience of the litigants even as his own rules curbed his exercise of authority. It was up to the conscience of the chancellor whether to issue the subpoena or decree the injunction, for "the lord chancellor must order his conscience after the rules and grounds of the law of the realm."[6] The maxim that equity follows the law—the subtext of this passage—thus grew out of the chancellor's prudence. By the mid-sixteenth century, the conscience that mattered was the chancellor's. Whether this made equity more regular and objective, or proved only that Elizabethan litigants were more stubbornly disputatious than their predecessors, is of less importance than the effect of the doctrine.

Undoubtedly, there were some grounds for the other central court judges to resent the emergence of the chancellor's court. Historians dispute the extent of this competition.[7] There is no question that the chancellor could intervene at various stages in a common-law suit. He could enjoin a litigant from bringing an action, step into an ongoing suit through his subpoena, and even prevent execution of a judgment by threatening the winner with a fine and imprisonment for contempt if he or she tried to collect from the loser. Such power to trump their own judgments rankled the judges of Common Pleas and King's Bench. So long as the chancellor saw his activities as an extension of the Council's administrative function, there were little grounds for such rivalry to fester; but under the Tudor chancellors, this deference began to erode. Cardinal Thomas Wol-

sey, chancellor under Henry VIII, was accused of misusing his discretion by issuing too many injunctions. Wolsey was a very active
chancellor, not only in his own court, but also in the Council, which
he dominated, aiding those without remedies at law. In such cases
the conscience of the court was decidedly his conscience.[8] Thomas
More, Wolsey's successor and the first of a long line of lay chancellors trained in the common law, continued to issue injunctions,
but more sparingly than Wolsey. More also insisted that royal courts
soften the rigor of law by adopting equitable principles. In his own
court, More's impartiality was celebrated. He certainly did not go
out of his way to challenge the authority of the regular courts.[9]

More's prudence also may be attributed to the rise of other
courts of equity abutting his own court's jurisdiction. The Court of
Requests, established by the Council in the late fifteenth century, was
a poor person's version of the chancellor's court. For the century
that it flourished, its doors were open to petitions for redress from
those who could not pay the fees in the chancellor's court and from
servants of the king. Its jurisdiction extended to all manner of legal
questions; its procedure was "civilian," much like its more celebrated
senior cousin among the Tudor prerogative courts, the Star Chamber; and its bench was composed of members of the Council.[10] The
king's Exchequer, the central court charged with royal fiscal matters, also had an equity side, as did the quasi-independent manorial
courts of Durham, Lancaster, Chester, and the regional Council of
the Marches of Wales.[11] The proliferation of quasi-administrative
courts was a Tudor innovation. All posed discretionary alternatives
to common-law adjudication.[12]

As some of these experiments in quasi-administrative dispute
resolution waned in the closing years of Elizabeth's reign, the business and influence of her chancellor's court soared. The number of
suits filed in chancery doubled between the beginning and the end
of Elizabeth's reign. In the first decade of her successor's tenure,
that of James I, the docket increased by another 50 percent. The
offices of the chancery spread all over London and Westminster. In
cluttered rooms filled with smoke and malodor and great halls
watched by milling solicitors and bystanders, the chancellor and his
many clerks, arrayed in a hierarchy marked by robes as well as functions, did their work. Court was held in the south end of the Great
Hall in Westminster. A 1620 woodcut in the British Museum shows a
knot of men gathered around the seated chancellor. The six clerks
and their underlings who kept the records of the court had their

offices off Chancery Lane, in the City; the pleaders often lived in Doctors Commons; and the chancellor made his home at York House, near Charing Cross. As the number of litigants and the paperwork skyrocketed, Thomas Egerton (later Lord Ellesmere), Elizabeth's last master of the rolls and James I's first chancellor, pressed for reform of the court. He established the chancellor's supremacy over the rival equity courts, instituted uniform rules for pleading, and tried to regularize the content of decrees. Although the reforms were popular, the overall success of his program was mixed. He left a court plagued by delay and inconstancy.[13]

The English Civil War brought the chancellor's court to its knees, a victim of judicial envy and parliamentary animosity. As a prerogative court, it was subject to the same suspicion as its far more obnoxious and politically active counterpart, the Star Chamber. The Presbyterian interest in the Long Parliament did away with the latter, but the court of chancery weathered the storm. Although it was attacked on all sides, threatened with abolition on at least three occasions, and restructured as a "commission" for a time, its functions were so vital, and thoroughgoing revision of the law to absorb its role so difficult for the lawyers in Parliament to swallow, that it survived.[14] The Restoration chancellor's court was far different from its pre–Civil War predecessor in one respect. Under the tutelage of the greatest of all chancellors, Heneage Finch, Lord Nottingham, the court voluntarily curbed its own discretion and conformed much of its jurisprudence to that of the courts of common law.[15] Nottingham's approach was adopted by his successors, a line of well-trained, respected, conservative chancellors in the eighteenth and nineteenth centuries. If the age of uncurbed assertion of discretion was over— conscience ripening into equity, equity "hardening" into law—chancellors continued to regard conscience as the basis of their jurisdiction and discretion as its legitimate expression.[16] Until its last days in 1873, through a period of troubles in the early nineteenth century so poignantly and sharply castigated by Charles Dickens in *Bleak House*, the chancellor's court asserted its vital role in English law.[17]

The buffeting of the chancellor's court in the constitutional crisis raised questions of both law and politics, not a new position for this court—recall Wolsey's fate—but one that ironically offered, in the context of parliamentary calls for fiduciary responsibility from the king's ministers, the possibility of an equitable reading of constitutional obligations. In the controversy over the chancellor's court, reformers linked the public debate over the accountability of officials to the efforts of private suitors to protect their rights as beneficiaries. The vocabulary for the language of public trust came from the chancellor's court.

PRIVATE TRUSTS AND THE PUBLIC TRUST

The word "trust" had a rich nexus of meanings in seventeenth-century English usage. From Middle English came "confidence" and "safety," to which was added, by the fifteenth century, a sense of expectation for the future. These words echoed in instruments for transmitting property from one generation to another enforceable in equity. The precise origins of the "trust" in English law are obscure. One source undoubtedly was the jurisdiction of the chancellors to protect the interests of a *cestui que use*, the beneficiary of the medieval "use."[18] The use was a common device by which the propertied tried to evade the restrictions on feudal land tenure. The use gave control over the future of the interest in land to the holder and took that control away from the Crown. The Crown also lost revenue when "feoffors" transferred land through uses. Chancellors recognized the intended beneficiary's interest by creating an "equitable estate." Indeed, it may be said that the protection of uses was the first occasion the chancellor had to develop his own jurisprudence. Henry VIII, strapped for funds, tried to close this loophole in his laws with a Statute of Uses (1535), surely one of the most obscure statutes ever fashioned, but then gave way to established practices.[19] The chancellor continued to protect "trusts" of all kinds, including "uses upon uses" for the same reason that chancellors began to protect the *cestui que use*: the law courts could not compel the trustee to act in good faith, for the trustee had legal title to the property. In good conscience, however, the trustee had bound himself to manage it for the best interests of the beneficiary, a binding pledge in the eyes of the chancellor.

Throughout the turmoil of the seventeenth century, including the closing of the courts of law for a time in the 1640s, the trust business of the chancellor's court continued to grow. The explanation for this phenomenon may be a technical one—lawyers advising their clients that the trust was a good way to pass the fruits of their labors on to a new generation without exposing the principal to royal taxes, wasteful habits of heirs, dispersion through division in a will, or the disposition of the common-law judges to permit an heir at law to break up an estate and sell off the pieces.[20] Despite all the attacks upon the chancery by the Puritans, the chancellor (or the "Commissioners in Chancery" during the Interregnum) continued to protect beneficiaries. After the Restoration, chancellors transformed the trust from a fiduciary relationship into a legal interest, which could be transferred or sold by the beneficiary under certain conditions.[21]

Despite the self-constraining view that chancellors after Nottingham generally took of their discretion, particularly their pains to avoid a confrontation with the law courts, they continued to expand the concept of trusts in their own court. By the eighteenth century, a category of "implied" trusts had emerged. When a testator conferred a benefit on another, the chancellor could construe the intent of the donor to have been the creation of a trust.[22] The origins of the "constructive trust," in which the court made a party unjustly enriched into a trustee for the unwitting donor, lay in Nottingham's tenure and were well known by the early eighteenth century.[23] That view of the trust persists to this day. The superintendency of privately arranged trusts was a model of the efficient and fair use of equitable discretion—a principled discretion, not a vagarious one. It was so vital an aid to the distribution of family property through the generations, even in the midst of civil war, that one may say the trust saved the chancellor's court as much as the chancellor's court saved the trust.

How did such technical matters in court become part of a public controversy over the shape of government, vaulting the divide between law and politics, courts and parliaments? Actually, in this period the divide was illusory. The series of dichotomies—law is neutral and legislative politics are partisan, courts deal with private quarrels among individuals and legislatures deal with public matters affecting the entire people, courts remedy past damages and legislatures provide for prospective entitlements—that conventionally distinguish judicial from legislative activity disguises the effect of politics on courts and ignores Parliament's role as an adjudicator of private quarrels. The boundary between private and public, individual and general, retrospective and prospective was often crossed in both directions. On the judicial side of the boundary, the central courts' decisions influenced public policy, changing the status of entire classes of men and women. Courts occupied a central position in the political controversy, for they were the most vulnerable and most accessible organs of government. On the other side of the boundary, Parliament's time was often taken up with "private bills" granting relief or special privileges to individuals. A final, most striking violation of the separation of adjudication and legislation was the fact that Parliament was the highest court as well as a legislature.

The dispute among parliamentary factions and the royal party over the "public trust" was not just a suit over a private trust writ large. The connections were embedded in a much more complex transfer of legal ideas from one context to another. Equity was borne onto the center of the political stage by Chief Justice Edward Coke's controversy with Lord Chancellor Ellesmere. The impeachment of Ellesmere's successor, Francis Bacon, Viscount St. Albans, for violation of his fiduciary duties—his trusteeship of the public weal—allowed Parliament to appropriate the very language Ellesmere had used to defend his court. The continuing involvement of the chancellor's office in the constitutional crisis rendered the abolition of the court of equity a prime objective of Puritan legislative reformers. In this last and most comprehensive struggle, the concept of the public trust entered the discourse of politics for generations to come.

The story begins with two proud servants of the Crown, a slick operator, and a fake gemstone. From his appointment to the chief justiceship, Coke, who bore no affection for Ellesmere, had led the charge against the court of the chancellor.[24] At one level, the dispute concerned which court would be the final arbiter of individual lawsuits. The power of the chancellor's court to enjoin litigants from bringing suit and to intervene in the course of trial went largely unquestioned, but its authority to bar a successful litigant from enjoying the rewards of a favorable decision at common law was not so clearly established. If certain defenses or documents were not admissible in common law, and the loser there did not think to raise these defenses or seek to enlist the aid of the chancellor in obtaining the evidence during the trial, could the chancellor, upon the loser's petition, enjoin the winner from seeking execution of the trial court's judgment? Coke feared such late intervention would not only subordinate every order in his court to the chancellor's whim, but also delay the final settlement of every lawsuit and undermine the authority of every common-law judge.[25] One must not substitute the great constitutional reformer of 1624 for the chief justice of 1615. Coke had professional reasons for opposing the intervention of chancery. In addition to his general aversion to the uncertainty of equity, he preferred common-law remedies to equitable remedies.

The issue came to a head in *Courtney v. Glanville* (1613–14). The defendant in the law suit, Francis Courtney, was trying to avoid paying the "penalty" bonds he had left with an untrustworthy London jeweler, Richard Glanville. The bonds—customarily twice the amount of the actual debt—were a common form of insurance that the buyer would pay what he owed. In fact, Glanville had misrepresented a topaz as a diamond to Courtney. An agent for the seller, one Davies, first fooled Courtney and then lied to the common-law courts. While a writ of error in the Court of Common Pleas was pending, Courtney, the defendant in law, became a petitioner in equity when he asked the chancellor to prevent collection on the bonds.[26] Ellesmere agreed that fraud was a bar to recovery and imprisoned Glanville for contempt when he refused to respond to a subpoena in chancery. Coke, incensed at Ellesmere's disregard for the decision of the central common-law courts, released Glanville from the Tower. Coke insisted that Courtney had plenty of time to assert his rights in equity before or during his trial, but he had waited too long; even equity required that the petitioner not sleep on his rights.[27] What was more, decisions in the high courts were final and binding; that was settled law in England.[28] Coke did not hesitate to use his power to challenge Ellesmere.[29] Coke's justification was simple: "the law is reason and equity, to do right to all, and to keep men from wrong and mischief, and therefore the law will never make construction against law, equity, and right."[30]

The chancellor was not without his weapons. In the *Earl of Oxford's Case*, he hurled his own thunderbolt at Coke:

> And yet here in this Case, such is the Conscience of the Doctor, the Defendant, That he would have the Houses, Gardens, and Orchards, which he neither built nor planted: But the Chancellors have always corrected such corrupt Consciences. . . . And (his Lordship) the Plaintiff in this Case only desired to be satisfied of the true Value of the new Building and Planting since the Conveyance. . . . And Equity speaks as the Law of God speaks. But you would silence Equity. 1st Because you have a judgment at Law. . . . To Which I answer. . . . The Office of the Chancellor is to correct Mens Consciences for Frauds, Breach of Trusts, Wrongs and Oppressions, of what Nature soever they be, and to soften and mollify the Extremity of the Law, which is called *Summum Jus*.[31]

The chancellor did not enjoin the common-law judges nor set aside their order; this would have been beyond his power. He did have jurisdiction over the person of the winner of a lawsuit, however, and asserted it to prevent unjust enrichment through fraud. Ellesmere maintained that equity had always relieved against sharp dealing, fraud and misrepresentation included. Without equitable redress, there could be no justice. James I, hearing both sides of the quarrel between the courts and a report from Attorney General Francis Bacon (shortly to succeed Ellesmere as chancellor), determined that the chancellor had acted correctly.[32]

As King James's intervention demonstrated, a deeper constitutional question was hidden beneath these squabbles over jurisdiction. Indeed, formal relations between the two kinds of courts were generally cooperative, even in this era.[33] The really troublesome question that *Courtney* and the *Earl of Oxford's Case* exposed was which court could be trusted by the people to protect their rights. The chancellor conceived his jurisdiction as a public trust. As Nottingham wrote in his *Prolegomena of Chancery and Equity*, "Equity being opposite to regular law, it is in a manner an arbitrary disposition administered by the chancellor in the King's name as a special trust committed to the King, the power of which court is absolute and unlimited, though out of discretion it entertains some form, which it may justly leave in special cases."[34] If the king had created the trust and the chancellor was his agent, acting in his stead, then the beneficiary must be the people. This was the very argument counsel for the defendants in the "ship-money" cases would assay to avert punishment of their clients. Oliver St. John, counsel for John Hampden, insisted that "His Majesty is concerned in the way and manner of execution of the highest and greatest trust which the law hath reposed in him, the Safety and Preservation of the Kingdom."[35] Hampden should not be fined and imprisoned for holding a trustee to the terms of his office. Neither Nottingham nor St. John made clear whether the king was the trustee or merely the creator of this trust, but whatever the king's role the chancellor was charged to protect the people.

A court so closely tied to a monarchy under siege could not be a viable superintendent of the public trust as far as Coke was concerned. The chief justice, the foremost interpreter of fundamental law of his day, insisted that the common law—not equity—mirrored natural law. It captured in maxim and precedent the rights of all English people; its word must be final in public as well as private disputes.[36] The intervention of the chancellor after the common-law courts had spoken violated his own trust—his duty as a judge—because he raised his own authority above that of the common law. The chancellor's court rested not on fundamental law (that is, for Coke, on common law), but on the caprice of the Crown. The chancellor was incapable of resisting political pressure. The monarch could make and unmake courts; such tribunals could never be as safe a repository for the rights of English people as the regular courts of law. In 1610, Coke, then chief judge of Common Pleas, opined that the common-law courts must be supreme over the legislative side of Parliament as well, for "it appears in our books, that in many cases, the common law will controul Acts of Parliament and sometimes adjudge them to be utterly void: for when an Act of Parliament is against common right and reason, or repugnant or impossible to be performed, the common law will control it, and adjudge such Act to be void."[37] Ellesmere prepared a draft opinion rebutting Coke but never found the occasion to publish it.[38]

Coke's view of the law courts was colored by recent politics; he had lost the ear of the king. In theory and fact, the common-law courts were no less a child of the king's Council than the court of the chancellor, for all derived authority from the prerogative of the Crown to hear and determine cases touching its property, peace, or majesty.[39] In terms of established protocol, Coke had a better case, for chancellors before Ellesmere had generally deferred to the common-law judges.[40] Sir Matthew Hale, Coke's successor as the foremost interpreter of the common law, celebrated its claim to supremacy in the last years of the seventeenth century: "This [common law] is that which asserts, maintains, and with all imaginable Care, provides for the Safety of the King's Royal Person, his Crown and Dignity, and all his just Rights, Revenues, Powers, Prerogatives and Government . . . and this law is also, that which declares and asserts the Rights and Liberties, and the Properties of the Subject; and is the just, known and common Rule of Justice and Right between man and man, within this Kingdom."[41] No voice was raised on the chancery side to dispute Hale's opinion.

Ellesmere had rested his position as trustee of the public good on his conscience; a chancellor's conscience was the essence of his jurisprudence. In 1621, Francis Bacon, Lord Chancellor St. Albans, stricken, he said, by conscience, admitted to Parliament that he was taking bribes. The chancellor's court was again subjected to political attack. Bacon, made keeper of the rolls and then chancellor after Ellesmere, had long lobbied for the post and gloried in it; he had reached the office his father Nicholas had held before him. Bacon's genuine desire for fair dealing, based in part on his professionalism and in part on his philosophical commitment to justice, was bent by his love of luxury and his fawning desire to please James I and his chief minister, the avaricious and unscrupulous Duke of Buckingham. Falling in with Buckingham's schemes to fill his family's pockets with the proceeds of illicit monopolies, Bacon sealed documents which would later haunt him. He was also open, as his own testimony revealed, to bribes in pending cases. When the Parliament of 1621 convened, it had a shock in store for him. The spokesman for the reformers in the Commons was none other than Sir Edward Coke, now banished from the bench and a bitter enemy of equity and Bacon. Under the prodding of Coke, the lower house investigated the monopoly scandal and rumors of bribery in the chancellor's court. Bacon, knowing that there was truth in both accusations, sought the protection of James I and Buckingham, but they were advised by Bishop Williams (who would replace Bacon as Lord Keeper) to expose him to the enmity of the Commons in order to protect themselves.[42] Willingly they stepped aside, leaving Bacon to his enemies. Parliament had already impeached, tried, convicted, and punished another of Buckingham's henchmen, Sir Giles Mompesson, for abuse of public trust.[43] The Commons swiftly drafted a bill of impeachment against Bacon, charging him with "breach of trust."[44] Fearing that the impeachment could not be stayed and that the verdict at trial in the House of Lords was a foregone conclusion, Bacon confessed. His "conscience," at last stirred to life, dictated that he bow to the censure of his peers in the House of Lords.[45] Even his abject submission did not prevent the Commons from seeking a formal trial, at which Bacon had to repeat his confession to the specific charges. From the height of power and luxury, Bacon was reduced to near penury. His reference to his own conscience-stricken recollection, intended to gain the pity of the Lords, sounded like an ironic and distorted echo of origin of the chancellor's authority. Prophetically, Bacon had seen the pitfalls of "great place" a decade before: "the standing is slippery, and the regress is either a downfall or at least an eclipse, which is a melancholy thing."[46]

Bacon had abused his trust, for which he was held accountable by the representatives of the people. In the process, the concept of public trusteeship came clearer. Bacon was not a trustee for the king, but for the people. His removal for corruption in office was accomplished by the representatives in Parliament of the beneficiaries of his trust. In a series of impeachments of royal ministers leading to the impeachment, conviction, and execution of Lord Strafford, adviser to Charles I, primarily for misdeeds in his office as administrator of Ireland, opponents of the Crown rehearsed the theme of officials' accountability to the representatives of the people according to the public trust.[47]

As the breach between Crown and Parliament widened, the chancellor's court was again thrust into the limelight by a tug-of-war for the Great Seal. Without the seal, official documents were not legal. The chancellor was always the keeper of the seal, which he carried in an embroidered bag. Parliament insisted that the chancellor use the seal to give authority to its acts, even though the king and Parliament were waging war against each other. When Chancellor Littleton would not accede, Parliament appointed a commission to handle its secretarial duties. Insofar as these involved adjudication of suits in equity, Parliament had created its own equity court. The Lords Commissioners of the Great Seal, in one form or another, continued to exercise this jurisdiction until the Commonwealth was swept away in the restoration of Charles II in 1660.

From 1649 through the end of the Protectorate, eleven years later, ordinances to reform procedure in the chancery were regularly prepared, debated, and, in some cases, actually passed. William Sheppard, Lord Protector Oliver Cromwell's personal legal adviser and the drafter of the last and most comprehensive of the reform bills, glimpsed the future of equity. In his monographic plea for law reform, *England's Balme* (1657), he argued that equity courts should consider pleas and defenses based on common law as well as equity, and that the central courts should have jurisdiction over all matters legal and equitable. He even argued, anticipating the Judicature Acts of 1873 and 1875 in England, that pleading should be factual, leaving the distinction between equity and law to the judges.[48] If taken seriously, Sheppard's proposals would have streamlined the court system and facilitated private pleading, but Sheppard could not overcome the inertia of lawyers in Cromwell's own entourage. A combination of political partisanship and juristic inertia defeated this thoughtful and prescient program of reform.

During the Civil War the court's reputation remained—justly or unjustly—synonymous with arbitrary and overweening discretion. The accountability of the chancellor to Parliament, a source of dispute throughout the 1640s, merged with a rising controversy over the accountability of Parliament itself at the end of the decade. In the process, arguments developed to justify reform or abolition of equity courts fed into the broader debate over parliamentary accountability to the people. As reformers and factions pressed toward an answer from all sides, a general doctrine of public trusteeship began to take shape.

Early in the Civil War, Henry Parker, a conservative parliamentary reformer, equated the duty of governors with the duty of private trustees:

> I conceive it is now sufficiently clear, that all rule is but fiduciarie, and that this and that Prince is more or lesse absolute, as

he is more or lesse trusted, and that all trusts differ not in nature or intent, but in degree only and extent: and therefore since it is unnatural for any Nation to give away its owne propertie in it selfe absolutely, and to subject its self to a condition of servilitie below men, because this is contrarie to the supreme of all Lawes, wee must not think that it can stand with the intent of any trust, that necessarie defense should be barred, and naturall preservation denied any people.[49]

Parker had drawn an analogy between a private trust and a commonwealth. Two years later, William Ball made the analogy even more explicit. He argued against the resuscitation of royal authority, for "by [the people] reposing or granting such Trust [in the king], they doe not disinvest themselves of their *right naturall* (no more than one that passeth an estate to foefees in Trust for some causes and considerations disinvesteth himself of the use intended or reserved)."[50] Ball had confused somewhat the trust, which was settled without "consideration" (that is, something of value in return for the trustee consenting to serve), with a contract, which required such consideration. The source of his analogy should not be mistaken, however.[51] It was the equitable trust.

As Parliament assumed more of the powers of government, critics of its Presbyterian bias and its political conservatism began to question its accountability to the people. Though the radical attack on the royal and aristocratic presence in the English government had emerged by 1644, a fully critical exploration of parliamentary rule itself did not appear until 1646.[52] The spokesmen for this position developed a power base in the "New Model Army" of the Commonwealth and in the City of London. Among these men was a small cadre of political reformers whose enemies called them "levellers." The precise importance of these incendiaries remains a matter of controversy, and much of their influence dissipated after 1647, but within the radical tradition in England and America their advocacy of direct accountability of government to the people resonated through the centuries.[53]

More than one man led the movement, but its heart was John Lilburne, an advocate of radical political reform from the late 1630s, an officer in the Puritan army, and a brilliant autodidact. In 1646, with the Presbyterians ousted from control of Parliament by a more radical combination of freethinkers, Independent Puritans, and republicans, Lilburne wrote and distributed his *Remonstrance*—a warning to the leaders of the new parliament to avoid the sins of their predecessors: "But ye are to remember, this was only of us but a

Power of trust, which is ever revokable, and cannot be otherwise and to be imployed to no other end, then our owne well-being: Nor did we choose you to continue our Trust's longer, then the knowne established constitution of this Commonly-Wealth will justly permit."[54] Lilburne, an avid reader of law books, used "trust" in both the literal and the figurative sense. The "revocable trust" is a term of art referring to a certain kind of trust. It could be revoked by its creators on their own volition, or automatically when certain conditions were violated. Lilburne was suggesting, by analogy, that the people were the grantors of the trust as well as its beneficiaries—a version of a "life trust"—and could revoke the authority of the trustees, here Parliament, for violation of the terms of the trust. In particular, by overstaying their term in office, members of Parliament would automatically dissolve the trust. This was a novel and clever addition to the growing vocabulary of public trusteeship. Lilburne also summoned up the commoner meaning of trust—reliance on those one has come to respect. Parliament had lost the confidence of the people and could only regain it by seeking their approval at the polls.[55] Emotional and self-sacrificing, Lilburne served with distinction in Cromwell's army, then turned to it for support in his attempt to reform Parliament.

For its part, Parliament feared a standing army, even its own, and tried to disband it in 1647. Refusing to be sent off without pay or privileges, the army gathered at Putney Green in November to debate its future. While radical army officers tried to convince Colonels Richard Ireton and Oliver Cromwell, both country gentlemen, that further reform was needed, Richard Overton, a freethinking leveller of middle-class origins, published his own *Appeale from the Degenerate Representative Body* in the City. Overton directed his appeal to the army, whose leaders he instructed in the equity of the laws. The problem was how to legally oppose a parliament that had arrogated to itself all authority. Overton first sought to establish that "*the equity of the Law is Superiour to the Letter.*"[56] Should law, by which he meant parliamentary ordinances, transgress equity, by which he meant Parliament's underlying promise to treat the army fairly, then law was invalid. His language borrowed force from the juristic convention that when a statute could not be easily applied to a case, the judge looked to the "equity" of the statute by standing in the place of the legislature and determining how it would have wanted the case handled.[57] Overton misapplied the rule; Parliament was quite specific about its intentions for the army.[58] The equity and the letter of its ordinance both required the army to disband and ran against his position. A more cogent argument for his cause was his insistence that Parliament was a trustee and its ordinances merely expressions of the terms of the trust. He continued: "*All betrusted powers, if forfeit, fall to the hands of the betrusters, as their proper center.*" So long as Parliament acted to discharge its trust, its power remained, "but no sooner the betrusted betray and forfeit their *Trust*, but (as all things else in dissolution) it returneth whence it came, even to the hands of the *Trusters*."[59] Overton did not suggest a method by which erring representatives could be called to account without disrupting the government. Impeachment and trial were such a mechanism, but they belonged to Parliament and could not be used by the army.

A year later, Lilburne and his associates joined in an *Agreement of the People* (1648) proposing a more structured accountability. A new parliament, to be elected biennially, would have the power "in calling to an account, and punishing publick Officers for abusing or failing their trust."[60] The House of Lords was abolished (and with it trials of impeachment), so that removal from office under the *Agreement* could not be the same as impeachment and trial in the old parliament. What was more, in the old Commons, anyone could be impeached, not just officeholders, and offenses were not confined to failing in the public trust. Under the *Agreement*, only officials could be reached by parliamentary recall. The penalty for such parliamentary recall was not defined. Ironically, lawyers were forbidden to practice when they sat in this new model assembly, a slap at the profession and a simultaneous proof that lawyers were playing a major part in politics. The commitment to legalism in the structure and language of the levellers' proposals is obvious and thoroughgoing. The appropriation of the ideal of the equity of the law and the even more explicit borrowing of the private trust showed that the language of law was open for use by nonprofessionals away from the court chamber.[61]

In borrowing and transforming the language of equity courts, the levellers did not mean to defend chancery itself or its procedures for gathering evidence and arriving at decrees. The chancellor operated without a jury, and no body of English political writers was more committed to trial by jury than the levellers. More than once John Lilburne himself was saved from the clutches of his political opponents by sympathetic juries determining not only facts but law as well. The levellers merely appropriated the conscience of an idealized chancellor, extended that conscience to rout out abuse of public trust, and made the process accessible to popular scrutiny.

The leveller program only briefly survived its enunciation.

Though Lilburne, Overton, and others pruned and shaped it to near perfection in their third *Agreement of the People* (1653), that pamphlet was published while they languished in the Tower. Once Oliver Cromwell had elevated himself to the Protectorate and driven the Long Parliament from its chamber, political radicalism no longer remained an option and the levellers were silenced. Lilburne and Cromwell had a perverse and ambivalent relationship, at one point in which the former regarded the latter as the savior of England. As Lilburne was incapable of sycophancy for very long and Cromwell thrived on it, there was no future to their alliance. Imprisoned, the levellers opted for more private occupations. Lilburne became a Quaker. Their last words were all but lost in the burr of noise emanating from so many political sources in the last years of the Protectorate and the first flourish of the Restoration.

The levellers were not the only, or even the most profound, radical critics of Parliament and Protectorate. Less obtrusively at first, because they were better connected and educated than the levellers and had more to lose, but ultimately more profoundly, John Milton, James Harrington, and Algernon Sidney also explored the problem of public accountability. They drew upon classical and continental sources rather than the legal constructs that so entranced the levellers, but they were not immune to equitable analogies. Harrington's own utopian essay, *Oceana*, like Machiavelli's *Prince*, from whose barely concealed longing for disinterested civic virtue Harrington drew inspiration, was crafted to convince a powerful leader to think in a republican fashion. In the end, Harrington had no more influence on Cromwell than Machiavelli had on Lorenzo de Medici, even if Harrington's reputation fared far better than Machiavelli's.[62] Harrington's thoughts on "The Judicial Part" in chapter 8 of *A System of Politics* showed a genuine debt to a Ciceronian ideal of natural law inseparable from equity. Harrington assumed that "natural equity" dictated the outcomes of lawsuits—"there is no difficulty at all in judging of any case whatsoever according to natural equity"—a species of naiveté that no lawyer or leveller would have exhibited.[63]

Around Harrington, Algernon Sidney and a host of other republican writers and politicians gathered, waiting and hoping for vindication of their theories. Sidney's *Discourses Concerning Government* (1689), published six years after his execution for treason, were the most moving and the most often quoted of these arguments.[64] Like Harrington, Sidney believed that tyrants must be opposed. Unlike Harrington, he advocated violence to do it. With Harrington, he shared the central dilemma of all these republicans: their fierce passion for accountability was never harnessed to any workable scheme for insuring accountability short of creating new governments (Harrington's proposal) or shearing away old ones (Sidney's threat). If they had made a mark on the conduct of government—Cromwell's own *Instrument of Government* (1653) had promised that all erring officials would be punished (in that respect alone it resembled the *Agreement of the People*)—the Protector and his Council were charged with ferreting out malfeasance in their own ranks.[65] Charles II's advisers were as partisan and corrupt as those of his father and grandfather. Had all the sacrifice and intellectual effort of the radicals gone for naught?

The wag who chides that historical hindsight has twenty-twenty vision misses an important truth about legal and political ideas. Despite their failure to avert the restoration of Stuart rule, with its indifference to popular opinion and official accountability, the radicals' arguments remained in circulation. One salutary immediate consequence was that Harrington's idealization of the contractarian beginnings of government, though based in his own admiration for ancient Solons, moved William Penn to envision a benevolent commonwealth. Penn's program became reality in his proprietary colony of Pennsylvania, a gentle trust whose beneficiaries were the first settlers of the province.[66]

Harrington's aspirations continued to resonate in the arguments of reformers during the Restoration, notably John Locke. Locke was a physician whose longing for a university professorship was never consummated, but whose attachment to the household of the freethinking and politically active Anthony Ashley Cooper, later Lord Shaftesbury, brought him into contact with the liberal religious and political reformers of his day. Locke acted first as Shaftesbury's personal physician, then as his secretary, then as administrator of a number of the organizations and special interests of which Shaftesbury was sponsor or director. Locke was more than an amanuensis; as Shaftesbury's grandson later recalled, "He [Shaftesbury] put him [Locke] upon the study of the religious and civil affairs of the nation with whatsoever related to the business of a Minister of State, in which he was so successful that my grandfather began soon to use him as a friend, and consult with him upon occasions of that kind. ... The Liberty he [Locke] could take with these great men was peculiar to such a genius as his."[67] Locke's influence followed the fortunes of his patron, save that the secretary was far more inconspicuous and cautious than the Lord. Shaftesbury's opposition to the Catholic interest—the exclusion controversy—earned him the enmity of Charles II's brother James and Charles's wife and brought Locke to the edge of ruin. In the wake of the discovery of the "Rye House Plot" against James, Whigs like Locke had to flee the realm. Shaftesbury was dead, but Locke found many of the conspirators safe and active abroad and spent the rest of the Stuarts' tenure in the Netherlands, returning to his home when Parliament deposed James II.

Before he fled, Locke had prepared a defense of the Whigs' program.[68] In part, Locke's *Two Treatises on Government* was a compendium of responses and adaptations of others' theories. The manuscript rejected Thomas Filmer's Bible-based analogies to patriarchs, with their call for absolute obedience to the Crown, and Thomas Hobbes's rationalism, with its grant of absolute power to a unitary magisterial discretion.[69] Locke appears to have bought into Harrington's "contractarian" vision of an agreement among people in a state of nature to submit themselves to government, reserving to themselves through the structure of their government basic rights of life, liberty, and property. Locke did not stop here, however. In the last sections of the *Second Treatise* he contemplated the theoretical basis of accountability. First, he likened the "prerogative" of the executive to the discretion of a trustee, moving easily and consciously from the legal to the political context. "This Power to act according to discretion, for the Publics good, without the prescription of the Law, and sometimes even against it, *is* that which is called *Prerogative.*" The power of the executive could only be exercised "suitably to the trust and ends of the Government." A good prince was mindful of this "trust" and did not abuse it. The power of calling parliaments was also part of this trust.[70]

What if the trust were abused by the Parliament or the prince? Locke contemplated the possibility of abuse of discretion squarely. If members of the legislature breached the trust by which they held power, they forfeited it to the people who gave it to them. So, too, corruption by the executive, using the public fisc to suborn the legislature or to buy votes of electors, traduced his public trust and opened him to removal. Who was to judge whether the public trust had been violated? "To this I reply, *The People Shall be Judge*; for who shall be *Judge* whether his Trustee or Deputy acts well, and according to the Trust reposed in him, but he who deputes him, and must, by having deputed him have still a Power to discard him, when he fails in his Trust? If this be reasonable in particular Cases of private Men, why should it be otherwise in that of the greatest moment;

where the Welfare of Millions is concerned, and also where the evil, if not prevented, is greater, and the Redress very difficult, dear, and dangerous?"[71] Locke had adopted the notion that the grantor of a trust may also be its beneficiary. Lilburne's suggestion that the mechanism for dissolving the trust may be built into it—the conditional or revocable life trust—here gained its most formidable statement. With abuse of power, the trust automatically dissolved. This formulation also averted the most pointed objection to any analogy between public accountability and removal of private trustees—the absence of a chancellor to decree removal of a public official. By making the public trust revocable and conditional, Locke implied that the chancellor (or the eminence behind him, the king) was not necessary to protect the public trust.

Though Locke cited the concept of trust far more often than that of contract and was familiar with the usage of public trust in the previous fifty years of controversy, modern scholars do not ascribe to him a literal appropriation of the equitable trust: "We need not assume, as is often done, that he was trying to describe a formal trust deed for government."[72] Although there is no necessity in this assumption, it is supported by the particular circumstances of Locke's relationship to Shaftesbury. In 1673, while Locke was his confidant and secretary, Shaftesbury was elevated to the office of chancellor. Though not a trained judge or a practicing lawyer, Shaftesbury had sweeping plans for revamping the central court of equity. He had sat on the parliamentary committees to reform the courts in 1652 and prepared for his inauguration as chancellor a comprehensive set of rules. What is more, Shaftesbury was convinced that his predecessors had lost their commitment to speedy and even-handed justice. Whatever the measure of his accomplishments, he must have discussed his hopes and plans continually with Locke. Locke was his Secretary of Presentations, an office related to Shaftesbury's many duties as the chancellor, and saw firsthand the workings of chancery. Shaftesbury's vigorous and somewhat untutored manner of conducting chancery court, and, even more, his partisanship, led to his dismissal at the end of 1673, another event that he and Locke must have endlessly rehearsed at dinner in the London townhouse they shared. Discussion in Shaftesbury's mansion was always full, frank, and politically pointed. Locke had every opportunity to familiarize himself with the trust as a concrete model for reforming English constitutionalism.[73]

Unfortunately for the Whig conspirators' agenda for constitutional reform, they had to flee the realm. Locke went into exile, and his manuscript, safe in his trunk, went with him. *Two Treatises* was published in 1689, after the Stuarts were driven from their throne and William of Orange, a staunch Dutch Protestant and husband of the deposed king's daughter Mary, was invited to assume the Crown under the condition that he accept the supremacy of Parliament in financial matters and preserve inviolate the rights of the English people. Parliamentary supremacy was henceforth assumed in a constitution that mixed monarchy, aristocracy, and popular representation. Shaftesbury was long dead, but Locke was honored by the new government and given a post in it. He never acknowledged that the *Two Treatises* was his work and went on to repute as an educational theorist, psychologist, and philosopher.

In the political context of its publication, not its actual composition, the *Two Treatises* was read as a vindication of parliamentary supremacy. Nothing could have been further from Locke's original purpose. He had condemned all untrustworthy government and demanded accountability from all branches of it. Instead, the eighteenth-century Parliament courted the image of a trustee—"No Whig could deny that government was in some sense a trust"—but not in the strict sense of an equitable trust.[74] Indeed, the equitable analogue could have no bite when Parliament regarded itself as its own monitor. If Locke was read in context, as an advocate of aristocratic rebellion or popular uprising, he would have been as threatening to the parliamentary settlement as the levellers or Tories like Henry St. John, Viscount Bolingbroke.[75]

A few hardy eighteenth-century critics of Parliament recognized Locke as a kindred spirit and from him and the levellers drew sustenance for their protest. For these radical "commonwealthmen," the ideal of accountability of Parliament itself was a realizable goal.[76] As James Burgh wrote in the first volume of his *Political Disquisitions* (1774): power in the hands of Parliament or ministers of the Crown "may be compared to the reflected light of the moon; for it is only borrowed, delegated, and limited by the intention of the people, whose it is, and to whom governors are to consider themselves as responsible." When the government "betray their trust," power reverts to the people. Burgh was not advocating revolution but reform. Parliament could not purify itself until it undertook to make itself accountable to the people; corruption would not brook reformation. The rotten boroughs had to be destroyed. The maldistribution of voting in the other electoral districts must be redressed. Bribery must be sternly punished, for "Members of Parliament have the properties, liberties, and lives of the nation in their hands, and hold themselves accountable to no man, or set of men, for the laws they make. Ought the trustees of so great a charge to be men capable of giving or receiving base bribes?"[77] Burgh called to his side the shades of Locke, Lilburne, and the leveller agitators in the New Model Army to insist that even Parliament was accountable for its trust. Impeachment and trial, the collar on ministers and members of Parliament alike in the preceding century, were not only the tools of Parliament but also had fallen into disuse after 1715. Burgh's proposal was to make Parliament more representative and accessible to the people, a constitutional remedy. The constituents would then instruct their members, preventing special interests from gaining control of the lower house. Annual parliaments, with a broadened franchise, would prevent unpopular and unjust acts from passing. What was more, greater freedom to publish criticism of the government would insure that enquiry "into the behavior of our *trustees*" and the ability "to call them to *account*" was not lost.[78]

No one would accuse Burgh's treatise of originality. Its great virtue, one that commended it to American revolutionary readers at least, was its compendious array of authorities.[79] Catherine Macaulay's *History of England* (1769) also paid its debt to the levellers and Locke. Her contemporary political message, cast in the form of an extended historical essay on the failings of the first Stuarts, noted with approval the agitators in the New Model Army, particularly their realization that government was "instituted for the protection of the people, for the end of securing, not overthrowing, the rights of nature; that it is a trust either formally admitted or supposed; and that magistracy is consequently accountable."[80] John Wilkes championed the same cause in the nineteenth number of his *North Briton* series of pamphlets. His style was not so pedantic as Burgh's nor so narrative as Macaulay's. Wilkes trumpeted: "but if the people's implements, to whom they have trusted the execution of those laws, or any power for their preservation, should convert such execution to their destruction, have they not a right to intermeddle? Nay, have they not a right to resume the power they have delegated, and to punish their servants who have abused it?"[81] John Almon, a third-generation commonwealthman, thundered the answer: "our government is a *trust* from the people, and someone must be *answerable* for the *exercise* of every part of it."[82]

Strong as these voices of dissent were, they cried out in a wilderness of corrupt, timeserving Whiggery. The commonwealthmen had no power to alter this state of affairs, any more than the levellers could impress their demands upon Cromwell and his lieutenants.

Locke's vision of an accountability based on equitable trusteeship was thus a lost opportunity in England. One of the great ironies of Anglo-American political theory is that, through a channel of communication manned by religious sectaries and political freethinkers, the commonwealthmen's ideas found a wider audience in Britain's North American colonies than they had in the mother country.[83] In the New World, calls for accountability of Parliament had a special and immediate force after 1763. The strength of the trusteeship theory developed in England and shipped to America was that its basic language was so commonplace and well rehearsed that it needed no special pleading to gain adherence. The weakness of the theory, a paralyzing weakness, was that it had little grip in the real world. The commonwealthmen could not put any of their ideas into practice—Parliament did not reform itself until early in the next century, and then under different prompting than the impassioned cavilling of the commonwealthmen. The links between equitable trusteeship—Locke's "deed of trust"—and the arguments of his disciples nearly a century later were too attenuated to offer reformers a concrete model of genuine accountability. The English chancellor was no longer a political symbol, either as the conscience of the law or as a target for reform, nor was his court in the center of constitutional quarrel. He had receded, with equity itself, into the labyrinth of precedent and rules in which Joseph Story found him two generations later. The alternative of impeachment and trial by Parliament, never a satisfactory guarantor of parliamentary accountability, had fallen into disuse. Thus the gift of the commonwealthmen's idea of trusteeship to the Americans was a gift of a terminology; persuasive but limited, it could confirm, support, and broaden, but not authorize any particular system of accountability in the increasingly restive colonies. Instead, Americans had to duplicate the English experience with equity—in court and out-of-doors—before they could fully utilize the conception of political accountability. In fact, this is what happened.

3 THEIR TRUSTEES AND SERVANTS

The rules of equity developed in the chancellor's court came to nearly every one of England's North American colonies, but conditions in these far-flung settlements altered the shape of equity. The hallmark of colonial reception of equity was a bewildering variety of equity courts. Central courts of general jurisdiction, special high courts of equity, assemblies and councils, and local courts all exercised some measure of equity jurisprudence. Governors and assemblies debated the division of these powers endlessly and acrimoniously. The result was an evolution of doctrine and practice punctuated by brief but bitter political controversies, a pattern more reminiscent of equity in Lord Ellesmere's day than in eighteenth-century England. Out of the quarrels between governors and assemblies over the proper boundaries of equitable jurisdiction came occasions for fusion of the workaday practices of equity lawyers and the higher ideal of an equitable state. Much as John Locke had reached into the language of equity courts to find a metaphor of public accountability, so colonial lawyers employed the precepts of equity to argue against the power of governors and imperial officers. In the revolutionary crisis, one of the colonies' most brilliant equity lawyers, Thomas Jefferson, linked Locke's vision of public trusteeship to the American experience with equity and produced a timeless evocation of equitable constitutionalism.

RECEPTION

Much as the formal apparatus empowering settlement and establishing order in the New World depended on English legal authority and models, the colonists very soon developed an autochthonous legal culture.[1] Though vast space—a "howling wilderness" the first English people in New England called their new abode—and easy movement certainly played a role in this development, the colonists neither sought to deconstruct the English legal system nor succeeded in doing so.[2] In part, American jurisprudence differed from its parent because the composition of the law-giving elite differed. Colonial population was not a cross section of England's.[3] Magistrates and legislators in New England were younger, less affluent, and certainly not as aristocratic as the judges in the king's commission and the members of his Parliament. Future colonial lawmakers thus brought with them an imperfect picture of the vast variety of English tribunals. They could not and did not try to duplicate that array of special courts derived from feudal grants, Saxon customs, and the king's prerogative. What is more, the settlers had far greater affinity for reform of courts and law than did the authorities in England, save for the brief period when Puritans controlled the English government.[4]

The difference in personnel and experience gave courts and law in America a distinctive structure. Here, a simple system of hierarchically arrayed forums of general jurisdiction replaced England's multiplicity of overlapping courts. English became the language of statute, code, and court pleading; Latin and Law French were banished to lawyers' and judges' libraries. Colonial elites quickly grasped the value of labor in their settlements; there was no surfeit of sturdy beggars to employ in seasonal agriculture as in England. Colonial lawgivers and judges mitigated the penalty for many felonies.[5] If Puritan exiles from religious persecution instituted their own inquisitions, Lord Baltimore in Maryland, Roger Williams in Rhode Island, and the Quakers in Pennsylvania allowed more religious toleration in their precincts than could be found anywhere in England before 1689. The paucity of lawyers, officially barred from receiving fees in many of the first colonies, and the amateurism that suffused local adjudication led to open-ended grants of jurisdiction to county courts.

A rich tradition of legal autonomy, worked out in interstices of imperial rule, marked colonial law and legal authority in these early years of settlement. Throughout the eighteenth century, better contact with England, a steadily increasing number of practicing lawyers, many of whom were trained in England, and closer English supervision of colonial courts led to an Anglicization of the colonial law,[6] but the process was never completed. True, much of the letter of England's case law and some of its statute law was received and incorporated into the superstructure of colonial judicature, but the colonies retained their juridical distinctiveness.[7]

The most important of these differences between colonial and English jurisprudence was the intimate tie in America between constitutional law and private dispute resolution. The former could never be precisely defined in the colonies, because they had no constitutions as such. They existed under positive grants, much like chartered corporations. England had a constitution, but, shorn of all rhetoric of Edward Coke, Matthew Hale, and William Blackstone, it was nothing more than the collection of all its statutes, court decisions, and royal ordinances. The colonists could bask in the glory of this constitution, but it was not quite theirs.[8] Perhaps because they did not fully share the rights of the English within the realm, the colonists were obsessed with the idea of a fundamental law embodied in constitutions—an obsession whose therapy was a passion for writing compacts and fundamental orders wherever they set down their feet. In the process, the fashioning of private law merged into the effort to control and order society through written instruments of government.

English equity was received and altered in this context of colonial legal particularity. Despite periodic difficulties and an occasional disaster, equity made its way into the jurisprudence of all the southern colonies. The first grant of equitable jurisdiction in the New World appeared in Maryland, the proprietorship Charles I conferred on the Calvert family. The Calverts' charter, which they helped to draft, allowed them to appoint "Praetorian Judicatories." They had borrowed from Roman jurisprudence the term for magistrates—a stylish show of their own erudition as well as an invitation to adjudicate "praetorian" (that is, equitable) suits.[9] The assembly created its own court of chancery in 1639, a harbinger of disputes between assembly and proprietor over the courts that would erupt throughout the history of the colony, but the proprietor promptly rejected such legislative assertiveness. The assembly mended its ways in 1642, passing a bill making the governor and his council into a court of equity. The governor became the sole chancellor in 1725. The Maryland court of chancery was even more active than equity courts in its larger neighbors. At the bar of that court the leading figures in the colony brought complaints and made responses on behalf of clients, including the proprietor himself.[10] Virginia's governor and council sat as a high court of equity throughout the colonial era. Although much of its early record was destroyed by fire, a remnant of cases edited by Thomas Jefferson demonstrates that the best and the brightest of the Virginia colonial bar practiced before its court of chancery. County courts of general sessions also had and used equity powers.[11]

The original charter for the Carolina proprietary (1663) did not create a court of equity, but it did apply to the colony the notion—already so commonplace as to be readily invoked in English political dialogue—that all Carolina officials "will truly and faithfully discharge their respective trusts." Without settlers, the grant would never fulfill its purpose—to line the pockets of Charles II's supporters. One of these was Lord Shaftesbury, and he commissioned Locke to write "Fundamental Constitutions" (1669) for the colony that would attract settlers as well as promoting profits for the proprietors. Locke introduced a colonial chancellor, who, among his other duties, would do justice in all "invasions of the law, of liberty of conscience, and all invasions of the public peace, upon pretense of religion, and also the license of printing." Locke and Shaftesbury were trying to have their cake and eat it: offering toleration while promising to prevent religious agitators from disturbing public order. Locke's constitution was soon forgotten, but the North Carolina high court of equity functioned from the end of the seventeenth century until the Revolution.[12] In South Carolina, an indigenous court of chancery was almost coterminous with the colony. Governor Stephen Bull simply asked the members of his council to sit with him as a court of equity and they all swore "in all things [to] demean and behave . . . as to equity and justice pertains." The proprietors ratified this arrangement, which continued with modifications through the royal colony and the statehood era until the Civil War.[13] Proprietary Georgia was a living example of equity: a trust for debtors whose government was a board of trustees. Ironically, the trusteeship colony had no court of equity (indeed, lawyers were barred from practice), but no sooner was a royal charter in place than a central court of equity was established.[14]

The Middle Atlantic colonies established courts of equity in a variety of ways. Pennsylvania county courts were granted equity powers by the earliest laws of the colony. William Penn proposed but never set up a central equity court. His lieutenants' efforts to this end in 1706 collapsed. A brief experiment with a central court of equity between 1720 and 1735, "for opening a way to the right and equity of a cause for which the law cannot, in all cases, make a sufficient provision," was also undermined by antiproprietary agitation, but local courts in Pennsylvania and the "lower counties" of Delaware retained their equitable jurisdiction. The colony's assembly also acted as a court of equity (perhaps one reason why its majority opposed a central court of equity), hearing and disposing of over seven hundred petitions for specific performance of contracts, production of documents, aid to minors and the mentally incapacitated, and regulation of trusts.[15] Both East Jersey and West Jersey had distinct courts of equity from their settlement. When the two proprietary colonies were joined as a royal colony in 1702, a central court of equity was fashioned. Though long thought to have functioned sporadically, evidence in the papers of James Alexander, surveyor general and counselor in the colony, reveals an active court. Alexander himself, a Scots emigrant who arrived in Perth Amboy in 1715, established a busy private equity practice in New Jersey.[16] New York gained a central court of equity through the initiative of Lieutenant Governor John Nanfan in 1701 after an abortive enabling act in 1683. The governor sat as chancellor. With a few notable breaks in its course due to the colony's intense factionalism, the court met through the revolutionary era and, with an altered bench, into the period of statehood.[17]

New England's experience with courts of equity was more troubled than that of the southern or Middle Atlantic colonies. Massachusetts' General Assembly, styled the General Court when it sat with the assistants of the colony, acted as a high court of equity until the Dominion of New England was formed and the colony's original charter was dissolved. County courts in the Bay Colony long exercised equity powers, but these were only formally defined by the General Court after the charter was lost, a hedge against the power of the Crown to reclaim its New England real estate. Edmund Andros, governor of the Dominion, attempted to create a central court of equity, but with his overthrow the court collapsed. After the second charter was granted, the General Court twice attempted to erect courts of equity on its own authority but was rebuffed by the Privy Council.[18] Though one attempt in New Hampshire to create a royal court of equity failed, in 1692 the colony's assembly agreed to let the governor and council sit as a high court of equity.[19] The Connecticut General Assembly retained an appellate equity jurisdiction until 1773, after which appeals in equity were to go from the district superior courts to the supreme court.[20]

The ideal of a public trust came to Rhode Island long before any equity court was established. The "Agreement" of 1640 bringing together the four towns on the Narragansett certified that the heads of the towns were "betrusted" to establish a fair and representative system of government. In an ironic echo of this self-generated trusteeship, the royal charter of 1663, lobbied for by Roger Williams at Westminster, returned the lands to the inhabitants, "Upon trust, for the use and benefit of themselves and their associates." The settlers were now trustees for themselves, a remarkable variant on a living trust. The Rhode Island General Assembly heard equity cases and created a high court of equity in 1741. Three years later the General Assembly dissolved that court.[21] In all of the New England colonies there was some demand for more autonomous high courts of equity,[22] but proposed arrangements were either negatived by the Crown[23] or opposed by local opinion.[24] In the absence of a distinct central court of equity, assemblies delegated specific equitable powers to the superior courts, including the authority to "chancer" penalty bonds on debts and provide equitable redemption of mortgages.[25]

The equity jurisdiction of lower courts was often disguised by the absence of technical terminology, expressing itself instead in a rough-and-ready interchange of legal and equitable remedies. Local courts were not staffed by professionally educated judges. The county justice of the peace sitting in quarter sessions with his fellow squires was rarely a lawyer. Nevertheless, examination of the records of lower courts in Virginia, for example, shows that they regularly heard petitions for equitable remedies, including discovery of documents, account of assets, and rescission or reformation of contracts.[26]

The operation of colonial central courts of equity would have been marginally more familiar to an English solicitor than the equity practiced at county court. The high courts of equity were not as busy as the supreme courts of law. In South Carolina, the records for the year 1692 show eight entries, some of which were orders for defendants to appear or complainants to replicate their suits, subpoenas for new witnesses, and other procedural business. Substantive matters included one order for an account to be made of an estate, two orders forbidding the sale of assets until the court could hear the case, two injunctions to stay a legal action in the common-law courts, one examination of trustees for malfeasance, and a petition for assistance in a marital separation suit. The docket for 1712 contained thirty-one cases; in 1733, twenty-four items of business were heard; in 1767, forty suits were pending. Not all of these suits were new; the average case returned slightly over four times. The original complaint, the demurrer or answer, the replication, an order for interrogatories, intermediate orders for new evidence, and possibly the report of a master appointed by the court all might precede a final decree.[27] In North Carolina, from 1696 through the early 1700s, there appear to have been seven or eight cases pending each year. By the 1720s this number had risen into the low teens. In the 1760s, twenty-five to thirty suits each year were docketed.[28]

In Maryland, whose chancery court was the most active across the entire span of the eighteenth century and whose records are by far the best preserved (a fact that may explain the comparatively large volume of business), the docket for 1699 contained 32 entries. In the mid-eighteenth century, the docket of each of the four yearly sessions held an average of 45 suits, 4 or 5 of which were new. On average, it took suits two to four years to reach final disposition.[29] The records of the Virginia court of chancery, the General Court sitting in equity, were burned by accident at the end of the Civil War, but Jefferson's *Reports* includes 5 cases in chancery before 1744.[30] The official manuscript docket and file papers of the colonial New Jersey equity courts are too fragmentary to estimate yearly caseloads, but a copy of the August 1723 docket in the James Alexander Papers notes 9 pending cases. Alexander himself handled 44 suits in the colony between 1718 and 1743.[31] In New York, the first chancellors were busy. The surviving docket book for 1701 shows that 84 items of business came before the court in its first year. Between March 1705 and September 1708, there were 147 suits pending at some stage. In later years, the number fluctuated, from 20 in 1722 to 51 in 1725; ahead were hard times for the court.[32] The Pennsylvania high court of equity heard 30 cases between 1720 and 1735.[33]

Equity court hearings offer a glimpse into a ritual of pleading whose formalities rested on inquisitional rather than adversarial process. Sometimes this gave aid to a lower-status litigant against his higher-status opponent that would not have been available in a common-law proceeding. In Maryland, renters were protected against their landlords in much the same manner as Cardinal Wolsey assisted copyholders centuries before, and the court appointed counsel when poor defendants did not frame their pleas correctly.[34] In proceeding after proceeding, the address of the petitioner intoning the formulaic plea for "right equity in good conscience" led to hearings into the reality of harms and hurts that common-law proceedings, still abounding in the abstractions and legal fictions of the writ-pleading system, could not duplicate. Pleading in equity could get complicated—bills in the English chancery were as complex as any in the Court of Common Pleas—but America's first equity courts were never as wedded to form and technical precision as its early courts of law.[35]

Leading lawyers regularly appeared at the bar of the chancellors' courts. James Allein in South Carolina, Daniel Dulany the Elder and his son in Maryland, James Alexander in New Jersey, William Smith, Sr., in New York, and a host of luminaries in Virginia all practiced in the equity courts. If the great were there representing the propertied, the least members of the community—orphans, slaves (by their "next friend"), women, and servants—could also seek justice by filing or getting another to file a complaint. The chancellor would not throw an improperly framed suit out of court but would order its revision and delay the hearing until the correct forms were observed. Equity court records display the willingness of the chancellor to undo fraud, rewrite injustice, and protect against coercion.[36]

The immense variety of presentation of the cases in these courts is striking. The chancellor heard one-hundred-page complaints composed in dense technicality and single-page petitions scribbled in heart-rending simplicity. The suits might concern a needy widow's subsistence or the claims of the king of Spain.[37] Certain general tendencies characterized these proceedings, however. Chancellors actively endeavored to convince suitors to work out their differences.[38] About one-fifth of all suits were dismissed by the consent of the suitors. The chancellor encouraged this amicable event by discharging both parties from paying court costs. Another one-fifth of the cases ended with the suitors' consent to the report of the master or commissioners appointed by the chancellor. Of the remaining cases, more than half were dismissed. The injunction was dissolved; the complaint was dropped by the complainant or was conceded by the defendant. Though these steps might drag out over many sessions, and most of these courts worked without juries,[39] equity was effective and trusted. Even common-law judges might be called to account in colonial courts of equity.[40] Indeed, on the eve of independence, revolutionary leaders cited equity as one asset of empire, though with uncharitable motives they twisted the argument to condemn London for withholding equity from some of the colonies. William Henry Drayton, a South Carolina Supreme Court justice, added to his "American Claim of Rights" that "of right there ought to be in each colony, constitutional courts . . . of chancery" lest claims of right be abandoned or lost for want of jurisdiction. When "the dernier resort" for justice was an ocean away, there was no justice.[41]

Despite some similarity in procedure and substance, equity in the eighteenth-century colonies was profoundly different in structure and implication from its English counterpart. First, equity in the colonies was derivative and indirect. England's courts of equity were prerogative courts; the authority for equity in the colonies was based largely on statute or a combination of statute and royal grant. From a colony one could always appeal a suit to the English chancellor or to the appeals committee of the Privy Council, seeking a decision from the king himself.[42] Second, unlike the educated, experienced, and craftsmanlike chancellors of the post-Nottingham era in England, high courts of equity in the colonies convened under royal governors (with or without their councils), most of whom had little interest or training in the law, and some a palpable distaste for the claims of suitors in equity when these challenged royal policy. Neither these judges, nor the inferior court magistrates who had equitable powers in some of the colonies, nor many of the lawyers who represented petitioners in equity, were as learned in law as their counterparts in the metropolis.[43] As William Livingston, then a New York lawyer and later governor and chancellor of New Jersey, wrote in 1753: "The Governors for the Time being, always act as Chancellors of those Provinces over which they respectively preside. And a very few instances can be assigned of their having been bred to the Profession, or Study of the Law; without a considerable Knowledge of which, it is impossible any man can be qualified for the important Office of a Chancellor."[44]

The consequences of this arrested and incomplete reception of equity were simultaneously disruptive and creative. On the disruptive side was the periodic politicization of courts of equity. Gabriel Johnston, for example, though governor and chancellor of North Carolina, refused to hear equity cases in parts of the colony distant from his home. Despite their remonstrances, protesters could not budge him or get him removed.[45] On the creative side was the fact that these political disruptions became opportunities for the colonial bench and bar to explore the larger implications of equity concepts in the same way as their English predecessors had during the Civil War.

TRANSFORMATION

In surveying the record of colonial equity courts from within, there is little to suggest that chancellors, lawyers, or suitors in equity had any consistent constitutional agenda. The vast majority of equity suits came before the local courts, often disguised in some way as quasi-legal petitions, and were handled in summary fashion. In complex ways, however, the relative lack of sophistication of the central courts of equity and their openness to political stimuli permitted political adaptation of the language of equity pleading.

The door to analogical thinking was pried open not by advocates of a new jurisprudence or political theory, but by working lawyers coping with real disputes. As in England, the wedge was the problem of public accountability. Throughout the long course of English rule in the colonies, a galling and intractable issue was the local unaccountability of imperial officials. These officials—only a minority of whom were qualified by talent or experience to hold their posts—personified the awesome authority of king or proprietor in the colonies. Indeed, after the Glorious Revolution of 1689, royal charters gave more power to the governor of a colony than the king possessed in his realm. When such agents of the Crown misused their power, appeal to England was the approved method for relief but often brought none. Quarrels between placemen and colonial leaders erupted often enough to convince the colonists of their incapacity to curb the corruption of the Crown's minions. The problem was acute, the damage irreparable and recurring. Colonial lawyer-politicians analogized the misconduct of imperial officials to a violation of their trust. The language for this identification was already available on both sides of the Atlantic.[46]

The equity bar in almost all of the colonies, unlike the mother country, included men prominent in politics. Politically active lawyers, trained to sue in equity and driven to political confrontation with Crown officers or with the mother country itself, dug into the vocabulary of equity to petition for redress. What began as a way of categorizing the issues (in the case at hand, defining the equitable grounds for a complaint) became a method of formulating general problems in equitable terms. The analogy went from shadow to reality. The language of the chancellor's courts rose bit by bit to a higher level of generality and found meaning in the ongoing constitutional discourse. A similar process was transforming Americans' understanding of common law, as disputes over particular rights to free speech or freedom from warrantless searches became disputes over a broad range of constitutional liberties.[47] Outbursts of Radical Whig agitation, prefiguring the movement for independence, often began in the courtroom.[48] In these clashes, professional lawyers expanded narrow legal briefs into constitutional discourses, a striking example of the close tie between private law and public law in America. Courtroom advocacy provided a training ground for constitutional dialectics.[49] Under such conditions, technical legal exchanges could quickly escalate into constitutional colloquia wherein counsel advocated their versions of good government. So, too, constitutional quarrels often found their way into the courtroom.[50]

The language of equity could lend itself to such constitutional confrontations under a number of circumstances. The chancellor, his agents, or his court might become the center of the storm, implicating as a matter of course his discretion and the usages of equity. Particular suits in his court or lower courts of equity might involve constitutional questions as well. Members of the equity bar embroiled in constitutional squabbles might reach for postulates modeled on equity when other lines of argument failed to persuade. So long as equity was the king's prerogative—its use in the colonies directly or indirectly derived from his right to mitigate the severity of his own laws—thrusts against Crown officers resting on equitable metaphors were just that, metaphorical. Should the king's authority be disavowed, his courts closed, and his judges driven off or made to renounce their oath to the Crown, the way would be open for the shift from metaphorical accountability to real accountability. The opportunity missed in England might then be seized in America.

An early and striking episode of the abuse of equitable discretion in the early colonies, Governor William Cosby's exchange of spite with Supreme Court Judge Lewis Morris in New York, did credit to neither of the protagonists but demonstrated the political volatility of the equity court issue. The New York Court of Chancery was born in a skirmish between assembly and chancellor-governor, remained a target of partisan snipers through the 1720s, exploded in a battle between Governor William Burnet and Speaker of the Assembly Adolph Philipse in 1727, and concluded with a war between Governor Cosby and his enemies. On November 25, 1727, Philipse, a New York merchant, walked into the assembly chamber and read a list of resolves condemning the conduct of the governor-chancellor. Philipse, furious over losing a suit before Burnet, sputtered that no one man should have the power the chancellor took for himself and asked the house to concur in a motion to declare all decrees in chancery null and void. Philipse's arguments generated much heat and gained applause from Burnet's opponents in the assembly, but they failed to check the governor's prerogative to sit as chancellor.[51]

If Burnet was stubborn, Cosby was grasping, shortsighted, and contrary. His short tenure as governor (1732–36) nearly brought the colonial courts to a standstill. He allied himself early with one faction in local politics, lobbied incessantly for more pay, and in 1733 created an exchequer side of the supreme court on his own authority. Cosby asserted that the new exchequer court ought to have equity powers, powers that would have allowed him to control much of the legal apparatus of the colony and not incidentally to collect back pay Cosby claimed was wrongly given his predecessor, Rip van Dam. Cosby's plan terrified his political opponents, the "Morrisites," for equitable remedies were discretionary and few trusted Cosby and his henchmen.[52] Morris himself denounced the intrusion into the supreme court's procedures. The essence of Morris's objection was the same as Philipse's—no court and no schedule of fees could be imposed by the governor without the consent of the legislature, at least as Morris read the precedents.[53] The associate justices, allies of Cosby, disagreed with Morris and Cosby got his way. Morris resigned his judgeship and later moved to New Jersey to assume the governorship and ironically became the target of barbs like those he had hurled at Cosby. Meanwhile, Cosby repaid Morris's insult; in 1735 he decreed against the Morris faction in the "equivalent lands" or "Oblong" suit.[54] The denouement of the decade of controversy featured the prosecution of the Morrisite faction's paid propagandist, John Peter Zenger. Zenger was acquitted by a jury that disregarded the instructions on seditious libel of Cosby's hand-picked chief justice, James Delancey, and decided instead that truth was a defense against the charge.[55]

Morris published from the bench his dissent against Cosby's proposals. The issues in Morris's opinion may seem forced, stalking horses for a partisan assault on Cosby's incessant factionalism and disdain for the privileges of the assembly. That is too narrowly grounded a dismissal of Morris's arguments. Morris did not oppose an equity court or the exercise of equitable powers; after becoming governor of New Jersey in 1738, he heard many equity suits. He opposed an equity side to the exchequer court because it did not rest on statutory authority. It mattered who created the court. Morris insisted that statutes must control and make accountable the court, allowing for removal of its presiding officers upon misuse of power. Executive fiat did none of these. The immediate issue of accountability of the equity court was transformed and elevated into the issue of governmental accountability as a whole.

Morris did not adopt the language of equity to frame his complaint, though a precedent for that step already existed in the colonies. In the same years as Burnet and Cosby jousted with the New York Assembly over equity courts, the proprietor of Maryland crossed swords with his assembly over the role of judges in the colony. No Maryland family was more powerful or more learned in the law than the Dulanys, and Daniel Dulany, Sr.'s examination of accountability on behalf of the assembly drew sustenance from analogies to equitable pleading.[56]

Dulany, Sr., founder of the family fortune, was an able lawyer, land speculator, and early in his career a spokesman for the assembly. In his last years he would be co-opted by the proprietary, but not before he published a defense of the right of the people to enjoy all the laws of England—with or without the proprietor's consent.[57] In 1727 the assembly had locked horns with the proprietor over the form of oaths the judges would take, the extent of common law received in the colony, and the necessity of proprietary consent to legal forms. The proprietor's younger brother, Benedict Leonard Calvert, had arrived in the colony as governor, confident that he could protect proprietary prerogatives. Backed by the lower-house party, Dulany insisted on the right of the colony to the common and statute law of England without restriction. Calvert answered that comparable cases, explicit royal instructions, and precedent ran against such incorporation.[58] In reply, Dulany wrote and published a short pamphlet, *The Right of the Inhabitants of Maryland to the Benefit of the English Laws* (1728).

The nub of the dispute was accountability. To whom would the judges be accountable if the governor, rather than the assembly, decided which laws were in effect? How would appointees of the governor be held accountable for their misuse of power if their master could pick and choose the laws received in the colony? Dulany's pamphlet was a legal brief advocating a position on the underlying constitutional issue. His lawyerly habits of mind,[59] rather than any passion for philosophical discourse, directed his answer to the questions at hand. Dulany argued that Marylanders had "an equal right" to the benefits of the laws of England. Without this equality, there could be no remedy for wrongs. The "love of equity, and justice" was the highest good in courts but could not be obtained without an extension of the common laws to the province. Echoing Locke, Dulany pronounced that men formed themselves into societies and passed laws of "equality" to protect their rights. The origin of Maryland government, Dulany continued, rested on a trust, the terms of which were violated when the laws of England were not equally enforced in the new province.[60]

Dulany did not mention the flourishing equity courts of the colony. From 1725 the governor was the sole chancellor of Maryland and from 1728 to 1733 Dulany's chief opponent in the debate was the younger brother of the proprietor himself. To cite the successful

reception of equity in the colony under the aegis of the proprietorship would have admitted that the governor-chancellor's discretion
had proven itself fair and expeditious. Why then should one de-
nounce the same individual's discretion to veto assembly bills? Dulany's dilemma was inescapable. As long as colonial lawyers pleaded
in royal or proprietary courts, they could not fully explore the anti-
imperial implications of equitable principles.

Dulany's immediate problem reflected a second theoretical dilemma: where did one bring suit against a violator of the public
trust? Analogies to equity precepts led to the chancellor's court, and
in Maryland the chancellor was the antagonist of the assembly. One
could always appeal to the Privy Council in England, which on occasion acted like a court of equity, but such an appeal meant a direct
affront to the Calverts, closing a door to high proprietary office that
Dulany might wish to enter. In the end, he found no relief—no
concrete remedy, at least—for the danger of misuse of power, although his caution did recommend him in later years to the proprietor's service.

Dulany's oldest son, Daniel, Jr., followed in his father's foot-
steps. Trained at the Inns of Court, he returned to Maryland to
practice law, acquire land, and amass offices. In 1765, the younger
Dulany became a vocal opponent of the Stamp Tax. Though he was
more conservative in politics than many of the protestors, he could
not allow the tax to go unchallenged. First and foremost, the new
tax raised the old question of accountability. Who could hold Parliament accountable if it misused the colonies' wealth? His *Considerations on the Propriety of Imposing Taxes in the British Colonies* (1765) was
not a stylish or moving piece, but it gained great fame and wide
distribution because it denied the validity of "virtual representation"
as a form of fiduciary supervision. The theory that Parliament represented the economic interests of all subjects of the king's colonies
in the same way it represented the interest of the nonvoting English
defended Parliament from the charge of taxing the colonists without
allowing them representation. Dulany denied the theory unequivocally and refuted the elegant pamphlets of its supporters.[61]

Dulany's arguments can be read as a dissertation in constitutional theory, but he wrote them as a legal counsellor whose clients
were the colonists. As a lawyer, he urged his clients to obey the law
while he instituted suit against it. He would not accept the opinions
of "court lawyers," by which he meant the king's Privy Council and
his legal advisers. As far as Dulany was concerned, these men were
not judges but advocates for the other side. Against his adversaries

he drafted a very rough facsimile of a complaint in equity. Dulany knew there was no forum to which he could take an equity suit against Parliament; he merely borrowed a way of arguing from his familiarity with equitable forms of pleading. His approximation of the terminology and jurisprudence of equity was suggestive, stylistic, and analogous rather than conclusive.

Dulany first needed to prove that the colonies had standing to bring the suit. If the colonies were totally dependent on the will of the Crown, they had no recourse—whether in law or in equity—to resist the king-in-Parliament. But if, as Dulany argued, the colonies did have privileges and immunities that limited the power of Parliament, they could indeed bring suit to defend themselves from unjust application of the laws. Even as Dulany repeatedly pledged his loyalty to the Crown (he would, in fact, stay neutral during the war for independence) and reiterated that Parliament had power to bind the colonies with statutes, he pointed out that statutes with discriminatory and unjust effects in particular cases—to wit, in the colonies—could be challenged in equity.[62] Dulany then insisted that the Stamp Tax worked special, particular injustice in the colonies. In effect, he sought an equitable exception from the law to remedy its supposedly unintended mischief. In aid of his case, he insisted that the idea of virtual representation was "unfair and deceptive." It was sharp dealing of the kind chancellors curbed in their courts. Dulany even hinted that the funds raised would be used for corrupt purposes, a telling point in an equity complaint. The Stamp Act abused colonists' rights, and the colonists ought to be relieved of that particular wrong.[63]

Was the Stamp Tax discriminatory in its effect as well as unsupportable in its rationale? Dulany asked his opponents to produce evidence on the expected yield of the new tax (a plea for "discovery"), for, "If a sum had been liquidated and a precise demand made, it might perhaps have been shown, if proportioned to the circumstances of the colonies, to be of no real consequence to the nation." Such an accounting would have permitted the colonies to devise more "equitable and proportioned" ways of assisting the royal treasury than a tax on official papers.[64] Dulany denied that the tax was an "equitable" measure, for "The colonies for a long course of time have largely contributed to the public revenue, and put Great Britain to little or no expense for their protection. If it was *equitable* to draw from them a further contribution, it does not therefore follow that it is proper to force it from them by the harsh and rigorous methods established by the Stamp Act, an act *unequal and dispro-*

portioned to *their* circumstances whom it affects" (italics added). Dulany explained that the Stamp Tax did not fall equally on each colony, a further burden of inequity. Indeed, such a tax turned equity upon its head by decreeing oppression rather than justice.[65]

Dulany had reached the place in his complaint for a plea for relief, that is, to name his remedy. Here his problem paralleled his father's: in what way could a provincial politician demand an accounting from the home government? The rest of his pamphlet explored the possibilities of such relief and finally concluded that only passive resistance, in the form of some sort of self-imposed economic sanction, could be employed. Self-denial was not illegal (nonimportation, for example, was not in itself a crime, though conspiracy to prevent others from importing English goods might be regarded as an offense). It was hardly a plea for relief that a chancellor, even an imaginary one, could countenance, but political reality left no other course open.

Dulany was forty-three years old when his *Considerations* appeared. It marked the high tide of his patriotic reputation. A cadre of younger lawyers was already vying with him for prominence in the provincial courts and in the 1770s they, not he, led the attack upon the Crown. The issue remained one of accountability, and analogies to equitable trusteeship were again pressed into service by both sides. In the tobacco inspector's fee controversy of 1773, Dulany found himself defending one variant of equitable analogy against a newer and more assertive version. First established by authority of the proprietor, the fees for tobacco inspectors were set by the assembly from the 1740s. In 1770, the lower house sought to reduce the fees and curb the patronage of the governor, for these officials were appointed by him, but the governor's council refused to concur. In the impasse, Governor Robert Eden set the fees at their old level by proclamation. The opposition "country" party attacked the proclamation as unconstitutional, likening the restored fees to a violation of the terms of a trust. The proprietary party answered that some regulation of fees was necessary and that without agreement of the two houses the governor—a trustee—had to act to protect the public interest. Dulany stepped forward as the spokesman for the proprietary position. A leader of the younger generation, Catholic lawyer and landholder Charles Carroll of Carrollton, pleaded the opposition case.[66]

The eight letters the two men exchanged in the *Maryland Gazette* as "Antilon" (Dulany) and "First Citizen" (Carroll) were pompous, scurrilous, and inelegant. In part their dudgeon may be attributed to the explosive dislike the two men developed for each other. In part the diffuseness of their arguments can be attributed to the diffuseness of their thinking. Not every pamphleteer wrote as wittily or trenchantly as Benjamin Franklin. All criticism to one side, Dulany and Carroll faced a genuine crisis in an already uneasy Anglo-American constitutional relationship. The issue for both of them was not just whether there was one constitution, governing both mother country and colony, or two constitutions, but what was to be done about corruption within the government. How were the inspectors to be curbed, Dulany asked, without some upper limit on their exactions? He answered: should corruption be suspected the established courts, including the chancellor's court, could investigate and prosecute. Carroll castigated such apologies for Eden's proclamation. The opportunities for collusion were too apparent. Were not the courts manned by the same officers—the governor and his council—who proclaimed the fees? What was to stop corruption from seeping up into the courts or down from the courts? Dulany replied that the chancellor in England and the chancellor in Maryland both set fees for their own courts with no complaint from litigants. If chancellors could not be trusted, he pleaded, who could be trusted? Carroll retorted that should suits over the misuse of fees come before the chancellors, they would be party to their own cause. Dulany rejoined that all official misconduct was accountable to higher authority; it would lead to removal. Carroll was not satisfied; only juries or the assembly could be trusted to remove erring officials. Shorn of insulting Latin epigrams and endless denials of personal cupidity, the arguments in these letters borrowed the terminology of the equitable trust to contest how citizens could hold officials to account for their actions.[67]

Dulany did not surrender his faith in the trustworthiness of chancellors. He had practiced in equity courts for too long. Carroll, an accomplished solicitor in his own right, saw that adherence to existing courts of equity compelled ultimate loyalty to England and its authority. This he could not accept. Groping for a new conception of trusteeship, he floundered. His literal-mindedness had a self-serving origin. Carroll could not abandon the oligarchic structures of existing equity because he was an aristocrat himself. Though his Catholicism barred him from office, he did not want to destroy the social and economic system that protected his family's property in the colony. There was no hint of radicalism in his letters. Thus, neither man was prepared to argue that a thorough reform of electoral rules, including a broadened franchise, or the binding of the assembly by the instructions of the electorate, was a viable alternative to misuse of public trust. On the verge of a vision of public trustee- ship, they faltered.

As Dulany and Carroll geared up for their campaign of mutual vilification, a crowd of "Mohawks" marched onto the quays in Bos- ton Harbor and dumped shiploads of tea into the water. Their dis- guises fooled few. These were "Sons of Liberty" protesting the pref- erential duty on British East Indian Company tea under the Tea Act. Lord North's ministry in England was not amused by this "tea party" and after some wrangling in Parliament secured passage of the Boston Port Act and the Massachusetts Government Reorganiza- tion Act. The Port of Boston was closed and a quasi-military admin- istration was set over the rebellious colony. Massachusetts' cries for assistance against these "Intolerable Acts," written by its committee of correspondence and transmitted to the other colonies, led to a Continental Congress to seek ways to repeal the obnoxious acts and reconcile a disaffected American people with king and Parliament.[68]

Lawmakers—legislators, judges, jurists, and lawyers—occupied a vital position in this crisis. They were the guardians of legal order, the repositories of wisdom and authority in a legal regime. Often, they were also players with much to lose or gain from alteration of that regime. If revolution, successful rebellion, always has its own legality—the winners write the laws and the treaties, convene the courts, and dispense justice; the losers acquiesce or flee—no revolu- tionary leader could be certain of the verdict of history in the winter of 1774–75, and no experienced revolutionary lawyer would want to risk life, liberty, and sacred honor in that cause without first don- ning the armor of legality. They thus faced a dilemma particular to their calling: how were men of law, sworn to follow the rules of court, schooled in English legal customs, authority, and ways of thought, to raise rebellion? In this moment of crisis, they must be counsel in a higher cause than they had ever before represented. Where were they to find authority for this most unlawful legal brief?

Lawyers were an assertive and influential cadre at the Con- gress.[69] They knew that the legal procedure for removal of erring officials and redress of grievances in the colonies was appeal to the king in Council, but attempts in the First Continental Congress to follow this course failed miserably.[70] George III would not hear a protest against the Intolerable Acts. Rehearsals of the rights of the colonists under the settlement of the British constitution at the time of the Glorious Revolution foundered upon historical fact: the British constitution had made Parliament supreme and Lord North's majority was not disposed to concede the point, not in 1774 at any rate. Appeal to a higher, natural law—one supposedly informing the British constitution though violated by Lord North's administration—was an appropriate next step, but flights of philosophical fancy did not win lawsuits, except perhaps for Patrick Henry, and then only before sympathetic juries.[71] Natural law might be (and was) incorporated into legal arguments, particularly when the law was not settled on the issue, but the revolutionary lawyers were not so much philosophes as practitioners with broad reading interests.[72]

The legal question went to the heart of the protest. The Continental Congress represented the people; it was their agent. In and of itself, it had no legitimacy—no legal existence—in imperial law; but as the agent of the colonists, pleading for their rights, it could claim to act within the conventions of civil—that is, adversarial—advocacy. The First Continental Congress petitioned the Crown in the name of the people for a redress of grievances. While in outward form this petition seems to resemble the parliamentary petitions of right in 1628 and 1689, the comparison is spurious. Parliament was the highest court in the English realm and made law. The king was expected to assent. The First Continental Congress was neither a court nor a legislative body in English law; it could only speak for those who had legal grievances against the imperial government.[73] A better analogy, though one not urged at the time, was that Congress represented an amorphous "class" of petitioners in something like a multiple bill-of-peace suit. In such a suit, petitioners seek to have their rights (usually to disputed parcels of land) declared and full use of the property restored to them. Such a "class action" is equitable, not legal, in origin.[74]

Even as it raised an army to resist the Crown, the leadership of the Second Continental Congress continued to seek redress within the law. Among its ranks were lawyers already distinguished for tenacity and brilliance in the colonial cause. Of these John Dickinson had emerged preeminent. Although he would not sign the Declaration of Independence, he returned to his native Delaware to join the revolutionary army, later winning election as "president" of the state assembly and continuing his career as a spokesman for a conservative republicanism.[75] As de facto chief counsel in the Congress, he was the very epitome of professionalism. Though outraged at the illegality of the Intolerable Acts, he enjoined a "strict and impartial Judgement" of all causes and consequences of Britain's policy upon those who planned to oppose it. Lawyers contributed firm, tempered, and well-directed counsel, Dickinson believed. Lawyers must work with the rule of law.[76]

In June 1775, after hostilities had commenced, Dickinson counseled the Second Continental Congress against "violent resentments and incurable animosities."[77] As late as January 1776, he viewed the greatest danger to the inhabitants of the colonies as the loss of the protection of the law.[78] In a speech prepared for Congress, he based the relationship between colonies and king on the common law of lessor and lessee. His notes survive:

> I would explain this Idea, by comparing [it] to a Case of our municipal Law, which will show, that things standing as they did at first, the Obligation between the Parties continued whatever . . . [impression] either or both of them were under at the Time of Compact. The principle is sufficient for Elucidation tho it may run on all four. Lease by Trade—by a man who has not a legal Title—good between them unless Lessor enters or the Lessee be ejected by him who has the Title. We at this Day enjoy the Grant—in part dissolved indeed, but We will not say the Lease is entirely broken. And I think it will do no Credit to our Cause at this Time of Day, to pry for Flaws into the Title of our Lessors, and upon the pretence to withhold those Rents which We and our Ancestors have ever been accustomed to pay. This Ground of the American Cause is not tenable.[79]

Dickinson, wedded to the common law, a cornerstone of which was the principle that rightful title to the colonies lay in the king, could not justify the ultimate form of resistance. He found himself in a cul-de-sac: common-law property analogies mandated subordination to the king's law.[80]

When Dickinson faltered, his progress blocked by the massive architecture of common law, Thomas Jefferson stepped forward to propose another line of argument. He averred that the Crown had violated its duties as a trustee, acting in a partial, self-serving, and mean-spirited manner, bringing ruin to the beneficiaries of the trust, the colonists. On the surface, his characterization of these violations of the colonists' rights resembled the commonwealthmen's invocation of John Locke. In its precise context and nuance, Jefferson's argument retraced and improved on the process by which Locke himself had come to his conclusions rather than just relying on Locke for authority. Locke had transformed the inept efforts of a liberally educated, reforming chancellor, impatient with technical niceties, into a program for constitutional accountability. Jefferson employed the equitable lexicon with far greater facility than Lord Shaftesbury and manipulated its forms with far greater precision than Locke. In the process, he resolved the problem of remedy which had stymied the Dulanys (though the younger Dulany withheld his support from Jefferson's conclusions).

Insofar as a provincial lawyer might be, Thomas Jefferson was an equity specialist. Trained by George Wythe, himself the possessor of a large equity practice, and referred cases by Wythe and others, young Jefferson was soon sought after for opinions on equitable questions.[81] From 1768 to 1774, the years that Jefferson practiced before the General Court, 78 of his 939 cases were brought in equity. Some of these involved major disputes over inheritance (the Custis fortune, for example), land surveys, and bonds.[82] When Jefferson represented Robert Bolling, the defendant in a suit initiated by Archibald Bolling, whose counsel was Wythe, Jefferson's learning was fully displayed. The case concerned a disputed construction of the will of Edward Bolling. Was Jefferson's client, the administrator, to bear the debts of the estate out of his portion, while the complainant got the emblements, the crops already in the ground, and various other disputed properties? A special master in chancery was treated to a long and exhausting display of scholarship by both counsel. Wythe won the day, but not before both men proved that they could dispute the reliability of the English chancery reports that they cited as well as the contents of cases. It was a final exam of sorts and the pupil did very well indeed.[83]

Instruction in Wythe's office not only had made Jefferson a superb litigator, it inculcated a love for the larger principles of equity. Indeed, Jefferson's intellectual interests ran in the same broad channels as Wythe's. In his Equity Commonplace Book, following 1,076 entries cribbed from English equity reports, Jefferson copied a long portion of Lord Kames's *Principles of Equity*. Wythe, Jefferson, and Kames shared a vision of the place of equity in a system of laws, and the selections Jefferson chose to copy stressed the ties between the mechanics of equity practice and the "other," higher equity. Kames believed that there were no rules in common law for handling "extraordinary" cases, and "equity, in its proper place, then, comprehends every matter of law that by the common law is left without remedy." These remedies rested on natural law and were steadily increasing in number, that is, they were a measure of the progress of society, not just the residue of some outmoded, primitive equity jurisdiction. "In the progress of society and course of practice [of law], many duties were evolved which, by ripeness of discernment and growing delicacy of sentiment, were found to be binding in conscience. As these were made no part of the common law, they came naturally under the jurisdiction of equity. These more refined duties of the law of nature, making at present a great branch of equity, shall be traced from their true source in human nature." Jefferson then copied Kames's conclusion: "It appears now clearly, that a court of equity commences at the limits of common law, and enforces benevolence where the law of nature makes it our duty. And thus a court of equity, accompanying the law of nature in its gradual refinements, enforces every natural duty that is not provided for at common law."[84] In fact, Kames did not press the claims of equity over common law where the common law provided an adequate remedy, but his insistence on the close connection between natural law and the practice of equity was very different from Blackstone's conservatism.[85] Jefferson's maturing predilection for reform of law based on egalitarian social values found Kames's approach congenial.[86]

Both Jefferson and Wythe appreciated the underlying discretionary character of equity, as Wythe, for his part, would prove in decision after decision when he was state chancellor. Jefferson himself leaned on equitable analogies, for example, in *Howell v. Netherland* (1770). In *Howell*, Jefferson acted *in forma pauperis* for the plaintiff, a mulatto servant, claiming that the act that bound the servant's grandmother to service until she was thirty-one years old (she was the offspring of a free woman and a slave) could not be construed to bind him to service until he was thirty-one. Jefferson brought an action of unlawful arrest, a common-law tort, but his argument was not based on common law. He turned instead to the equitable doctrine of the constructive trust. The servant's master, gaining the unjust enrichment of the servant's labor, ought to be regarded as a trustee by the court. Such a remedy came to equity from a noble source—nature itself: "I suppose it will not be pretended that the mother being a servant, the child would be a servant also under the law of nature, without any particular provision of the act. Under the law of nature, all men are born free, every one comes into the world with a right to his own person, which includes the liberty of moving and using it under his own will." Jefferson skirted the general rule that explicit statutory provisions could bar equitable remedies by arguing that the statute's silence on the question of children's status must be interpreted on the side of equality—though he knew well that the Virginia custom had always been to keep the children of mulattoes in extended servitude. To win Howell's freedom, Jefferson had to imply that hundreds of persons in Howell's situation ought to be free. In the face of the clear intent of the legislature to bind all persons of color, of whatever degree, to servitude, his closing sally—"that it remains for some future legislature, if any shall be found wicked enough, to extend it [the act] to the grand-children and other issue more remote"—was hardly likely to sway the court, and it predictably gave judgment in favor of the defendant. The case was not an earth-shattering one; Jefferson still represented slaveholders in cases of disputed ownership of slaves. Nevertheless, it is evidence that he had begun to think through the utility of analogies based on the equitable doctrines he had studied under Wythe.[87]

The widening revolutionary crisis presented Jefferson with a series of opportunities to explore, test, and refine the extension of equitable pleading to the public crisis. On July 27, 1774, the free-holders of Albemarle County sent him to the Virginia Convention with a resolution written by Jefferson himself calling for a restoration of the "natural and legal rights" of the colonists.[88] The exact content of this jointure of rights was not yet clear, but Jefferson required that both be addressed, for he did not conceive of them as distinct and separate. Both were expressed in the charters that the Crown negotiated with, not gave to, the settlers. The charters created duties on both sides, but Jefferson did not characterize the obligation of the Crown as a contract. There was no exchange of promises.[89] Where lay the intersection of legal and natural rights, then, if not in a contract? Put in other terms, it was the revolutionary lawyers' dilemma revisited at a more advanced stage of the crisis: if the charters were not contracts, on what basis did the colonists protest the home government's failure to perform its duties?

Jefferson began to think through this problem on his way to Williamsburg that summer. When illness interrupted his progress, he sent ahead a rough draft of a *Summary View of the Rights of British Americans*. It was a moving but unfinished performance. Jefferson broached the theory that the colonies originated in a royal "use" and proposed that redress be sought from the Crown on that basis. He was not hopeful of winning on this line (the *Summary View* was more a memorandum than a polished brief), but it seemed that this was the only way the colonists could proceed under color of law. Parliamentary encroachments on colonial property and liberty must be stopped by a just king. Jefferson listed example after example to demonstrate that England's laws were corrupted by the venality of its leaders and the viciousness of its politics. Alas, evidence without a fully developed legal doctrine floated in the air; it could not convince, much less command. A second piece of his argument followed from the first: parliamentary laws had unjust and unfair consequences in Boston, where "Not the hundredth part of the inhabitants of that town had been concerned in the act [the Boston Tea Party] complained of . . . yet all were involved in one indiscriminate ruin [by the Boston Port Act]. . . . This is administering justice with a heavy hand indeed! And when is this tempest to be arrested in its course?" The act for suppression of riots in Boston also worked hardship on innocent parties, forcing witnesses to cross the Atlantic to give testimony. Here Jefferson recast Dulany, Jr.'s thesis: equitable relief against the unjust and unintended effects of law on particular persons must be sought from the king. Jefferson pleaded that the Crown use its discretion to do right, for "the great principles of right and wrong are legible to every reader." Let a wise and merciful king "deal out to all equal and impartial rights."[90] Here was an appeal to the king's discretion to do justice in his own person, the very authority he had shared with his chancellors for 450 years.[91]

Late in the spring of 1775, Jefferson joined the Virginia delegation to the Second Continental Congress. There he was added to the committee already composing a "Declaration of the Causes of Taking Up Arms." His draft was not adopted by the committee, and he would not accede to John Dickinson's alternative wording of the document. Jefferson was already moving away from Dickinson's thinking with results apparent in Jefferson's subsequent draft reply to Lord North's "Compromise Proposal." Lord North had agreed to let colonial assemblies assess their own contributions to the Crown treasury in lieu of parliamentary impositions. Jefferson rejected the proposal outright, opening with an argument based on the equitable suit for an account of assets. If the colonists had the right of "appropriating their gifts [a sarcastic reference to Lord North's concession], so are they entitled at all times to enquire into their application; to see that they be not wasted among the venal and corrupt for the purpose of undermining the civil rights of the givers." Upon this equitable claim he built a second, larger demand for accountability—a higher order, as it were, of accountability—that an entire people may require of their government.[92]

This shift of levels in the argument from a technical ground for relief in a court of equity to the broader constitutional implications of the principles of equity was the process by which Jefferson developed a concept of public trusteeship. "Experience has invariably proved," he wrote in a part of the draft not ultimately published, "that it is not the best method of preserving the friendship and good offices of any part of government to render it independent by vesting it with perpetual revenue." How could a people check abuse in their government if they could not demand an account of its revenue? For a people to grant discretion to governors, they must always retain the right of calling the government to account. This was the essential principle of trusts that equity courts enforced. Contract failed as a model, as Jefferson knew (and Dickinson was learning from his own struggles with contract metaphors), because contract did not provide a mechanism for controlling erring governors short of dissolution and damages. The trusteeship model of government did provide a mechanism for calling governors to account—a regular voice of the people in government with the power to remove erring individual officials. Jefferson contended that such a mechanism was in place in the colonial governments, arrangements that "please ourselves, they answer the substantial purposes of government and of justice." Adopting bits and pieces of the language of a solicitor in the chancellor's court, Jefferson also claimed that Lord North's proposal was a deliberate deceit intended to misrepresent colonial rights and conceal British oppression. In equity, the misrepresentation or fraudulent representation of a transaction was grounds for its revocation or reformation by the chancellor, for such deceits confounded the operation of the common law and prevented justice in the regular courts. So, too, on a public level, deceit by a government confounded the sufficiency of ordinary political processes.[93]

By the late spring of 1776, Dickinson had found himself supplanted by other, more radical, spokesmen for Congress. Among these was Jefferson. Charged by the Congress with drafting a declaration to support Richard Henry Lee's resolution for independence, Jefferson at last had the opportunity to explore the full constitutional implications of his equitable language. Jefferson's Declaration of Independence was modeled on a "bill" in equity, following forms that he might have used to plead for a client before the General Court of Virginia sitting in equity. While too much can be made of this resemblance in form, it should not be dismissed. His choice of this form of pleading was neither inadvertent nor inconsequential and went a long step beyond the Dulanys' efforts. For two years Jefferson had experimented with the lexicon of equity to frame an effective protest in what today would be called public-law litigation. As he crafted this final brief for independence, the forms of pleading not only channeled and directed the flow of ideas, but they also highlighted the deeper structures of the argument. In effect, Jefferson had carried on a dialogue with the language of equitable pleading, extending and revising it, and the Declaration was the fruit of his endeavors.

Bills in equity followed a prescribed form in the colonies. Jefferson, under the pressure of the moment, appropriated the form entire. The bill had nine parts, some of which were optional. The first was the address, the most formulaic part of the bill, naming the court and appealing to its jurisdiction for justice. The second part introduced the complainants, mentioning all persons party to the suit and establishing their standing to bring the suit. The third part stated the grievances. It was entirely factual and often quite voluminous. The fourth, "confederating," part of the bill accused the defendants of a conspiracy against the complainants, preventing the latter from obtaining justice in the regular courts. This was optional. The fifth part, also optional, anticipated and refuted the arguments of the defense. The sixth part claimed that no other remedy but an equitable one would suffice; the common law did not apply, was inadequate, or had been subverted by some unjust conspiracy of the defendants. The seventh part, again optional, was the report of the interrogation of witnesses. The eighth part of the bill described the specific equitable remedy desired. The final part was the prayer for process—the request that the court enforce its decree immediately. An oath by the complainant to the truth of all the allegations and the necessity for the suit concluded the bill.[94]

In the Declaration, Jefferson added to the list of grievances he had developed over the past two years at both ends new material organized and given momentum by the bill-in-equity form.[95] In the process, the complaints that are the heart of the Declaration showed their equitable origins, fitting categories familiar in chancery. These Jefferson prefaced with the address and introduction that commenced bills in equity. At the close of the stating part—the list of grievances—he added an accusation against the British people for their complicity in the plot against American liberties—the confederating part of the bill. He closed with prayers for equitable relief and process, and an oath—all of which completed the bill in equity. It was a lawyer's Declaration, adapting a form of pleading that could overcome the hurdles of common-law–based loyalism. At the same time, it raised equitable concepts of trusteeship to the level of constitutional principles.

The opening of the Declaration of Independence would have posed the most difficult problem for Jefferson whether or not he elected an equitable format. What right had Congress to declare the people of the colonies independent? On what legal authority could such a claim rest? The bill-in-equity format aided him. A global version of the "address" formula allowed Jefferson to argue that, just as individual suitors had equal rights in the court of chancery, so nations had "separate and equal station" under "the laws of nature." Jefferson's approach harkened back to the era of English equity when Ellesmere held office and to the juridical foundations of equity: equity was justice under the law of nature. Yet even as imprecise and antique as Jefferson's address might be, he could not ignore the fact that, from their inception, equity courts were the king's courts, extensions of his moral authority and power to do justice. Ellesmere had been the king's man. If Jefferson's address in equity were strictly construed, he would have been appealing to the king's appointee for relief against the king's own views. Jefferson found a bold answer: he employed an equitable concept to overturn the royal foundations of equity courts and rebuilt equitable jurisprudence on a foundation of popular sovereignty.

Jefferson drew support for this transformation of the address stage of a bill from Locke's *Second Treatise*. There can be little doubt that Jefferson was indebted to Lockean constitutionalism.[96] When it came to discussing the working relationship between governed and government, Jefferson understood that Locke relied on the analogy of equitable trust, not contract.[97] When Jefferson declared the causes that impelled the separation, he used Lockean language (everyone in his audience could be expected to recognize Locke's arguments) the way a lawyer uses a citation to authority. The right of the people to create and abolish governments was analogous to their right to create and abolish a trust for their own benefit. The inherent and inalienable rights Jefferson cited were the terms of that trust. Should that trust fail to offer them security and happiness, it revoked itself or could be dissolved. Within the trusteeship constitutionalism that Locke and Jefferson shared, there was no illegality in removing erring trustees. Jefferson the advocate, with the assistance of Locke the theorist, had found an answer to the revolutionary lawyers' dilemma. The introduction of the bill also identified the complainants, none other than the whole people. The colonists had suffered the abuses of imperial power, and necessity induced them to dissolve the trust long before created for their lives, liberty, and happiness.

The central portion of the Declaration corresponded very closely to the stating part of the bill in equity. Though few of the grievances amounted to a cause of action in a common-law court, all, applied to a private trustee, might have sustained a complaint in chancery. The underlying charge was that the king had failed in his duty as a trustee. Throughout the crisis, Crown lawyers maintained that the colonies lay in the king's ancient domain, and, indeed, the king had spoken repeatedly as if he were a trustee for the colonies, creating from his domain a life trust for the benefit of the colonists. Part of the official rationale for the Stamp Tax and subsequent statutory impositions was that the funds would be spent to secure the safety of the colonists. If the king had legal title, the colonists, for whose benefit the colonies were administered, had equitable title to the land and its fruits, much as settlers in Georgia and Rhode Island claimed. The law of equitable trusts did not even depend on an explicit instrument of trust. Maitland, looking back at eighteenth-century English law, wrote, "we may well have a trust although no person has in any ordinary sense of the word placed trust or reliance in the trustee."[98] Did not the benevolence the king purported to show for his subjects abroad amount to an implied trust? And if a corrupt king had violated his duties as a trustee, should there not be an equitable remedy? The theme of corruption, everywhere used by the revolutionaries to prove the malign motives of the British authorities, dovetailed nicely into Jefferson's challenge to royal trusteeship.[99]

Jefferson iterated the king's violations of his duties: by creating new offices, allowing quartering of troops, imposing taxes, cutting off trade, interrupting immigration, plundering and ravaging towns and farms, and making war on the colonies; by refusing to assent to wholesome laws, forbidding governors to approve laws of pressing importance, disrupting the assemblies, subjugating the judges, and grinding the regular courts under the heel of martial law; by his assent to punitive measures, harming all rather than only those who might have violated his law; by employing foreign mercenaries, forcing slavery on the colonists for his own merchants' benefit, and inciting the Indians to war; by fraud and misrepresentation in denying colonial petitions and convincing the people of Britain that the colonists were wrong in their protest the king violated the terms of the trust. All of these grievances had weight in equity.

Of the optional parts of a bill in equity, the fourth, fifth, and seventh, Jefferson elected to include only the fourth, confederating part in his Declaration. He accused the British people of joining in the plot against American liberties. These "unfeeling bretheren" submitted supinely to Parliament while the king usurped American rights. They even returned erring ministers to power when they could have voted them out of office. By refusing to call for an accounting from Parliament and king, they had exposed the Americans to grave danger. Congress excised this portion of Jefferson's draft for reasons of exigency. He did not include the fifth part of the bill, the anticipation of the defendant's arguments, or the seventh part, the interrogatories.

The sixth part of a bill, that no legal remedy would suffice, was essential. Jefferson knew that during the long course of the controversy the ordinary courts of justice were unable to protect colonial rights. Indeed, the royal courts were used against the colonists. The colonists must now "acquiesce in the necessity" of separation from the mother country. The authority for this remedy was the will of the "good people of these states." Here Jefferson again profoundly altered the authority for equitable pleading, breaking equity's historical tie with the king and replacing him with sovereignty of the people. The shift was not mere sophistry for Jefferson, a convenient argument. Shortly after the Declaration won approval, Jefferson traveled to Virginia and proposed that Virginia's chancellor be chosen by the representatives of the people.

The eighth part of a bill named the equitable remedy. Jefferson did so as well: "Reject and renounce all allegiance and subjection to the kings of Great Britain and all others who may hereafter claim by, through, or under them . . . utterly dissolve all political connection which may heretofore have subsisted between us and the people or parliament of Great Britain; and finally . . . assert and declare these colonies to be free and independent states." This was a dissolution of the trust agreement between the colonies and the king and Parliament. Dissolution lay within the power of beneficiaries in a revocable life trust. Congress initiated and formalized the process, giving it the stamp of legitimacy. The reference to the court of public opinion (a "decent respect for the opinions of mankind"), which opened the Declaration, reappeared in altered garb. Congress was now recast: it was no longer a collegium of lawyers but a people's court. Jefferson was not the first revolutionary to make this argument. Earlier in 1776, South Carolina's Justice Drayton had addressed his "Freeman" essays to the "High Court of Congress," a reference to the jurisdiction of the High Court of Parliament.[100] If Congress did not have the judicial powers of Parliament, it did possess some of the executive powers of the Crown, particularly the conduct of war and diplomacy.[101] Jefferson was mindful that another of these monarchical powers was that of holding equity courts. Jefferson acted as though Congress had the quasi-judicial power some of its members, in later years, would explicitly confer on a truly federal judiciary. When that government was created, equitable jurisdiction was given to its Supreme Court.

The ninth part of a bill in equity was the prayer for process: "That as free and independent states they have full power to levy war, conclude peace, contract alliances, establish commerce, and to do all other acts and things which independent states may of right do." This part of the bill, again resting on the sovereignty of the people rather than the power of the Crown, made the Declaration into a harbinger of a national Constitution. Without the ninth part of the bill, it had no force, for without "free and independent states" independence was only a word. The legal authority of the Declaration arose from the legality of Congress, which in turn rested on the right of provisional colonial conventions to send and instruct delegates to Congress. This was exactly the same right on which the first states based their constitutions. Congress's unanimous approval of the revised Declaration stamped it with the approval of the state governments, an approval ratified by inclusion of the Declaration in many of the states' fundamental laws. The delegates turned an equitable analogy into a political reality.[102]

The bill in equity ended with an oath. So did the Declaration of Independence. Such oaths were also used to conclude revolutionary "associations." The oath at the close of the Declaration does not establish that Jefferson was using the bill in equity as his model, but absence of an oath would have been odd if Jefferson were using an equitable format.

For an attorney under great pressure serving his people in a cause of such moment, the Declaration of Independence must be accounted a magnificent achievement. In later years, Jefferson would describe his effort as a synthesis of ideas common at that time; it was not in his nature to dramatize his own work.[103] His transformation of the bill in equity from a commonplace of litigation to a unique statement of republicanism was remarkable, however Jefferson characterized it himself. His silence on the use he made of equity is therefore puzzling. One might conclude that his elevation of equitable concepts was less conscious advocacy than unconscious mimicry, as though he adopted equitable terms and forms without fully realizing the implications of his thought. Nothing in his "Notes of Proceedings" on the debates of that early summer hints that he was tinkering with equitable pleading, much less with the fabrication of a theory of constitutional accountability based on the analogy to a trust. In his autobiography he recalled that only George Wythe had understood that the colonies were not contractually subordinate to Britain, but Jefferson did not mention discussing equity with Wythe on this occasion.[104]

Subsequent events suggest a more self-conscious borrowing. When Jefferson went back to Virginia immediately after drafting and voting on the Declaration, he gave serious and prolonged thought to reform of the Virginia Court of Chancery. He drafted a bill for a chancery court and introduced it on November 25, 1776. That bill provided for a court of three judges chosen by the legislature to hear equity complaints, with appeal to a court of appeals. All matters of fact were to be determined by juries in the equity court. The House of Burgesses would amend the bill to effectively eliminate juries and later reduce the bench to one man (George Wythe), but the rest of Jefferson's draft became law. One may speculate that if Jefferson's effort to recast equity in Virginia was connected to his pre-1776 equity practice, he might easily and consciously have relied on the bill in equity when drafting the Declaration. A consciously equitable Declaration may then have stimulated Jefferson to recast chancery in his home state.

From their creation, the new states' constitutions bore the commitments to official accountability to which Jefferson had held George III. George Mason's draft for the Virginia Constitution insisted that "all Power is by God and nature, vested in, and consequently derived from, the People; that Magistrates are their Trustees and Servants, and at all times amenable to them."[105] The drafters of Pennsylvania's constitution used similar language: "all power being originally inherent in, and consequently derived from, the people: therefore all officers of government, whether legislative or executive, are their trustees and servants, and at all times accountable to them."[106] Spokesmen for both states likened government to a trust—not a contract—in which the grantors and the beneficiaries were the people and the officeholders were merely trustees, accountable for malfeasance. In neighboring Maryland, a more conservative revolutionary leadership also committed itself to the trusteeship model: "all persons invested with the legislative or executive powers of government are the trustees of the public, and as such, accountable for their conduct."[107] In an era when so much of state constitutionalism rested on vague promises of republican principles and easily gave way to repressive reasons of state,[108] such words of accountability could have been ignored, but they were not. Virginia and Pennsylvania provided for impeachment and removal of erring officials, and Maryland removed public miscreants through legislative address to the governor. In all three states, officials were called to account through these mechanisms before the end of the revolutionary era.[109]

The analogy from the equitable trust was not the only source of the language or the deployment of these supervisory devices; but when the lexicon of trusteeship did emerge in political discourse, it gave greater force to the demand for accountability. For example, when Maryland revolutionaries drafted the first state constitution changing a proprietorship into a republic, the analogy to private trusteeship reappeared and proved powerful in the hands of political moderates—the very outcome Charles Carroll had feared in 1773.[110] In continuing disputes over the accountability of officials after 1776, Carroll and other magnates called for open-ended delegations of authority to legislators. They wanted the electorate to trust their conduct implicitly, for they were men of honor. Assembly leaders disagreed. Popular party politicians, led by William Paca and Samuel Chase, called for genuine and immediate accountability.[111] In 1786–87, the issue exploded during debates over the paper money emissions that debtors in the colony desperately sought. In the ensuing election campaign Paca told his constituents that officials were but trustees and if any of them neglected the strict instructions of the beneficiaries of that trust, they should be removed. The people were not to be denied access to information about debates and votes in the houses of the legislature. To the consternation of Carroll and his allies in the senate, leaders of the paper money faction in the lower house joined Paca in his appeal. Equitable principles defined a trustworthy government; accountability provided a cornerstone of revolutionary representation. Paca and Chase, accomplished solicitors and drafters of the Declaration of Rights, merely had gone further than their predecessors toward giving revolutionary constitutionalism an equitable shape.[112]

Trust and accountability, accountability and trust, indissolubly linked by two hundred years of controversy and speculation on the shape of constitutions, an effort fusing philosophical speculation and technical pleading skills, were built into the republican constitutions of the states. For equity lawyers who were also framers of constitutions, the combination of trusteeship and accountability had become second nature by the end of the revolutionary era. When Virginia ratified the federal Constitution, it proposed that the document be prefaced with a declaration that "Magistrates . . . are their [the people's] trustees and agents and at all times amenable to them."[113] When Secretary of the Treasury Alexander Hamilton, an accomplished solicitor in New York's courts, wanted a model for the funding and assumption of the outstanding federal debt, he turned to the trust. "To equalize the contributions of the states [to the fund], let each be then charged with its proportion of the aggregate of those balances, according to some equitable ratio." Should some states become creditors and others debtors, the federal government could be trusted to manage a reapportionment of the differences. "The whole of this arrangement [is] to be under the superintendence of commissioners, vested with equitable discretion, and final authority."[114] The public finances were to be managed as an equitable trust; that was what republican government was all about.

John Locke and Thomas Jefferson, faced with constitutional crises and armed with a working vocabulary of equitable remedies, elevated trusteeship from a private arrangement to a rule of public office. They took the language of equity from the courts and applied it to fundamental structures of government. Locke approached by analogy; Jefferson borrowed more closely from forms of pleading. Locke had written for a coup that failed and later was widely read but misunderstood. Jefferson wrote for a revolutionary Congress, and his message of accountability was everywhere understood, though its equitable origins were merged with more pressing concerns of constitution making and ultimately were lost to his own generation. In the fifty years after Jefferson's death, the process of elevation of equitable language and remedy from court practice to constitutional paradigm would repeat itself with even more striking consequences for American fundamental law.

PART TWO EQUALITY

Revolutionary American republicanism explained itself in the language of trusteeship. As Supreme Court Justice Joseph Story boasted, "by enabling the people to remove public functionaries, who abuse their trust, and to substitute others more faithful, and more honest, in their stead" the framers protected the beneficiaries of the public trust—the people.[1] Other, more visionary interpreters of the revolutionary achievement expanded the metaphor, making American leaders the stewards of a national trust that contained more than real estate and personal property. A way of life based on political and economic equality and opportunity was the gift of this trust to future generations.[2] Not all Americans shared in its bounty, however. Disfavored minorities suffered personal indignity, legal debility, and psychological damage. The courts, charged with redressing individual grievances, gave little comfort to the victims of these blows. If, for example, a slave woman wished the courts of North Carolina to punish the man who rented her from her master and shot her down, she would be disappointed.[3] If a free black woman besought the aid of state and federal courts to free her children from a man who bought them thinking they were slaves, she would beseech in vain.[4] Without equality of persons before the courts, trusteeship constitutionalism was an empty promise to the most oppressed Americans.

The chancellor's oath of office committed him to do "equal right to all manner of people, great and small, high and low, rich and poor, according to equity and good conscience,"[5] and advocates of chancery courts in the new states commended the humane and fair inclinations of equity. Nothing in their praise hinted that unleashed and unconstrained chancellors would or ought to remedy

the injustices of the world outside their chambers. Erastus Washington, lobbying for courts of equity in Story's home state of Massachusetts, merely offered that "the comparison [between law and equity]
may show that the practice of chancery is more easy and safe for the
parties, more favorable to justice, and more consonant to sound and
unfettered reason."[6] Frederick Brightly, a legal writer in Pennsylvania, another state without separate courts of equity, confided that so
egalitarian a government as Pennsylvania's had automatically incorporated equitable principles into its jurisprudence. The spirit of
equitable treatment of the disfavored was always there, although a
want of formalities had made equitable relief uncertain.[7] These ad-
vertisements for equity courts were milk-and-water things; why, then,
did Story go out of his way to blast the unconstrained and moraliz-
ing license of early equity?[8] Who was advocating such conduct? The
foremost student of equity in his country—he "wrote the book" on
it—and a chancellor himself when he rode circuit in New England,
Story had no reason to censure the jurisprudence of Lord Ellesmere
or Lord Nottingham. Yet Story plainly envisioned a latent, intrusive,
uncompromising force in equity poised to reshape private relationships and public policies.

Hidden in what appeared to be technical caviling among
learned legal writers lurked a far more controversial issue: the
chance that a chancellor troubled by conscience would reach out
beyond the suit before him to reorder social and economic relationships in the society as a whole. Such systemic, institutional relief
might overthrow social custom and political structures and tumble
the entire judicial system into the cauldron of political crisis.

There was cause for Story's uneasiness about courts of equity.
In his lifetime, he witnessed a veritable explosion of political and
economic energy. Such fundamental changes had to reach into the
courts. In the wake of the independence movement, revolutionary
America committed itself to egalitarian innovation. Freedom of worship replaced establishment of religion in many of the new states—a
real reform that chancellors could not mistake, for it thrust upon
them complicated suits between disestablished ministers and their
former vestries. The confiscation and sale at auction of loyalist property redistributed some of the wealth, a process in which equitable
claims and defenses played a part. The end of entail of estates and
primogeniture in descent freed some real estate from the grip of
great families, a fact chancellors hearing disputes over wills could
hardly miss. Chancellors also witnessed the movement for abolition

of slavery; case after case of disputed wills emancipating bondsmen and women forced chancellors to confront issues of conscience.[9] The generation that inherited the achievement of the founders combined an attachment to democratic reform with a passion for social experimentation. The opening of the West, the disappearance of property restrictions on free white male suffrage, and a myriad of private and state-sponsored reform projects for the handicapped and the deprived buoyed reformers and worried conservatives.[10] Both sides in these contests over the allocation of resources and distribution of wealth trooped to the chancellors' courts.

The same deep changes that promoted democratic reform triggered a surge of entrepreneurial ingenuity. In the first half of the new century legislative charters of monopoly to banks, road and bridge companies, and other public service enterprises crumbled before this onslaught of entrepreneurship. A multitude of transportation, land development, and commercial ventures transformed the look and pace of business. A business class emerged, distinctive in dress, education, speech, and manners from workers and servants. The mills, factories, and railroads built by the business class spilled their waste products and fired off their sparks onto the houses and farms of the very working men whose political rights were vindicated by legislative reforms. State governments gradually bowed to the insistence of business. Democratic equality elevated the ordinary man to the political privileges once held by a few; liberalization of law allowed the strong to accumulate more wealth at the expense of their poorer neighbors.[11]

Chancellors might stay this headlong pursuit of entrepreneurial gain by insisting that older forms of communitarian land use and business exchanges prevail over more "modern" ideas of development and contract. They might defend gemeinschaft against gesellschaft. Overall, the historical record of courts of equity in the new nation revealed the chancellors' disposition to aid the entrepreneur rather than the laborer, the master rather than the slave, but on noteworthy occasions individual chancellors also promoted the equality of persons. In doing so, they reached into the language of equity that regarded mutual fairness not efficiency, justice not enterprise, as its touchstone. In a series of cases involving trusts for slaves chancellors faced particularly agonizing choices bringing together all of the issues of equality and entrepreneurship, modernity and custom. When the intractable slavery controversy brought on a civil war, lawyers in Congress followed the chancellors into the equity of trustccship. The Freedmen's Bureau, the Civil Rights acts, and the Reconstruction amendments all appropriated concepts of public trusteeship and linked these to the goal of equal civil rights for blacks. Story's fears, rooted in his love for the Union, became the freedmen and women's best hope.

4   IN LAW AND EQUITY

—————

"Procedure"—rules governing access to the court, standing to bring a suit, definitions of who bears the burden of proving what fact, and choices among available remedies—theoretically flattens social and economic distinctions among litigants. Procedure keeps the court impartial. Suitors start on an even playing field. In practice the rules of pleading in courts favor one side or another, one sort of litigant or another, one kind of claim, or defense, or motion. It is thus no surprise that interested parties always vie to control the drafting and emendation of the rules of court. Judges celebrate the goal of neutrality and deplore capture of the rules by special interests by distinguishing procedure from substance, but such distinctions are labored and draw a bright line where none exists.[1]

From the inception of the new nation, rule making for equity courts was especially controversial. The historical accident giving rise to the authority and jurisdiction of the chancellor also gave him the power to revise the rules of his court at will. Early English chancellors allowed suitors to frame their complaints far less precisely than in common-law courts. The discretion that the chancellor had under the English rules to hear suits when he thought there was genuine harm for which law gave no remedy, his power to determine facts without the aid of a jury, and his willingness to openly make or ignore precedent in the name of justice to a particular claimant were troublesome to an American revolutionary leadership struggling against the unchecked discretion of Parliament. After all, the English chancellor only held court because the king could delegate his personal authority to a subordinate. Revolutionary ideology welcomed public trusteeship, a substantive borrowing from equity, but republicanization of the procedures of a royal prerogative court seemed another matter entirely.

The peculiarities of equity courts in the colonies had largely, though not completely, diffused the discretion of chancellors. Inferior courts mixed equitable with common-law process and allowed local juries to find facts. Assemblies used political means to curb discretion in central courts of equity. Nevertheless, assuming that the revolutionary framers decided to re-create courts of equity, the lawmakers would not be able to avoid a procedure that enshrined discretion. If equity were to function, it would have to remain flexible. If the chancellor or chancellors were to peer behind the pleadings, they would have to investigate records, compel the production of evidence, and interrogate witnesses. This intrusion into the lives of Americans, far exceeding that in a contemporary common-law court, raised questions of substance as well as procedure, of politics as well as efficiency in the courts. Would courts of equity become an engine of elitist oppression, bypassing juries? Or would demagogic chancellors mount an assault upon property to appeal to the restless masses?

REPUBLICAN EQUITY

Given the theoretical basis for resistance to courts of equity, the ease with which this most English of courts passed from imperial imposition to republican fixture was remarkable. Hostility to the common law was overt in New Jersey, Delaware, Pennsylvania, and New Hampshire, where statutes prohibited citation of postrevolutionary English decisions. Prerevolutionary English common law might be received insofar as it had been accepted in colonial courts, but the odium of royal exactions was still fresh in the revolutionaries' nostrils. State constitutions also insisted on jury trial of facts.[2]

For all this, equity courts resurfaced in the American republics. In wartime South Carolina, the lieutenant governor and his Privy Council acted as chancellors; with peace, they were replaced by a three-member equity court.[3] A similar movement to conserve a central court of equity in North Carolina foundered, but equity relief was made available in the district superior courts.[4] In Virginia, the new state court of equity had three chancellors. This arrangement, the work of Thomas Jefferson and a committee to reform the laws, soon gave way to a single chancellor whose decrees might be reviewed by a supreme appellate court.[5] In Georgia, which had no central supreme court until 1845, equity was exercised in the district courts under statutory authority.[6] Delaware, after 1776 fully independent of its ties to Pennsylvania, created a central court of equity that exists to this day.[7] Pennsylvania's courts and its assembly continued to exercise broad equity powers based on the explicit rationale that where no court existed to deliver equity the courts of law and the legislature must fill the gap. As Chief Justice Thomas McKean reasoned, "As there is no positive law, no adjudged case, nor established rule, or order, to direct the Court in this point [whether damage done by the invading British forces relieved a lessee of the duty to keep the leased premises in good repair], we must be guided by the principles of the law; by conscience, that infallible monitor within every judge's breast, and the original and eternal rules of justice. For equity is part of the law of Pennsylvania." Using English precedent, McKean ordered the lessee and the lessor to split the cost of the damages to the property caused by the British army.[8] New York and New Jersey continued to operate with high courts of chancery, the former convened by a specially appointed chancellor who was the titular head of the entire judiciary, the latter presided over by the governor of the state.[9] Massachusetts' General Assembly conferred specific equity powers on its regular courts of law.[10] Connecticut provided for a more comprehensive program of equity relief before the eighteenth century ended.[11] The new states, Tennessee in the van, conferred equity jurisdiction on their courts of law.[12]

After the lawgivers had spoken, the judges added their voices: convenience outweighed ideological qualms. As Chancellor William Henry DeSaussure argued in his South Carolina equity reports, states without equity had a "sensible defect" in their laws, for only equity could supply complete relief "in many important cases." There was no alternative to retention of equity. The common law resisted change, and wholesale incorporation of equitable procedures and remedies into common law would have been too much for even the most adventurous revolutionary legal reformer to champion. DeSaussure explicitly warned that partial experiments of that sort in various states "have increased the delay and expense of suits to an intolerable degree."[13] James Wilson, lecturing on the law at the College of Pennsylvania, pressed for a state court of equity precisely on grounds of convenience and efficiency. In particular,

> liquidating accounts judicially at common law [through individual jury determinations], is obviously exposed to many disadvantages and delays; and, for this reason, the action [in common law] of account has, in great measure, fallen into disuse. In England, the parties in unsettled and litigated accounts have recourse to chancery; in Pennsylvania, to arbitrators, or to

jurors acting in the character of arbitrators. The numerous em-
barrassments, which arise from the want of a proper commercial forum, are well known and severely felt both by the gentlemen of the bar, and by the gentlemen of the exchange. Impressed with these truths, the committee who were appointed to
report a draught of a constitution for the consideration of the
late convention of Pennsylvania, included, in their report, the
plan of a chancery establishment.[14]

The committee lost its bid for a separate equity court, but the common-law courts proved themselves receptive to the motives behind
the proposal and adopted equitable procedures when appropriate.

In addition to convenience for litigants, there was the question
of fees for litigators. In the commonwealth of Virginia, for example,
elite lawyers like John Marshall and Edmund Randolph solicited equity suits, as Thomas Jefferson, Peyton Randolph, Edmund Pendle-
ton, and George Wythe had in earlier years.[15] Fees for the most
intricate and substantial of these cases, based on the number of papers drawn up and filed, were lucrative, for such suits required a
mountain of paperwork and dragged on for years. Resistance among
the members of the Richmond equity bar to the division of equity
suits among district courts of equity proved that any threat to the
lawyers' livelihood was taken seriously indeed. Virginia lawyers
should not be singled out for criticism. Equity practice was a business like any other. For example, New Jersey Governor and Chancellor William Livingston appointed his son a clerk in chancery. The
clerk (really a scrivener) prepared all the written pleading for one
side or the other throughout the life of a suit—each document
bringing a fee. After all, everyone was entitled to recompense for
work performed.[16]

Despite their willingness to provide practical aids to suitors and
a source of income for the bar, state legislators were wary of an
independent judiciary. There remained too much discretion in equitable decree making to suit newly established revolutionary assemblies—always jealous of their supremacy over the courts in any case.
A practical compromise was struck: the legislators allowed equity to
function but retained control over rule making in the chancellor's
court.[17] Over time, the legislators either mired themselves in pica-
yune rule changes or grudgingly conceded the authority to regulate
process in the courts to the judges and chancellors themselves. In
Connecticut, whose courts dispensed both equity and law under distinct rules, the legislature fine-tuned the rules for fifty years. In

Massachusetts, whose regular courts had very limited equitable powers, the legislators conferred additional powers bit by bit until the judges were full-fledged chancellors. In New York, whose distinct high court of equity was a powerful institution in its own right, the assembly generally allowed the chancellors to regulate their own procedure until 1846, when a reformist constitutional convention swept away the court and the chancellor. The advent of "code pleading" in New York, soon copied by over half the states in the nation, seemed a triumph of procedural equity, but that triumph was illusory.

Connecticut's county court judges had equity powers in small claims (under thirty-five dollars), and its superior court judges had equity powers in more substantial claims. The state legislature did not fiddle with the substantive powers of these courts so much as with their procedure. Title 20 of the 1821 state code allowed no appeal from decrees but did permit a defendant to bring a writ of error to a higher court (the court of errors, in the case of appeal from a superior court). The colonial practice of obtaining a rehearing *de novo* on the merits in the higher court was thus abolished in equity. Judges could issue temporary restraining orders *ex parte*, or might, at their own discretion, notify defendants and arrange a hearing. All facts in the pleading were to be recorded, a mirror of the heavily factual nature of the chancellor's jurisdiction; he found facts without a jury. He might also allow a retrial if convinced that newly uncovered facts warranted it. In 1827, the legislature amended the equity title, spelled out the conditions under which a hearing on the temporary injunction might be held, and set the fees due the judge who decided to call the hearing. There must have been irregularities, confusion, and complaints about the old rule. In 1829, the lawmakers again amended the section on injunctions to provide that chief judges in the county courts could supervise the issuance and dissolution of injunctions when their courts were not in session. Two years later, the legislature ordered that cross-bills could not be filed without fair notice to the parties involved and when a money judgment resulted from a hearing in equity, the judge could order attachment of property "as in actions at law." By 1844, enough resistance had been raised to the power of lower court judges to issue or dissolve injunctions that the legislature allowed a party to go to the supreme court of errors instead of the appropriate local judge. Provision was also made for the court to adjourn the auction of attached property in order that the defendant might find an alternative method of payment. The lien remained in force during the adjournment. The legislature finally merged law and equity fully in 1879.[18]

Massachusetts had neither established courts of equity nor given its courts of law a full panoply of equitable powers. Instead, a statute specifying "Remedies in Equity" allowed mortgagors to redeem their interest in their property despite late payments. Bit by bit, that substantive jurisdiction was statutorily enlarged to include rules for fair notice to debtors, protection against unfair penalty bonds, a setoff of debts among parties in an ongoing suit, equitable jurisdiction to order the discovery of evidence and the production of documents in court when these could not be obtained through common-law process, equitable jurisdiction over partnerships when the common law did not afford a remedy, and appointment of masters in chancery to "do and perform all the duties, which, according to the rules and practice of Chancery, are usually performed by a Master in Chancery." To these powers, the legislators later added jurisdiction to prevent waste of assets or nuisance by equitable means when there was no remedy at common law, judicial supervision of corporations as well as more conventional trusts, and the hearing of cross claims among coexecutors or administrators of an estate. In chapter 81 of the Revised Statutes of 1835, the legislators threw up their hands at the prospect of drafting precise rules for equitable joinder of suits and declared that "All other cases in which there are more than two parties having distinct rights or interest, which cannot be justly and definitely decided in one action at the common law" might be joined in the same proceeding, at which time the court could hear cross claims and counterclaims and adjudicate class actions. The minutia of procedure burdened the legislators so long as they insisted on drafting the rules for the courts. In 1841, they had to determine the rule for court costs when the plaintiff only wanted to discover evidence rather than seek a full hearing on the merits of a suit. In 1843, they set a time limit for oaths in redemptions of mortgages. Six years later, the General Court explicitly authorized the conversion of equitable estates into legal estates. In 1857, legislative control of equity ended with a whimper: the assembly conceded that "the supreme judicial court shall have full equity jurisdiction, according to the usage and practice of courts of chancery, in all cases where there is not a full, adequate, and complete remedy at law." The next step was inevitable, and section 26 of Chapter 113 of the General Statutes reported that "The Court may make rules regulating the practice and conducting the business of the court in matters of equity, so as to simplify the proceedings, discourage delays, lessen the expenses and burdens of litigation, and expedite the decision of causes."[19]

The General Court labored in fear of a more sweeping revision of judicial practice along the lines followed by its neighbor, New York. Until 1846, New York had the most respected central court of equity in the country. Its reports were widely read and its chancellors, particularly the redoubtable James Kent, fashioned American equity precedent.[20] Although the state legislature periodically tinkered with the structure of the chancery court (for example, in 1823 giving equity powers to circuit court judges subject to appeal),[21] the chancellors could and did write their own rules of court.[22] In 1846, a new state constitution abolished the central equity court—its expense and delay, the revisors claimed, were notorious—and invited the legislature to reconsider the traditional differences between equity and common-law pleading.[23]

A commission appointed by the state legislature drafted a comprehensive new Code of Civil Pleading, which the state adopted in 1848. Under it, all equity powers were given to the regular courts. Equity procedure was also merged into legal procedure. The single form for bringing an action was to be the "complaint," which need only state the identity of the complainant, "the facts constituting the cause of action, in ordinary and concise language, without repetition, and in such a manner as to enable a person of common understanding to know what is intended" and "a demand of the relief to which the plaintiff supposes himself entitled." Gone were the specialized common-law writs with their obsessive Latinate precision. "In construction of a pleading, for the purpose of determining its effect, its allegation shall be liberally construed, with a view to substantial justice between the parties." Throughout the act were what appeared to be telltale signs of a triumph for equitable pleading. Amendment was to be liberal, without costs before the opposing party's answer, and discretionary after that answer, as justice allowed. Appearances were deceiving, however. Along with the chancellor, discovery, interrogatories, and pre-trial process were banished, and that with malice of purpose. The drafters of the act had no use for equity.[24]

Behind the code was the tireless energy of David Dudley Field and the more diffuse but equally compelling force of the "codification" movement. Field was an indefatigable Jacksonian, a Connecticut-born, New York City–based lawyer whose intensely moralistic vision of what the law should be coexisted comfortably with his service to clients like Jim Fisk and Jay Gould.[25] Ambivalence seemed to suit

Field. Though he had publicly scorned the southern wing of the Democratic party and supported Free Soil candidates, he defended the right of slaveholders to do what they wished with their human chattel within the South.[26] Though he regarded secession as rebellion, and rebellion as a crime, he challenged the legality of the Reconstruction acts. An effort might be made to bind up his views under the label of traditional Jacksonian strict-construction doctrine were it not for Field's own advocacy of loose construction when it suited him, for example, in defense of the Legal Tender acts.[27]

In his desire for codification, however, Field was consistent. It spanned his entire professional life and its most notable success came in the adoption of a code of civil procedure by New York. When the commission appointed by the state in 1847 floundered, Field stepped in to replace one of its number, and his inspiration and determination shaped the finished product. Field's call for a code was in surface accord with the sentiments of more radical reformers. He knew that reform of pleading was necessitated by the constitutional revision of the courts and conceded that "radical reform in legal proceedings has long been demanded by no inconsiderable number of the people." Lest this be considered advocacy of a protopopulist upheaval, however, Field continued that "none can reform so well as we [the lawyers on the commission], as none would be benefitted so much." The great charm of a code for lawyers, he confessed, was the uniformity, efficiency, and expeditiousness it would foster. He reassured his brethren at the bar that no substantive right of any party would be lost, drawn-out bills of interrogatories would disappear, and evidence would be tested in cross-examination under oath at trial.[28]

Clearly, Field's approach to the code was not nearly so leveling in purpose or effect as that of other codifiers in his day. Field knew that the radical ideal of a new law, shorn of all English anachronisms, had not made much progress,[29] despite the avidity of its proponents. In the 1830s and 1840s the movement was still strong; David Hoffman, Robert Rantoul, Jr., and William Sampson labored to create a truly egalitarian private law in America.[30] Field looked to other goals. Fed to the teeth with delay and extra expense growing out of poorly edited collections of statutes and irregular publication of judicial opinions, Field demanded certainty and authority in written sources. The code also did away with much of the fee system. Henceforth, leading lawyers could charge whatever they could get. The New York code was a victory for the elite of the bar, not an invitation to a democratic revolution in legal procedure.[31]

Nevertheless, given this mischievous and unpredictable imp at its door, Massachusetts' piecemeal revision of its equity rules was grudging indeed. Unlike in New York, the Bay State's conservative bench and bar, led by Joseph Story and Rufus Choate, had successfully resisted major substantive reform. For Story, the goal was professionalism—to keep rule making in the hands of a newly emergent profession of lawyers and judges. For Choate, democracy itself was the enemy. Reformers could count on the support of Governor Edward Everett, whose commission for revision of the laws periodically reported to a divided state legislature.[32] Despite the enthusiasm of its advocates, the general failure of substantive revision was only partially redeemed by the gradual merger of law and equity. Perhaps all the combatants in the codification struggle wearied of their labors as another struggle of far greater moment loomed in front of them. Theodore Sedgwick, a New York Democrat of conservative sympathies, spoke to that consensus in 1857:

it is plain that the matter [of who will determine the rules of court] is of great moment. On the one hand, the nature of the case, the frequency of doubt, the impossibility of recurring to the legislature or to the popular sovereignties for the removal of difficulties, and the general analogies of our system [to common law and the authority of precedent], require the power of the judiciary to be extended over the subject; while, on the other hand, unless their authority be very carefully exercised and confined within strict limits . . . the most valuable parts of the law-making power [would] practically fall into the hands of that branch of the government [that is, the courts] which is not intended to have any share whatever in the enactment of laws.[33]

Setting aside the hortatory language of the statute, what was gained and what was lost by the merger of common law and equity in New York and its sister states? It surely was not an unalloyed victory for traditional rules of equity. One need only compare the rules for taking depositions compiled by Chancellor Robert Lansing and emended by Chancellor James Kent with the foreshortened procedures for discovery in Title XII, chapter 6, of Field's code. Lansing and Kent afforded the suitor a chance to gather evidence the defendant had concealed. The code emphasized trial of the factual issues in court, reducing the plaintiff's capacity to breach the defendants' wall of secrecy. The judge became a mere arbiter, called in at the trial stage. If the ideal was efficient disposition of cases through simplification, nothing in the revision aided the less well-financed party against a wealthier opponent. Indeed, under the code the litigant who could afford the better counsel had a greater advantage than he or she had before the code, because more depended on management of the trial.

The struggle between legislatures and courts over the rules of equity had been deflected. Story need not have worried. An egalitarian challenge to the rules was co-opted by the lawyers, they in turn were led by a codifier who did not seek egalitarian reform at all. The reformers of the New York State Constitution may have done away with the chancellor in order to make all the courts receptive to the popular will, but when Field was done the result left rule making effectually in the hands of the courts. When the judges wished to narrow the scope of the code to protect either vested property rights or traditional social mores, they ignored the original purpose of constitutional reform.[34] The new rules—henceforth commonly called the "Field Code"—framed the structure and flow of litigation, but equity procedure in state courts, whether under codes like New York's or traditional regimes of chancellors, did not succumb to the rage for democratic reform.

After 1789, state interest in equity rules gained a rival, which assemblies and state judges could not control. The creators of the new federal government opted to give independent equity powers to its judges, creating another arena in which the judges, counsel, and litigants could do battle over the rules. Federal equity jurisdiction added, moreover, a wholly new issue to this debate over equity procedure—the issue of federalism.

FEDERAL EQUITY JURISDICTION

The basis of federal equity jurisdiction is Article III, section 2, of the United States Constitution. The Supreme Court obtained jurisdiction over all cases "in law and equity" arising under the Constitution, federal statutes, treaties, diplomatic controversies, and disputes between states, citizens of different states, a state and citizens of a different state, as well as suits to which the United States was a party.[35] The framers of the Constitution directed Congress to define the shape of equity jurisdiction in the lower federal courts, a task the Senate undertook in its first session. Contemporaries recognized that the equity clause not only gave the federal courts the power to decree equitable remedies but also enlarged the discretion of federal courts. Some political observers feared that this discretion might lead to an expanded role for the courts within the new federal government at the expense of the other branches, to intrusion of the federal courts into the internal affairs of state governments, or even to federal chancellors' redistribution of private wealth. As in the states, the rules of equity became a focus of controversy.[36]

Delegates to the Constitutional Convention in Philadelphia spent relatively little time on the "least dangerous branch" of their new government.[37] On August 27, 1787, the committee of detail reported its revisions to the convention without any mention of equity. Connecticut lawyer William Samuel Johnson then moved to add "both in law and equity" after "the judicial power of the United States" in section 1 and before "arising under" in section 2.[38] George Read, a Delaware lawyer, objected to vesting both legal and equitable powers in the same court and was joined by the Maryland delegation in voting against the amendment to the committee of detail's report. Read may have been thinking along the same lines as John Blair of Virginia when the latter prepared a motion for a distinct federal high court of equity.[39] Virginia and Maryland had separate courts of equity. Despite the opposition of Delaware and Maryland, Johnson's motion carried, with New Hampshire, Connecticut, Pennsylvania, Virginia, South Carolina, and Georgia voting for it. The committee on style, to which Johnson was appointed, retained his proposal in its report of September 12 to the convention, although it excised the first reference to "both in law and equity."[40] Article III, section 2, clause 2, of the engrossed version of the draft still contained a provision granting an undefined equity jurisdiction to the Supreme Court and by implication allowed Congress to grant similarly broad equitable jurisdiction to any lower federal courts it might create.[41]

Anti-federalists immediately seized upon the proposed equity power to warn against the dangers of uncontrolled discretion in the federal courts. They cited as proof of that danger the absence of juries in the chancellors' chamber. "Centinel" (Samuel Bryan, son of a radical Pennsylvania anti-federalist and judge) reminded his readers that federal courts' equity powers reached everyday questions like the construction of the meaning of a will. Would Americans accept such discretion unchecked by a jury?[42] A "Democratic Federalist" from Pennsylvania agreed: "it seems to me that there is much more *equity* in a trial by jury, than in an appellate jurisdiction from the fact."[43]

Alexander Hamilton rushed to reply to these and similar objections to the planned equity clause. In *Federalist* No. 80, he admitted: "It has also been asked, what need of the word 'equity'? What equitable causes can grow out of the Constitution and laws of the United States?" His answer was gentle but patronizing, as though to say that those less experienced in the ways of the practicing litigator must concede: "There is hardly a subject of litigation between individuals which may not involve those ingredients of *fraud, accident, trust,* or *hardship* which would render the object a matter of equitable rather than of legal jurisdiction, as the distinction is known and established in several of the states."[44] Hamilton could have applied the lesson immediately. Article I, section 8, clause 8, of the Constitution gave to Congress the power to protect copyrights and patents. Without equitable decrees to compel the production of evidence that might not be required of the same party in a court of common law and injunctions to bar future infringement in copyright and patent suits, federal courts would not be able to fulfill the dictates of congressional action in those areas. Hamilton concluded that there was nothing untoward in the equity power and nothing required the presence of a jury to insure fair play. In *Federalist* No. 80, Hamilton did not respond directly to the anti-federalists' underlying fears of judicial discretion unchecked by juries.[45] He dealt obliquely with these deeper reservations about the equity clause in *Federalist* No. 83. There, in the midst of an explanation of the varying state provisions (or lack thereof) for jury trial in cases of probate, admiralty, and other civil matters, he brushed away objections to the equity clause by laying its origin in existing state equity courts.[46] Indeed, such suits in equity might be too technical for the average juror. Obviously, Hamilton's own extensive equity practice had tutored him in the utility of equitable procedures, but he was not the man who added the equity clause to the new Constitution.[47]

What had motivated William Samuel Johnson to promote equitable jurisdiction for the federal courts? Was it personal interest or a more "civic," public interest? Ideally, the "publian" policymaker unites these two kinds of purposes, but there is nothing in Johnson's personal correspondence or that of anyone else connected with the Constitutional Convention to fix his motivation.[48] Johnson was a quietly busy member of the Connecticut delegation who had worked behind the scenes to prevent controversy over slavery and representation from dissolving the convention. Indeed, after a brief and professionally devastating brush with loyalism early in the revolutionary war he had avoided controversy in his legal practice and his public life.[49] The relative absence of controversy over equity at the convention suggests that Johnson enunciated a generally perceived need among the delegates, not to say a neutral, that is, wholly disinterested, purpose.[50]

A review of Johnson's career in the law suggests the practical, professional value he might have seen in the equity clause—the real-world needs he meant it to answer. Long before William Henry DeSaussure and James Wilson wrote about equity courts, Johnson's own practice as a collection agent and litigator for New York commercial interests in Connecticut had grown immense. When necessary, he sued delinquent Connecticut buyers. The latter often had paid with promissory notes, which they later were unable to honor. In response to their creditors' demands for payment on the penalty bonds attached to these notes, Connecticut merchants raised equitable defenses, for Connecticut superior courts could "chancer" the notes down to the actual amount advanced. Johnson's practice required vigorous and skilled refutation of equitable defenses, for which he had tutored himself early in his career.[51] He might well have surmised that federal courts hearing these suits would need to have equitable jurisdiction to dispose of defendants' arguments. It was a matter of efficiency.

In 1782, Johnson extended his equity practice from private suits to a public dispute and from demolition of equitable defenses of individual merchants to construction of an equitable defense for an entire community. The state of Connecticut asked him to uphold the titles of its settlers in the Wyoming Valley of Pennsylvania. In 1754, the Susquehannah Company of Connecticut had purchased the tract from the Delaware Indians. The company, part get-rich-quick scheme and part political machine, seemed on its face to realize the dreams of land-hungry Connecticut men and women. Its directors enrolled settlers in the colony and sent them off to cultivate their frontier parcels. The settlers soon found themselves locked in struggle with Pennsylvania claimants holding land under titles issued by their own colony, later reaffirmed by the state of Pennsylvania. Johnson briefed himself on the issues, a task eased by his own earlier involvement in the Susquehannah Company, and prepared for the hearing, in November 1783,[52] authorized by the United States Congress under Article IX of the Articles of Confederation.[53] The most experienced lawyer in the Connecticut three-man delegation, Johnson recognized that Pennsylvania might have a superior legal claim to the tract under its charter of 1682. He posed the equitable rejoinder that the Connecticut men and women had relied on the Connecticut Charter of 1662 in which Charles II had

granted to Connecticut land in what would later be northern Pennsylvania. Although subsequent royal grants had given the same land
to William Penn, the Connecticut settlers could reasonably have relied on their own charter to occupy the Wyoming Valley. And they
did, Johnson claimed—investing their energy, wealth, and, in many
cases, their lives, to hold, cultivate, and improve the land.[54] When a
rival claimant (here, Pennsylvania's speculators) stands by and lets
another improve land and only then claims that land, the cultivator
may seek relief from the chancellor under the doctrine of equitable
estoppel.[55]

Johnson's brief sounded in equitable principles and if not inge-
nious was at least moving and thoughtful. Unfortunately for his clients, he could not convince the commission that the dispute ought to
be resolved in their favor. Had the suit been brought in a regular
court of equity, the chancellor might well have asked why the Connecticut settlers made no effort to confirm their titles with Pennsylvania authorities. Such a show of good faith would have told in their
favor. Failure to make the effort in the face of requests from Pennsylvania could hardly be weighed in the scale for the settlers. In later
years, Johnson nevertheless blamed his defeat on the ignorance of
the commissioners.[56]

Viewed in broad perspective, Johnson's equity practice touched
two of the most important sectors in the economy of his region:
trade and land acquisition. Interstate trade was a necessity for Connecticut, wedged as it was between two commercially active neighbors.[57] Courts of equity enabled merchants to settle accounts over
long spans of time and across great distances. Equity also played a
major role in Connecticut farmers' desperate quest for land inside
and outside the state. Within Connecticut, equity allowed the mortgagors to prevent foreclosure when they missed payments on the
principal of the loan. Remittance of the interest and principal due
and payment of court costs forestalled the mortgagee. Pressure
from population density within Connecticut and speculative opportunities outside the state led to land fever among Connecticut's investors. Their duel with Pennsylvania over the Wyoming Valley was
prefigured in a long-standing quarrel with New York over the "Oblong." The giant parcel was disputed in the New York Court of
Chancery and the Connecticut General Assembly, the latter's final
court of equitable appeals, for almost one hundred years. Both of
these high courts of equity strove to construe the meaning of the
royal grants given the two colonies.

Connecticut's investment in commercial and real estate ventures tied its fortunes to the other states' throughout the Confederation period. All suffered the debilities of interstate tariffs, states taxing each others' produce when it crossed state borders.[58] Rampant land speculation, with resulting uncertainty of titles and disputes over settlers' rights, pit state against state and slowed development of western land.[59] A lawyer like Johnson could see that interstate commerce and land transactions required equity courts to resolve commercial disputes and quiet land titles. If individual states' courts were the only source of this equitable jurisprudence, there would be no way to decide between different state chancellors' reading of equitable claims—leading to endless rounds of injunctions by one state's courts against the proceedings of the other state's residents.[60]

Even assuming that these surmises on Johnson's own purposes are accurate and that his thinking reflected a consensus among the delegates, the legitimacy of public law rested not on the perceived need of individuals or the interest groups they represented, but on conventional sources of authority. In postrevolutionary America, law derived from constitutions, statutes, and precedent, supplemented by a handful of treatises and essays.[61] The framers of the federal Constitution had already exceeded the authority that Congress vested in them by creating a wholly new form of government.[62] However strong the sense of commercial crisis they shared, the framers could not hope to gain broad acceptance of the new Constitution in state ratifying conventions if they created it without regard to existing practices of governance and law. There were two striking novelties in Johnson's equity clause that had to be legitimated. The first was the assumption of equity jurisdiction itself. The second was the merger of law and equity in the same court—initially the Supreme Court of the United States, prospectively the entire federal system when it was elucidated by the Congress.

If serious constitutional objections to reestablishment of equity courts—based on recollection of monarchical excesses, fear of the absence of juries, or concrete examples of the dangers of discretion—were widespread, they would have deterred state lawmakers from reconstituting equity courts long before the framers met in Philadelphia. Nevertheless, the anti-federalists mounted just such a critique and continued it even after ratification. Senator William Maclay of Pennsylvania, no lawyer and proud of it, opposed giving equity jurisdiction to the lower federal courts. He was certain that federal chancellors would become tools of the commercial elite and promote inequality. Such cavils fell before Hamilton's plain truth: many courts in the colonies and the new states, both of English and of native origin, already dispensed equity.[63] A generation later, Justice Story regarded Hamilton's argument for the legitimacy of equity courts as so compelling that it need only be cited to quash any reservations about the inclusion of equity jurisdiction in the federal system.[64] State equity practice had thoroughly republicanized equity in the same way that the states' adoption and use of impeachment procedures domesticated that uniquely English method of removing erring officials. As in the incorporation of impeachment in the federal Constitution, state equity statutes and structures served as models for a corresponding grant to federal courts.[65]

The merger of equitable and common-law jurisdictions in a single court was a second, distinct question before the framers. To some jurists, notably Thomas Jefferson, allowing merger presented a far greater peril than conferring jurisdiction. Jefferson trusted equity courts but wanted equity preserved as a distinct corrective to law. He reasoned:

> It has often been predicted in England that the Chancery would swallow up the Common Law. During many centuries however that the two courts have gone on together, the jurisdiction of the Common law has not been narrowed in a single article; on the contrary it has been enlarged from time to time by acts of the legislature. But jealousy uncorrected by reason or experience, sees certainty wherever there is a possibility, and sensible men still think that the danger from this court overweighs its utility. Even some of the states in our Union have chosen to do without this court, and it has been proposed to others to follow their example. In this case, one of two consequences must follow. Either 1. The cases now remediable in chancery must be left without remedy, in which even the clamours for justice which originally begat this court would produce its re-institution; or 2. The courts of common law must be permitted to perform the discretionary functions of the Chancery. This will be either by adopting at once all the rules of the Chancery, with the consent of the legislature, or, if that is withheld, these courts will be led, by the desire of doing justice, to extend the text of the law according to its equity as was done in England before the Chancery took a regular form. This will be worse than running on Sylla to avoid Charybdis. For at present nine tenths of our legal contestations are perfectly remedied by the Common law, and can be carried before that judicature only. This pro-

portion then of our rights is placed on sure ground. Relieve the judges from the rigour of text law, and permit them, with pretorian discretion, to wander into its equity, and the whole legal system becomes uncertain.[66]

Despite the similarity in their politics, Jefferson did not agree with Maclay that chancellors were fated to increase inequality. Quite the contrary: Jefferson wanted to insulate equity from the ordinary business of common law in order to preserve the special egalitarian character of equity. Political conservatives like James Iredell of North Carolina and Alexander Hamilton ignored the ideological subtext of criticisms of merger. They insisted merger would make a well-established technical tool more efficient. Their focus on efficiency was not necessarily an attempt to cloak partisan motives,[67] but efficiency was not in itself a precedent.[68] Once again, it was the experience of William Samuel Johnson that was essential in the proposal for merger. In 1772 Johnson was named to the Connecticut Superior Court bench.[69] That court already possessed common-law and equity jurisdiction. It was no accident, thus, that Connecticut Chief Justice Zephaniah Swift was the foremost exponent of merged jurisdiction: "If the good of the community required the perpetuation of the distinction, between law and equity, they ought to be administered by distinct tribunals: but as this distinction in many instances is merely verbal and in all, the jurisdiction might be blended, it is strictly proper, that these different powers should be vested in the same tribunal, for the purpose of forming a coalition."[70] In Connecticut, the equity bar had no special fees to preserve and no special claim on a chancellor, for there was none. Johnson's idea of merger was another example of state experience directly informing the fashioning of the federal Constitution.

The issue of merger continued to excite some controversy after ratification. As if to beat Jefferson's contentions into the ground, James Wilson assured critics of merger that

law and equity are in a state of continual progression; one occupying incessantly the ground, which the other, in its advancement, has left. The posts now possessed by strict law were formally possessed by equity; and the posts now possessed by equity will hereafter be possessed by strict law. . . . In this view of the subject, we shall find as little difficulty in pronouncing, that every court of equity will gradually become a court of law; for its decisions, at first discretionary, will gradually be directed by general principles and rules. . . . The particulars, in which they still differ, are, indeed, of importance; but I see no reason why the separate powers of chancery, placed there very properly, indeed, should be thought incommunicable to the courts of common law.[71]

Wilson, an associate justice of the new Supreme Court, lectured to an audience of grandees and advocates. His account of the future of equity was well calculated to calm whatever remained of the opponents of merger's qualms.

If the states' experience provided legitimacy for incorporation and merger, the state courts could not dictate the precise rules for federal equity procedure. The problem of defining the procedural scope of the equity clause was hardly unique. The Constitution overflowed with open-textured grants of power, which the framers assumed practice would delimit. As James Madison admitted in *Federalist* No. 32: "The jurisdiction of her [England's] several courts, general and local, of law, of equity, of admiralty, etc. is not less a source of frequent and intricate discussions, sufficiently denoting the indeterminate limits by which they are respectively circumscribed." How much more indeterminate would be the novel arrangements of a new nation? Madison interjected, pleading for good-faith reception of the framers' efforts.[72]

Working federal courts had to delineate rules of proceeding. At the threshold was a question peculiar to equity's history: did the weight accorded precedent in common-law courts under the self-imposed rigor of stare decisis obtain on the equity side of the docket? As authoritative a chancellor as Lord Nottingham had refused on occasion to be bound by prior rulings in chancery.[73] Nonetheless, by 1789 few American jurists would argue that equity rested purely on the chancellor's conscience rather than on settled rules and practices.[74]

The practical problem remained: what rules and practices of equity should the federal courts adopt? Federal judges might elect to use the rules of the state courts in which the federal district or circuit court sat. Congress had the chance to dictate this practice; it had done just that with common-law procedure in section 34 of the Judiciary Act of 1789.[75] During debate over the Judiciary Act in the Senate, William Samuel Johnson argued for unfettered equity jurisdiction in the federal courts, a rule-making power independent of state courts' and legislatures' decisions.[76] The circuit courts did obtain such jurisdiction under section 11 of the Judiciary Act. At the same time, Johnson and his Senate allies had to concede that a "plain, adequate, and complete remedy" at law should bar application to the federal chancellor. In the Judiciary Act of 1789, Congress ordered that equity conform to civil procedure but did not say whose civil procedure.[77] Desperate to avoid conflict between state and federal courts, Congress found itself tongue-tied. In the Process Regulation Act of 1792, equity in the federal courts was made coincident to the "rules of equity." This two-step reduced to the statement that equity courts should follow their own rules.[78] Plainly, Congress was allowing the federal courts to choose their own rules for equity proceedings. Unlike the state legislatures' claims to supremacy over the judicial branch, derived from the premier position of the state assemblies during the Revolution, Congress here bowed to the initiative and expertise of the judiciary.

An American law of equity was beginning to emerge in some of the states, but other states had no equity courts.[79] What were federal courts sitting in these latter states to do when disputants sought equitable remedies? Before a uniform policy emerged, at least one federal circuit tried to adopt the equity rules of the state where it sat.[80] The federal courts might have organized and refined the precedents and rules of states that did have equity courts and imposed these on all the states. The problem with this solution above and beyond the herculean labor of synthesis it imposed was that no one state could be confident that its own equity rules would apply within its own borders once the litigants had removed the suit to the federal courts. States without equity would have it clamped on them, a signal invasion of the state's sovereignty as some understood it at that time. Relations between the states and the new central government would be strained by this imposition.[81] Indeed, it smacked of the loose construction of the Constitution that anti-federalists dreaded and would lead to a political crisis during the Alien and Sedition Acts.[82]

Faced with this intractable conundrum and pressed by the need to find some acceptable source of rules, federal courts turned to the one readily available, fully documented source of equity precepts—England's court of chancery. In 1791, Chief Justice John Jay decided, in a reply to Attorney General Edmund Randolph, that "this court [will] consider the practice of the courts . . . of chancery, in England, as affording outlines for the practice of this court."[83] When the question of the content of federal equity was finally confronted directly, in *Robinson v. Campbell* (1818), Justice Thomas Todd did not have to conceal his high regard for English equity. Indeed, he used Jay's decision to rely on English equity rules to defend the autonomy of the federal court system. Subtle irony this was. Evidently the reputation of England's chancellors had not suffered in the revolutionaries' attack on royal placemen and ministers of state, perhaps in part because the chancellor had receded so far into the shadows of English rule.[84] The case presented a three-cornered dispute over land titles in the new state of Tennessee among claimants holding grants from Virginia and Tennessee. Was the federal circuit court bound by the Judiciary Act of 1789 and the Process Regulation Act of 1792 to apply Tennessee equity rules? Todd hypothesized: if federal courts were to confine themselves "in their mode of administering relief to the same remedies, and those only, with all their incidents, which existed in the courts of the respective states" and the state had no equitable remedies, the consequence would be to abolish equitable claims. Todd rejected this inference. The federal circuit courts had equity jurisdiction under section 11 of the Judiciary Act of 1789 and that jurisdiction could not be nullified by the incidents of state rules. Todd reasoned that federal remedies, as the enabling act had stated, were available "according to the principles of common law and equity . . . distinguished and defined in that country from which we derive our knowledge of those principles."[85] This result was confirmed cursorily in Justice Joseph Story's opinion in *Boyle v. Zacherie* II. Story wrote: "the acts of Maryland equity . . . are of no force in relation to the Courts of the United States" for "the settled doctrine of this Court is, that the remedies in equity are to be administered, not according to the state practice, but according to the practice of Courts of equity in the parent country as contradistinguished from that of Courts of law; subject, of course, to the provisions of the acts of Congress, and to such alterations and rules as in the exercise of the powers delegated by those acts, the Courts of the United States may, from time to time, prescribe."[86] Todd and Story regarded this process as entirely appropriate, a conclusion that Congress's silence seemed to warrant.[87] The Supreme Court thereafter laid down its own rules for equity, publishing them in its own reports. The high court also established rules for equitable process in the district courts and circuit courts, though the latter were permitted after 1822 to make "any further rules and regulations not inconsistent with the rules hereby prescribed, in their discretion." What is more important, the substantive relief afforded by federal courts sitting in equity remained the preserve of those courts and does to this day.[88]

Not quite hidden in this triumph of traditional common-law method in which the Court made law but insisted that the Constitution and statute dictated the result was the old problem: which English equity rules was the Court to follow? On its answer to that puzzle rested the resolution of the fundamental dilemma facing the federal courts—how to constrain the discretion of the chancellor. For his answer Story drew inspiration from William Blackstone and the decisions of post-Restoration chancellors, notably Lord Eldon.[89] Story led the charge to limit the discretion of future chancellors. Four years after *Boyle*, in his first volume on equity jurisprudence, he denounced wide-ranging discretion, whether founded on natural law or conscience:

> The . . . proposition, that every matter that happens inconsistent with the design of the legislator, or is contrary to natural justice, may find relief in equity, is equally untenable [as the proposition that equity might overturn settled principles of law]. There are many cases against natural justice, which are left wholly to the conscience of the party, and are without any redress, equitable or legal. And so far from a Court of Equity supplying universally the defects of positive legislation, or peculiarly carrying into effect the intent as contradistinguished from the text of the Legislature, it is governed by the same rules of interpretation as a Court of Law, and is often compelled to stop where the letter of the law stops. It is the duty of every court of justice, whether of law or of equity, to consult the intention of the Legislature. And in the discharge of this duty a Court of Equity is not invested with a larger or a more liberal discretion than a Court of Law.

It was a settled, conservative science of equity that Story discovered in the English reports and attempted to incorporate into federal jurisprudence.[90]

Story's effort to move Johnson's open-textured equity clause away from the precipice of unrestrained discretion was successful insofar as his treatises on equity became standard works, standing alongside reports of James Kent's decisions in the New York Court of Chancery.[91] Story's studied detail of the technicality of equitable jurisdiction did not obscure the fact that from its inception the equity clause had demonstrated that equity procedure under the Constitution was neither self-restraining nor self-actualizing. Federal courts were equity courts because lawyers serving merchants and speculators needed federal equity courts.[92] As with the state legislatures' periodic intrusion into their own courts, Congress occasionally reminded the federal bench that Congress regulated process, though in general Congress allowed the judges to set their own course. State and federal chancellors were thus free enough to decide between values like equality of persons and liberty of contract when the conflict arose between them and could not be mediated. Statute and precedent framed equitable quarrels in the courts but did not dictate their outcome. Procedure neither dictated equal treatment nor undermined it. The chancellor was still as free to hear the still, small voice of conscience as he dared to be.

5 EQUAL PROTECTION

The rules laid down for procedure in equity were not hard and fast, nor did they prefigure greater or diminished equality. Instead, procedure bled into substance and substance filled in the interstices of procedure. Joseph Story knew this and called upon chancellors for self-restraint. In the "private law" of individual exchanges, most notably in contracts, the discretion of the chancellor abutted the jurisdiction of common-law judges and was confined thereby. But the public and the private spheres of law inevitably overlapped, and chancellors adjudicating highly charged political issues had more scope to promote equality of persons. That was the discretion Story feared.

For all the rules that Story's *Commentaries* imposed on chancellors, their guide remained their conscience, though that "conscience" was increasingly regarded by most chancellors as an artifact of judicial culture rather than a personal moral faculty. Still, some chancellors read the maxims of equity to promote the factory and the railroad,[1] while other chancellors regarded themselves as the embattled guardians of a fast-receding, golden age of harmonious social relationships and mutual respect, a gemeinschaft threatened by milldams and canals. No matter that the gemeinschaft was a myth of their own making and to their own liking, these chancellors resisted the emerging American gesellschaft.

In the van of the entrepreneurial assault on a rural premarket culture was a newly triumphant judicial characterization of contracts. Under common-law rules of pleading, agreements between parties to perform services, buy and sell goods, and perform other market transactions were linked to limitations of the "writ" under which a wronged party could bring suit for damages. The writ was the initial claim filed with the court alleging the breach. The writs were the preserve of common-law courts, but a party could aver in the course of the suit that a contract was so unfair that the court should either rescind it or refuse to enforce it. These remedies were available only from the chancellor. If the consideration for the contract was so inadequate as to constitute proof that buyer or seller had misrepresented or concealed a material fact, a chancellor might intervene. Conversely, if one of the parties had substantially performed on the contract but not fulfilled every detail, the chancellor might find that the performing party was entitled to some payment under the contract. Finally, when one of the parties refused to perform, the chancellor might order it to do so if "specific performance" was a fairer remedy than monetary damages. In the antebellum era, a theory of contracts coalesced that sharply curtailed the chancellor's intervention. This was the "will" theory of contracts, and it was disarmingly simple. If the parties to a contract understood what they were doing (if there was a "meeting of their minds") and neither practiced open fraud on the other, the court would enforce every particular of the contract. The doctrine had precedents before the nineteenth century, but it gathered momentum in common-law courts after 1810.[2] A few chancellors stood in its way.[3]

In *Britton v. Turner* (1834), New Hampshire Chief Justice Joel Parker used equitable reasoning to afford a building contractor payment for partial satisfaction of a contract.[4] The will theory of contracts refused to let contractors or laborers claim any payment for a contract they voluntarily breached. Thus, if a contractor had failed to finish every detail of a job, a seasonal agricultural worker failed to stay for the last day of the season, or a sailor did not complete the whole voyage for which he had signed on, they were entitled to nothing at all from their employers. Parker rejected such reasoning, preferring instead the old equitable doctrine of *quantum meruit*— payment for what had been earned.[5] The contractor was entitled to a fair portion of the contract price, commensurate with his performance, otherwise his employer would have been unjustly enriched. Though the case did not concern farm laborers, it applied to them as well, as Parker undoubtedly knew. *Britton* lodged itself in the path of the will theory in employment contracts. Parker did not rest his decision on an explicit vision of a preindustrial community— chancellors rarely revealed their social preferences even in this era of "grand-style" judging—but dilated instead upon immutable rules of traditional equity.[6]

There was a second ground on which a chancellor might stand

to resist the incursions of entrepreneurial volitionism. In protecting the weaker party against the stronger party in a contract, the chancellor also might be guarding his own jurisdiction against the common-law courts. Lord Chancellor Ellesmere's combat with Chief Justice Edward Coke was no mere by-product of early Stuart politics; for the two of them, it was inherent in the nature of a dual court system. Chancellor James Kent of New York excelled in policing the boundaries of his court's jurisdiction, and the most famous antebellum decree concerning the doctrine of inadequate consideration came from his hands. *Seymour v. Delancey* (1822) was from its inception a leading case,[7] and it took two years to wend its way from the court of chancery to the New York Supreme Court of Errors. In January 1821, Thomas Ellison, old, feeble, and frequently intoxicated, exchanged two farms worth $14,000 (or somewhat less, depending on whose assessment the court believed) for a third interest in a lot in the town of Newburgh, New York, worth no more than $6,000. Four months later he was dead. His heirs refused to carry through the exchange, claiming that it was unfair. The purchasers brought suit in the chancellor's court for specific performance— they wanted the deal to go through—rather than accept damages for breach of contract, the only remedy available in a court of law. Chancellor James Kent refused to order the exchange. The chancellor's intervention rested on his "sound judicial discretion." He need not order performance if he thought that the contract was fraudulent; that much was not in question. Was such disproportionate value —inadequate consideration in technical terms—evidence of actual fraud? For Kent it was presumptive evidence that the buyers had taken unfair advantage of Ellison's diminished mental capacity: "and [it] is clearly sufficient, within the view of all the [English equity] cases [cited and examined by Kent], to render it highly discreet and just to refuse the aid of the court to a specific performance of so hard and so extravagant a bargain, gained from a habitual drunkard, in the last year of his life, and just before his infirmities had begun to incapacitate him entirely for business."[8] Kent had looked behind the formalities of the agreement to find the factual context of the contract. He buttressed his finding with English cases, although every one of those cases could be viewed in different terms or met with cases decided by the same English chancellors that told against Kent.[9]

Kent used authority to support a conclusion he had already reached: the contract was patently unfair, even if arrived at through the volition of both parties without fraudulent misrepresentation, and a chancellor did not have to enforce an unfair contract. Kent noted in passing a vital point: he did not have to undo the contract, for neither side had performed its part in it. What would the chancellor have done if the transaction had been irreversibly completed, the lands exchanged and improved? According to Kent, the chancellor would then have used another of his tools: the constructive trust. As he later wrote in his *Commentaries on American Law*, "And if a weak man sells his estate for a very inadequate consideration, equity will raise a trust in favour of him, or his family."[10]

The court of errors divided sharply when the buyers appealed. Kent had retired, but Chief Justice John Savage persisted that the chancellor need not order enforcement of a contract that, in his judgment, was unfair. Though nine senators (the state senate sat with the supreme court in the court of errors) followed Savage, fourteen were convinced by Senator John Sudam that a contract entered into by parties "at will" and without fraud was binding. Without assurance that such contracts would be fulfilled, he argued, all commerce would rest on the discretion of the chancellor. Sudam's opinion echoed the warning issued by James Duer, counsel for the appellants: Kent had subjected his clients "to the mere arbitrary discretion, the caprice and humor of the judge."[11]

Kent was not protecting the poor against the rich; he was protecting the discretion of the chancellor, which, properly applied, could aid the mistreated weak against the unscrupulous strong. The bargain was hard, but no fraud was involved, and, as Senator Sudam pleaded so persuasively in the court of errors, Ellison went into the deal with his eyes open (though his vision was very likely blurred, since his drunkenness was "notorious").[12] Yet on its face the exchange was unfair, and that had been enough for Kent to find evidence of undue influence. There were limits—severe limits—to his willingness to intervene; he was not about to effect Aristotle's distributive justice by decree: "A state of equality as to property is impossible to be maintained, for it is against the laws of our own nature. . . . Liberty depends essentially upon the structure of government, the administration of justice, and the intelligence of the people and it has very little concern with equality of property."[13] Indeed, "natural equity" might lead to greater inequality in wealth, for to Kent the right of an individual to hold property against more needy potential users was as much a tenet of equity as of common law.[14] Kent's successor, Reuben Walworth, allowed the railroads, as licensees of the state, to take prime land for their right-of-way under the rationale that private "eminent domain," despite its special benefits to the railroad and its owners, justified dispossession of less productive users.

In the public interest the chancellor could cabin his own powers to allow economic development. Belatedly, the state legislature followed suit—the railroads got what they wanted.[15]

Nevertheless, where the weaker party was in any way duped or misled equity would still subordinate productivity to fairness. In this era of speculation, duplicity abounded. For example, in the sale and purchase of Maine timberland after the country had recovered from the panic of 1837, a venture much resembling modern futures speculation, ordinary investors relied on the representations of timber brokers to buy lots sight unseen. Justice Story heard one of these cases on circuit in 1845, just before he died. He rescinded the purchase agreement and warned future sellers:

> It appears to me, that it is high time, that the principles of courts of equity upon the subject of sales and purchases should be better understood, and more rigidly enforced in the community. It is equally promotive of sound morals, fair dealing and public justice and policy, that every vendor should distinctly comprehend, not only that good faith should reign over all his conduct in relation to the sale, but that there should be the most scrupulous good faith, an exalted honesty, or as it is often felicitously expressed, *uberrima fides*, in every representation made by him as an inducement to the sale. . . . The vendor acts at his peril.[16]

Story knew that even as he protected the misled buyer, state courts of law were bridling equity with the common-law doctrine of *caveat emptor*. Nevertheless, equity still spoke when there was duplicity abroad. Story himself rebuked "the gambling spirit of speculation, that now unhappily prevails."[17]

THE CHANCELLOR AND SLAVERY

When the chancellor rescinded or reformed a contract, he aided a private party mistreated by another private party, but the effects of the chancellor's intervention rarely extended beyond the parties at the bar and the transaction they disputed. He tried to prevent unjust enrichment and restore the parties to their original position, an effort that did not in itself redistribute wealth or promote equality in any sweeping way.[18] The chancellor's jurisdiction over contracts was private law par excellence. In part this was due to the fact that he shared jurisdiction over contract disputes with courts of common law. The old and still active maxim that equity followed the law limited what chancellors could do in contract cases. In one area under his sole jurisdiction, supervising trusts for slave beneficiaries, he did not have quite the same degree of constraint upon his discretion. In the antebellum period, this area of equity jurisdiction was in flux, with two consequences. The first was that the chancellor faced many cases of "first instance," cases without clear rules to guide him. The second was that these cases were never wholly private, for each raised unresolved issues of public policy. Although his decrees in these cases might be directed to the parties before him, they were watched suspiciously by legislatures. Disputes over the manumission of slaves put chancellors to the task of constructing the intentions of testators and weighing these against the claims of heirs and demands of state statutes. Slave law raised complicated, bifurcating questions of domestic affection and commercial exploitation. Were slaves servants or property? Could they be beneficiaries of trusts, capable of suing for breach of either express or implied trusts, and of receiving bequests from a probated estate at some future time? Slaves' suits under disputed constructions of such wills and bequests threw these questions into the lap of the chancellor.

Under the "domestic" law of slave states, slaves were chattel in the stream of commerce, property accumulated by entrepreneurial skill and good fortune.[19] Could a chancellor, so disposed, use equitable doctrines and equitable powers to grant relief to slave petitioners as though they had capacity to bring suit? One must remember that the chancellor could not reach into the world outside his chambers and pluck out suits posing these questions. Moreover, equity was bound by statutes and constitutions as well as certain conventions of interpretation of documents. Nevertheless, even Story admitted that equity was far more flexible within its constraints than common law.[20] Could that area of extra discretion be employed to challenge the institution of slavery where it existed, or to manumit slaves within the state against the will of the legislature expressed in statutes? There was no bright line between private sentiment and public callousness in slave cases, and appeals to humane feelings like those expressed by Chief Justice John Rutledge of South Carolina in *Sally v. Beaty* (1792) grew increasingly rare by the 1850s.[21] As slave suits became national issues, this blurring of private and public made manumission suits in chancery into major crises of public policy.

The chancellor or the judge sitting in equity could employ a jurisprudence of benevolence alien to the common-law judge: the trust. The explicit trust created by the testator to free the slave at some future time when statute would allow it, the implied trust created out of the testator's manifest intent when she did not use the proper words, and the constructive trust fashioned by the chancellor to protect the interest of the slave wrongfully kept in bondage all played their parts in these intense courtroom dramas. Chancellors in the 1790s wrote the script. In *Pleasants v. Pleasants* (1799), Chancellor George Wythe, Thomas Jefferson's mentor, discerned an implied trust and ruled in favor of equality. The testator, a Quaker, wished to free his slaves in his will but was frustrated by the laws of Virginia. He thus wrote a will that gave the slaves freedom at such time as the legislature would allow it. At his death, the slaves passed to his legal heirs according to the will. After the legislature altered the slave code to permit testamentary manumission, the next friends of the slaves, other Quakers, brought suit in the chancellor's court for the slaves' freedom. In *Pleasants*, Wythe not only construed the bequest as a trust with the slaves as beneficiaries but also ordered the heirs to pay the slaves wages for the period of their servitude.[22] Perhaps the old teacher recalled his pupil's argument in *Howell v. Netherland*. More likely, Jefferson learned that argument during his studies under Wythe.

Wythe's equity jurisprudence, with its sweeping reformist commitment and its high regard for equality, was very personal, but Virginia chancellors moved part way toward his views under the prompting of testators who proved over and over that their humane instincts were far stronger than their regard for the reasons of state that forbade testamentary manumission. Virginians who desired to free their slaves in their wills sought and found in trusteeship a refuge from the rigor of the "peculiar institution."[23] The will either spelled out the terms of this trust—requiring "my good friend A" to free the slaves when the state allowed it and in the interim to let them work for themselves and keep their earnings; when they were freed to give them the use of funds from the estate set aside for them; and if necessary to take them out of the state to free them—or referred to these and other promises in more cryptic fashion. In South Carolina and North Carolina, testators had to rely on "secret trusts" to morally induce their executors to free slaves after the states' legislatures barred testamentary slave trusts.[24]

In the face of such statutes, testators and their counsel persisted in trying to couch the will in such a way that it would not be defeated by the heirs' desire to keep the slaves or sell them off.[25] Dr. Umstead of Orange County, North Carolina, asked his friends and executors, "in special trust and confidence," to take his "negro slave Dicey, and her two children Emeline and Harriet" and as soon as they found it "expedient" to free and liberate them, and, in the meantime, "it is my will and desire, that the labour of such slaves, and the profits, and proceeds thereof, shall enure to the use and benefit of the aforesaid slaves only." If the trust failed (for Umstead's lawyer must have warned that it would, as it happened, fail against the challenge of the heirs at law), the executors were to insure that the return of the slaves' outside employment was to benefit them alone. In these wills, the testators sought to impose their conscience on the state.[26]

Traditional equity doctrine, speaking in the voice of trusteeship, read a message of equality into the Southern law of manumission. T. R. R. Cobb, no friend to emancipation of the slave—he thought blacks were well suited to slavery[27]—conceded in his influential treatise, *The Law of Negro Slavery* (1858), that the chancellor might relieve a slave wrongfully held in bondage after manumission by deed or will:

> We may add here, that if a slave is bequeathed to a legatee for the purpose of manumission, this is good reason for a court of equity to decree a specific performance, if the executor, or other person having him in possession, refuses to deliver him up. In those States where domestic manumission is forbidden and foreign emancipation is allowed, a question may arise, how a direction to executors to remove slaves to a foreign State for this purpose, can be enforced? In the absence of the statutory enactment, both public policy and the principles of justice require, that the courts should devise some means by which a faithless executor should be compelled to execute the trust.[28]

Cobb imposed crucial qualifications to the discretion of a chancellor—state policy embodied in statutes forbidding domestic manumission voided the deed or will and defeated the intention of the late owner. Further, the manumission must not take the form of an executory contract, for the slave had no power to enter into a contract with future conditions. Finally, the slave's freedom depended on the solvency of the estate, for she could be sold to pay its debts before she was freed by probate of the will. Nevertheless, trusteeship doctrine was a still, small voice for equality and testators heard it.

On rare occasions, the testator's humanity, embedded in the doctrine of trusteeship, triumphed in the courts. Judges like South Carolina's John Belton O'Neall deemed the secret trust permissible despite his state's statutory repugnance to slaves' power to contract, elect the benefits of contracts, or gain their freedom from trusts. Seated briefly on a three-man court of general appellate jurisdiction,

he found ways to effectuate the testator's manumission of slaves despite apparent violations of state manumission laws. As his tortured
construction of these documents—always in aid of freedom—proved,
equitable discretion could mitigate the positive law of slavery. Even
after the state legislature explicitly repudiated O'Neall's views by dissolving the equity court on which he sat and passing laws voiding all
bequests to slaves that anticipated their manumission, he struggled
to honor the humane designs of testators. As he wrote in his own
treatise on *The Negro Law of South Carolina* (1848): "The right of the
master, to provide as comfortably as he pleases for his slave, could
not be and ought not be abridged in the present state of public
opinion."[29]

The doctrine of constructive trusteeship allowed judges and
chancellors to redress some of the nastier frauds practiced on pow-
erless former slaves by unscrupulous whites. Although Judge Alexander Handy of the Mississippi Supreme Court did not lean to the
side of liberty, he deplored whites' fraudulent attempts to obtain
property given to former slaves freed by their masters. In *Shaw v.
Brown* (1858), Handy turned property willed to a freedman by his
white father and later seized by other whites into a constructive trust
for the freedman. Handy simultaneously upheld the doctrine of
comity, giving full faith and credit to the judicial decisions of other
states' courts. Other chancellors protected estates for slaves until
they were taken out of state and freed.[30]

When state law did not forbid the manumission trust, chancellors had a freer hand. In Tennessee, judges sitting in equity allowed
slaves, through their "next friend," to bring a bill asserting their
freedom. Using trust doctrine, albeit under strict parameters, the
judges vindicated the intentions of manumitters.[31] In Georgia, a
trust fund for a slave freed by the testator himself (though he died
at the very moment he and the former slave set foot on the dock in
Cincinnati) was kept safe against the suit of heirs. The slave was held
to be free, though one dissenter on the bench would have nullified
that manumission.[32] Where the plan of the testator was not barred
by statute—for example, a trust created to give slaves to the American Colonization Society for the purpose of manumitting them and
sending them back to Africa—even a judge disposed against equal
protection for slaves like Thomas Ruffin of North Carolina could
not refuse to honor the will, though he required that the estate be
clear of debt before the slaves were transferred to the society and
that they give their consent to their manumission.[33]

Despite a few shining counterexamples, even the Southern chancellor disposed in favor of equality was driven back by the reality of slavery. John Belton O'Neall guarded his rear by announcing that his objective was merely the preservation of the peculiar institution; only by a kindly spirit, which presumably included solicitude for the wishes of manumitters, could slavery resist internal pressures and external attacks.[34] In Mississippi, *Shaw* was shortly overturned by *Mitchell v. Well*, Justice Handy dissenting.[35] The few cases upholding equitable pleas were bent nearly flat by a gale force of decrees against equality of slaves and former slaves in the chancellor's court.[36] Indeed, Wythe's contemporary, Chancellor DeSaussure of South Carolina, was far more typical in his view of slavery than Wythe or O'Neall. In decree after decree, culminating in *Frazier v. Executors of Frazier* (1835), DeSaussure upheld the strictest possible view of the impossibility of in-state or out-of-state emancipation without explicit, prior permission from the state.[37] In striking down wills and contracts that violated his view of state policy and social order, DeSaussure took particular aim at secret trust agreements designed by would-be manumitters to guarantee the freedom of their slaves against lawsuits by disappointed heirs. DeSaussure's decree in *Frazier* was reversed by O'Neall, but O'Neall's efforts hardly dented the outworks of slave law. It was DeSaussure's vision that captivated almost all of O'Neall's brethren. One of these South Carolina circuit chancellors became so frustrated at the evasive tactics of humane testators that he began his decree: "This is another of those cases, multiplying of late with a fearful rapidity, in which the superstitious weakness of dying men, proceeding from an astonishing ignorance of the solid moral and scriptural foundations upon which the institution of slavery rests, and from a total inattention to the shock which their conduct is calculated to give to the whole frame of our social polity, induces them, in their last moments, to emancipate their slaves, in fraud of the indubitable and declared policy of the State."[38]

The reality these chancellors saw behind the pleading of trustees seeking to carry out the manumission of slaves is not difficult to recapture. George Washington Dargin of South Carolina shared his vision in an extraordinary decree—extraordinary not because of its outcome, but because of its frankness:

A free African population is a curse to any country, slaveholding or non-slaveholding; and the evil is exactly proportionate to the number of such population. This race, however conducive they may be in a state of slavery, to the advance of civilization, (by the results of their valuable labors,) in a state of freedom, and in the midst of a civilized community, are a dead weight to the progress of improvement. With few exceptions they become drones and *lazaroni*—consumers, without being producers. Uninfluenced by the higher incentives of human action, and governed mainly by the instincts of animal nature, they make no provision for the morrow, and look only to the wants of the passing hour.[39]

Few decrees matched the chilling candor of Dargin's outburst, but in his many other decrees, and in those of his colleagues, the callousness of the racist state was imposed on the more caring consciences of dying would-be emancipators. Equity doctrine of itself, without the active hand of a sympathetic chancellor, could not promote systemic equality in slave cases.

Federal district and circuit trial courts were created in part to protect litigants against local judges' prejudices, but in manumission cases their decisions differed little from the state courts'. Federal courts heard petitions for freedom under their diversity jurisdiction. In the District of Columbia, for example, the federal circuit court sitting in equity disposed of a continuous stream of petitions from slaves. The judges did not lean in favor of equality; indeed, blackness constituted a rebuttable presumption of slave status as far as the court was concerned. Gifts to slaves in bequests did not constitute an implied manumission; an executory contract with a slave for his freedom was not binding on a master; nor would a disputed portion of a will manumitting a slave be read as an act of emancipation taking effect before the will was probated.[40] Nevertheless, equity opened some doors to equality that common law and statute could not. When a free black petitioner imprisoned as a runaway and sold into slavery by the state of Virginia claimed that she had been emancipated but had lost the deed of manumission, the circuit court ordered an investigation on its own authority. When the court was satisfied that she was once free, the federal judge voided the sale and barred the new master from bringing any suits to try to recover her.[41] Counsel for slave petitioners found trust doctrines useful. Francis Scott Key, a fervent enemy of the slave trade and an ardent supporter of colonization who often represented slaves in these cases, argued that such trusts need not be explicit. "Equity will not regard the want of an intervening trustee between the master and slave . . . equity will consider the master himself as a trustee for the benefit of the slave" when the master has promised freedom upon some condition.[42]

Roger Taney, Chief Justice of the Supreme Court succeeding John Marshall, understood exactly where Key's argument might lead. Key had not convinced the court that it should impose a constructive trust on the master, but many state courts, including Virginia's and Maryland's, had upheld a wide variety of charitable trusts. Should federal courts follow the lead of state chancellors in protecting charitable trusts? The implications for testamentary manumission were pointed, and Taney did not miss their application in *Fountain v. Ravenal* (1854). On its face, the case had little to do with slavery. Frederick Kohne, a wealthy Philadelphian, willed that the bulk of his estate, after the death of his widow, should go to such charitable purposes in Pennsylvania and South Carolina as his executors determined. These might include the relief or purchase of slaves, though the will did not mention such aims. In the actual event, his wife and executors died without deciding what to do with his charitable trust. The wife's heirs took the property, and Fountain, an heir at law of Kohne, brought suit in federal court to regain the property and apply it to charitable uses. The Supreme Court, to which the suit was appealed, decided that the trust could no longer be maintained without trustees or explicit objectives. Justice John McLean wrote the opinion for the Court and turned the case on very narrow grounds of trust law. The Court could not exercise the *cy pres* power to construe the intentions of Kohne because the will was too vague. McLean conceded that the court of chancery in England would have effectuated the trust, but only because that court shared the king's prerogatives as *parens patriae* and traditionally the king favored charitable uses of private funds. Taney, joined by another avid defender of slaveholders' rights, Peter Daniel of Virginia, concurred with the result but dissented from McLean's reasoning. Taney saw the issue as a public one, extending far beyond a technical distinction between the "judicial" and the regal power of chancery courts: "These prerogative powers, which belong to the sovereign as *parens patriae*, remain with the states . . . but state laws will not authorize the courts of the United States to exercise any power that is not in its judicial nature; nor can they [the state] confer on them [the U.S. courts] the prerogative powers over minors, idiots, and lunatics, or charities, which the English chancellor possesses." Taney did not mention slaves, but he knew that they were the objects of many charitable trusts in the states. If the states wanted to allow such grants, so be it, Taney conceded, but he would not permit the equitable discretion of federal chancellors to challenge a state's refusal to sanction charitable trusts for slaves. Though his opinion spoke in the language of "states' rights," his voice had the stridency of proslavery. Where Story urged chancellors to step gingerly, Taney forbade chancellors to venture.[43]

The temptation became more and more explicit. The efforts of individual counsel for slave plaintiffs in the 1820s blended into a more thoroughgoing legal campaign against the institution of slavery in the 1830s and after. Antislavery lawyers led by Salmon Chase, William Seward, and Charles Sumner began to challenge slave law in the federal courts. Attempting to read natural-law principles of human equality back into the Constitution, often citing the Declaration of Independence as their source, antislavery lawyers pleaded for the legal equality of slaves.[44] While the plight of the slave touched the conscience of individual justices on the Supreme Court, notably Gabriel Duvall, William Johnson, Joseph Story, and, after abolitionism had become a national force, John McLean and Benjamin Curtis, the Court as a whole protected the "peculiar institution."

Under Chief Justice Marshall, the Court had abstained from theorizing about public policy in slavery suits. Whenever possible, Marshall's decisions rested on technical jurisdictional grounds, the rules of evidence, or close reading of statute. Sometimes this method led to freedom for the slaves,[45] more often to continued bondage.[46] In slave suits involving private individuals, the Marshall Court proved a less than avid chancellor, defending its jurisdiction in the abstract but eschewing broad decrees based on theories of abstract fairness. When the Court was confronted directly with a claim for broad equitable relief in a public-law suit like *The Cherokee Nation v. Georgia*, the Marshall Court opted for dismissal on the narrowest possible grounds.[47] The Cherokee had wanted the federal government to enforce its own "Nonintercourse Act" protecting tribal lands from invasion by the state of Georgia.[48] The Court refused to intervene in equity, though later it would futilely uphold the Cherokee's treaty rights against state invasion.[49] Marshall tried to steer his Court away from the shoals of political controversy, though he knew that law courts were part of a highly political system of government.

Joseph Story's response to the issue of slavery is particularly instructive, because he was the Court's expert on equity. Like so many of his brethren on the federal bench, Story was a conservative in many senses of the word—an elitist in education, a Whig in poli-

tics, and a traditionalist in social outlook. Perhaps even more important, he was an ardent unionist.[50] Though a conservative, Story recognized that the framers understood that many clauses of the Constitution would be interpreted in changing fashion over time and
that some of these clauses were meant to be adapted to future needs.
Story's conservatism on equity was not matched by his view of other
fields of law, particularly when he had the chance to broaden the
foundations of the national government. As Story himself proved in
the cases involving criminal and commercial law, federal courts
could significantly expand their substantive purview within the
grand, open-spaced architecture of the Constitution.[51] What, then,
troubled him about an open-textured equity jurisdiction?

Story argued that the equity clause was limited in its scope not
by the Constitution or by Congress, nor by the content of equity
itself, but by the self-regulating discipline of the chancellor. He did
not fetter the chancellor's discretion in cases of constructive fraud
or in private trusts. Story feared the public questions into which
chancellors might be drawn. He worried that sweeping equitable discretion promoting equality of persons would undermine the Constitution and the Union—he had heard the "firebell in the night" toll-
ing its threat to national unity and obedience to law. Though
personally opposed to slavery, Story recognized that it was sanc-
tioned by municipal law in the South.[52] Article VI, section 1, of the
Constitution and the federal Fugitive Slave Law of 1793, strength-
ened by the Fugitive Slave Law of 1850 after Story's death, forced
citizens of free states to acquiesce in recapture and rendition of slave
runaways.[53] He realized that abolitionists' efforts in the free states
circumventing or disregarding the Fugitive Slave Law were an ironic
inversion of prior Southern states' rights positions.[54] Requiring return of slaves to their masters and punishment of those who had
helped the slaves escape or remain at large was painful for Story, but
he clung to the rationale that only respect for existing law throughout the land could save the Constitution and the Union.[55]

Story and other Northern judges, whatever their sympathies,
were compelled under the dictates of comity,[56] or the letter of federal statutes and Supreme Court decisions, to accede to the legitimacy of Southern slave law, at least regarding runaways.[57] The antislavery bar was eloquent, committed, and persistent, but it lost case
after case in federal forums. By the mid-1850s, it could claim a few
signal victories, but these victories were less precedent than provoca-
tion. Such cases seemed to promote equality at the price of reality,

for news of each inched the South closer to secession—hardly the intention of most of the antislavery bar.[58]

Northern chancellors might be touched by the plight of runaways but stayed their hand, for (they told themselves with good reason) the Union, the Constitution, and law and order hung in the balance. It may be true that "the judicial conscience is an artful dodger, and rightfully so," but such aphoristic wisdom was no help to the chancellor whose conscience gasped for breath beneath the weight of Story's cautions.[59] Did fidelity to oath of office, precedent, and positive law mandate a chancellor's acquiescence to slavery? By 1850, most chancellors were also judges—they had, under code pleading, lost the special office assigned their predecessors long ago by the kings of England. Would a decision against slavery be, as counsel for the purchasers in *Seymour* had argued in another context, a tyrannical and unrestrained discretion, taking from the slaveholders their lawful property?

There were a few exceptions to the Northern chancellors' self-denial. One is illustrative. In it, partly camouflaged by a discussion of the rules of evidence in equity, Chancellor Reuben Walworth spoke for equality. In *Jack v. Martin*, the New York Supreme Court denied the slave Jack's petition for freedom from his mistress, Mary Martin. Jack did not gainsay that he had been a slave in New Orleans. He merely asserted that once he stood on the free soil of New York, Mrs. Martin could not use the processes of the Fugitive Slave Act of 1793 to return him to Louisiana. Though she had already detained him, the New York court heard his petition, for the judges agreed that he did not lose his right to sue under New York law merely because he might still be a slave under Louisiana law. Nevertheless, the court found that the Fugitive Slave Law was constitutional and therefore trumped New York law freeing slaves who were brought into the state by their masters.[60] Jack appealed to the New York Court for Correction of Errors.

The majority of that court recognized that the case was a significant one for comity purposes and upheld the New York Supreme Court ruling. The chancellor filed a separate opinion. He could not prevent the rendition of Jack, because Jack had admitted running away from Louisiana. Nevertheless, a chancellor often investigated questions about the sufficiency of evidence, and from this ground Walworth launched an attack on the rules for rendition of slaves under federal law. The process outlined in the Fugitive Slave Act of 1793 was capture, production of the captive before a magistrate without a trial or equitable hearing of facts, and the issuance of a certificate upon which the slave catcher or the master might carry away the suspected slaves—"under which law," Walworth thundered, "any free citizen of this state may be seized as a slave or apprentice who has escaped from servitude, and transported to a distant part of the union, without any trial except a summary examination before a magistrate." The spectacle of the chancellor defending jury trial against magisterial discretion may seem faintly ludicrous (after all, no jury sat with the chancellor when *he* decided facts), but Walworth's object was no mere technical cavil. He conceded the factual point in Jack's case because Jack had admitted the facts that the trial would have established. The general issue of insufficiency nevertheless gave Walworth the opportunity to go beyond the case itself into the outside world where no black person was safe from the cunning of slave catchers. "Suppose, as is frequently the case, that the question to be tried relates merely to the identity of the person claimed as a fugitive slave or apprentice, he insisting that he is a free native born citizen of the state where he is found residing at the time the claim is made? . . . Can it for a moment be supposed that the framers of the constitution intended to authorize the transportation of a person thus claimed . . . upon a mere summary examination before an inferior state magistrate, who is clothed with no power to compel the attendance of witnesses to ascertain the truth of the allegations of the respective parties?" Lest Walworth's underlying message be misread as a complaint against the investigatory incapacity of inferior judges, he continued: "Whatever others may think upon this subject, I must still be permitted to doubt whether the patriots of the revolution who framed the constitution of the United States, and who had *incorporated into the declaration of independence, as one of the justifiable causes of separation from our mother country, that the inhabitants of the colonies had been transported beyond seas for trial* [italics added], could ever have intended to sanction such a principle as to one who was merely *claimed* [italics in original] as a fugitive from servitude in another state."[61]

Walworth was free to issue these dicta—his decree did not determine the outcome of the case, and in any event he did not argue that the Fugitive Slave Act was unconstitutional. His argument nevertheless demonstrated that the chancellor's insistence on full disclosure of evidence equalized in some small measure the difference between whites and blacks (the only litigants ever presumed to be slaves) in court. Allowed to choose between his state's assumption that all its residents were free and the assumption of Southern statutes and precedent that all blacks were slaves unless proven otherwise, he opted for equality of the races. Equity enhanced that opportunity.

Secession curtailed the liberty with which such choices might be made. Abraham Lincoln's forecast that the nation could no longer remain half free and half slave soon came to pass. In the course of a ferocious civil war a presidential decree partially ended slavery. Two years later, the Thirteenth Amendment to the Constitution forever banned slavery in the nation. Antislavery arguments became acts of Congress. In the years before the war, trust doctrines had been used to further the equality of persons, and in the legal reconstruction of the South they would again play a leading part.

THE EQUITY OF RECONSTRUCTION

Slavery hovered over the secession crisis of 1861 like the ghost of Banquo at Macbeth's coronation feast. President-elect Lincoln admitted "one section of our country believes slavery is *right* and ought to be extended, while the other believes it is *wrong* and ought not to be extended. This is the only substantial dispute."[62] He foreswore abolition of slavery where positive law established it, but secessionists bolted the Union when Lincoln's party won the presidency. Confederate President Jefferson Davis discerned in Republicanism the hypocritical, self-interested culmination of a Northern campaign to subjugate the South, in which "a persistent and organized system of hostile measures against the rights of the owners of slaves" initiated over a course of years was brought to fruition.[63] Davis was wrong about the Republicans' plans for slavery. Moderates and conservatives within the Republican party resisted more radical colleagues' demands for emancipation of slaves until the necessities of war dictated confiscation of secessionists' chattels. When it came, emancipation initially was framed as a wartime measure and applied only to areas in actual rebellion.[64]

The constitutional basis of emancipation was President Lincoln's power as commander in chief, but the fate of the slaves once the insurrection ended was not a prime subject of interest to his successor, Andrew Johnson. Johnson wanted speedy restoration of a white supremacist South and preferred that the freedmen and women serve that South as docile and cheap laborers. Bound by a limited theory of the powers of all governments and disposed to suspect federal intrusion into state domestic affairs by the orthodoxy of prewar federalism, all but a handful of Republicans acceded cautiously, if sometimes reluctantly, to Johnson's "Presidential Reconstruction" of 1865–66.[65]

Republican Radicals in and out of Congress answered the legal conservatism of their comrades with an argument based on conscience. George Washington Julian, an uncompromising Radical from the "burnt district" of eastern Indiana, told conservative Republicans in 1862, "If we expect the favor of God we must lay hold of the *Conscience* of our quarrel."[66] Throughout the turbulent sessions he and other Radicals stressed the issue of conscience: moral duty—religious righteousness—infused their interpretation of the Constitution. Lawyers among the Radicals in Congress joined with antislavery clergymen to argue that conscience demanded aid to the slaves, and, after emancipation, that freedmen could not be left to the goodwill of former rebels.[67]

Before the end of the war, Republicans had debated among themselves and with their president the form that good conscience should take. Lincoln prudently abandoned his initial suggestion that the freedmen and women be apprenticed to their former masters, flirted briefly with the notion of federally supervised labor contracts, and arrived at benevolent temporary guardianship of former slaves coupled with gradual extension of the franchise to the worthy among them. Abolitionists resisted such guardianship so long as it implied an inferior legal and political status for the future freedmen and women.[68] More radical members of his party leapt ahead of the chief executive to survey the possibility of enfranchising all freedmen. On a practical level, by 1864 Republicans became committed to permanent emancipation and joined in support of the Thirteenth Amendment. It passed both houses with sufficient majorities in January 1865.[69]

Most Republicans' conception of emancipation, quite distinct by 1865 from their (and Lincoln's) earlier concern for military advantage, resonated in a doctrine of self-help. Prewar liberalism, reinforced by the abolitionists' faith in the perfectibility of the individual, informed this exercise in wishful thinking. Self-help was the civil religion of the antebellum American; but would newly reconstructed Southern governments allow the freedmen and women to help themselves? Some provision must be made, Republicans concluded, for former slaves' equal protection before the law. This credo became the sine qua non for Radicals by the end of the war: whoever directed Reconstruction, however many former Confederates entered the reconstructed governments or voted in their elections, the equal protection of the former slave must be insured.[70]

Equal protection before the law for Afro-Americans was not a new concept. The same Republicans who pressed for it in 1864 and 1865—Massachusetts Senators Henry Wilson and Charles Sumner, for example—had argued for it during the long battle to desegregate Boston's primary schools. Though they lost the single great judicial test of the unconstitutionality of segregated schools, *Roberts v. City of Boston* (1850), the cause of black parents triumphed in the Boston school board elections and legislative contests of 1855.[71] Almost a decade later, Sumner regularly added a provision for equal protection of the races in public accommodations and the polling place to every budget and administrative bill in the Senate. Henry Wilson joined Sumner as the Massachusetts senatorial delegation stood firm in 1864 for what its members had advocated in 1844 and 1854: the law must not make invidious distinctions based on race.[72]

Radicals had supported the Wade-Davis bill of 1864, recognizing at its core a federal commitment to equal protection of freedmen and women.[73] Their assumption that good-faith implementation of federal laws would come in the South was undermined by the treatment of former slaves in federally occupied Louisiana and shattered by the resurgence of racial discrimination in the first states reconstructed after the war. Vainly did Brigadier General Eliphalet Whittlesey write to Washington, D.C., from North Carolina: "All laws should apply to all races alike. Give equal rights to whites and blacks; impose the same taxes, the same duties, the same penalties for crime, and then execute the laws with simple justice; and the result will be peace, safety, and prosperity. . . . But the white people in this state are not yet ready to treat black men justly."[74] Legal prescriptions for equal treatment presuming that former slaves could rely on the reconstructed state courts were doomed from their inception. Good faith without a mechanism for enforcement and a will to use it was willful naiveté.

The argument from conscience against the limitations of law led both implicitly and explicitly to an experiment in equitable remedies for the burdens of freedmen and women. Implicitly, it revived the antislavery arguments Seward, Chase, and Sumner had advanced before the war. During the school integration struggle, for example, Massachusetts abolitionists had asked why a little black girl had to walk miles past five white schools to reach the school for blacks.[75] Was this not an abuse of the discretion given the school board to act as trustee for the best interests of the beneficiaries of public education as well as an inequitable misapplication of a facially neutral law against a disfavored class? Radicals recognized that equality before the law would not leap up, like the genie from the bottle, when the black man and woman heard the words of the Thirteenth Amendment. Some comprehensive public relief was needed to insure the safety and aid the progress of victims of slavery.

Though conservative Republicans were at first satisfied by Secretary of State William Seward and President Lincoln's wholehearted support for the Thirteenth Amendment, Radicals in Congress and Union commanders who dealt directly with refugees and freedmen and women, albeit from very different perspectives, grasped that full freedom, much less equality, could not be attained by pious exhortations or paper pronouncements. Humane exigency demanded that some assistance be rendered the masses of freed slaves. Isolated solutions in the Sea Islands off the coast of Georgia and South Carolina, the Mississippi Military Department, and elsewhere proved that education, land grants, and financial assistance could begin to turn former slaves into productive and able citizens of a republic. In all of these cases, control of the land remained for the moment with the confiscating authority—the army. Food and clothing were provided to the refugees, and work was found for them, for which they were paid.[76]

Congress created the Freedmen's Bureau (the Bureau of Refugees, Freedmen, and Abandoned Lands) in March 1865 to administer this assistance on a broad scale. It was the first national relief plan, an experiment in social engineering unparalleled in earlier American history.[77] Its managers were army officers, who were paid their regular salaries, acting under their commissions. They received no special bonus to administer the bureau. Its assets were a trust fund, according to Oliver Otis Howard, its first and only commissioner. Agents were given great discretion under the enabling act and the encouragement of the commissioner to suit their actions to the conditions they found in their various districts. The beneficiaries of the trust were primarily the freedmen and women, but any needy person might obtain similar assistance according to Howard's reading of his powers.[78]

The bureau's framers and administrators agreed that the core of the program must be the transfer of confiscated and abandoned lands to the freedmen and women. That task was folded into the original charter of the bureau. When Howard sought the opinion of the attorney general on the freedmen's right to retain confiscated lands in the face of returning Confederates' clamor for restoration of their old titles, James Speed replied that the bureau must act as trustee of the lands for the use of the freedmen and women.[79] In

Congress, George Julian, himself a lawyer, had anticipated the trusteeship land transfer. Long an advocate of homestead laws giving settlers title to land they improved in the national domain, he opined that the federal army held the confiscated lands "In trust for the people," including the freedmen. His conception of trusteeship was both political metaphor—advocating a congressional policy—and technical term, much as John Lilburne, John Locke, Thomas Jefferson, and John Belton O'Neall envisioned trusteeship. Congress would define the beneficiaries and the federal courts would protect them.[80]

In confiscating and distributing abandoned lands under army orders and congressional statutes, the Freedmen's Bureau did act as a trustee. Legal title to the land might remain with former Confederate soldiers and officials, but the freedmen and women gained an equitable right to the soil when they entered, worked, and improved the land relying on the promise of the army and the bureau. Conceived of as beneficiaries of this federal "use," they could claim the right to receive or buy the plot or equivalent land at fair market prices. At the end of 1865, slaves learned from the bureau that President Johnson had ordered return of these lands to former legal owners. Oliver Otis Howard and other agents of the bureau held out as long as they could for some other equitable solution, perhaps an exchange of the confiscated lands actually worked by the freedmen and women for federally owned lands, a kind of setoff in which the federal government compensated the former slaves for what they gave back to the original owners. Technically, if the slaves had "notice" that their possession of the lands was temporary, that is, that their claim was tainted, they might not be able to assert an equitable right.[81] In any event, Johnson's decision to return the lands fell upon them like a thunderbolt, so sudden and so shocking that, when Howard broke the news to gatherings of former slaves, he confronted angry and bewildered crowds. He remembered to the end of his life one sturdy black farmer on Edisto Island who pleaded: "Why, General Howard, why do you take away our lands? You take them from us who are true, always true to the government. You give them to our all time enemies! That is not right."[82] Hindsight might plead that government had made an agreement with the former slaves on the Sea Islands as binding as the contracts the freedmen and women later made with their former masters. In dealing with contracts whose terms had not been performed, courts of equity regarded that which was agreed upon as already done and ordered specific performance, particularly in land sales.[83] A homestead bill for the freedmen and women was actually passed in 1866, but it was never effectuated and died in the year of the Great Compromise of 1877.[84]

Evolving trust law gave a twist of a different sort to the legal significance of the land taken back from the freedmen and women. Some trusts were devices to preserve the property of an older generation from dispersion or waste by a new generation, hence the sobriquet "spendthrift trust" for a trust whose assets could not be touched by the beneficiary. The beneficiary of the restricted trusts could not lift the dead hand of the donor from the lid to the strongbox. Such trusts preserved family wealth against public and private intrusions. Other trusts locked up land and chattels in charitable reserve for religious uses. These charitable trusts flourished early in the antebellum period. One may even regard the secret slave trust as a species of charitable trust. Nevertheless, in the 1840s, 1850s, and after the war, a period of entrepreneurial impatience with traditional views of spendthrift and charitable trusts, democratic capitalism spoke for the cause of the former Confederates. They, not the former slave subsistence farmer, were more likely to fully develop the commercial potential of the land. Insofar as the triumphant reentry of the white owners was analogous to a repudiation of the trust, it fit the arguments of pro–laissez-faire jurists.[85] In the context of evolving trust law, President Johnson, perhaps unwittingly, argued the case for the liberalizers; the Radicals contended for a more traditional view of trusts.

The bureau's commitment to education for the freedmen and women was another expression of the trusteeship concept. It united ideals of self-help, Christian charity, and federal protection, though often teachers working for the bureau were too harassed by white assailants, and schoolhouses were too quickly reconverted to their former use as private homes, businesses, and churches, to allow the experiment to work well. Nevertheless, freedmen and women devoured such morsels of education as the bureau was able to provide, demonstrating the love affair between many Afro-Americans and education that would ultimately lead to *Brown v. Board of Education* and beyond.[86]

Nominally free to negotiate for their own services, former slaves found some of their former masters to be unscrupulous employers. White planters, often acting in concert, refused to pay black farm workers the same wages as white workers and used coercion to induce compliance with harsh terms of employment.[87] Again the Freedmen's Bureau came to the former slaves' aid, with mixed results. The bureau tried to regulate economic transactions between the races by basing them on written contracts among white landowners and black workers, though in many cases the program led not to bargained-for exchanges but to an inversion of one of the hallmarks of slavery—the task system. In this lowland labor system, slaves could use their time as they saw fit after their tasks were done. Freedmen and women now lost this liberty even as they gained the freedom to contract.[88] The bureau courts enforced contracts as though both sides had equal bargaining power and benefited equally from the arrangement. Former slaves gained when the bureau forced employers to pay what they owed, but in many cases the former slave found himself working for his former master, doing the same tasks as he had in slavery without adequate compensation, free in name but not allowed to leave the premises. Many of these contracts, which the freedman could not read, were unconscionable or based on mutual mistake and misrepresentation. Rather than inquiring into the reality behind the labor relationship, a reality that made former slaves dependent on their former masters for credit and employment, bureau courts ratified a remnant of peonage. In defense of the bureau, it must be recalled that it was born in the age of the will theory of contract law; courts all over the North ruled that voluntary contracts were valid and voluntarily negotiated terms must be performed. The ironic result was that the bureau treated a relic of slavery as though it were a necessity of modern commerce. Without the bureau's willingness to rescind or reform these contracts along more equitable lines, there could be no equal protection.[89]

Though its debilities were admitted by all but Howard, the bureau traveled down an equitable road to greater equality. At its best, it operated as a public charitable trust. Too often, its good-faith efforts were weakened by the implicit racism, or at least the unthinking paternalism, of its agents and far more destructively by the diehard resistance of former Confederates. Howard believed that good-faith compliance with bureau directives by his subordinates as well as all those touched by the bureau would bring equality in time. His personal faith in others' conscience was deeply rooted in Christian zeal and more distantly in the perfectionism he shared with far more Radical Republicans. Good-faith compliance is a necessity for equitable decrees to be effective, but behind that maxim must stand the personal jurisdiction of a chancellor willing and able to use his jurisdiction over persons to compel obedience.

Even as the Freedmen's Bureau established petty tribunals to enforce its decrees, which in theory would cease to function when civil courts were restored in the Southern states, and handled minor civil disputes and misdemeanors, the quickly reconstructed states passed "Black Codes." These reincarnations of slavery informed the freedmen and women that they had no prospect of political identity—no right to vote, hold office, sit on juries, give testimony in court against nonblacks—and precious few civil liberties. The right to equal access to civil process, to pursue certain professions and businesses, to move about freely, and to receive a public education—all the rudiments of citizenship in a modern republic—were denied former slaves. As state courts, under Andrew Johnson's lenient plan for Reconstruction, refused to honor the property rights of the freedman, the bureau courts were forced to remain in service. Even so, violence outside the court and the bureau judges' own prejudices limited the justice available to freedmen and women. Though emancipation was a giant step forward for the former slaves and the nation, the local quest for equal legal rights was accompanied by great personal danger. Some freedmen and women who resisted the insults of white Southerners were beaten, raped, and murdered. The Black Codes were an official excuse for a scourging of former slaves who protested their maltreatment against which the bureau was all but helpless. Only Congress could intervene.[90]

Radicals, joined now by moderate and conservative Republicans, recognized that further legislative steps—federal intrusion of another sort—must be imposed on the South to assist the former slaves. The Democrats in Congress, supported by President Johnson, resisted. Federal intervention would slow the reconstruction of the South (and hinder their party's rehabilitation). Conservative Republicans wavered; evidence of continuing white Southern disregard of both the freedmen and women's rights and the interests of the Republican party swung these Republicans into line behind the Civil Rights Act of 1866. Johnson vetoed the act on February 19, 1866, but Congress passed it over his veto.[91]

The act enumerated certain personal liberties that the Southern state authorities might not violate. It wedded a continuing commitment to protect the interests of the freedman to the older vision of equality through self-help.[92] The first section of the act gave to freedmen and women an avenue of self-help that the bureau could not provide. Senator Lyman Trumbull of Illinois, never an advocate of racial equality, but a stubborn and courageous defender of legal equality, drafted the act.[93] In it, he gave expression to the concept of "civil rights"—those rights that every citizen of the United States possessed. These included (though the list was perhaps not exhaustive because rights not mentioned were not explicitly denied anywhere in the bill)[94] the right "to make and enforce contracts, to sue, be parties, and give evidence, to inherit, purchase, lease, sell, hold and convey real and personal property, and to full and equal benefit of all laws and proceedings for the security of person and property, as is enjoyed by white citizens." The legal debilities of the freedman or woman defrauded of pay for labor or of title to land might be heard in a bureau court, but the bureau had little power to compel civil authorities to enforce its orders. Much was left to negotiation. The Civil Rights Act allowed freedmen or women to remove a suit from state courts to federal courts when as plaintiff they could demonstrate discrimination against them in the state court. The act aligned the federal courts behind the bureau as a source of assistance to former slaves—signaling a major shift in the division of powers between federal and state governments.[95]

The Civil Rights Act of 1866 did not provide for "civil" remedies, including equitable ones, instead imposing mandatory fines and prison sentences on those who thwarted the civil rights of the freedmen and women. The focus on a "public," that is, a criminal sanction, rather than the private remedy of damages or injunctive relief, was a deliberate choice of the framers of the act. Section 2 of the act implied that officials in the newly reconstructed state governments might not claim "color of law" in their persecution of blacks, hoping thereby to escape correction through the doctrine of "sovereign immunity." Even the most radical Republicans could not deny that officers of a state government were all but immune to civil suits when performing their official duties, particularly when they acted within the scope of their discretionary authority. Thus police officers arresting suspects, sheriffs attaching property, and judges enforcing court orders under color of law could not be fined or enjoined in the postwar South. They could, however, be tried and punished for violating federal criminal law, assuming that federal juries and federal judges were willing to apply the law. Penalties for the denial of civil rights to freedmen and women under the act of 1866 were thus made wholly criminal. Section 6 of the act also punished private citizens who aided and abetted in discriminatory practices. Whether the denial of civil remedies demonstrated the framers' solicitude for states' rights in the North, or was a necessary concession to conservative Republicans' fears of the rise of an all-powerful federal judiciary, are fair questions, but the framers did not openly debate them.[96]

The same Congress that overrode the president's veto of the Civil Rights Act of 1866 framed and passed the Fourteenth Amendment. Johnson had no say in its creation, though he uttered a gratuitous reproof of it when it passed. The meaning of the amendment's first and fifth clauses was then and remains to this day the single most controversial area of American constitutional law. The first clause made citizens of the United States into citizens of the various states where they lived and forbade the state to make any law that denied equal protection—in context a clear reference to racial discrimination. The imposition of a due process requirement on the states also reinforced the Civil Rights Act of 1866. Finally, states were barred from making or enforcing any law denying the privileges and immunities of citizens of the United States. The amendment struck at the Black Codes and raised the Civil Rights Act to the status of unquestioned constitutionality. The due process clause, in later years extended to protect a fictional "person," the corporation, from unreasonable regulation by the states, was intended to secure the rights of freedmen and women in Southern state courts. Potentially, the last-named admonition to the states was the most potent. It imposed the privileges and immunities clause of the Constitution on the states, albeit without defining those privileges and immunities. Broadly conceived, they might entail the first ten amendments to the Constitution, guarantees of political rights and even those "social rights" (such as integrated schools) that most Republicans denied that they favored. The fifth clause of the amendment gave Congress the power to enforce the other clauses with legislation—a last body blow at the recalcitrant leaders of the first reconstructed state governments.[97]

Whether the proscribed practices had to be state directed or sponsored, or might apply to purely private discrimination (if there be such a thing), was a sharp point upon which Congress soon impaled itself, but the Civil Rights Enforcement Acts of 1870, and the Ku Klux Act of 1871, primarily designed to criminalize hooded night riding and conspiracy to violate the civil rights of freedmen and women, also permitted victims to seek remedy "in an action at law, suit in equity, or other proper proceeding for redress." In the congressional debates over the Ku Klux Act, no consensus emerged over its application to wholly private discrimination, but as the damages provided for by the Enforcement acts were likely to be small at law, and the aim of the plaintiff was to end discrimination, the equitable remedy could have become the tool of choice.[98] The federal judge's injunction could be deployed against whole systems of discrimination, from vagrancy laws that reenslaved unemployed blacks to discrimination in court proceedings.[99]

The Civil Rights Act of 1875 extended the reach of the federal chancellor into discrimination in public accommodations, but plaintiffs under all the Enforcement acts preferred to seek criminal penalties rather than injunctions against future discrimination.[100] Indeed, the Civil Rights Enforcement Acts were major additions to a hitherto slender body of federal criminal law. They protected black citizens and voters from interference with their rights on pain of fines and jail sentences for convicted violators.[101] Control of unwanted behavior through fines in the Anglo-American system is at least as old as Henry II's justiciars' power to fine villages for their failure to enforce his laws, but juries in civil rights cases, whether in the North or the South, did not prove eager to carry on the work of integration. Federal trial court judges were willing to sit in judgment of suspects, but some of the former worried aloud about the constitutionality of the Enforcement acts.[102] In a few Northern states, notably Iowa, state supreme courts ordered integration of public facilities, citing the Civil Rights acts and the Fourteenth Amendment, but in these cases the plaintiff did not seek nor the court employ equitable means to change an entire system of discrimination. If individual plaintiffs obtained relief, the massif of racial segregation in the North and subjugation in the South remained unscaled.[103]

Behind the facade of federal enforcement of freedmen and women's rights was a majority of Republicans' inability to probe the realistic consequences of their logic.[104] Committed to equal protection of blacks' rights, they erected a structure of self-help. Whether from a lingering regard for prewar federalism and state sovereignty, a persistent affection for economic liberalism, or a faith in the perfection of society through the education of individuals, religious revival, and hard work, the makers of the Civil Rights acts assumed that, ultimately, minorities persecuted by majorities would be able to protect their rights by bringing their own suits in the courts or using their votes in democratic elections.[105]

The ultimate act of faith for supporters of this course was political as well as legal—the Fifteenth Amendment, intended to guarantee to black men the vote. The amendment merely stated that race could not be used to deprive otherwise qualified men of their franchise, but in 1870 the Republicans tried to insure the safety of black voters with another Enforcement Act.[106] Its fate was the same as the Civil Rights Act that preceded it and the Ku Klux Act that followed it. The suspicion that massive white Southern violence against black voters might dissuade the freedman from voting either failed to sway supporters of the amendment and the Enforcement acts or, more likely, they were so wedded to the illusion of liberalism that they failed to fully appreciate the extent of white Southern resistance. Republican officials in the South certainly overestimated their own state governments' capacity to protect themselves from violence. Continued outrages led a growing exhaustion and cynicism on the part of some Northern congressmen and senators of all persuasions.[107] In the end, only a saving remnant of Radicals, abolitionists, and jurists, primarily those in Republican ranks, kept full faith with the freedmen and women in the equitable public trust that was Reconstruction.[108]

THE END OF RECONSTRUCTION

The Enforcement acts of 1870 and 1871 and Charles Sumner's Civil Rights Act of 1875 offered the victims of private discrimination an equitable remedy—provision was made for "all" remedies available in federal courts. Freedmen and women might seek an injunction against the person or institution barring their access to a public facility. Under the 1875 act, the facility need only cater to the public— an amusement park or a theater, for example; state funding or management was not required.[109]

Such statutes blurred distinctions between public and private claims and prospective and retrospective relief, because judicially ordered equality of access was never a wholly private, retrospective remedy. Were the injunctive relief confined to the plaintiff named in the complaint, the defendant would be able to discriminate against the very next customer fitting the plaintiff's description. When this occurred, the new victim would have to bring his or her own suit on the same issue in the same court, and the court would find itself adjudicating an endless stream of homologous claims. To a series of plaintiffs wronged in the identical manner by the same defendant, chancellors had long granted multiple bills of peace. "A bill of peace is sought to prevent useless litigation by settling in one suit a question that is common to many actions."[110] The bill of peace was the father of the class action.[111] Every suit under section 1 of the Civil Rights Act of 1875 thus was effectually a class-action suit and therefore a suit in equity.

Judicial relief under the act of 1875 could also become a form of public lawmaking, for it challenged the entire institution of racial discrimination, the systemic pattern of slights, offenses, and denials that made some men and women wear badges of inferiority every day. Investigations into the reality of publicly condoned injustice verged upon the domain that antebellum jurisprudence reserved for the legislature, but in Sumner's act Congress had apparently delegated that broad, intrusive role to the courts. After 1875, if not before, federal courts could go where the Freedmen's Bureau, a temporary, extra-judicial agency, could not. The federal judge was reminded of his predecessors in chancery; he could peer deeply into the infrastructure of inequality, bringing together a wide variety of facts to determine and then undo covertly state-sponsored or state-encouraged discrimination. Lyman Trumbull and the other framers of the Civil Rights Act of 1866 had recognized that discrimination can never exist without the connivance of the state when they added the phrase "under color of law" to section 2 of their bill. They plainly intended to reach the conduct of state officials conniving to deprive the freedmen and women of their civil rights.[112] If public trusteeship was the central metaphor of American revolutionary republicanism, Sumner demanded the realization of the metaphor in race relations.

Sumner's vision shimmered and was gone. In the *Civil Rights Cases* (1883), the Supreme Court, with one dissenter, overturned four convictions for discrimination based on race in access to public accommodations and amusements brought under the Civil Rights Act of 1875. The Court found that the provisions of the first article of the 1875 act exceeded the bounds of the Fourteenth Amendment, since private railroads, theaters, and inns were not state sponsored. When Justice Joseph Bradley wrote for the majority in the *Civil Rights Cases* that the time had come for the former slaves to stand as equals with other citizens without the helping hand of the federal government, he ignored the reality of blacks' inferior legal status, earning power, and political influence. Still more damaging to the cause of civil rights, he denied the deliberate systemic public basis of that inequality. There were tenable constitutional grounds to argue, as Bradley did, that the public accommodations provisions of the Civil Rights Act of 1875 went beyond the scope of congressional intent in the Fourteenth Amendment, but there was no factual basis to Bradley's assertion that blacks could gain equality without federal assistance.[113] Bradley rode circuit in the Deep South; he knew that local government underwrote the denial of full equality for the freedmen and women.[114] In his dissent, Justice John Marshall Harlan asserted matters of social fact: blacks were the victims of discrimination, and amusement parks were licensed and regulated by the state. He pleaded for evenhanded justice—surely the federal government could do for the freedmen and women what the federal government had done in past years for the slaveholder under the Fugitive Slave Acts.[115]

Given the opportunity to begin to enforce an equitable trusteeship for blacks, the federal courts instead erected doctrinal barriers against unpleasant facts. Justice Bradley drew upon these doctrines to fashion his opinion in the *Civil Rights Cases*. Recent studies of his thinking have stressed his genuine regard for federalism—the diffusion of nonenumerated powers among the various states, limiting the intrusion of the federal government into the domestic affairs of localities.[116] For him, the Reconstruction amendments had shifted the boundaries of federalism but not weakened the core concept of a division of powers among multiple sovereignties. Bradley assured the freedmen and women that they could take their claims to state courts and get a fair hearing. As prophecy this failed even if it was doctrinally consistent with Bradley's understanding of the federal system.

Bradley and the court were not sitting in equity in the *Civil Rights Cases*; but were they called upon to rule on the constitutionality of injunctive relief against discrimination, they could have cited a growing body of theory against equitable judicial intervention in public matters. Contemporary jurisprudents summarily declared that equity was restricted to "private civil rights . . . it has no jurisdiction over public rights."[117] Even were this limitation brushed aside as historically inaccurate, the doctrine of sovereign immunity of state officers protected them from suits in federal court so long as they acted under authority of their office and within their lawful discretion.[118] In addition, chancellors had avoided political questions as defined in *Luther v. Borden*,[119] refused to intervene in criminal prosecutions,[120] and sent claimants in public nuisance cases to local authorities to seek criminal indictments.[121]

Though Bradley did not raise the issue directly, the experiment with trusteeship equality thrust upon the federal judges an unprecedented and largely unwanted power to systemically reorder local institutions. In the past, the chancellor had intervened in individuated terms even if his decree dealt with public matters. Particular injustices, brought individually to the chancellor's court, had gained his ear. Even the class-action suit was based on an individual injustice and sought an individual remedy, though the party structure was extended. Indeed, courts of equity in America had struggled throughout the nineteenth century to articulate a general theory of "representative" suits.[122] There was little precedent for the federal judge sitting in equity to order a state or a county to remedy an institutional injustice, much less for him to monitor compliance with that order. If the rhetoric of public trusteeship continued to flourish in the politics of the Gilded Age—Grover Cleveland supposedly accepted the Democratic nomination for the presidency with the line "a public office is a public trust"—freedmen and women were not its beneficiaries.

There were undoubtedly broader economic and intellectual reasons why the federal courts backed away from a commitment to public trusteeship. The increasingly influential canon of laissez-faire played a part. A strong attachment to the emerging economic orthodoxy of liberalism was another influence on the courts. According to contemporary jurists as prominent as Christopher G. Tiedeman and Thomas M. Cooley, liberty of contract, not intrusive equity, best ordered a free society.[123] An insidious racism, the more dangerous for its advocates' denial that they were racists, added to the disinclination of federal judges to upset social folkways.[124] The circumscription of all governmental intrusion into private business dealings had also become a great desideratum among some federal judges as Populist state legislatures began to squeeze the profits (and regulate the unscrupulous conduct) of speculators.[125]

Charles Sumner had marshaled the last of his strength in support of the Civil Rights Act of 1875. He died before its passage clinging to the belief that a sweeping expression of congressional solicitude for the freedmen and women would be his monument.[126] History honored his dying gift. The Civil Rights acts of the 1950s and 1960s built upon the foundations he laid. In his own time, with George Julian, Henry Wilson, Thaddeus Stevens, and a handful of others, Sumner had tried to do what Jefferson had done—rework the language of equitable relief into a more just model of American constitutionalism. He knew that trusteeship was an empty promise without equality before the law. What he did not see was that equality before the law was nothing more than empty words unless real judges in real courts were willing to enforce it.

PART THREE REALITY

Business in equity courts flourished in the last quarter of the nineteenth century, an unwitting tribute to Oliver Wendell Holmes, Jr.'s dictum that law did not promote good conduct so much as punish misconduct.[1] Equity courts were overwhelmed with evidence of a society corrupted by its own disillusionment. If the North and the South for different reasons viewed the coming of war as a purging of sin, the end of the Civil War reopened the speculative mania in railroads, banks, and manufacturing corporations. Many of these floated bond or stock issues with the connivance of state legislatures. Bloated northern stock ventures and undercapitalized southern enterprises soon collapsed. The Bankruptcy Act of 1867, designed to regulate the pooling and distribution of defunct businesses' assets, flooded federal courts with bankruptcy petitions, real and feigned, particularly after the depression of 1873. To the doors of the federal courts also marched shareholders seeking injunctions against the supposedly unscrupulous receivers appointed to liquidate corporate assets. In theory, the receiver was neutral, part of the court-ordered relief. In fact, many receivers had a financial stake in the defunct venture and used their position to fatten their own accounts.[2] The war had also spurred inventors to patent all manner of machines and would-be inventors to infringe those patents. In record numbers the patentees sought federal injunctive relief against the infringers.

From an average of twenty petitions a year reported before the war, the number of equity petitions reported in federal district and circuit courts skyrocketed to seventy per year from 1865 to 1880. Fully 40 percent of these petitions sought some manner of injunctive protection of patents, trademarks, and copyrights, and 20 percent were pleas to prevent waste by a bankruptcy receiver. (One must bear in mind that bankruptcy, patent, and copyright were the exclusive preserve of the federal courts.) All these cases involved claims of fraud, corruption, and venality.[3]

Some of these suits also documented the decay of fiscal standards in public institutions. Disputes over receivership for insolvent corporations and controversies about repayment of wartime bonds raised questions of state and municipal complicity in fraud, or at least self-dealing. Bankruptcy cases involving the Confederate war debt coupled official avarice to more subtle questions about the legal capacity of the rebelling states.[4] Reconstructed state governments' default on railroad bond issues also raised equitable questions: for example, what were the rights of subsequent purchasers of the bonds who paid for them without knowledge of their often corrupt parentage?[5]

Chancellors were hard put to discover the truth behind the pleading in these cases, much less to fashion equitable remedies, because powerful interests obtained the aid of political institutions to cover their tracks. In the worst of these suits chancellors had to untangle conspiracies between iniquitous state legislatures and pet corporations. These were endemic in the Reconstruction and "Redeemer" South and swept through the North during the Grant administration.[6] Though best known for narrowing the privileges and immunities clause of the Fourteenth Amendment, the *Slaughterhouse Cases* were a prime example of equity immobilized by public peculation.[7] The details of the litigation reward close scrutiny, for they demonstrate that courts of equity themselves were not safe from the influence of corruption.

In 1869, the extortionate legislature of Louisiana created a monopoly for a handful of New Orleans butchers and then protected the interests of that monopoly by "regulating" competing butchers out of business. On its face, the statute was a health measure restricting the landing of cattle and the treating of carcasses to one facility, though in fact the act was bought and paid for by the Crescent City Stock Landing and Slaughterhouse Company. The Butchers' Benevolent Association, a lobby for butchers left out of the monopoly, got an injunction against enforcement of the Crescent City monopoly from the Sixth District Parish Court. Crescent City lawyers, watching the unincorporated butchers' every move, sought an injunction from the Fifth District Parish Court and succeeded. The two preliminary injunctions caused one newspaper wag to complain about abuse of the injunction power by the lower courts, but more injunctions were on the way. Members of the Live Stock Dealers' Association, a third party in the dispute, had already contracted to buy land from Charles Cavaroc to build their own butchery. They marched into the Seventh District Parish Court and obtained an injunction against Crescent City. At this point, the state attorney general jumped into the fray to protect the state's interest by enjoining the Live Stock Dealers. The Fifth District Parish Court accommodated him. Fearing rescission of his contract with the Live Stock Dealers' Association, Cavaroc sought an injunction against enforcement of the health regulation. The Third District Parish Court obliged. Behind the diversity of courts' rulings may have been a division between English-speaking butchers, French-speaking butchers, and their respective allies in the courts, but the performance of these courts was a parody of equity.

Chancellors are accustomed to mendacity and bad faith, but the *Slaughterhouse Cases* invited local chancellors to shop in the marketplace of special interests. The district courts stayed their injunctions while the issue was heard by the Louisiana Supreme Court. Not surprisingly, it upheld the monopoly and reinstated the injunctions of the Fifth District Parish Court against the Butchers Benevolent and the Live Stock Dealers. The latter were not finished, however. Using as their grounds the Fourteenth Amendment's guarantee of citizens' privileges and immunities against state action, the unincorporated butchers brought their plea to the federal circuit court. Supreme Court Justice Joseph P. Bradley, sitting with federal district court Judge William B. Woods, took the case on a writ of error and found for the petitioners. The court dissolved the injunctions against the butchers and reinstated those restraining the police of the city from interfering with butchers' pursuit of their trade. Bradley dismissed the state's claim that it was merely regulating the health of its citizens; the object of the monopoly was plainly greed, not public duty. The state appealed, and the rival petitions for equitable relief wended their way over a leisurely course of four years to the United States Supreme Court. There the butchers lost their suit—a bare majority of the Court restricted "privileges and immunities" to those granted the former slaves—but equity was the real loser. The maelstrom of public cupidity and private avarice reaching down from the governor of the state to the lowest local official blasted the power of the chancellor to provide an adequate remedy. Insofar as the issues in the *Slaughterhouse Cases* were typical of those in municipal and state bond defaults, railroad stock jobbing, and

other corrupt alliances between public agencies and private interests, the Gilded-Age chancellor faced a critical test of his jurisprudence.

Courts of equity traditionally provided mutual, flexible, realistic
remedies for suits in which legal remedies were not completely adequate. That, after all, was the reason for their existence. In certain
obvious ways, the courts in the *Slaughterhouse Cases* had failed in that
duty. The lower courts of equity and the state supreme court did not
entertain a wide range of factual presentations to determine how to
deal with health problems in the industry while allowing legitimate
butchers and packers to earn their bread. The majority of the
United States Supreme Court not only ignored the reality behind
the state claims of health regulation, it refused to probe the machi-
nations of the fixers. Justice Bradley and Justice Stephen J. Field
maintained that corruption was the root of the state charter, but
they did not link their reading of the sordid facts to principles of
equity. All the justices regarded the case as a matter of constitutional
interpretation, but not as an opportunity or a duty to read the Constitution in an equitable way. The injunctions were just matters of
procedure, not markers of a special vision of mutuality or a deeper
immersion in social reality.

The debility of equity demonstrated in the *Slaughterhouse Cases*
was in certain ways common to post-Reconstruction equity courts.
They failed to grapple with reality, becoming inflexible and one-
sided, for two distinct but not independent reasons. First, some of
these courts retreated from the rules of discovery once used in equity. Traditionally, the chancellor allowed suitors to depose as many
witnesses and obtain as much documentary evidence as was necessary to bring the whole story before him. Indeed, the adjudication
of the suit was based on these depositions and documents. Bills of
discovery and account in his court were designed to go where "writs"
and testimony at trial in law cases could not penetrate, to prevent
deception and forestall trickery. The limitation of these forays in
Gilded-Age courts was partly due to the restrictions on pre-trial
interrogatories under the Field Code of 1848 and its imitators, for it
was widely adopted by other states. The purpose of the nineteenth-
century codes of procedure was to replace the intricacies of writ
pleading with simple complaints and defenses. Under the Field
Code one pleaded those facts that demonstrated that a preexisting
right had been violated by someone who had a duty or an obligation
not to violate the right—a trespass, for example, or a breach of contract. Under the codes of procedure, the old writ system was dis-

mantled, but the facts pleaded still had to be the appropriate ones to sustain the claim and no others, putting a plaintiff at risk to lose the suit at the pleading stage. Equity traditionally gave petitioners and respondents a chance to avoid traps and surprises; under the Field Code, setting traps again became a valuable tool for the good counsel. In fact, the better trained and the cleverer the counsel, the better off his client was. Gone was equitable discretion to promote and weigh broader factual inquiry, banished with the chancellor himself to the archives where the old reports gathered dust.

In part, the incapacity of Gilded-Age courts of equity to probe the reality behind the pleading was also due to some judges' solicitude for certain types of property under attack from a wide range of sources. The United States Supreme Court demonstrated this tender concern on more than one occasion in the post-Reconstruction era in cases involving railroads, trusts, and major industrial enterprises. One striking example illustrates the relationship between the narrowed scope of relevant factual information, an emphasis on protecting certain types of property rights, and the outcome of equity suits. In 1909, the state of Kansas outlawed the "yellow-dog" contract whereby a prospective employer forced an applicant to agree not to join a union as a precondition of employment. The Populist government of the state regarded these contracts as coercive and indicted employers for using them. The employers sought injunctive relief in federal court. The Supreme Court, sitting in equity, accommodated them. Justice Mahlon Pitney, formerly the vice-chancellor of the state of New Jersey, wrote the opinion for the Court. "On this record, we have nothing to do with any question of actual or implied coercion or duress, such as might overcome the will of the employee. . . . Granted the equal freedom of both parties to the contract of employment, has not each party the right to stipulate upon what terms only he will consent to the inception, or to the continuance, of that relationship?"[8] In fact, both parties did not have "equal freedom" to bargain, but the actual bargaining strength of the employee and the employer was of no moment to the Court. The only evidence allowed before the Court were proofs of physical coercion. The state was concerned with the broad context of economic coercion, a concern Pitney ignored by restricting the admissibility of facts.

As Pitney's opinion in *Coppage v. Kansas* demonstrated, self-limiting approaches to factual investigations by courts were well served by the emergence of "legal formalism," a particular style of exposition of opinions, and "conceptualism," the ideal of a wholly internal, perfectly formed logic of the law. Formalism and conceptualism attracted judges seeking or claiming certainty in an era when disobedience to law in the South and aggressive regulatory tactics by legislatures in the North appeared to imperil the independence and authority of the judiciary. For the formalist judge, the "picture is clean and clear: the rules of law are to decide the cases; policy is for the legislature, not for the courts, and so is change even in pure common law. Opinions run in deductive form with an air or expression of single-line inevitability. 'Principle' is a generalization producing order which can and should be used to prune away those 'anomalous' cases or rules which do not fit."[9] Not every Gilded-Age judge nor every case exhibited such formalism and conceptualism; but where it did appear, it subjugated equity to a set of substantive legal values about property and human volition that were as absolute as they were unrealistic.[10]

Equitable maxims were not fixed principles; they could never be. Equity, if it was to be remedial, had to remain flexible. Abstraction ill suited an effective chancellor. The courts' narrowing of those facts deemed relevant to disputes and adoption of the formalist style and conceptualist canon hamstrung equity, for they denied the chancellor's power to fashion new remedies or do full justice to all the parties. The consequences of formalism in the codes were neither matters of arcane legal science nor limited to public-question suits, as cases like *Wood v. Boynton* (1885) illustrated. In the volitional theory of contracts best loved by conceptualism, each side bore the burden of its own folly. Commercial transactions and the development of resources were supposedly expedited by the will theory, all parties certain that the courts would not undo what the parties had decided. The consequences of this theory, unchecked by an independent court of equity, could be as poignant as they were pointed. Mrs. Wood had brought "a small stone the nature and value of which she was ignorant" to a jewelry shop, and though the jeweler professed not to know what the stone was, he offered to buy it from her for a dollar. After hesitating for a day, she agreed. The stone turned out to be an uncut diamond worth over one thousand dollars. The Wisconsin Supreme Court refused to rescind or reform the sale; it was a contract, made willingly by both parties, neither intending to defraud the other, neither possessing superior knowledge amounting to fraud, and made for consideration—the dollar. The inadequacy of consideration—the difference between the value of the stone and what the jeweler had paid—did not impress the justices despite their equitable jurisdiction under the state code of pleading. For them, unlike Chancellor James Kent in *Seymour v. Delancey*, a clear rule was balm in Gilead: without actual fraud or mistake there were no grounds for intervention in equity. The plaintiff would just have to suffer the "unfortunate" consequences of her loss. Even if she relied on the expertise of the jeweler, and even though he might be expected to have known what an uncut diamond looked like, the court was bound by the doctrine it enunciated for itself. The court's reasoning threw all parties to a contract upon their own abilities; the court would not pretend to inquire into fair price or fair practices, much less the reliance of a weaker party on the expertise of the stronger party. Unless patent fraud, accident, mistake, or coercion could be proven, there was no remedy.[11]

The second reason why some equity courts failed to grasp reality was their arbitrary and capricious erection and flattening of barriers to relief. In these courts the barrier went up in civil rights cases and came down in labor and rate regulation cases. In the *Civil Rights Cases* (1883) the Supreme Court opined that nothing in the cases could be regarded as a state-sponsored activity; "The wrongful act of an individual, unsupported by any such authority, is simply a private wrong, or a crime of that individual." Punishment for such private acts, whether civil torts or crimes, must be left to the state; the Fourteenth Amendment did not authorize federal intrusion into these private matters. Civil rights guaranteed against state action— that is, rights enforceable under the Fourteenth Amendment—could not "be impaired by the wrongful acts of individuals, unsupported by state authority in the shape of laws, customs or judicial or executory proceedings."[12] In the same decade that the Supreme Court refused to cross an equitable bridge into the domain of public law to aid freedmen and women, state and federal judges, including the majority of the Supreme Court, leapt into private disputes between capital and labor to issue injunctions against striking workers. In a series of somersaults worthy of younger intellectual acrobats, these judges defined labor union picketing and strikes as public nuisances in order to levy criminal contempt penalties on union leaders and then redefined the same acts as private nuisances, enabling mine and railroad owners to enjoin the unions.

Yet the course of the law is anything but logical, and within the very language late nineteenth-century jurists used to refashion the shape of equity to undermine the Civil Rights acts and promote industrial expansion was the prototype of a very different approach to equitable relief. A new generation of judges began to transform formalist equity into a managerial, balancing style of adjudicating public disputes. As one of these, Charles E. Clark of Connecticut, later wrote, "We ought to make a solemn covenant with ourselves that never again will the concepts of our law be allowed to become so divorced from reality as to permit such a condition of . . . exploitation of the masses . . . to exist not merely untrammeled, but with well nigh complete judicial support."[13] Formalism and conceptualism were never wholly replaced, but a new model of sensitive, realistic intrusion into local economic and social tensions, balancing the equities of all parties in the name of communal fairness, took shape. In a second round of civil rights cases a half century after *Plessy*, the federal courts reversed the retreat of the Reconstruction judges. To be sure, the public road equity traveled from Reconstruction to *Brown v. Board of Education* and beyond was less a triumphant parade of legal reform over the highway of humane statism than a twilight march along a twisting path of expediency and uncertainty. Nevertheless, in the course of the journey the chancellor returned to a central place in American jurisprudence by coupling reality to equality and trusteeship.

6 BALANCE OF EQUITY

Formalism disparaged discretion; the judge merely reasoned his way from basic principles to logical outcomes. The only relevant, hence admissible, factual content was that which narrowed the issue to its core. From this precision perfectly proportioned remedies supposedly followed.[1] Formalist equity fulfilled both Joseph Story's ideal and David Dudley Field's rules: equity became a science. Apparently in vain academic critics caviled that equity had become "decadent," a mechanical caricature of its old flexibility, or worse, that formalism masked very real and frightening forms of judicial discretion.[2]

Nevertheless, within the very language of the decrees of chancellors in the 1890s and early 1900s was the basis of an entirely different vision of equity. Out of the terse quasi-penal, antilabor, and antiregulatory injunctions and the refusal to enjoin industries from dumping their wastes would come a deeper, more caring "structural" injunction, encouraging fair play, compromise, and good faith. The equitable doctrine of Balance of Equity, initially deployed in a formalist effort to deny relief in nuisance suits, was transformed into a supple and penetrating tool of economic and social readjustment. The inherently flexible and mutual character of equity overflowed the embankments of formalism.

A TALE OF TWO INJUNCTIONS

In the same decade that federal courts had erected an impenetrable barrier between private injustices and public responsibility in civil rights cases, some judges on these courts rushed to aid what one critic called "government by injunction."[3] Gilded-Age judges revived a long moribund equitable jurisdiction over criminal contempt to enjoin labor unions from striking and state officials from enforcing rate and welfare regulations. The antilabor injunction and the anti-regulatory injunction thrust the equity courts into the very mael-strom of large-scale economic oversight that prewar chancellors had shunned. Chancellors who issued the antilabor injunction and the antiregulatory injunction agilely vaulted the barrier between public and private law in both directions, prohibiting some private groups from challenging one set of public priorities and aiding other pri-vate parties to overturn another set of government policies.

Labor unrest was endemic in the Gilded Age. In the name of private property and liberty of contract, judges used injunctions to prevent labor organizers and their followers from interrupting the operation of railroads, mines, and factories. Although the union was no longer regarded as a criminal conspiracy per se, some courts closely scrutinized union activity for evidence of criminality. When these courts found such evidence, they fined and imprisoned union leaders for criminal activities. Employers did not want to wait for this event, fearing that strikes, picketing, and boycotts would work irreparable harm—the watchword of the preliminary injunction—upon their enterprises. On the eve of strikes, they petitioned the courts for injunctions, which strikers would violate at peril of con-tempt citations. Manufacturers, railroad owners and managers, and mine owners sought and obtained preliminary relief in the courts, and union organizers leading strikes duly fell afoul of the injunc-tions. Reformers condemned the antilabor injunction as partisan and unfair, but state and federal courts persisted in their prohibition of strikes and other labor union tactics.[4]

The United States Supreme Court upheld the antilabor injunc-tion in *In Re Debs*. The lock-step reasoning of the Court, its eager-ness to define its equitable powers by a simpleminded formula, dem-onstrates the way in which equity could be blinded by formalism, behind which, hidden in the shadows of doctrine, were highly struc-tured and aggressive economic theories. Eugene V. Debs had orga-nized the railway workers, won significant battles at their head, and led them on a sympathy strike when negotiations at the Pullman sleeping car factory broke down. Debs favored negotiation; indeed, his vision of labor-capital relations recaptured the origins of equity: "mutual justice between employer and employees," good faith, har-mony, and fairness.[5] The owners sought an injunction against the strike, which the federal district court granted to prevent obstruc-tion of the United States mails. On appeal, Justice David J. Brewer spoke for the Supreme Court: "any public nuisance may be forcibly abated either at the instance of the authorities, or by any individual suffering private damage therefrom."[6]

The struggle between capital and labor agitating a nation and threatening class war (to listen to some of the doomsayers), or promising a new world of equality (to hear the more radical union organizers), was reduced in the Supreme Court to a public nuisance. Debs had violated a temporary restraining order, issued *ex parte* by the federal district court, that is, without allowing him or the union to speak in its defense. Such orders were and remain common in nuisance suits to prevent irreparable damage to the plaintiff's property from the defendant's conduct until a full hearing can be scheduled. Debs and the American Railway Union were not to interfere with the federal mails carried on the trains. The real issue was the legitimacy of general strikes, but nuisance was the category Brewer selected, and reasoning by analogy to nuisance he proceeded in quick march to the remedy. The chancellor could enjoin a nuisance at the behest of anyone (here, the railroad owners) who proved that they suffered a special injury from the nuisance. In vain Debs's counsel, the venerable Republican Senator Lyman Trumbull, converted to political liberalism and returned to private life, argued that if the strike were a public nuisance, Debs was liable to criminal penalties only. The owners should neither be able to bring suit nor gain an injunction, because equity did not concern itself with the prospect of crime. He too avoided the underlying issue of the horrific working conditions of the Pullman employees, the underlying problems of the industry, and the repression of organized labor. He did not add any of these quantities into the scales to weigh against the injunction. For Trumbull as for the Court, the injunction remedy either did or did not follow from the relevant set of abstract conditions that governed each entirely self-sufficient category of law.[7]

In the Sherman Anti-Trust Act (1890), the Erdman Act (1898), and the Clayton Anti-Trust Act (1914) Congress attempted to exempt unions from injunctive interference when the union activity was legal, but successive Supreme Courts construed those acts narrowly, allowing as much room as possible for the antiunion injunction. The Norris-LaGuardia Act explicitly barred federal court injunctions against strikes, but in 1947 the Supreme Court declared that even that barrier was not insurmountable.[8] The antilabor injunction marched where wiser chancellors had feared to tread.[9] Injunctions had hitherto been enforceable only against named defendants and their agents, with notice, that is, those who had been informed of the suit and summoned to court or informed of the outcome of the case. None of these safeguards appeared in the antilabor injunction. Those who engaged in the proscribed behavior brought themselves under the injunction and so risked jail for contempt of court.

The antilabor injunction framed the debate over the employment of equitable relief in public questions for an entire generation of liberal law professors. Felix Frankfurter of Harvard Law School inveighed against the injunctive powers of courts because of their intervention against organized labor and called for even stronger legislative prohibitions on the discretion of chancellors.[10] Roscoe Pound, Frankfurter's colleague and far more committed to judicial discretion and equitable relief than Frankfurter, insisted that there must be some way to retain the preliminary injunction in restraint of trade and infringement of copyright cases yet dampen the ardor of antilabor judges.[11] Zechariah Chafee, Jr., a dedicated friend of free speech and Harvard Law School's leading expert on equity, condemned the antilabor injunction in the *New Republic* as an unwanted invasion of the criminal courts' jurisdiction. The next year, he admitted to Sidney Post Simpson, a New York lawyer and future colleague, "I am no friend to the unions or to [Robert] LaFollette's attacks upon the courts, but the increased hardening of the judges toward the unions in the last few years lend support to the belief that the administration and judges appointed by it are excessively influenced by the ideals of manufacturers' associations."[12] Chafee, always balanced in his public expressions and on this subject particularly cautious, finally condemned the antilabor injunction because it was too vague. He decided that good law assists those it governs to avoid illegal acts; the antilabor injunction was too diffuse to aid union officials and organizers.[13] However they approached the subject, this generation of reforming, liberal scholars feared public-question injunctions because of the apparent abuse of the antilabor injunction.

The antiregulatory injunction was far less common than the antilabor injunction but even more ominous to Progressive reformers. It plunged equity into public-law disputes without regard for consequences or context, the anodyne of the chancellor's traditional jurisprudence. Ironically, its target was the tenet of federalist theory that states might regulate domestic affairs—the very idol of Reconstruction federalism to which the Civil Rights Act of 1875 was sacrificed. In a series of cases between 1880 and 1920, railroad owners and their stockholders (or their receivers, if they were bankrupt) sought federal injunctive relief against state rate regulation. The petitioners argued that the rate regulations violated their due process rights under the Fourteenth Amendment, and district federal courts agreed. On appeal, the Supreme Court concurred. The Court barred state officers from enforcing the rate regulations. In *Reagan v. Farmers Loan and Trust* (1894), the Supreme Court found "illegal, [and] unreasonable" a Populist Texas government's attempts to curb its railroads' rate hikes.[14] Four years later, in *Smyth v. Ames*, the high court struck down a state rate statute, finding that the rates amounted to a legislative taking of property.[15] *Ex Parte Young* (1908) was the high water mark of the antiregulatory injunction. A reformist Minnesota government had directed its attorney general to enforce a railroad rate law. When the attorney general attempted to do his duty, the railroad obtained a preliminary injunction from the federal district court. The Supreme Court, on appeal, upheld the injunction and the contempt citation against the attorney general.[16] The justices' "reason" convinced them that the trial court had not abused its discretion in issuing the preliminary injunction, though the test for "reasonableness" was a constitutional one based on substantive due process,[17] not an equitable one based on proof of the likelihood of irreparable harm.

At the same time as antilabor and antiregulatory injunctions reestablished the criminal jurisprudence of many chancellors, others began to refuse injunctions where once they had been available. Again the issue was one of public policy, though the litigants might be private parties. The issuance of injunctions against major industrial polluters for "nuisance" was curtailed by the discretion of the chancellor under the novel doctrine of Balance of Equity. The "strong arm of equity" poised to strike against the worker and the Populist state official was stayed when the defendant was a manufacturer.[18]

By the end of the Civil War, the eastern portion of the nation had changed its face from broad expanses of agriculture and pockets of commerce to a more mixed economy pitted with industrial plants of great size.[19] The latter had long used natural water courses to dispose of waste and belched chemical fumes and soot into the air. Chancellors had recognized the threat these waste products posed to landholders, homeowners, and water users. The reality was plain to them and, faced with it, antebellum chancellors grudgingly conceded that traditional equitable remedies against nuisance must accommodate themselves to the advance of industrialization, but they still granted injunctions when the nuisance was substantial and likely to continue.[20]

After the Civil War, industrialization and formalism assaulted nuisance doctrine shield to shield, inducing some chancellors in industrial states to rethink the nuisance injunction. Like all formalist doctrine, the "Balance of Equity" that resulted reduced a complex story to a simple test: if the petitioner's prospective advantage from the nuisance injunction was small compared to the defendant's loss, the injunction would not be granted.[21] The discretion of the chancellor would thus favor profitable commercial and industrial enterprises over the suits of homeowners and farmers with less property to protect. No such balancing was attempted in the antilabor and antiregulatory injunctions; the laborer's plight and the reformers' goals had no weight against the manufacturers' and the railroad owners' property rights.

The first case in which an American judge sitting in chancery used a Balance of Equity analysis to deny an injunction against a nuisance was *Richard's Appeal* (Pennsylvania, 1868). L. Harry Richard, the petitioner, was a cotton manufacturer whose small works and family home were situated below the smokestack of the giant Phoenix iron foundry. Soot from the latter poured through the windows of Richard's house, rendering it unlivable, he claimed. The lower court refused an injunction until the petitioner could prove that a nuisance in fact existed, for which he was sent to a court of law. Instead, he appealed. Chief Justice James Thompson, writing for the Supreme Court of Pennsylvania, found that although a nuisance undoubtedly existed and was likely to continue, "It is elementary law, that in equity a decree is never of right, as a judgment at law is, but of grace. Hence the Chancellor will consider whether he would not do a greater injury by enjoining than would result from refusing and leaving the party to his redress at the hands of a court and jury."[22] The suit was then dismissed.

Justice Thompson's tone implied that Balance of Equity was a well-established doctrine. The confidence of the court belied the weakness of the precedent for its holding. In the string citations of counsel for the defendant there was much precedent for the chancellor using his discretion but no case or treatise to substantiate refusal of relief from an established nuisance. The court cited *Hilton v. Earl of Granville* (1841), an English chancery suit, and a number of Pennsylvania cases, none of which was really decided on a balancing test. In *Hilton*, the chancellor was asked to enjoin a mining company from tunneling under a home. Although he did note the great expense entailed in mining operations and their importance to the nation and continued, "I have to determine, whether, balancing the question between these two parties, . . . the extent of the inconvenience likely to be incurred on the one side and the other," he did not claim that such balancing could deter the outcome of the case. Instead, he looked at relative hardship as a threshold question, part of the definition of a nuisance. Far from balancing the equities and giving a decree, he merely stayed his hand until a court of law could tell him whether there was a nuisance.[23] The Pennsylvania Supreme Court, in *Bell v. The Ohio and Pennsylvania Railroad Company* (1856), denied a petitioner injunctive relief against a railroad's intrusion upon the commons in the city of Allegheny. Bell wanted to graze his cows on land recently given to the railroad. The court mentioned a "balance of conveniences" test but left the exercise unfinished. Two of the justices argued that the chancellor could exercise a "sound discretion" in granting or withholding the injunction, but the court split on the chancellor's jurisdiction when the nuisance had yet to be proven in a court of law. In the end, the petition for the injunction was denied by a divided court.[24]

Without doubt, chancellors before *Richard's Appeal* asserted that remedies in equity were discretionary. Discoursing on the relationship between the petitioner's rights and the chancellor's power to tailor a remedy to a wrong, Supreme Court Justice Noah Swayne, in *Parker v. Winnipiseogee Lake Cotton* (1862), pronounced that "After the right has been established at law, a Court of Chancery will not, as of course, interpose by injunction . . . it will consider all the circumstances, the consequences of such action, and the real equity of the case."[25] Swayne, like his brethren in the state courts, stopped short of balancing the equities—he did not allow the relative inconvenience of the injunction to the defendant to enter into his calculations.[26]

The text of *Richard's Appeal* shows that the facts themselves provided the spur and the warning to which the articulation of Balance of Equity replied. The spur was a familiar clash of equal rights: lawful use of land by one owner against the enjoyment of land by another, a situation that was becoming increasingly common in industrial central Pennsylvania. Some formula to avert decrees of sweeping economic impact had to be found, or the chancellor would become the arbiter of the future of entire local economic systems.

Such a burden would force the chancellor to step outside the confines of formalist adjudication into a denser world of nonlegal discourse.

The warning in this case was sounded by the threat the case posed to formalist conventions of how one side prevails in a lawsuit. The formalist language of rights and remedies did not accommodate nonlegal interests, yet, if some winner and loser were to be named in these nuisance suits, the consequences of the remedy in the world outside the immediate boundary of the dispute had to be recognized. Balance of Equity permitted some of the realities of that world to enter the courtroom without challenging the limitations of formalism. Under Balance of Equity, defendants' claims could include such consideration as the court in *Richard's Appeal* gave to the amount of capital invested in the defendant's ironworks, the number of people he employed, and the value of the plant to the community in which it was situated. An injunction closing the plant would have crippling effects on the local economy—an irrelevant matter under the traditional regime of nuisance (though the notion of "reasonable use" of land had already appeared in an increasing number of nuisance cases),[27] but a response that counted in Balance of Equity.

The doctrinal novelty of *Richard's Appeal* rapidly spread through the reports on injunctive relief for nuisance, the good tidings pollinated from suit to suit by defense counsel. Three years after *Richard's Appeal*, the same court reaffirmed Balance of Equity in *Huckstein's Appeal* (1871).[28] Thereafter, *Richard's Appeal* became a standby in the string citations defendants' counsel presented to avert injunctions. Sporadically, the doctrine found adherents. In *Fox v. Holcomb* (1875), the Michigan Supreme Court refused to enjoin defendant's dam construction despite evidence that water backed up onto petitioner's land. There was no need for equity to slavishly enforce "every legal right" when a slight injury would, if enjoined, create great hardship.[29] Homeowners in Keokuk, Iowa, tried to enjoin the city waterworks when it built a boiler next to their homes, but the court in *Daniels v. Keokuk Water Works* (1883) found that equity required the public good to take precedence over personal comfort. Judge William H. Seevers did not believe that a higher smokestack, sought by the petitioners, would abate the nuisance, but he did concede that "each case must be determined by its own special circumstances."[30] Although Seevers was willing to hear argument on the possibility of abatement, the cost of abatement, the savings to the public arising from the new boilers and similar, extralegal, matters, in the end he sent the petitioners to a court of law to seek damages.

Some states modified or abandoned the riparian doctrine of a downstream water user's right to untainted and undiminished water supply in favor of Balance of Equity. In *Clifton Iron Works v. Dye*, an 1888 Alabama suit, the court decided to "weigh the injury that may accrue to the one or the other party, and also to the public, by granting or refusing the injunction." The defendant's "washers" were necessary for its smelting operation, and in Alabama, slowly recovering from the economic dislocation of the Civil War, "the court will take notice of the fact, that in the development of the mineral interests of this state, recently made, very large sums of money have been invested." While the industry was not a public works, "the great public interest and benefits to flow from the conversion of these ores into pig metal should not be lost sight of."[31] In its reasoning the Alabama Supreme Court also virtually erased the long-standing distinction between public utilities and private industry, so great was its eagerness to promote industrialization.

Whether Balance of Equity may be regarded as an intentional aid to large-scale entrepreneurs or not (courts did not need them to provide a "subsidy" for insecure investments and technologies; other anti-plaintiff rationales in nuisance cases would serve as well), the new doctrine did ease the court's burden in justifying the refusal of an injunction by thwarting older conceptions of liability for nuisance.[32] In the process, *Richard's Appeal* and its immediate successors expanded the "locality exception" to liability for a nuisance—petitioners must expect some pollution if they live in an industrial area.[33] The defense of regional development through Balance of Equity continued strongly in the South and the West well into the early twentieth century. The former region was still scarred by the Civil War and its legislatures and courts favored and fostered entrepreneurial development. *Clifton Iron Works* expressed those public policy priorities as well as any legislative enactment could or did. Promoters of the economy of the western states were similarly active in this period, as one can read in western mining cases.[34]

The most striking example of the connection between regional industrial development and the initial stage of Balance of Equity decrees arose in the mining district of southern Tennessee. Farmers long resident in the valleys between the spurs of the Smoky Mountains sought the aid of the chancellor to enjoin a major copper smelting operator in *Madison v. Ducktown Sulphur, Copper, and Iron*

Company (1904). The court found a substantial and continuing nuisance but further decided that the value of the farmland was small compared to the investment in capital, jobs, and production of goods in the defendant's plant. The court then argued that sound equity discretion did not require an injunction. The latter would "blot out two great mining and manufacturing enterprises." The decision may be read as a triumph for unbridled entrepreneurship, though the judges were mindful of the farmers' loss. They not only invited the petitioners to seek a remedy at law but also ordered the defendants to put up bonds for the prospective damage award, or the court would impose the injunction. The petitioners had still to bring their suits at law, but the court had all but foretold the outcome of that action.[35]

In *Ducktown Sulphur*, the court dealt with industrial pollution in a rural area. When the petitioners came to the nuisance or lived in an industrial area, Balance of Equity almost always tipped in favor of the defendant.[36] Some courts preferred to decide the dispute on the threshold question, that is, denying the existence of a nuisance in fact or in law.[37] Courts had an easier time weighing the scales in favor of polluters when they acted under a municipal or state license or were public servants. Despite the fact that New Jersey's chancery court had rejected Balance of Equity unequivocally,[38] the supreme court of the state would not enjoin a defendant acting in the public interest if the injunction was "without corresponding advantage to the complainants."[39] In effect, the public interest acted as a geometric multiplier of the benefits of defendant's conduct. As Justice Brewer noted in *New York City v. Pine* (1901) before he refused to grant an injunction against a city reservoir dam despite manifest damage to a neighbor's land, "this is not a case between two individuals in which is involved simply the pecuniary interest of the respective parties." The petitioner might go to law to obtain damages, but the injunction would cripple "a municipality undertaking a large work with a view of supplying many of its citizens with one of the necessities of life."[40]

Whatever significance the historian of economic policy assigns to these parallel, though inverted, approaches to labor and regulatory activity on the one hand and nuisances on the other, the doctrinal impact of the antilabor and antiregulatory injunctions and the Balance of Equity doctrine was confusion. Equity had reached an equipoise, a "moment" between the classical vision of an equity limited to individual suits in private matters, but always delivering a remedy where there was a right, and Gilded-Age equity, thoroughly entwined in public issues and capable of vastly expanded reach, but hobbled by formalist pleading and special interests. The plaintiff whose face was darkened by nature or coal dust pleaded in vain for relief, as the old paradigm of the chancellor treating all before him equally and insisting that all involved come before him to plead their cause was dissolving. The realism that had animated equitable intervention, a conscientious inquiry into the actuality of injustice, struggled for a foothold on the polished marble surface of formalism.

REBALANCING THE EQUITIES

A generation later, Balance of Equity had turned 180 degrees from a formalist doctrine of few words used to deny injunctive relief and protect great industries to an extensively researched and argued invitation to the chancellor to manage controversy over industrial pollution and waste disposal for the benefit of the public interest. A new generation of judges had responded to a combination of the blooming, buzzing reality of litigation in their courts and a changing reality outside that court. Beset by petitioners seeking abatement of industrial nuisance, warned by legislative committees and popular spokesmen of the dangers of pollution, prodded by well-organized reform groups, chancellors and judges changed Balance of Equity from a narrow rationale for refusing an equitable decree in a private dispute over property rights to a powerful tool for analyzing public and private contests over broader issues.

In this second wave of Balance of Equity decrees, chancellors began to probe social realities and respond to deeper community needs than those immediately presented in the pleadings. The judges developed a style of contextual analysis and managerial intervention—balancing the rights of those at the bar with benefits to employees, landowners, communities, and entire regions unmentioned in the formal pleadings. Balance of Equity, in part consciously, that is, because the chancellor elected to utilize it, in part because the doctrine lent itself to investigation of actual harms, induced chancellors to confront their own and their communities' policy priorities. In the process, policy considerations leached into the language of rights and the rationales of remedy, gradually replacing abstract reasoning with a more supple idiom of social facts and communal values.

Judges generally regard rules—clear applications of statute, constitutional provisions, and relevant case law—as dispositive of the vast majority of cases that come before them.[41] Yet rules are not written, for the modern judge at least, in some heaven of legal forms, but in the broader context of human activity. As Justice Benjamin Cardozo, one of the first and most influential of this new generation of jurists, concluded (quoting Munroe Smith with approval): "The rules and principles of case law have never been treated as final truths, but as working hypotheses, continually retested in those great laboratories of the law, the courts of justice. Every new case is an experiment; and if the accepted rule which seems applicable yields a result which is felt to be unjust, the rule is reconsidered." Justice, Cardozo implied, lies in the relationship between legal rules and areas of human conduct and values not wholly embodied in law. Cardozo argued that the formalist judges and courts that preceded him worked in this way, though "the ends to which courts have addressed themselves, the reasons and motives that have guided them as they made new law have often been vaguely felt, intuitively or almost intuitively apprehended, seldom explicitly avowed." Cardozo then chided his predecessors for concealing, by convention or personal reticence, what his successors would more readily admit: that their vision of "social welfare" plays a major role in their view of the proper function of law.[42]

In deep and pervasive fashion the world makes its way into the judge's chambers. As Cardozo revealed early in *The Judicial Process*, "All their [the judges'] lives, forces which they do not recognize and cannot name have been tugging at them—inherited instincts, traditional beliefs, acquired convictions; and the resultant is an outlook on life, a conception of social needs . . . which, when [legal] reasons are nicely balanced, must determine where choice shall fall."[43] Though Cardozo verged on mysticism in this passage, the realist in him was not content to believe that the origins of such choices are totally hidden from the judge's own mind. At the end of his essay, he returned to the subject of the judicial mind: "I have spoken of the forces of which judges avowedly avail to shape the form and content of their judgments. Even these forces are seldom fully in their consciousness. They lie so near the surface, however, that their existence and influence are not likely to be disclaimed."[44] Judges and chancellors are creatures of their times, their opinions and decrees as much historical documents as they are precedent in the ongoing discourse among lawmakers and law consumers. Judges not only make law, they make policy decisions about how law should function in society. Though these policy positions may be covert, as they often were in the heyday of judicial formalism, and perhaps, as Cardozo suggested, are still semiconscious in the work of many judges, they pervade the shift in the shape of the Balance of Equity decrees.

Between 1877 and 1900, the world around the judges changed. America lurched, sometimes violently, toward hitherto inconceivable concentrations of wealth and population. Though many in the elite legal community pined for the gentler, more orderly past they thought they remembered,[45] only stubborn indifference to reality could deny the impact of immigration, urbanization, and radical agitation on the law. The frontier, as its admirers sorely lamented, was disappearing. In 1890, the Bureau of the Census decided that population density in the West exceeded the minimum dispersion needed by the bureau's own estimate for frontier conditions.[46] An equally significant demographic shift was occurring in the cities. Immigrants from southern and eastern Europe and young people from rural areas swelled urban population. Three decades after the frontier closed, a majority of Americans would live and work in urban centers. In these growing metropolises, ethnic neighborhoods emerged, sometimes antagonistic toward each other and often alienated from the city itself.[47] The old forms of city government creaked and groaned under the strain of burgeoning population.[48]

In the new metropolises and the older mill towns economic activity had grown in size, technical sophistication, and capital investment.[49] Sooty sky and blackened buildings testified to the new factories' capacity to pollute the air, water, and land. Great combinations of these industries formed trusts to reduce competition and control markets, raw materials, and labor supply. Reformers decried, with some reason, collusion between courts and great industries in defense of capital. Without the compliance of the courts, legislative efforts to improve the quality of life for working classes and dissolve monopolistic cartels would fail.[50]

In these years, many of the country's leading jurists feared the direction of the nation. Outbreaks of political radicalism, reinforcing these judges' own conservatism, persuaded many of them to resist any reform of the law. The Supreme Court's decisions in labor, taxation, hours and safety regulation, and a host of other cases demonstrated antipathy to the claims of workers, reformers, and the local governments they had captured. Powerful minds on the bench made very creative use of law to defend corporate accumulation of wealth and power.[51]

Even as this conservative orthodoxy was emerging triumphant in the courts, newer currents in juridical thinking were appearing.

With the rise, in the latter portion of the nineteenth century, of professional social science,[52] particularly the science of public administration, public policy was weaned from its subservience to political theory.[53] Younger scholars, led by Woodrow Wilson, searched for ways to isolate emerging government bureaucracies from the corrupting influence of partisan politics.[54] A more socially realistic jurisprudence, following Oliver Wendell Holmes, Jr., began to preach that the law rested on considerations of public interest, not abstract moral truths.[55] Law was to be regarded as an instrument by which entrepreneurial energies were released, faults were made good, and human relations were regulated. Its life was not abstract rights and duties, but political and economic experience. New forms of governmental regulatory activity confirmed scholars and jurists' emerging conception of the interdependency of law and public policy.[56] The courts did not merely adjudicate rights, they also allocated resources in the society.

Holmes's thoughts on the nature of law were, when uttered, understood and influential in a fairly small and elite circle, but the force behind them, the demand that law reconcile itself to its roots in public policy, was beginning to flow through legislatures and courts. Although industrialization had originated in the Northeast, after 1900 northeastern state legislatures began to recoil from the coarsest form of industrial boosterism. Faced with the prospect of social unrest, overcrowding, and exhaustion of energy supplies, the courts of these states now began to allow antipollution injunctions, or at least entertain argument for them. This, in turn, was the product of a rapidly developing science of public health, among whose findings was the genuine danger of toxic chemicals and biological agents to personal health.[57] Holmes had given this new medical technology a brisk workout in *Missouri v. Illinois* (1900) before deciding that there was insufficient proof of biological contamination to warrant an injunction.[58] In later cases, judges routinely weighed evidence of disease-producing nuisances.[59]

The courts in these northeastern states were also open to broader currents of contemporary technological and scientific thought, and, under their influence, the role of factual analysis (if not always the outcome) of Balance of Equity decisions began to shift. Three of these movements directly touched questions of nuisance. The first was the drive to conserve national resources, primarily forests. Gifford Pinchot, director of the Bureau of Conservation in the Department of Agriculture, led a crusade to replenish national forest reserves.[60] The thrust of his effort was probusiness, but it gained urgency from the discovery of the second law of thermodynamics—entropy—and the implications of this dire prediction of the ultimate dissipation of all forms of energy.[61] A more radical counterpart of the conservation movement was the wilderness movement. Prompted by John Muir and other western naturalists and promoted by Theodore Roosevelt, the wilderness movement led to congressional protection of large forest tracts as national parks.[62] Finally, the Green-Belt and Garden City concepts, inaugurated in England but rapidly absorbed into American urban reform, flowered in the development of city suburbs, new styles of more open urban design, and the cultivation of green spaces—parks and playgrounds—throughout the country.[63]

Less subtle pressure on the courts came from political reformers. Critics of industrial excess in two overlapping assaults directed their fire at conservative judges. The Populists, adherents of a late nineteenth-century reform movement largely agrarian in support and anticorporate in outlook, began the campaign for recall of judges. Their objective was to make the courts more responsive to the needs of poorer citizens.[64] The Progressives, somewhat more affluent, educated, urban, and business-oriented in their approach, joined in the clamor for recall. Their target was the corrupt judge, but they also wished an end to judicial countenance of oligopolistic industrial trusts and unscrupulous speculation.[65] The influence of these movements on federal and state judges was significant, but it would be easy to overestimate the politicization of the Progressive courts just as it would be easy to overstate the political motives of pre-Progressive benches.[66] In fact, there were two kinds of judicial conservatism at work in this era, an older Jacksonian laissez-faire ideology, opposed to radical reform but also opposed to bigness itself, and a newer corporatism, favoring the trusts. The old conservatism wrote the Sherman Anti-Trust Act. The new conservatism refused to enforce it except when business combinations acted in "unreasonable" restraint of trade.

The combined weight of the new social science and various political exigencies did not crush Balance of Equity but altered its form. The doctrine had a life of its own—like all doctrines in law—and bent rather than broke under criticism. Some jurisdictions never accepted Balance of Equity,[67] but in those jurisdictions where the doctrine was adopted or at least made some headway, its shape began to conform to the new reality of the judges' world. The very nature of the doctrine, loosened from its attachment to formalism, allowed and even encouraged courts to engage in wide-ranging examination of factual issues behind the pleadings. What had started as a simplifying doctrine to reduce the danger of overbroad injunctions in cases where the nuisance was quite minor became a complex thicket of explanations and exceptions, in part because Balance of Equity invited counsel for both sides to produce mountains of detail to sustain the plaintiff's prediction of damage to come and the defendant's reckoning of future economic losses.

Judges with varying sensitivities to the economic and policy issues wrestled with Balance of Equity in this protean era. In Pennsylvania itself, courts sharply narrowed the applicability of *Richard's Appeal*, then expanded it, then narrowed it again. In *Pennsylvania Lead Company's Appeal* (1880) the court granted a farmer an injunction against the lead company's fumes, supposedly because the nuisance was more substantial than that in *Richard's Appeal*, but in actuality the court was retreating from the latter decision without admitting as much.[68] In *Pennsylvania Coal v. Sanderson*, Sanderson petitioned to enjoin a coal company from polluting a stream with sulfuric acid. Three times the court issued the injunction.[69] In 1886, with newly arrived judges joining the old minority, a majority of the court decided that the "necessities of a great public industry," which, though in private hands, "subserves a great public interest," outweighed the claims of lower riparian owners. Sulfuric acid in the water was a "trifling inconvenience," which homeowners in Scranton would have to bear in return for the wealth the coal and iron industry brought to all.[70] *Sanderson* IV was not the last word on the doctrine in Pennsylvania, however. Balance of Equity forced the judges to dig deeply into each situation, because counsel were encouraged to detail the prospective harms on both sides. In *Evans v. Chemical Fertilizing Company* (1894), the state's high court again shifted direction, finding that the malodor produced by the plant and the dust it spewed into the surrounding farmland was a continuing and substantial nuisance, and no balancing of conveniences could deny a petitioner the right to complete relief. In the opinion, Balance of Equity appeared to have been marginalized, for "the chancellor can no more withhold his grace than the law can deny protection and relief, if able to give them."[71] Even so, some of the judges clung to the original version of Balance of Equity.[72]

In the 1920s a managerial Balance of Equity reemerged in Pennsylvania. Typically, in *Quinn v. American Spiral Spring* (1928), the court ordered a manufacturer whose newly built plant caused a neighbor's home to vibrate to move its heavy machinery to the other side of its lot or face an injunction. The court noted that "mere money value" of the defendant's investment could not extinguish the plaintiff's rights—apparently rejecting Balance of Equity. The court knew that after the plaintiff refused to sell his house to the defendant for a price below its market value the defendant had placed his loudest machinery next to the plaintiff's lot. This was bad faith, and bad faith never won the good opinion of the chancellor. Nevertheless, the court did not shut down the factory.[73] It used a Balance of Equity test that was implicit, and the threat of the injunction was a club poised over the head of the defendant.

Faced with the same combination of increased litigant pressure and internally generated doctrinal impulses as in Pennsylvania, the New York Court of Appeals at first resisted any analysis relying on Balance of Equity, then, without fully admitting its course, gradually swung toward the doctrine. When *Richard's Appeal* and *Huckstein's Appeal* were first cited to the New York Court of Appeals, in *Seaman v. Campbell* (1876), Justice Robert Earl refused to accede. Instead, he awarded an injunction to a farmer against a brick factory on the grounds that the defendant did not use his property reasonably. If irreparable damage was likely or substantial damage would continue, the chancellor had no grounds to deny relief.[74] By 1900, the New York high court could no longer ignore Balance of Equity. In *Strobel v. Kerr Salt Company* the defendant diverted and vaporized water from a stream to manufacture its salt. The trial court found no nuisance—merely reasonable use, an honest effort at abatement, and little diversion of water—but, speaking through Justice Irving Vann, the court of appeals reversed and issued the injunction. At trial and again in the high court the defendant had pressed *Sanderson* IV on the justices, to which Vann retorted: "that case had a varied history and it was not until it came before the court for the fourth time that, influenced by the necessities of a great industry, the rule [Balance of Equity] was laid down as stated." Vann continued that Balance of Equity never made any headway in New York against riparian doctrine. He was not insensitive to the policy behind the *Sanderson* decision, however, and he did not dispense altogether with it, despite his rejection of the precedent. Instead, he cited the "plastic powers" of the chancellor as grounds for issuing a temporary injunction, conditional on the defendant constructing a reservoir and taking greater care in preventing the escape of saltwater.[75] In *McCarty v. Natural Carbonic Gas* (1907), Vann further explored the potential of Balance of Equity. The defendant burned soft coal in his factory, customary in the industry but a nuisance in the rural district where the petitioner lived. Vann issued the injunction, but he conceded that "the law of nuisance is a law of degree." In such a case as *McCarty*, it was "better, however, that profits should be somewhat reduced, than to compel a householder to abandon his home."[76] Vann had begun to balance the equities without formally invoking the doctrine, clothing his version of balancing in the garb of older nuisance standards.

The New York Court of Appeals was inching toward Balance of Equity, though the outcome of cases still favored the petitioner. The case most often cited to show the state's resistance to the doctrine, *Whalen v. Union Bag and Paper* (1913), in fact opened the door wider to Balance of Equity. The petitioner was a lower riparian owner whose farmland was damaged by waste from an upstream paper mill. Though the defendant employed four hundred to five hundred workers and had sunk over $1 million into its operations, the high court appeared to reject the Balance of Equity calculation applied in the trial court. "Such a balancing of injuries cannot be justified by the circumstances of this case," the court of appeals admonished the lower court, which had dismissed the suit, for "if followed to its logical conclusion it [Balance of Equity] would deprive the poor litigant of his little property by giving it to those already rich."[77] What sounded to the untutored ear like a wholesale rejection of Balance of Equity was in fact a refined and subtle application of the doctrine. The court found that the mill's damage to the creek was extensive and affected every downstream owner.[78] By expanding the scope of the adjudication to reach all riparian owners, the court multiplied the plaintiffs and the damages, thereby rebalancing the equity in favor of the named plaintiff and all those whom he virtually represented. The court's self-initiated inclusion of fictional petitioners compensated for defendant's inclusion of all its employees in its claim of hardship from an injunction.

Recognizing how the New York court rebalanced the equities, it is easier to understand how the same court refused an injunction in *McCann v. Chasm Power Company* (1914). The petitioner's claim that the power company had flooded his land was technically valid, the court admitted, but there was no "rigid rule in equity that a court will compel a trespasser to undo a trespass. . . . A Court of equity can never be justified in making an inequitable decree. If the protection of a legal right even would do a plaintiff but comparatively little good and would produce great public or private hardship, equity will hold its discreet and beneficent hand and remit the plaintiff to his legal rights and remedies." The court then calculated the money spent by the utility and the value of its dam to the public and balanced this against the "profitless" gain to the petitioner from the injunction. There were no other, unnamed, parties to this suit who might have benefited from the decree. The outcome of the case was wholly in keeping with older nuisance doctrine, but the court's analysis was thoroughly in accord with Balance of Equity. In a dictum, the court acceded to the force of its own language: an equity court is not bound to decree an injunction "where it will produce great public or private mischief, merely for the purpose of protecting a technical or unsubstantiated right."[79] The court's addition of the words "private mischief" clearly distinguished its opinion in this case from older holdings protecting public charters or services from nuisance suits.[80]

Federal judges also transformed Balance of Equity from a formalist on/off switch into a managerial exercise in court-aided fact-finding and mutual fairness. In a series of mining and industrial waste disposal cases, federal courts first resisted, then adopted, and finally modified Balance of Equity to probe the reality behind the growing confrontation between wilderness and farming interests on the one hand and industrial concerns on the other. Federal trial courts first confronted the Balance of Equity defense in *Woodruff v. North Bloomfield Mining* (1883). The circuit court for the central district of California enjoined a mining company whose accumulating silt caused a dam to overflow, thereby flooding the petitioner's hotel downriver. The court was cognizant of the great value of mining to California even without counsel for the defendant raising Balance of Equity as a defense, for the court had appointed a special master to determine the extent of the damages and weighed alternative remedies after the master's report was made. Nevertheless, the court did not accede to Balance of Equity. "These are considerations with which we have nothing to do. We are simply to determine whether the complainant's rights have been infringed, and, if so, afford him such relief as the law entitles him to receive, whatever the consequence or inconvenience to the wrong-doers or to the general public may be."[81] The court's opinion was thoroughly formalist in style, although the outcome did not favor the more heavily capitalized party. Nine years later, across the continent, a federal circuit court for Rhode Island, in *Tuttle v. Church* (1892), conceded that a fish oil manufacturer's activities were a proven nuisance to a cottager but continued, "Among the considerations which should influence a chancellor is the relative effect upon the parties of granting or refusing the injunction."[82] The cottager was sent to file a claim in law to obtain damages, if he could convince a jury to award them.

For a time, different federal districts adopted both *Woodruff* and *Tuttle*. In *McCleery v. High Land Boy Mining Company* (1904), a federal court for the district of Utah followed *Woodruff* explicitly, allowing a farmer injunctive relief against a smeltery. Dismissing the defendant's Balance of Equity argument, Judge John A. Marshall wrote, "I am unable to accede to this statement of the law. If correct, the property of the poor is held by uncertain tenure, and the constitutional provisions forbidding the taking of property for private use would be of no avail." The court founded its aversion to Balance of Equity on considerations of "public policy,"[83] but it could no longer ignore the interests of the defendant. The court allowed the defendant to seek an easement by compensating the petitioner for depositing the acid waste on his soil. The plaintiff acceded to this as an alternative relief, and the court held the injunction as a club over the head of the defendant to induce him to concede to the arrangement. Two years later, the court of appeals for the Ninth Circuit juggled the equities somewhat differently from *McCleery*. The case, *Mountain Copper Company v. U.S.* (1906), involved a smelter's pollution of United States forest reserves. Judge Erskine Ross, for the court, found the issue to be one of "comparative convenience," in which it was "well established doctrine" that the court weighed the relative hardships of petitioner and plaintiff resulting from the injunction before issuing it. The federal lands had little value and the defendant's company was an essential part of the economy of northern California. The court cited, with approval, *Ducktown Sulphur*, decided two years before *Mountain Copper*. At the same time, even the dissent in *Mountain Copper* felt compelled to deal with Balance of Equity, if only to insist that the details of the present case were sufficiently at variance from *Ducktown* to warrant a different outcome.[84]

The irony of the majority holding that *Mountain Copper* must follow *Ducktown Sulphur* was that the United States Supreme Court was at that moment overturning *Ducktown*. In *Georgia v. Tennessee Copper* (1906), Justice Holmes, writing for the Court, refused to "balance the harm" because of the extent of the petitioner's grievance. "The case has been argued as if it were one between two private parties; but it is not." No sooner had he thrown Balance of Equity out the door than Holmes smuggled a variant of it into the opinion through a back window. He calculated that the harm from the Ducktown factory was far more widespread than the Tennessee courts had realized. The pollution not only fell upon Tennessee farmers, the petitioners in the original suit, but extended well into northern Georgia. Seven years before *Whalen*, Holmes was retallying the Balance of Equity by adding the hardship of petitioners virtually represented by the sovereign state of Georgia to that of the actual petitioners in the Tennessee court.[85] Holmes also arranged for the lower court to manage resolution of the dispute. The trial court was to give the polluting factories a short time to try to remedy the nuisance, with the threat of the injunction hanging over their heads.

The fact that the federal courts' choice between *Woodruff* and *Tuttle* depended on close attention to the details of cases meant that precedent framed but did not dictate individual judges' readings of the effects of the injunction. Public policy and equitable discretion were bound together by Balance of Equity. For example, in *McCarthy v. Bunker Hill Mining Company* (1908), a court for the district of Idaho found that recent production increases by a smeltery on the Coeur d'Alene River were a substantial and continuing nuisance. At the same time, counsel for the defendant persuaded the court that millions of dollars were invested in the plant, hundreds were employed by it, and an entire region depended on the smeltery for its welfare. Indeed, the defendant insisted that the injunction would "depopulate one of the largest producing and richest mining regions of the United States." The court made its way carefully but inexorably toward a Balance of Equity. Judge Ross began by saying, "If the established principles of equity entitle the appellant to this drastic relief, it must, as a matter of course, be awarded them, however disastrous the consequences. . . . But is the case made by the record such as to demand or even justify the injunction sought?" The chancellor protected the weak, but he also preserved the "just rights" of the strong. "Usage, custom, and law . . . in mining states" conferred the right to use flowing waters to dispose of waste. If the defendant acted in a lawful manner, "the court should give due consideration to the comparative injury which will result from the granting or refusal of the injunction sought." Part of this consideration was the effect of the injunction on third parties—fictive plaintiffs and defendants. Just as Holmes had added the hardship of all farmers in the area to the petitioner's side of the scale in *Georgia v. Tennessee Copper*, so Ross added the inequities of "throwing out of employment thousands of men, practically wiping out the existence of important towns" to the costs of the injunction.[86] Of course, if the petitioners represented "large and prosperous agricultural interests," which would be ruined by a copper plant's pollution, as was alleged in *Arizona Copper Company v. Gillespie* (1912), Balance of Equity would speak for the injunction.[87]

Balance of Equity in federal courts not only protected traditional forms of property. The judges had begun to take account of the quality of life that pollution threatened. The health and welfare of the poor constituted the core of petitioners' complaint in *DeBlois v. Bowers* (1930). The homeowning petitioners of Clinton, Massachusetts, had proven that the defendant's steelworks polluted the air. The court mused that "just where the line should be drawn between, on the one side, the interests of a community in its industrial establishments which give occupation to its inhabitants and revenue in the form of taxes and in other ways, and on the other side, individuals who are annoyed or rendered uncomfortable by the operation of such establishments, is, as the cases say, not easy to define." The court then asked, in the managerial vein now quite common in this analysis of equities, whether the defendant had done all in its power to abate the nuisance and told the defendant to make better provision for the fumes or the court would impose an injunction. Indeed, the court ended with a strong suggestion to the parties to sit down and work out suitable arrangements between them.[88] The implication was that the court would play a continuing role in the suit if such an accommodation was not forthcoming.

On the Second Circuit, Judge Learned Hand demonstrated that Balance of Equity was truly judge-made doctrine and rested squarely on discretion in *Smith v. Stasco Milling Company* (1927). Hand was a superb judicial craftsman of progressive leanings and liberal instincts. His reputation among his peers was equaled only by Benjamin Cardozo. When the defendant in *Smith*, a roofing manufacturer, polluted the stream running through a summer resident's retreat and filled the surrounding air with dust and noise from his blasting, Hand diligently searched for bright-line rules and only found that slate sludge did not exist "in a state of nature."[89] He concluded that a nuisance did exist, but what was to be done? Vermont, whose law should govern the dispute, did not allow for balancing the equities, but Hand was not deterred by this lacunae in local law. He treated the litigants to an exegesis of the doctrine drawn from federal cases and the jurisprudence of neighboring New York. In an exhibition of the reach of federal common law before it was reined in by *Erie Railroad Co. v. Tompkins* (1938),[90] Hand admitted, "In other jurisdictions, the law is in great confusion," but he believed "the balance of convenience is a determining factor." In a final masterful touch, Hand protected his dictum on Balance of Equity by actually deciding the case on another equitable principle—reliance. When he had finished balancing the equities, the inconveniences, and the hardships, "a reasonable principle" if one still foreign to Vermont, he based his decision on the fact that during construction of the plant the roofing manufacturer had made a promise to the petitioner that there would be no pollution, a promise on which the latter relied in allowing the defendant to continue construction unimpeded by a lawsuit. Defendant's soon abandoned promise, not the complex balancing of qualitative values and interests which took up the bulk of the opinion, premised Hand's decree: no further pollution until defendant cleaned up the slate in the river, tried to abate the dust, and refrained from blasting in summer, when petitioner was in residence.[91]

By 1933, the new-style Balance of Equity had entrenched itself in the federal courts, as Justice Louis Brandeis, a progressive jurist and socially sensitive policymaker, demonstrated in *Harrisonville v. W. S. Dickey Clay Manufacturing Company*. Although the case was a riparian suit in which there was a nuisance in fact and law, Brandeis concluded that "where substantial redress can be afforded by the payment of money and issuance of an injunction would subject the defendant to grossly disproportionate hardship, equitable relief may be denied, although the nuisance is indisputable." When the defendant was not a private individual but a public corporation acting in the public interest, "the reasons for denying the injunction may be compelling." The defendant, a city sewage company, could not be asked to cease its operations or to pay more for an addition to its plant than the petitioner was losing in damages. At the same time, as was the rule in these cases, denial of the injunction was conditioned on the defendant agreeing to pay damages equal to the value of petitioner's land. In effect, the court was arranging a buy-out to adjust the equities.[92]

The transformation of Balance of Equity was prudential, not academic. The judges led the professors. Indeed, the first treatise writer to comment on *Richard's Appeal* misunderstood the opinion to hold that the damage was trifling. The author, Horace Wood, corrected his mistake in his next edition but condemned the new doctrine. Other scholars followed suit.[93] The third (1907) and fourth (1917–18) editions of John Norton Pomeroy's *Equity Jurisprudence*, both edited by his son, John Norton, Jr., continued to insist that the weight of authority was against allowing a balance of injury as a means of determining the propriety of issuing an injunction.[94] Pomeroy displayed a formalist resistance to the new shape of the doctrine, but George Boke, a California Law School professor who was no formalist, strongly seconded Pomeroy's judgment.[95] By the mid-1920s, some scholars were willing to make the doctrine a bit more welcome. Spelling and Lewis's final edition of *Treatise on Injunctions*, published in 1926, conceded that "no general dependable rule can be deduced from the decisions or expressions of the courts" on Balance of Equity.[96] Chafee waffled on the question. In his lectures in Equity III at Harvard Law School, he presented the doctrine without comment but reported in his teaching diary that students seemed opposed to it. He concluded, "it is wrong to burden courts with this class of problem . . . but while they are, they should decide as well as possible, considering all factors and weighing expert advice."[97] In a later series of articles on equity for the *Harvard Law Review*, Chafee noted the spread of the doctrine, but his own casebook favored the sharp limitation on Balance of Equity in New Jersey.[98]

Such waffling did not satisfy the critics of Balance of Equity in academe. William Walsh continued to denigrate the doctrine.[99] A *Yale Law Journal* "Comment" on *Smith v. Stasco* disputed the generality of Hand's dictum and anticipated with regret future opinions like Brandeis's. The author of the "Comment" used Hand's own words to describe his method as "a quantitative comparison between two conflicting interests." The student commentator was correct in one sense; Hand had supplied a checklist for judges drawn from the tool kit of the chancellor: examine the context of the damages, look for all data, weigh remedial efforts of defendants, estimate the probability of future damages, ferret out fraud and misrepresentation, determine if the petitioner acquiesced, and assess good faith by all the parties. The commentator misunderstood Hand's apparent pragmatism, however, and complained that, in the process of weighing harms, the injunction as a matter of right was submerged, or at least made secondary, to the balancing of interest.[100] Actually, Hand had seen "rights" on both sides, rather than only one, and took them all into account. The "Comment" nevertheless concluded that Balance of Equity gave too much power to judges and created too much uncertainty for litigants.[101]

By 1930, when the judges had not only come to terms with Balance of Equity but also transformed it into a managerial tool of some social sensitivity, some academics were still arguing about the original version of the doctrine. Henry McClintock disputed the conclusions of the Yale "Comment" in an article for the *Minnesota Law Review*. He championed Balance of Equity, calling it essential to proper adjudication of equitable questions. He persisted, however, in regarding Balance of Equity as though it were wholly proindustrial in effect: "the interest in the security of individual property," he wrote in 1948, "must yield, to some extent, particularly in a newly developing community, to the necessities of industrial progress." It was the court's job to "balance all of the equities, which include not only the relative hardships to the parties" but also all the equities in the situation.[102] Equally unaware of the true dimensions of the newer version, an annotator of *Quinn*, writing in 1929 for the *American Law Reports*, persisted that "while there is some confusion on the subject, due very largely to the influence of the facts of the particular case . . . the weight of authority . . . established that with material, substantial, and irreparable injury with no adequate legal remedy" an injunction was mandatory.[103] The critical issue, the annotator did grasp, was the adequacy of the alternative to the injunction, but more and more courts dictated and supervised complex combinations of equitable and legal remedies under Balance of Equity. Finally, a decade after *Quinn*, a brilliant "Note" in the *Texas Law Journal*, the handiwork of W. Page Keeton and Clarence Morris, recognized that Balance of Equity allowed judges to manage appropriate solutions to otherwise intractable problems. The threat of the injunction behind the arrangement was enough to induce polluters to pay off petitioners, and, if recurring nuisance could not be avoided, the power to withhold the injunction induced petitioners to accept the defendant's offer of compensation.[104]

Traditional academic jurisprudence did not lead the judges to the new Balance of Equity, but the "Legal Realism" of Karl Llewellyn, Jerome Frank, and Thurman Arnold created an atmosphere in some classrooms, law schools, and law reviews conducive to the general project of judicial inquiry into the actual stakes of lawsuits. The Legal Realists pressed chancellors and judges to weigh the social consequences of their decisions. As Arnold, one of the Yale Law School Realists, and later a judge, wrote to Felix Frankfurter, the goal was to get the courts to see beyond the particular case, to plan, to be "more practical." When the Realists themselves rewrote the law or ascended to the bench, as Charles Clark and Jerome Frank did in the late 1930s, they were able to put some of this preaching into practice.[105] One must note, however, that Legal Realism entered the jurisprudential lists after the courts had begun to refashion Balance of Equity. Despite the crucial role of legal academics in giving a scholarly rationale for such doctrines and styles of judging, it was the chancellors and judges who had muddled on, piecing together the revised doctrine as they went.

As chancellors and judges were forced by petitioners to confront the reality of naphtha and soft-coal pollution, dangerous nuisances that did not confine themselves to a neighbor's field or streams, they could not help but begin to weigh the interests of persons not named in the pleadings. In the traditional regime of equity, chancellors always bore the burden of probing beneath the legal forms to the facts of the transaction, seeing the dispute from below, as it were. The new Balance of Equity applied that approach to quasi-public contests. The reality in the latter, the number of people involved and the prospective (as opposed to retrospective) consequences of the decree—the scope and the stakes of conflict in these cases—was different from the reality in earlier nuisance injunction cases, and that reality pushed the chancellor away from abstract, deductive theories of rights and deeper into the world outside his chambers. The chancellor who visited the site of urban blight, as more and more did, to hear the noise and smell the fumes of nearby factories from the steps of dilapidated row houses,[106] made Balance of Equity into a tool of policy, a way of reallocating social and economic values.

The chancellor and the judge still had to find words to express the managerial-style decree. Even modern judges particularly sensitive to social reality sincerely avow craft constraints on judicial conduct.[107] The old paradigm of a judge's function—to determine standing, admit or disallow factual claims, declare the rights, and deliver judgment—could not be discarded when the judge acted as a supervisor and mediator. Even as traditional roles for judges were expanded and transformed by managerial activities, the internal language by which the transformation was justified had to conform to conventions of judging. The chancellors had to piece together a rationale for the new Balance of Equity to justify the additional discretion it seemed to confer on them.

When Hand argued, in *Smith v. Stasco*, that Balance of Equity seemed the best rule, he meant that it helped him to frame and then resolve the issues. At one level, Hand had found Balance of Equity a more elegant, aesthetic way of expressing the stake both parties had in the litigation. The doctrine enabled him to go beyond the ethereal analysis of absolute, abstract rights and obligations between neighbors and portray their quarrel more accurately. Its sure grasp pulled in more relevant facts, a bigger piece of social and economic reality. Hand, Brandeis, Cardozo, and the other transforming lights of the new Balance of Equity were great lovers of facts. With the social scientists of the Progressive Era, men like Wesley C. Mitchell of Columbia University, Hand, Brandeis, and Cardozo believed in the autonomy of data. Objectively discovered, neutrally presented facts would convert the most reluctant formalist. The Progressive ideal of social science fit the new, managerial equity hand in glove, for, traditionally, chancellors allowed very broad inquiry into background facts through depositions and interrogatories. The problem for the modern chancellor was to fit this burden of evidence gathering into the confines of the complex modern suit, for delayed justice was no justice at all. The Federal Rules of Civil Procedure drafted in 1938 by advocates of equitable methods blessed this marriage of traditional rules for discovery with managerial judging.[108]

At the same time as it expanded the scope of factual presentations, Balance of Equity enormously extended the reach of the chancellor into the domestic and economic affairs of entire regions. The enlarged reach of the remodeled Balance of Equity answered the debilities of formalism in nuisance cases, but it also appeared to challenge the original jurisprudential basis of equity. The first chancellors had derived their power to act from their moral authority to remedy injustice in particular cases. This limitation on traditional equity was consonant with the chancellor's power to bring malefactors before him and compel them to make concessions. He was not asked or expected to deal with perspective classes of offenders or offenses. In the modern nuisance case, certainly complex cases of industrial pollution, the chancellor knew not only that he could not bring all the parties together before him, but also that the very essence of his balancing of equities lay in calculations of consequences to parties who might not yet be alive.

The remodeled doctrine of Balance of Equity answered this challenge by blurring the very distinction between public and private adjudication formulated in the nineteenth century to handcuff the judiciary. In the formalist model self-imposed by late nineteenth-century courts, there was a sharp distinction between private suits and matters of public interest. Public questions were the preserve of the legislatures. Courts might step in to prevent the assembly from taking away a vested right or abridging a contract, but the courts did not allow the litigant to bring suit to change public policy.[109] The court's reach was back into the past, not into the future and not out into society as a whole. In later Balance of Equity cases, the scope and nature of the evidence forced judges to look forward to the consequences of injunctions and beyond the litigants to classes of potential losers and winners under the injunction. Insofar as the relief sought involved a calculation of prospective harms (the continuing nuisance and irreparable harm requirements for the injunction), the courts found themselves standing in the stead of the legislative branch. The reach of modern Balance of Equity was prospective as well as retrospective, reordering macrosystems as well as mandating or prohibiting individual conduct.

In second-stage Balance of Equity cases, the courtroom filled with a spectral army—unnamed victims of the injunction jostled uncounted victims of the polluter. The defendant alleged that the injunction would work a hardship not only on him but also on all his employees, the communities in which they lived, the local governments that taxed him and them, and the economies of the entire region. The petitioner summoned up legions of virtual litigants, similarly injured homeowners, farmers, and workers whose interests the petitioner represented, even though the suit might not be a class action in form. The need to insure that the provisions of a conditional injunction, or a conditional denial of an injunction pending some form of abatement or compensation, were obeyed meant that the judge could not let his jurisdiction end with a simple decree. Instead, the judge continued to supervise the conduct of the litigants until satisfied that they had complied with his orders.

The changing grasp and reach of courts under evolving Balance of Equity doctrine worked because it fit the real world—the demands of suitors, the claims of defendants, the needs of communities—in an age of complex social and economic organization. As with all paradigms, it allowed the pieces of perceived truth to come together into a whole. However provenanced, the new Balance of Equity showed that the courts could be sensitive to a wide variety of local needs and aspirations. These need not involve property rights.[110] Equity could protect the quality of life, an elusive but increasingly vital concern in an industrial society.[111] The transformation of the role of equity and the chancellor was profound. Equity ceased to be a last resort when law did an injustice and became a first tool to get at the human situation behind abstract pleadings.

Defenders of the formalist model of equity still raised a valid caveat: would not the chancellors and judges fall prey to self-serving interests once their decrees lost their formalist armor? Venturing beyond the safety of their chambers to manage their decrees, could they not be captured by the very same armies of partisans that divided legislatures and wrestled for executive power? The basis for good-behavior tenure of judges was their supposed insulation from such ephemeral interests. Would the judge's independence not be compromised when the judge became the most visible actor in public controversies?

THE CLAMOR OF THE INTERESTS

In eighteenth-century political discourse, private "interests" were regarded as sinister, subterranean cabals, seeking their own good at the expense of the public. Parties were the vehicles of private interests, carrying on clandestine activities in behalf of the few against the many. In the *Federalist* papers, James Madison and Alexander Hamilton tried to recast the notion of interests, calling them an essential if not entirely welcome part of the republican landscape. Roscoe Pound carried the argument further. In 1915 he wrote that "the problem ultimately is not to balance individual interests and social interests, but to balance . . . [diverse] social interests and to weigh how far this or that individual interest is a suitable means of achieving the result which such a balancing [of larger group interests] demands."[112]

By the mid-1930s, Pound had begun to worry about public (that is, New Deal–inspired) invasions of private rights, and his advocacy of balancing interests came back to haunt him. At a dinner celebrating fifty years of the *Law Review* at Harvard Law School, Justice Harlan Fiske Stone, late of Columbia Law School, treated Pound to a lesson on public-interest adjudication drawn from the old dean's very words but revised to apply to the New Deal. "We are coming to realize more completely that law is not an end but a means to an end," the Supreme Court justice told his audience, and "that end is to be attained through the reasonable accommodation of law to changing economic and social needs. . . . If our appraisals are *Mechanical* and superficial . . . the law which they generate will be like wise *mechanical* and superficial; the judge has the liberty of choice of the rule which he applies, and that choice will rightly depend upon the relative weights of the social and economic advantages which will finally turn the scales in favor of one rule rather than another" (italics added).[113] Stone had pointedly reminded Pound of Pound's earlier attack on "mechanical jurisprudence." No one could mistake Stone's advocacy of balance of interests—Dean Pound certainly did not, for he and Stone clashed over publication of the address in the *Harvard Law Review*.[114] By the 1950s, leading American political theorists posited that diversity of social interests was the engine of the democratic system. American democracy was pluralistic.[115]

Twentieth-century American courts often decided cases by balancing interests. The controversy was hottest when claims made under the Bill of Rights were balanced against the interests of the state.[116] In deciding whether to enjoin certain forms of speech or uphold contempt citations for ignoring injunctions against civil rights marches and antiabortion demonstrations, "the court does a social welfare calculation" at whose center are "trade-offs between collective and individual ends."[117] Despite the fact that an injunction is at stake, however, such balancing has been only tangentially equitable. The court is primarily concerned with the constitutional right claimed, not the equitable remedy employed. Nor in these cases does the court manage systemic relief, as in Balance of Equity cases.

A far closer parallel between Balance of Equity and interest balancing appeared in government regulatory law, or, as it has been called since the 1920s, "administrative law."[118] Well before the New Deal, Congress had begun regulating segments of the economy without the benefit of supporting ideology, indeed, quite without theory of any kind save a lingering regard for nineteenth-century liberalism.[119] Federal administrative activity was as old as the Constitution itself, but in the 1880s a new urgency motivated federal legislative policymakers. Railroads, a key industry in the maintenance of the national market, had become a worst-case example of unscrupulous speculation, illicit rate fixing, and mismanagement. More menacing still, large industrial combines—trusts—violated many legislators' amorphous attachment to small-scale entrepreneurship. Trusts swallowed up competitors, cornered supplies of raw materials, rigged prices, and otherwise dominated markets. These functions the market itself was supposed to perform, an invisible hand prompted by laws of supply and demand, wages and prices, allocating to each entrepreneur what he or she deserved.[120]

When the Supreme Court struck down state legislative regulation of interstate commerce,[121] Congress intervened. The Interstate Commerce Act of 1887 created a commission to hear complaints about interstate rail lines. This first independent regulatory agency banned rebates, collusion, and other practices that restrained trade, though the commission itself restrained trade when it acted, a basic contradiction in the very structure of all economic regulation. Whatever the awkwardness of regulatory activity based on preindustrial ideals of competition, the Interstate Commerce Commission (ICC) did create a record through investigation of the actual conduct of the railroads. In an age increasingly devoted to gathering data under the assumption that better information was the first step in curing social ailments, ICC investigations provided an eye-opening tour through the underside of corporate conduct.[122]

The Sherman Anti-Trust Act of 1890 also conferred on the regulators the authority to bring suit. Intending to reopen opportunity for smaller entrepreneurs driven to cover by the trusts, Congress directed the Department of Justice to initiate suits against trusts without waiting for injured parties to complain. In effect, the act regarded the public interest as the victim of the trusts.[123] Nevertheless, with the initiative in the hands of an executive branch either beholden to corporate interests or wedded to an ideology that accepted the inevitability of large-scale industrial cooperation, few trusts were busted. Congress' belated answer was another regulatory agency, the Federal Trade Commission (FTC), created in 1914. The commission could, like the ICC, compile its own record. It was not dependent on the facts presented to a court of law by interested parties. Between them, the antitrust division of the Department of Justice and the FTC undertook a campaign against the most obnoxious cases of price-fixing, interlocking directorates, and other monopolistic practices.[124]

To be sure, long before 1890 suits against unfair trade practices were entertained in common-law courts, where judges ordered relief for some plaintiffs,[125] but the federal antitrust statutes added a new dimension to the common-law right. Under the former, the government could act in place of the injured party, including the consumer. What is more, the government could obtain preventive, injunctive relief, breaking up monopolies. The actual impact of the acts was narrowed sharply by early twentieth-century Supreme Court opinions, but when the high court found unreasonable restraint of trade, it ordered divestment of assets and rescinded contractual obligations.[126]

The "rule of reason" introduced in these cases was in reality a balancing test, weighing the actual restraint of trade and the harms it caused against the gains in productivity and competitiveness such activities might bring. As the circuit court that heard *Standard Oil of New Jersey v. United States* (1909) observed, "The court must steer as best it may [citations omitted] between its duty 'to prevent and restrain violations of' this Act of Congress and its duty not to deprive defendants of their right to engage in lawful competition for interstate and international commerce."[127] The rule of reason was also a rule for remedy in antitrust cases. When the defendants were found guilty of restraining trade, the courts attempted to frame remedies that preserved as much of the industry as possible—fair to the defendants as well as those injured by their practices—although even the courts sometimes disagreed on the content of the injunction.[128]

When the government debated whether to bring the suit, whether through the Department of Justice or the Federal Trade

Commission, its lawyers carried on informal balancing tests. More and more often, these tests took place within the confines of regulatory agencies like the FTC. In the 1920s, the FTC was largely remade into the adviser of business rather than a regulator of business abuses. When revived in 1933 under guidance from academics like James Landis of Harvard Law School, the purpose of the FTC was couched in balancing terms: "the disposition of competing claims by contending parties . . . with a keen sense of the practicalities of the situation."[129] The New Dealers' answer to an economy in crisis was even more expert management through additional independent regulatory agencies. The number of regulatory agencies grew steadily, a behemoth from the sea to which clung law professors from all the elite schools in the country: for example, the Securities Exchange Commission directed by William O. Douglas, the Legal Realist from Yale. Frankfurter, Landis, and other New Deal talent spotters cajoled the best and brightest young lawyers to enter the public sector. Some senior professors of law became special assistants to the attorney general or the Department of Justice; others sat with the new regulatory agencies. All had a genuine sympathy for public policy goals of the New Deal and learned to balance the demands of different interest groups.[130]

In practice, balance was hardly achieved. Before the 1930s the agencies, staffed by former or future servants of the industries under supervision, became increasingly receptive to the arguments of prospective defendants. This "capture" of agencies was and remains a problem of administrative law.[131] The New Deal agencies and the agencylike divisions of the Department of Justice, particularly the antitrust division, were far more suspicious of corporate conduct. Antitrust suits like *United States v. Alcoa Aluminum* (1937) were cast as Manichaean struggles between heroes and villains.[132] The government agency and the interested party were hardly equals in this proceeding, and agencies' decisions against private parties were routinely reviewable in the courts. For the courts, the issue was the discretion of the agency, but the reversal of an agency ruling was usually based on grounds of "unreasonableness," another balancing test.[133] Congress attempted to remedy the imbalances in balancing with the Administrative Procedure Act of 1946, requiring full public hearings, attended by all interested parties; full reports from the agency; and a standard of reasonableness in its determinations matching that imposed by the courts on themselves.[134] The demand for a full record, based on a hearing of all parties, grew more complex in the 1960s and 1970s. The Supreme Court began to insist that the agency itself develop a vision of appropriate balance, rather than reflecting and choosing among those perceptions presented to it.[135]

Both agencies and courts carried on balancing tests in regulatory suits, and the managerial style of these agencies certainly resembled that of judges in Balance of Equity cases. So, too, the concern for a full record, deeply probing the realities behind the parties' claims and the consequences of any decision, was shared by the two types of adjudication. Both Balance of Equity and administrative decision making were hybrids of private and public law, or rather proof that there was no sharp division at the boundaries of the two types of adjudication. Yet Balance of Equity was distinguishable from a balancing of interests precisely because Balance of Equity was equitable in origin. Balance of interest worked within rules of statutory origin; Balance of Equity would entertain novel remedies based on fairness to all. Balance of interest in the agencies chose between sides and gave the palm to one of them. Balance of Equity strove for mutual justice. Balance of interest could be swayed by expediency and political influence. Balance of Equity did not look for offenders, it corrected human weakness. Balance of interests sought to "police" miscreants.[136] Balance of Equity was synoptic; it assumed good faith or worked to create it.

In Balance of Equity the chancellors had forged a powerful weapon; it did not suit the struggle between the regulatory agencies and the businesses they supervised and licensed,[137] but it had the potential to engage a far more entrenched and determined enemy. Equity is mutual and Balance of Equity had become a doctrine of mutuality par excellence. It was thus uniquely fabricated to untangle and remedy long-standing, deep-rooted, systemic social injustices. After World War II, the federal judges were summoned to bear witness to a "second Reconstruction" in civil rights bringing together trusteeship, equality, and reality in equitable constitutionalism.

7 *BROWN* II AND ITS PROGENY

Balance of Equity proved unsuitable for antitrust and regulatory law, but it flowered in adjudication of complex civil rights suits. These call upon the essence of equity. Damages—purely economic remedies—are not as important as the rearrangement of the parties' social relations with each other. The petitioner seeks fair play. The court probes deeply into the reality of social harms and tries to make the world whole. Defendants are given time and assistance to act in good faith, for the object is not to punish or deprive wrongdoers but to promote mutual justice. The civil rights injunction must be a structural remedy, reaching deeply into people's lives and broadly into their society. Can and ought chancellors to assay such intrusive judicial strategies? The nuisance cases pointed the way, but they did not entail explosive political repercussions. The regulatory cases were inherently political, but they did not reach deeply into the social structure of local communities. Once again, it was the pressure of petitioners—pressure from below,[1] and the argument of facts—stubborn, sad, compelling facts,[2] that touched the chancellor's conscience and triggered his resolve.

After World War II, federal courts became increasingly busy civil rights forums.[3] The Legal Defense Fund (LDF) of the NAACP brought case after case asking federal courts to undo long-standing, deeply entrenched Jim Crow education laws. Even before they brought their claims to the courts, petitioners had to make hard choices. Desegregation could cost black teachers and principals their jobs and decrease the quality of education for black schoolchildren.[4] Defendants might choose to stonewall the suits or spend more money on segregated schools.

Federal and state courts had before them *Plessy v. Ferguson* (1896), a not insuperable obstacle—the Supreme Court had already vaulted it in a series of cases involving segregation of professional schools—but an obstacle nonetheless. *Plessy* was judge-made law, a doctrine that judges could revise. The customs and statutes that adorned *Plessy* in the South were a more formidable barrier to desegregation because they foretold the difficulty of enforcing a desegregation order. Even the best-intentioned judges knew that compliance would not come easily. The equitable enforcement of desegregation would become a test of conscience within which Balance of Equity guided mutuality and good faith.

The LDF had won in *Sipuel v. Oklahoma* (1948), *McLaurin v. Oklahoma* (1950), *Sweatt v. Painter* (1950), and *Belton v. Gebhart* (1952); lost in the lower federal courts with *Brown v. Board of Education* and the Virginia, South Carolina, and District of Columbia School desegregation cases; and then triumphed when *Brown* was finally decided by the Supreme Court. *Brown* was a landmark victory for the principle of desegregation, but the Court delayed its enforcement decision. Could the justices have foreseen that *Brown* II and its progeny would put to the test the wisdom, patience, and ingenuity of the entire federal bench?[5] The old maxims of equity, filtered and channeled into Balance of Equity, were refitted for two generations of federal civil rights suits.

BROWN V. BOARD OF EDUCATION II

The justices' concern about the enforceability of a decree ending segregation directly affected their approach to the constitutionality of "separate-but-equal" school facilities. By severing the decision on the constitutional issue from the enforcement decree, a tactical decision fully within the authority of the Supreme Court, the justices tacitly conceded that they were still struggling to frame an appropriate remedy a year after they had promised relief to the petitioners. It is impossible, even with the historian's wonted hindsight, to determine whether delay was fatal to local school boards' early and full compliance with *Brown*. It is possible to trace the roots of the decision to issue a separate enforcement decree. From its first hearing on *Brown* in 1952, the Court was searching for the appropriate equitable mechanism. Even when the constitutional principle became clear, the equity of enforcement eluded the Court. Only when the justices began to read the Constitution in a fully equitable way almost two decades after *Brown* II, could the Court move swiftly and surely toward a mutual, realistic set of directives to local boards.

Then and only then did the entire federal court system begin to realistically wed trusteeship and equality.

The decision to delay the enforcement decree was prefigured early in the Court's hearings on the cases. The LDF bridled at the prospect of delay and said so in its briefs to the Court: "Even if the Court should decide that enforcement of individual and personal constitutional rights may be postponed, consideration of the relevant factors discloses no equitable basis for delaying enforcement of appellants' rights."[6] The LDF wanted a deadline for full compliance. When overt defenses of segregation were no longer possible, states with segregated school systems fell back on delay as a tactical weapon. As the attorney general of Florida told the Court, "the wise recognition by the Supreme Court in the past of the need for time in effecting certain economic changes [a reference to balance of interest cases, particularly antitrust suits] in our society in order to allow a period of healthy adjustment in sensitive areas . . . show[s] a recognition of the need for adequate *local* discretion in the same areas. This line of reasoning should be applied to the even more sensitive area of desegregation which presents a vast problem of human engineering to resolve the social changes sought."[7]

While petitioners and respondents wrangled over the extent of delay, the Court sought help of a more explicit nature. The justices were trying to determine what consequences would follow from various sorts of decrees.[8] The justices edged toward Balance of Equity from the inception of their deliberations, but Balance of Equity was a doctrine that originated in trial courts, courts that could expand the scope of factual inquiry until they could piece together the harms all parties had borne or might suffer and arrange a mutually fair remedy. To approximate this approach, the Supreme Court directed five questions to the parties.[9] The questions were prepared by Justice Felix Frankfurter, but they may have been suggested by Frankfurter's former clerk, then special assistant to the solicitor general, Philip Elman. Questions Four and Five addressed the problem of enforcement. Elman recently has admitted that he was in constant contact with Frankfurter from the inception of *Brown*. Frankfurter had warned Elman, at least in general terms, of the other justices' concern for noncompliance. Elman, responding to the suggestion, added a section to the government's 1952 "friend-of-the-court" brief that called for delayed, gradual, decentralized decrees from the district courts, reassuring local school boards that their special needs would be given due weight. Whoever originated the questions, Question Four asked the litigants to respond to two possibilities: immediate desegregation, or, in the alternative, "may this court, in the exercise of its equity powers, permit an effective gradual adjustment to be brought about from existing segregated systems to a system not based on color distinctions?" Question Five assumed an affirmative answer to the second alternative in Question Four and followed with a series of specific inquiries: should a time limit be given; should specific questions of detail be discussed; should a special master be appointed by the Supreme Court; and, if the Supreme Court merely remanded the cases to the district courts for decrees, what instructions should be given to these courts?[10]

Initially, the Frankfurter-Elman collaboration leading to Questions Four and Five jumbled together the formalist Balance of Equity cases like *Madison v. Ducktown Sulphur* (1904), antitrust and regulatory balance of interest suits, and managerial Balance of Equity. Elman's amicus brief for the United States government against segregated schools had cited without distinctions both antitrust and antinuisance injunction cases. Elman had either not seen or not bothered with the difference between balance of interests and Balance of Equity, much less the distinction between formalist Balance of Equity and managerial Balance of Equity. By confusing the different kinds of approaches, he appeared to be defending delay in enforcement as a sort of breathing space for defendants to accustom themselves to their fate.[11] As Elman had written in the first amicus brief of 1952, "A decision that the Constitution forbids the maintenance of 'separate but equal' public schools will necessarily result in invalidation of provisions of constitutions, statutes, and administrative regulations in many states . . . a reasonable period of time will obviously be required to permit formulations of new provisions of law."[12] Once the new law was in place, Elman implied, local boards would simply implement it. Arguing before the Court in December 1953 from a brief that Elman wrote, Solicitor General F. Lee Rankin used the antitrust cases as precedent; like corporations that had to rid themselves of monopolistic holdings, local school boards needed time to rearrange schedules and facilities.[13]

This was a straightforward reading of some of the injunction cases, but it compounded the Court's confusion of balance of interests with Balance of Equity. Local school boards were part of a political and social fabric that stretched throughout an entire community. They were not discrete legal entities, like corporations, nor could they simply cease illegal practices like a board of directors of a corporation. By citing antitrust cases as models, Elman and Rankin misrepresented the way in which defendants might expect a decree to work. The government brief did not do justice to the ingenuity that courts of equity had to exercise in managerial Balance of Equity suits. The government brief missed the way in which such courts penetrated deeply into the lives of entire communities.

The concatenation of the solicitor general's brief and the questions posed by the Court misled the parties to the desegregation suits. After some soul searching (Thurgood Marshall asked his staff for briefs both accepting some delay and rejecting any delay), the petitioners conceded that some delay in enforcement might be necessary. They still insisted on a terminal date for full compliance, as though the Court's decree would resemble an antitrust divestment order.[14] Encouraged by the federal government's misreading of the latent powers of chancellors in Balance of Equity, defendants agreed that the very best enforcement decree would give complete discretion to federal district court judges, often former local lawyers and politicians closely tied to the sentiments of the white elites in their communities, and allow these judges to set the pace of desegregation in accord with prevailing white sentiments. Perhaps the historian ought to read the briefs filed by attorneys general of the segregated states skeptically—they were political appointees elected by segregationist majorities—but it is likely that these men ultimately expected to desegregate their schools and wanted time to soften the blow to the more extreme segregationist elements in their midst. As Richard Ervin, the attorney general of Florida who had asked for time to handle the "sensitive" matter of desegregation, wrote to Chief Justice Earl Warren after *Brown* II came down, "the decision has met with wide approval in our state. There will be many difficulties encountered in complying with the decision of course, but everything considered, this wise decision will make these [problems] far less hard to solve than otherwise."[15] It is not difficult to credit Ervin's concern for violent resistance, though privately he strongly opposed integration. Across the South, the first local response to *Brown* I was muted, sometimes respectful and affirmative, sometimes quite cynical. Few influential white business people, clergy, or politicians stepped forward to work out desegregation plans, however, leaving local boards with the option, eagerly grasped, of doing nothing.[16]

How did the Court intend that *Brown* II be read? Although all the justices took part in the deliberations, two among them wrote its text. From his initial contacts with Elman, Justice Frankfurter had worked indefatigably to shape the enforcement decree. Frankfurter believed that the needs of localities must play some part in the resolution of segregation, or there would be no compliance at all. As the

Court pondered the shape of *Brown* II, he told Warren, "I think it is highly desirable to educate public opinion—the parties themselves and the general public to an understanding that we are at the beginning of a process of enforcement and not concluding it."[17] The justice prepared a prescient memorandum for the conference on January 15, 1954, the tenor of which was characteristic of Frankfurter's prudence and legal craftsmanship. Frankfurter distinguished the desegregation cases from Elman's antitrust cases and the earliest of the nuisance cases, as they turned on balance of interests or the formalistic version of Balance of Equity. In *Ducktown Sulphur*, for example, Frankfurter noted, the initial version of Balance of Equity allowed "public inconvenience" to bar injunctive relief. Frankfurter wanted a remedy in line with the spirit of later Balance of Equity cases. In part, this meant that the court must prepare itself and the lower federal courts for many grueling seasons of managing compliance with its decrees. A "declaration of unconstitutionality is not a wand by which such transformations can be accomplished," Frankfurter warned, even "assuming the best will in the world." Leaping a decade ahead of his time, the justice envisioned the goal of an "integrated" system of education. The "aim is summarized in the phrase 'integrated' schools," combining high-quality education and "social betterment." With these goals and not mere desegregation in mind, the Court had to act with "all deliberate speed." The crucial labor for the chancellor in such a situation was to gather facts, and here Frankfurter certainly preferred caution to haste. The high court could not do this for itself in every case. The "total situation" required the appointment of local masters to amass data and recommend a course of action. The needs of students and teachers, budgetary matters and educational matters, and the smooth operation of the school systems must all be factored into any decree. Plainly Frankfurter did not expect good-faith compliance. He feared that entire school systems would be closed down by recalcitrant local boards. He was right in his surmise about many of the school boards affected, though he kept scrapbooks of newspaper articles on voluntary compliance. He even anticipated "problems caused by shifts in population"—the white flight that followed enforcement of *Brown*. Like the Progressives of his generation, he placed a premium on data gathering. Facts would save the Court from the disobedience of diehard racists; facts would induce the South to act in good faith; facts would aid the district federal courts to protect the rights of plaintiffs, defendants, and all others touched by the decree. For this reason he wished all suits heard on a one-by-one basis in the district courts.[18] For the same reason, he wanted the Court to collect facts on school segregation in the North as well as in the South.[19]

Chief Justice Warren assumed the leading part in drafting *Brown* II. Warren assigned the opinion to himself.[20] He wanted full compliance but recognized that unanimity on the Court and conditions in the South would be strained by a demand for immediate desegregation. He signaled this in the second paragraph of his opinion in *Brown* II: "Because these cases arose under different local conditions and their disposition will involve a variety of local problems, we requested further argument on the question of relief."[21] Thus far, Warren's thinking was in accord with Balance of Equity. The highest hurdle remained, however: how was the high court to manage its injunction? Warren elected to retain jurisdiction over the project of desegregation but not, in any effective way, over the cases themselves. The Court distanced itself from the relief. It thereby husbanded its political capital as best it could, holding itself above the fray. Warren offered some guidelines to assist the lower courts in framing appropriate decrees, but these merely restated the duties of chancellors under a traditional regime of equity. The lower court judges were to act, in effect, as masters in chancery, gathering information, prodding the defendants, and overseeing compliance. Their decrees, fashioned according to "equitable principles" (in reality a redundant and hence rhetorical invocation in *Brown* II), were to be practical, flexible, and balanced. They were to show facility in adjusting and reconciling public and private needs.[22]

Like Frankfurter, Warren knew that he was engaged in public-law litigation in its most complex form. He did not wish a remedy based on Balance of Equity to be taken as a repudiation of the constitutional right and thereby excuse evasion, either by overly cautious district courts or mean-spirited local authorities. His opinion made clear that the decrees were to be obeyed. The defendants were to begin desegregation promptly and reasonably; and though additional time might be granted at the discretion of the district court, the burden for proving the necessity of such delay was to rest on the defendants. They must establish that the public interest required delay. Warren spelled out the conditions under which some delay might be needed. During these delays, however, the district court would retain jurisdiction over the cases and insure that ultimate compliance came.[23]

The crucial issue remained the pace of desegregation. Instead of the command to begin desegregation "at the earliest possible date" under the supervision of the lower courts, Warren adopted the phrase that Frankfurter preferred.[24] Unfortunately, Frankfurter's "all deliberate speed" was ambiguous, an attempt to load a few already ambivalent words in a compact and simply written opinion with more complexity than they could bear. Warren was convinced by Frankfurter's pleading and impressed by the older man's experience, but later events would prove that the chief justice had made a mistake.[25] The mixture of the language of remedy, derived largely from the Frankfurter-Elman collaboration, and the constitutional phraseology from *Brown* I began to blur each other's meaning. In either the idiom of constitutional rights—"it should go without saying that the vitality of these constitutional principles cannot be allowed to yield simply because of disagreement with them"—or the idiom of Balance of Equity—that "courts of equity may take into account the public interest in the elimination of such obstacles in a systematic and effective manner"—the meaning of the opinion would have been clearer. Superimposed on each other, the former read as mere rhetoric and the latter as an inducement to do nothing. At the end of this farrago, the phrase "all deliberate speed," instead of coupling a speedy remedy for plaintiffs who wanted to attend desegregated schools with the understanding that more systemic relief would take a little time and study, was misread by opponents of desegregation. Herbert Brownell, President Dwight Eisenhower's strongly pro-*Brown* attorney general, regarded "all deliberate speed" as "an invitation to stall and delay."[26]

Folded into this confusion was the Court's retreat from class-wide relief in *Brown* II. *Brown* I's plaintiffs had sought relief for themselves and all others similarly situated. In *Brown* I, the Court had agreed with that request. Federal courts could decertify as well as certify class-action suits, however, and this is what the Supreme Court did in *Brown* II. Warren based the decision on the variability of local circumstances, but the reason why Warren adopted this course may be that Justices Hugo Black and William O. Douglas pleaded for decertification.[27] Warren's opinion in *Brown* I, following the motion of the plaintiffs and certification in the lower courts, had treated the suits as class actions. In his unpublished draft opinion for *Brown* II, Warren had continued to regard the suits as proper class actions.[28] Perhaps he was finally convinced by Black and Douglas, the most strenuous defenders of equal rights and civil liberties on the Court, that local school boards in the South were not alike enough to fit under the Federal Rules of Civil Procedure provision

for class relief, or, if not convinced himself, he may have been anx-
ious to maintain the unanimity of the Court in the face of resistance
from Black and Douglas.

In hindsight, one can see that Warren's concession on decertification obscured the nature of the original complaint—the reality of
its systemic, institutional nature—which the Court had labored so
long and hard to explicate in the two opinions. Civil rights suits are
not only equitable, the injunction being the remedy of choice, they
are inherently class-action suits. With some exceptions, they benefit
not only the named plaintiff but also all those similarly victimized by
discrimination.[29] At the same time, there were black losers in desegregation—for example, schoolteachers and principals arbitrarily deprived of their jobs when segregated schools were closed. Warren's
decertification decision slowed these losses. Decertification also relieved the named plaintiffs and the NAACP of the burden of notify-
ing all those whose interests were affected by the suit, a requirement
under Federal Rule of Civil Procedure 23 as it then stood, and
placed an incredible financial strain on plaintiffs. An amendment to
Federal Rule 23 governing class-action suits would eventually ease
this burden. In 1966, responding to the increasing number of civil
rights suits of all sorts, the Federal Rules Advisory Committee proposed and Congress accepted a new Rule 23(b)2, allowing a class
action without notice to the represented (but absent) plaintiffs when
relief "with respect to the class as a whole" was more appropriate
than relief limited to the named plaintiff. Nowhere does the rule
mention civil rights suits, but its object was to expedite these suits.[30]
In certifying such suits under the revised 23(b)2, courts undertake
the role of trustee for the rights of the absent class members. This
trusteeship is equitable, based on a penetrating, realistic discretion.
By 1966, however, the barn door had been unlocked for a dozen
years.

The confusion of idioms in *Brown* II was compounded by later
scholarship. *Brown* II has been mistermed a compromise, or, worse,
an equivocation supposedly produced by the internal politics of the
Supreme Court as its members sought unanimity and placated
states' rightists. This judgment rendered, scholars have traced the
way in which the members of the Court gave different meanings to
the decision, and the way, more tragically, that local school boards
and politicians were left prey to the most virulently racist elements
in their midst. One example of the consequences of this false trail is
the notion that *Brown* II was a concession to federalism, that is, deference to the sovereignty of the states in a federal system. Although

Warren had invited states with segregated school systems to file amicus briefs, and these amici were asked during the oral arguments of December 1954 to explore, with the Court, what would happen under various possible enforcement decrees, the Court did not invite them to participate as partners in the process of ordering relief. They were there as interested parties to assist the Court in its investigation of local conditions as it sought guidelines for the lower courts. The states' rights in these matters had been preempted by the federal courts under *Brown* I. The decentralized structure of the decrees handed down after *Brown* II did not follow state lines, nor were they in any way conditioned by the actions of states as sovereignties. Localities did have some impact on the orders in the district courts, but only because the district courts were courts of equity and Balance of Equity took account of hardships to those whose conduct it enjoined.[31]

The opinion was not an equivocation, a concession to unanimity or federalism. On the contrary, it was highly ambitious. It sought to fuse a very technical conception of equitable discretion based on the Balance of Equity doctrine with Warren's highly personal vision of equitable discretion. Into the latter, Warren introduced the element of higher equity, "an attitude . . . a profound sense of justice and human dignity"[32] traditionally appropriate to any great chancellor. Balance of Equity was prudential—that is, it had its origin in the chancellor's discretionary power *not* to issue an injunction when it would be more equitable to provide some other remedy. The second stage of Balance of Equity deepened the doctrine, making it truly equitable—that is, concerned with mutual fairness, flexibility, and compassion. Warren's vision of a higher equity infusing the chancellor's powers had roots deeper in the origins of equity, but Warren was no Utopian. At least for the time being—in 1955—he heartily approved the Kansas district court's plan to send children involved in *Brown* to neighborhood schools, whether or not those schools remained largely segregated (though, in fact, Topeka was already politically committed to integration).[33] Frankfurter's view of equity was more technically nuanced than Warren's, but more suspicious, the residue of a lifetime of antipathy to the antilabor injunction. When Balance of Equity cases were presented to the Court in Elman's brief, Frankfurter grasped the centrality of judicial discretion—the managerial side of Balance of Equity—in them. Warren, tutored by Frankfurter, added this material to his own vision of higher equity.[34]

The Court had at hand another equitable weapon against delay—a declaratory judgment. In its brief on reargument in 1953, the

Legal Defense Fund had seemed to ask for a declaration of rights pure and simple, but this tactic was at odds with the LDF's earlier briefs and was dropped in its brief for *Brown* II. The LDF was never happy with the Elman approach but accommodated it in the end. In a world of pure good faith by defendants, or alternatively of unswerving national will to enforce school desegregation, the Court might have rested with a simple declaratory judgment that state-sponsored segregation (or even segregation per se) was unconstitutional and allowed local school boards to violate the judgment at their peril. Federal district court judges would then be in no doubt about the legitimacy of contempt citations against recalcitrant local authorities, though the contempt citation would remain entirely discretionary (and, as experience since the 1950s has proved, would rarely be used to promote civil rights compliance). Such a declaratory judgment might have appeared in *Brown* I or been the result of the further study that came between *Brown* I and II. The Court not only eschewed this course but also did not regard it as a serious option. One may speculate why this was so, but such speculation cannot change the fact that no declaratory judgment issued. It is valuable to keep in mind that the Court was thinking about remedial action in ways that bound it inextricably to the question of rights. In good Legal Realist fashion, the justices made no bright-line distinction between rights and remedies. Though the two were separated in time, they were not separated in the justices' minds.

IN THE WAKE OF *BROWN*

Although Court watchers knew that segregation's official days were numbered, *Brown* burst upon the nation like a bombshell. While waiting for it, Judge Learned Hand, then senior judge on the Second Circuit and the mentor of two generations of judges, warned Frankfurter about intrusive judging: "modern societies ought not to give judges the last word in such issues; if they do, they will end up with Blacks, Douglases, Rutledges, and Murphys, and . . . the other leaders in the 'Make this a Better World Movement.' "[35] On this occasion, Hand need not have troubled; Frankfurter prevented the Court from trying to make the world better in one great leap. What was more, the liberal justices whose inconstant activism on the bench Hand feared—Douglas and Black—joined Frankfurter's cautious approach.

Outside of the conference chamber, one doyen of the scholarly community publicly found fault with the Court's gradual, diffuse

use of its equitable powers. Though dying from heart disease, Zechariah Chafee took the Court to task in a memo he circulated to its members. "I have great dissatisfaction with the present situation as to segregation. Once the Supreme Court had laid down the general principle of integration in the first case, I think that everything depended on the framing of a satisfactory scheme to carry out that principle. . . . Instead of framing a scheme, it turned all the dirty work over to the local United States courts. Consequently, every school district and almost every school house was made the occasion for separate law suits, which had to be brought by private persons." In shifting its own burden to the shoulders of the lower federal courts, the Supreme Court effectually passed that weight on to the petitioners themselves. This was as unfair as it was unnecessary, Chafee implied. Chafee wanted President Eisenhower to step into the fray to urge the South to cooperate.[36] In fact, Eisenhower had not only declined to involve himself, he also did not agree with the Court and privately expressed his disapproval of its desegregation decisions.[37]

Frankfurter, long Chafee's colleague and friend at Harvard, judged Chafee's remarks unhelpful. Frankfurter queried his former law clerk, Alexander Bickel, "I wonder if you have seen the enclosed memorandum by my beloved Zech Chafee. It's all right as what he wrote in a letter to a friend, but to circulate it as a memorandum— well, is that the best one can do who has been deeply preoccupied with problems of procedure and civil rights for nearly half a century? In addition to all that, I must say he gets the progress of desegregation not a little out of perspective."[38] Bickel, Chafee's student and, briefly, his colleague, counseled Frankfurter: "Mr. Chafee's memorandum is, I agree, not his most impressive work, although his indignation at the President and his indignation with Virginia (rather, perhaps, disgust) are well taken."[39]

Chafee was right about the pace of compliance; desegregation moved at a snail's crawl. Local boards read *Brown* II to require careful study rather than action.[40] Worse, at first some federal district court judges covertly delayed desegregation. In South Carolina, the court impaneled to rehear *Briggs v. Elliott* (1955) understood *Brown* II to permit pupil placement programs based on "choice"—a burden imposed on black students but not on whites. Blacks could elect to leave their old schools and be bused to white schools; white students did not have to go anywhere.[41] Still more patently evasive was the conduct of federal district court judges like William H. Atwell in Dallas. He continued to regard separate but equal as good educational policy.[42] A few district court judges, like J. Skelly Wright of New Orleans and Bryan Simpson of Jacksonville, pressed school boards for real progress, but such impatience was the exception.[43] A decade later, Bickel overoptimistically wrote that "the South miscalculated badly." If by 1964 only Mississippi stood where it had stood in 1954,[44] official state resistance had been replaced by the obstinacy of local boards. Despite increasingly strenuous efforts by a liberal wing of the Fifth Circuit, in much of the Deep South there was still only token integration.[45] By 1968, the high court's patience had run out, and in a series of opinions beginning with *Green v. New Kent County* it directed lower courts to expedite local desegregation plans.[46]

Though Frankfurter, and after he retired others on the Court, continued to advocate self-restricting, gradual, diffuse equity—they did not believe it the Court's business to impose its own vision of social justice on local boards—in segregation case after case, a unanimous Court insisted on local obedience to district court judges. Even after Warren himself retired, his initial collaboration with Frankfurter—a fusion of subtle injunctive technique and conscientious striving for fair play—fueled the high court's reading of trial and lower appellate court opinions.[47] The operative terms mutated from desegregation to integration, but the vision behind them of one society, with equal opportunity for all, had not changed at all.

Faced with continued intransigence, a court of equity cannot avoid involving itself in the particulars of enforcement, as the federal courts demonstrated in *Swann v. Mecklenberg* (1971).[48] A half decade before the case arrived at the Supreme Court, parents of black children in the Charlotte-Mecklenburg school district of North Carolina had sought federally imposed integration of the schools. Under earlier federal court orders, a voluntary assignment plan had resulted in a largely unchanged pattern of segregation in the schools. In 1969, federal district court Judge James B. McMillan looked at the pattern of segregation and knew that the school board had not tried to comply with the spirit of the *Brown* decision. A decade later, he recalled his impression of the high court's directive: "though it may have been technically 'bad' law when read purely against those precedents [that is, *Plessy*] it would be hard to challenge its basic message from the standpoint of strict construction of the Constitution, of equal protection of laws, of morals, of economics, of *equity*, fairness and justice, of the progress of society as a whole and of its individual members, and of the Judeo-Christian ethic (perhaps not unique, but ours) which professes to treat men as equal in the sight of God regardless of their conditions or fortune" (italics added).[49] It would be hard to find a more moving concordance of the oath of the chancellor and the language of *Brown*.

McMillan knew that *Green* had mandated that school boards immediately take positive steps toward the creation of unitary school systems. He proceeded straightforwardly with Charlotte's school board, seeking to involve it fully in desegregation planning. This entailed the presumption of good faith. When the board procrastinated, McMillan asked John A. Finger, an expert educational administrator, to advise the court as a master in equity. The board's half-hearted efforts induced the judge to impose on Charlotte the Finger plan for busing students to achieve racial balance. Busing was long common in the South. Blacks were often bused past nearby white schools to reach regional black schools. Nevertheless, McMillan knew that there would be a storm of public protest and was prepared to weather it. He did not anticipate that the Fourth Circuit Court of Appeals would divide over his order and that a majority would vote to reverse it.

The Supreme Court debated the case in its 1971 term. From the first, Justice Douglas relied on Balance of Equity. Remedies must be flexible, and trial judges must have discretion to formulate effective remedies. Justice John Marshall Harlan emphatically agreed. In the balance, the commitment to purely neighborhood schools could not be permitted to outweigh the duty to integrate schools. Justices William Brennan and Thurgood Marshall joined Douglas and Harlan, Brennan reading from portions of his opinion for the Court in *Green* insisting on unitary school systems. Chief Justice Warren Burger had his doubts about busing; initially, he wanted to affirm the circuit court. In particular, he was disturbed about the scope of discretion the district court exercised. His first draft opinion distinguished traditional equity suits, in which he found such discretion wholly proper, from desegregation suits. When Justice Potter Stewart joined the majority, arguing that traditional equitable discretion was as suitable in a civil rights case as in any other, Burger began to capitulate. The final opinion in *Swann* fully supported Judge McMillan and reaffirmed that managerial Balance of Equity applied to civil rights suits.[50]

The embattled old Fifth Circuit Court of Appeals—the Deep South—had borne the heaviest burden of appeals from defendants seeking more time and plaintiffs demanding simple justice long delayed. Inspired by "the Four"—Judges Elbert Tuttle, John Minor Wisdom, John Robert Brown, and Richard Taylor Rives—panels of the court had anticipated the high court's demand for immediate compliance from the local boards, even when individual district court judges on the circuit hesitated. A few of the other judges on the circuit consistently resisted desegregation. Some called themselves "Jeffersonian Democrats," a term of ideological art that masked aversion to court-ordered integration with a doctrine of strict construction of the Fourteenth Amendment. Such rigor in exegesis of federalism's scripture did not prompt these Jeffersonian jurists to hinder the southerly flow of less socially controversial federal funds and services.[51] At the district court level, where *Swann* seemed to legitimate the discretion of trial judges to press for integration instead of merely ending state-sponsored segregation, judges battled with local school boards bent on continued evasion of *Green*. The judges compelled local boards to produce evidence about the imbalance of pupil placement, creating the "record" characteristic of the modern administrative agency. Such evidence documented the bad faith with which these boards had greeted *Brown* II.[52]

If southern resistance had expressed itself overtly, northern opposition to integration was based on denial that segregation was intentional. In theory, neighborhood schools merely reflected the ghettoized distribution of minority housing. In the 1970s, northern federal judges responded to *de facto* segregation in the same way that their southern brethren struck down voluntary pupil placement. In northern cities like Dayton and Columbus, Ohio, Wilmington, Delaware, and Detroit, Michigan, judges like Carl Rubin, Robert Duncan, Murray Schwartz, Stephen Roth, and Robert DeMascio managed major programs of redistricting, busing schedules, and teacher reassignment to insure integration.[53] The United States Supreme Court limited the geographic reach of such plans in *Milliken v. Bradley* (1974) but continued to allow trial judges immense discretion in formulating remedial plans within traditional school board boundaries.[54] When local boards ingenuously asked for further time, a tactic that had already delayed unitary education for two decades, federal judges threatened to place the schools under federal supervision. One federal judge used a board's record of delay and misfeasance as a basis to remove the board from its post and put the school district into a federal receivership. That case was tried in the media as well as the courts and deserves a second look.

On June 21, 1974, Federal District Judge W. Arthur Garrity found that the Boston school board had not only engaged in thoroughgoing segregation, keeping black students in Roxbury High School separate from white students in South Boston High School, but also had deliberately ignored earlier state court orders to formulate a plan for integration. The city school board had even allowed overcrowding of white schools to avoid integrating black schools—a lesson in bad faith that the children learned firsthand. In *Morgan v. Hennigan*, Garrity nevertheless allowed the school board to manage the first stage of what would be a three-stage plan for integration of the two inner city school districts.[55] Some white parents in South Boston displayed a fury at the plan reminiscent of Citizens Councils in Selma and Montgomery, Alabama, and for three years there was violence in the schools, sometimes provoked by black students, sometimes by white students. In the streets, protests by whites became riots. State troopers and city police were stationed around and in the schools to prevent fights, but a handful of students were stabbed and many more were beaten. After a year of fear and poor attendance, Judge Garrity placed the district under federal control, removed the board and the school administrators, and replaced them with his own nominees. In 1985 he finally returned a much scarred but more integrated school system to local control.[56]

In any equitable analysis of busing, the ruling tenets of mutuality and good faith dictate that the judge and the scholar consider the consequences of decrees for all those affected, not just the plaintiffs. Busing has sometimes left teachers and administrators whose primary concern is the welfare of their young charges on dark and bloody ground, and the quality of education for black and white has suffered.[57] In a poignant account of her own effort to care for her students, Iona Malloy, a marvelously sensitive teacher of English and modern literature at South Boston High School from 1974 to 1977, captured one side of that many-sided controversy. Her portrait of the damage that segregation, racial animosity, and sudden, unwanted intimacy did to blacks, whites, and professional educators cannot be dismissed in any defense of busing. As a foot soldier in the war against racism, she had every right to complain that Judge Garrity often flew too high over the terrain, particularly in his treatment of the teachers and principals in the schools. In 1977, she accepted a position at Boston Latin, a veteran not quite retired from the war.[58]

If the cost of going slowly was to rob an entire generation of minority students of their right to an integrated education, and the cost of going swiftly was to unleash deep-seated racial animus, only full and vigorous exercise of their equitable powers allowed federal judges to make any inroads at all against discrimination where local prejudice was deeply rooted and local elites refused to promote integration. Whether or not Charlotte or South Boston appreciated these powers, they are the working tools of the modern chancellor.[59]

THE SAFETY OF COMING TO THE JUDGMENT DAY

Armed only with the authority of their courts, a handful of marshals or bailiffs, and the mores of a people professing fidelity to the rule of law, federal and state chancellors are not the most powerful government officers. Without political support, if not directly from the other branches of government, then indirectly through the assistance of political parties, interest groups, and local elites, court orders in public-law disputes may be reduced to nullities. In truth, effective desegregation of the schools owed as much to the civil rights movement, the Civil Rights Act of 1964, the Voting Rights Act of 1965, and the sometimes grudging acquiescence of local leaders, as to the persistence and authority of the federal courts. Nevertheless, without the intervention of the courts, the moral tone and vision of civil rights reform would have gone for naught.[60]

The desegregation decree and the managerial stance of the judges behind it led public-question equity into the 1970s. With the elaboration of modern Balance of Equity doctrine, equity moved from Joseph Story's dull science to a revivified judicial art. The "conscience" of the chancellor, embedded in increasingly sophisticated arguments about Balance of Equity, refashioned old remedies into powerful tools for enforcement of public-law decisions. A veritable revolution in the role of the judge-chancellor in public-law litigation, wherein petitioners challenge the conduct of government agencies, municipal authorities, and state educational, prison, and mental health facilities, had the flexible, probing remedies of equity at its center. The mandatory injunction, aimed at structural, systemic, institutionalized harms, became the centerpiece of equity, and federal judges, acting as chancellors, remade a large piece of our social and economic world.

Federal Judge Frank Johnson of Alabama's Middle District and later the Fifth Circuit played a leading role in this transformation, at one point putting the entire Alabama state mental health program under federal receivership in order to secure decent conditions for the patients.[61] Reflecting on this case and others, he has written:

> In confronting such questions [raised in suits on discrimination, equal protection, and so forth, against large institutions and state governments] and after deciding that under the facts of a case the Constitution mandates that the litigants are entitled to

relief, a judge cannot discharge his oath of office without seeing to it that relief is provided. It will not suffice in these cases to make an award of monetary damages to the litigants for the injuries that they have suffered in the past. Often such monetary rewards are not even requested. Relief of a more affirmative nature is sought by these litigants. . . . The judge has no alternative but to take a more active role in formulating appropriate relief. Fortunately, in doing so the judge has access to a tremendous number of aids. . . . The comprehensive remedial decrees that in recent years have received so much attention— for example, reapportionment, desegregation, and public employment decrees, as well as decrees establishing minimum standards for prisons and mental illness and retardation facilities, compliance with which is necessary in order to eliminate the constitutional violations that necessitated court intervention— are in this sense not new.[62]

Johnson claimed that the federal judge simply reused the tools the chancellors had once used to remedy harm in private lawsuits against the erring agencies of local and state government. Whether these were new remedies or adaptations of old ones, the historical lesson lies in the way in which these tools are employed in public-law questions.

Over the past two decades since *Green*, scholars have laid out many roads to the constitutional principle in *Brown* and beyond without stopping at "equitable principles." Some of the roads traversed in the essays of legal academics bear the signposts "structural due process," "the Anti-discrimination Principle," and "democracy re-enforcing."[63] The moment one recognizes the inseparability of rights from enforcement, however, one realizes that there is no way to provide relief for petitioners in these public-law cases without reading equity into the Constitution. Consider the question from the bottom up. Even critics of the Court admit that compliance in cases like *Brown* came grudgingly and piecemeal.[64] Private lawsuits, portaged on the backs of the NAACP Legal Defense Fund, went on for decades. To defendants, learned disquisitions on the rights question were meaningless. Special masters gathered and delivered truckloads of facts, but without some rod to compel compliance, no right was vindicated and no principle assured. The answer that some district courts arrived at in the school cases—busing—was an extension of the very means by which many school boards had implemented segregation. If busing was "dirty"—as in the "dirty hands" maxim of the old chancellors—southern school boards could hardly complain about its imposition on them to attain racial balance. District court judges do not normally engage in celebrations of poetic justice, however, and busing was ordered not as a punishment but as a remedy familiar and fair to all. The storm over busing raised the constitutional question again, but only because busing proved, in some cases, onerous for all parties.[65] White resistance to integration took forms that negated the busing remedy. White flight from cities into suburbs and registration of children in "academies" created for the sole purpose of avoiding integration re-created overwhelmingly black schools in the inner cities. Efforts of integration leaders to penetrate into the suburban school systems were rebuffed by the post-Warren Court.

In all of this cut and thrust, much of it political in the most immediate sense of the word, federal district courts transformed the rudimentary Balance of Equity in *Brown* from a remedial tool to a way of reading the Constitution. There was little evidence of an unrestrained, unresponsive, or abusive wielding of the injunctive remedy in these cases. Good-faith community plans were almost always accepted. The courts' patience was tried, but few persons— even those who deliberately set out to sabotage the court rulings— were punished with contempt of the resulting equitable decrees. In a system where those who resist court orders to pay simple debts still can be imprisoned, critics of the federal courts of all political persuasions might well regard the forbearance of federal chancellors in the face of the antics of antiheroes of the civil rights movement as an argument for equitable discretion, not against it. The Constitution not only allowed such intrusive, systemic judicial enforcement, the Constitution mandated some such relief. Courts of equity were trustees; equality required their intervention; reality necessitated that intervention reach deeply into the rhythms of everyday life and up to the "other," higher equity. As Judge Robert A. Merhige recalled, sixteen years after ordering busing in Richmond, "I did what I did not only because it was law, but because it was right."[66]

EPILOGUE BALANCE OF EQUITY AND AFFIRMATIVE ACTION

Historians often speak of the "cycles" of history—cycles of reform and retrenchment, of Jacobinism and Thermidor. If there are cycles in constitutional law they are Ptolemaic, not Copernican. The law does not transcribe neat orbits of growth and decay but weaves through involuted loops and whorls.

At the height of congressional Reconstruction Charles Sumner pressed his Radical comrades to write guarantees of social equality, including protection against segregation of the races in schools, into the Civil Rights acts. The proposal never became law, but the fire that infused the acts was relit in the Legal Defense Fund's war of attrition against Jim Crow and burst into flame in the civil rights movement of the 1950s, 1960s, and 1970s. *Brown* II and its progeny walked step by step if not quite hand in hand with the many men and women, parents and children, toward mutual justice for all the races. In a series of modern civil rights statutes, Congress committed itself to redress the inequities of racism. By the 1970s, civil and political discrimination had given pride of place on the reform agenda to economic deprivation. State-directed and state-sponsored racism had retreated to the dark corners of American life, but the unjust effects of earlier economic subjugation of minorities still kept whole segments of the American people in thrall. Congress responded with affirmative action programs. The national legislature, relieved of the long nightmare of the Vietnam war, confronted the mandate of equitable constitutionalism, a trusteeship combining equality and reality. Throughout the country, in schools, municipalities, and industries, public and private employers and authorities either anticipated or followed the federal government's lead. It was a start, but only a start.

Sumner's dream had died as he did, unfulfilled. "Redeemers"

razed Reconstruction with a thoroughness that was almost unparalleled in American political history. In the decade of the 1980s, there have appeared unmistakable signs that the nation is sliding back toward a second "redemption," not as blatantly racist as the first but unraveling the "second Reconstruction" of the 1960s and 1970s just as surely as the first Redeemers dismantled Radical Reconstruction. The signs are everywhere—in the mounting tide of racial violence on college campuses, the rise to power of once and future leaders of white supremacist organizations, and increasing maldistribution of the nation's wealth. During the administration of President Ronald Reagan, the Civil Rights Commission was reduced to a near nullity and the Civil Rights Division of the Department of Justice was hamstrung.[1]

The language of redemption of the Constitution in our courts is not racist, nor can one assume that opponents of affirmative action advocate racism; that is not the issue.[2] The issue is the way in which our judges elect to read the Constitution. A renewed infatuation with legal formalism serves judicial redemption of a facially neutral but deeply inequitable reading of the Fourteenth Amendment. In a series of cases that started to arrive at the Supreme Court in the 1970s, the justices have been asked to use their equitable powers to bar enforcement of racial affirmative action quotas. The Court's opinions in these cases are almost always fragmented, unlike the desegregation cases of the Warren and early Burger courts. The precise fault line runs along the question of equitable remedies: plaintiff wants an injunction against the affirmative action program, defendant claims that the program is warranted by past harms. For the majority of the Court, in opinions that call to mind the formalism of the late nineteenth century, the equitable goal—a remedy that looks deeply into the social context of discrimination, traces out all its malign effects, and uncovers its covert corruptions—bows before a prudentially derived test of strict scrutiny. To pass the legal, not the equitable, test, the program must be justified by a compelling state interest in undoing its own past discrimination. For defenders of the second Reconstruction on the Court, a dwindling number of graying lions now at bay, the equitable question enfolds the constitutional one. Quotas and benign racial distinctions of other types are justified when the injury to the class of beneficiaries of the program is demonstrable in the larger historical context of race relations. In this sense, the affirmative action cases are closely akin to the desegregation cases: a trusteeship for equality resting on the reality of past harms and present deprivations.

Not surprisingly, colleges and graduate schools, the targets of successful desegregation suits before *Brown*, were among the first public institutions to assay the use of quotas to address inequality in educational opportunity. The larger picture of minority access to "equal resources" of education, so vital in our society (as the Court emphasized in *Brown*), motivated a number of universities to set quotas for minority recruitment.[3] Candidates accepted under these incentives might not have the same qualifications on paper as nonminority candidates, but this inequality could be and often was attributed to inequalities in socioeconomic standing of the candidates' families, cultural biases in the standardized tests of aptitude and achievement, and similar evidences of prior discrimination against minorities. That is to say, inequality in minority candidates' preparedness for higher or professional education could be attributed to a diffuse but pervasive effect of prior economic and social discrimination.[4]

Nonminority candidates for admission to schools sought injunctive relief against quotas that denied them entrance despite their possession of stronger traditional qualifications for entrance than the minority students admitted under the quotas.[5] One of these applicants was Allan Bakke, a thirty-two-year-old engineer from Minneapolis who wanted to change his career to medicine. He was able, well spoken, and bright, and no one at the University of California–Davis (UC-Davis), where he sought entrance to medical school, doubted the sincerity or zeal of his interest in medicine. Davis had established its medical school in 1968 and soon named a special task force to recruit minority students. Minority applicants were evaluated separately from nonminority applicants, and sixteen places in the class of one hundred were reserved for the best qualified of the minority applicants. Bakke came close to acceptance, but his own excusable delay in finishing his application put him behind other equally qualified nonminority students. He just missed the cutoff. Informed of his fate and urged to reapply, Bakke edged toward legal action. Possibly encouraged by a friendly member of the faculty, Bakke sued when a second application the next year failed.[6]

In the California courts, the university defended its racial quota by citing the pervasive social effects of past discrimination. UC-Davis accepted the general principle that all racial discrimination was invidious and stigmatizing, but it argued that some racial distinctions were allowable when a compelling public interest outweighed the more diffuse general principle of equality before the law—in particular, there were too few doctors in minority areas of the state because there were too few minority doctors. A California superior court rejected that claim; racial quotas were unacceptable. Judge F. Leslie Manker did not order Bakke admitted, however, for Bakke had not proved to the judge's satisfaction that he would have been admitted had no places been set aside for minority applicants. Both sides appealed the judgment, and the California Supreme Court heard the case in 1976. The result vindicated Bakke's position, and the court ordered him enrolled. The state supreme court required not only that a compelling public interest be served by a racial quota, but also that other, less invidious means be tried and found wanting to achieve the same result before any school instituted a quota. The university had neither shown a compelling state interest nor explored other avenues of providing minority applicants with a medical education.[7] The university appealed to the United States Supreme Court.

Bakke was not the first case of racial or implicitly racial quotas that the Supreme Court had heard. Until the 1940s, the Court had allowed southern voter registrars to exclude all minority voters, the strictest form of quota.[8] So, too, state apportionment lines that acted as quotas against urban voters were left in place under the "political question" doctrine.[9] In these suits against implied quotas, the high court deferred to the states under a self-denying interpretation of federalism. Later, in the wake of *Brown*, such state-sponsored or state-supported racial distinctions were gradually pulled down, though private and quasi-private barriers were left in place.[10] Nevertheless, *Bakke* was a cause célèbre by the time the Supreme Court, after some wrangling, granted certiorari on the university's appeal.[11]

Chief Justice Warren Burger and Justice William Rehnquist, ultimately joined by Justices John Paul Stevens and Potter Stewart, opined that no racial quotas were tolerable unless a compelling state interest could be found that only those quotas could satisfy. Burger was willing to "leave open whether and to what extent indirect consideration of race is compatible with constitutional or statutory proscriptions" but remained convinced that "rigidly cast" quotas failed the strict scrutiny of racial discrimination imposed by the Fourteenth Amendment.[12] Rehnquist wrote a far more sweeping disapprobation of the Davis plan. Race could never be the determinant of access to education, he insisted, at least so long as the discrimination was public, not private. Minorities benefited from the equal protection clause insofar as it took race out of politics; that was what the framers of the Fourteenth Amendment wanted. Only when courts could identify the specific victims of specific prior public discrimination was a racially reflective remedy allowable, and then it had to pass a strict scrutiny test to insure that the remedy exactly fit the injury. Past injuries to minorities as groups, often called "societal discrimination," did not pass such muster, for no minority could claim an exact correspondence between all its members and the supposed discrimination. "I am unwilling to agree that every member of a minority has been discriminated against, in the sense that under the Fourteenth Amendment it is permissible for the state to provide a remedy." The object of strict scrutiny was perfect mapping of injury and remedy, a result rarely obtainable when the injury was diffuse, long standing, often concealed, and damages the victims before they come to the remedial stage (for example, lowering their standard examination scores, a debility when applying to medical school). Nevertheless, Rehnquist continued, "The fit between the two groups . . . is far from exact and thus an insufficient basis for use of racial classification." The damage to the liberty interests of the innocent nonminority losers in such quotas was "something out of George Orwell" and by itself convinced the justice that the Davis plan was unconstitutional.[13]

In *Bakke v. Regents of California* (1977) the Court struck down the Davis plan in a five-to-four vote, Justice Lewis Powell, the swing vote and the author of the crucial opinion, voting with Rehnquist, the chief justice, Stewart, and Stevens. The permissibility of giving some advantage to minority candidates was not struck down, however, Powell joining Justices William Brennan, Byron White, Thurgood Marshall, and Harry Blackmun on this point. Powell found the Davis program unconstitutional because it made race the sole criterion of admission for a set quota of the entering class.[14]

Powell's voice was again crucial in the Court's resolution of *Fullilove v. Klutznick* (1980),[15] a challenge to the congressional 10 percent set-aside of all federal public works contracts to minority contractors or subcontractors. To Chief Justice Burger, who assigned himself the opinion for another much divided court, the intent of Congress was compelling. Congress worked to deliver on "a century-old promise of equality of economic opportunity."[16] Justice Powell subscribed to the chief's reasoning but wrote a short concurrence to explain how *Fullilove* could rest alongside *Bakke*. The difference was simply that the government in *Fullilove* had shown that actual discrimination in the past led to actual harms. In *Bakke* there was no such proof. Powell believed that Congress had the authority to provide a remedy for past employment discrimination. The Board of Regents of California had no such authority. Congress tailored a remedy to reasonably fit the wrong. The Board of Regents did not tailor its remedy.[17] Justices Marshall, White, Brennan, and Blackmun stood on their opinion in *Bakke* and strongly supported the set-aside.[18] Justices Stewart and Rehnquist similarly reiterated their opposition, expressed in *Bakke*, to any racial distinctions. Justice Stevens dissented as well, not because he thought the Fourteenth Amendment barred any racial distinctions, benign or malign, but because he required strict scrutiny and, under it, found no evidence for the specific and continuing discrimination that the quota might remedy.[19]

Justice Powell's test was pressed into service again in *Wygant v. Jackson Board of Education* (1986),[20] with a very different outcome. Again, Justice Powell was worried about the practical issue—the effect on innocent third parties of a contract negotiated by a teachers' union and a local school board to hire and retain minority teachers in order to achieve racial balance in the teaching force. The crisis came in the early 1980s with retrenchment and dismissals of nonminority teachers with more seniority than the more recent affirmative action appointees. The school board of Jackson, Michigan, argued that the lay-off plan was tailored to keep minority teachers in the schools as "role models" for minority students. The district court for the Eastern District of Michigan found for the school board in a summary judgment, short-circuiting the compilation of evidence— the proof of prior discrimination by the board that would have allowed it to pass the strict scrutiny test. The Sixth Circuit Court of Appeals upheld the district court, but Powell disagreed. Instead, he argued that layoffs ignoring seniority, contract or no contract, were a burden to nonminority Jackson teachers innocent of wrongdoing. This was no "benign" remedy; its victims paid for others' misdeeds. He did not give weight to the argument that the dismissed teachers might have owed their jobs in the first place to a discriminatory hiring policy.[21] The Court, Blackmun, Brennan, Marshall, and Stevens dissenting, followed Powell.

In *City of Richmond v. Croson* (1989),[22] a majority of the Court, following *Wygant* and reversing *Fullilove* in part, demanded that local government play no racial favorites in awarding municipal contracts. Municipalities were not to attempt to remedy diffuse, long-standing injustices through quotas, unless those injustices were the direct, conclusively proved results of that municipality's racial discrimination and precise victims and culprits could be identified, notwithstanding the possibility that such victims and culprits were long dead or retired from the marketplace and the city hall. Like the hedgehog in Tolstoy's fable, antidiscrimination programs know one great truth: evidence of particular intent often hides its face, leaving behind only statistics of deprivation and gross evidences of misery. The majority on the Court instead reminded municipalities and reassured minorities that "the deviation from the norm of equal treatment of all racial and ethnic groups is a temporary matter, a measure taken in the service of the goal of equality itself. Absent such findings [of explicit wrongdoing by the municipality, which racial quotas would redress] there is a danger that a racial classification is merely the product of unthinking stereotypes or a form of racial politics."[23] Giving preference, through a quota, to one race over another was an affront to the equal protection clause.

In 1983, the Richmond City Council had adopted a municipal "set-aside" ordinance requiring anyone submitting a bid for a city contract to assure the city that at least 30 percent of the contract (or the subcontracts under it) went to minority business enterprises, businesses whose ownership was at least 51 percent Oriental, Indian, Hispanic, Eskimo, Aleut, or Afro-American, a provision in conformity with federal definitions of minorities. The mayor and a majority of the council were, for the first time, black, and at public hearings there was opposition to the plan. The city attorney replied that black businesses had received only 0.67 percent of the city's contracts in the past and black businessmen had been systematically excluded from contractors' associations. The city attorney also cited the congressional set-aside plan upheld in *Fullilove v. Klutznick*. The intention of the city of Richmond was to encourage minority business enterprise, a step-up or bootstrap approach to self-help. The plan was thus to have a limited life of five years. The city council believed, and the federal district, appellate, and supreme courts were told, that nonminority contractors had for a century prevented black craftsmen from becoming businessmen, refusing them loans and finding ways to regulate them out of the market while yet using their labor. Its advocates might regard the set-aside plan as a form of systemic restitution, for Richmond was built, repaired, and rebuilt in part by minority employees who gained little from their labor save continued economic subordination. Such prior discrimination might be termed unjust enrichment, for which one appropriate equitable remedy was the set-aside. Opponents of the plan then and throughout the litigation retorted that no one had produced conclusive evidence that nonminority contractors in Richmond discriminated against minority businesses, or that the city, when under white control, had discriminated against black contractors. Indeed, in the past there had been few minority contractors against whom to discriminate. The ordinance placed a burden on the shoulders of nonminority business people to find such minority contractors and include them in the city jobs. Minority contractors did not have this burden, nor did they have to find nonminority contractors to share the bids they won.[24]

In September 1983, the J. A. Croson Company bid for the job of replumbing the city jail. Croson tried to find a minority plumbing subcontractor but had not succeeded until the day before bids were due. At that time, after a good-faith search by Croson, Continental Metal Hose, a minority business enterprise, asked to subcontract the fixtures. Croson was the only bidder on the job and its bid was accepted. But Continental, whose bid was essential if Croson was to fulfill the 30 percent minority subcontract requirement of the ordinance, was having a hard time getting a price for the fixtures from nonminority suppliers. In fact, they would not give Continental the same price they had offered to Croson. After a month's wrangling, Continental finally arranged to purchase the fixtures from a supplier at a price $6,000 higher than Croson had included in its bid. Croson had sought a waiver from the set-aside while Continental was dickering with its suppliers, but when the Continental bid arrived, Croson asked the city to include the extra $6,000 in the price for the entire job. The city refused and Croson sued, claiming that the ordinance violated its Fourteenth Amendment rights.

The federal courts took two years to hear and decide the case, the Supreme Court opinion coming a year after the set-aside plan ceased to exist. The Supreme Court was concerned with the apparent conflict between *Fullilove* and its decision in *Wygant v. Jackson Board of Education* (1986). The federal district court for the District of Eastern Virginia found the ordinance constitutional under *Fullilove*. The appellate court for the Fourth Circuit upheld the district court. The Supreme Court, having reversed *Fullilove* in part in *Wygant v. Jacksonville School District*, remanded the case to the Fourth Circuit with instructions to reconsider it in the light of *Wygant*. The Fourth Circuit did just that, its majority deciding that the set-aside was contrary to *Wygant*. The Supreme Court upheld the majority of the Fourth Circuit. When district and appellate federal courts appear unable to distinguish between earlier and later Supreme Court rulings, the high court uses a case like *Richmond* to clarify its position. *Green v. New Kent County* and *Swann v. Mecklenberg* were such cases.

Writing for the majority of the Court, Justice Sandra D. O'Connor distinguished *Richmond* from *Fullilove*. She judged that a generalized assertion of past discrimination could not sustain a quota without proof of close correspondence between the number of individuals harmed by the past discrimination—in this case, the number of minority businesses denied public works contracts—and the percent of future contracts set aside for minority businesses. Without calculation of this internal quota, there was no fit between the remedy and the past injury. Without such tailoring, there would be no limit to the scope of duration of the remedy—no logical stopping point. Broadly stated proofs of societal discrimination amounted to "sheer speculation" when applied to the precise question at hand— strict scrutiny of the city's quota. Justice O'Connor ruled out any argument that pervasive, private discrimination, countenanced by the city, prevented minority craftsmen from becoming minority businessmen, and the nonminority contractors benefited thereby, if only through reduced competition. There had to be a direct connection between evidence produced at trial and the plan itself to sustain it. She chided Richmond for not doing its homework. The city did not know how many minority business enterprises were affected by past discrimination, nor had it, as Davis had failed to do in *Bakke*, attempted to use more race-neutral means to aid black entrepreneurs. "The gross overinclusiveness of Richmond's racial preference strongly impugns the city's claim of remedial motivation." Reading between the lines of O'Connor's opinion, one finds her suspicion that the city's set-aside was nothing more than a form of political patronage. Such "shifting preferences" in the political marketplace could not sustain strict scrutiny. When minorities or majorities used racial quotas to further political ends, they violated the Fourteenth Amendment. The argument from congressional intent that protected the public works set-aside in *Fullilove* did not avail the defendant here, for "The history of racial classification in this country suggests that blind judicial deference to legislative or executive pronouncements or necessity has no place in Equal Protection analysis."[25] The chief justice, Justice Stevens, and newly appointed Justices Antonin Scalia and Anthony Kennedy concurred in the opinion of the Court, reiterating their adherence to an exacting standard of no racial quotas except those remedying the state's own prior discrimination and giving redress to the precise victims of that discrimination.[26]

What had happened to the language of Balance of Equity? Had the doctrine so vital to settlement of school integration cases proved useless in dealing with affirmative action cases? The majority in *Bakke*, *Wygant*, and *Croson* had not tried to balance the equities, concluding instead that discrimination on the basis of race was constitutionally impermissible unless certain mitigating criteria were met. Without proof of prior discrimination against the petitioners by the defendants—the test that switched on the compelling state purpose proviso—these criteria could not be met. The minority in these cases (joined by Powell and Burger to make a majority in *Fullilove*) clung to a Balance of Equity approach. In *Bakke*, Justices White, Brennan, Marshall, and ultimately Blackmun agreed that the Court need not require strict scrutiny of a quota whose purpose was benign. They rejected formalism in favor of a standard resting implicitly on equitable grounds—prior unjust enrichment and restitution. The equities of the case, its deeper reality, influenced Justice Brennan: "To read the Fourteenth Amendment to state an abstract principle of color-blindness is itself to be blind to history." Congress was giving special privileges to freedmen and women "before and after the adoption of the amendment." The goals of the Davis plan were in accord with this reading of the amendment: a genuinely egalitarian society. *Brown* had rested not on abstract principles, but on social facts and an equitable remedy. It was the racial stigma, the badge of inferiority, that was the injury, not the racial discrimination per se. "The constitutional principle I think to be supported by our cases can be summarized as follows: government may not on account of race, insult or demean a human being by stereotyping his or her capacities, integrity, or worth as an individual." Discrimination far more widespread and pernicious than the prior denial of admission to medical school had disabled potential minority applicants. Davis could hardly be a party to such discrimination—its medical school had only been founded in 1968—but minority applicants to Davis suffered nonetheless the injury of long-standing racism in California.[27]

Though disabled by illness during much of the exchange of memos on *Bakke*, Justice Blackmun submitted his own thoughts to the conference on May 1, 1978. He had decided, after much soul-searching and legal research, that admissions policies had to take race into account if any realistic progress toward equality in professional opportunity was to be had. He captured the essence of equal concern in simple prose: "I yield to no one in my earnest hope that the time soon will come when an 'affirmative action' program is unnecessary and only a relic of the past. I would hope that we could reach this stage within a decade, but history strongly suggests that that hope is a forlorn one. . . . This is not an ideal world. It probably never will be. It is easy to give legislative language a literal construction when one assumes that the factual atmosphere is idealistic. But we live in a real world." The equal protection clause was designed to counter entrenched racial prejudice, not to erect a facade of unreality in front of racial injustice. "The Davis program is a benign one and carries no stigma. Its race-conscious aspect could be far better formulated, but the numbers it employs are reasonably acceptable to the necessary social goal."[28]

Justices Brennan and Blackmun used Balance of Equity to fill the spare language of the Fourteenth Amendment. They wrote in the tradition of the great chancellors, and their arguments strongly influenced Justice Powell, the swing vote in the case. Powell was an experienced lawyer who knew firsthand how hard the state of Virginia had labored to put off integration of public facilities. He was sympathetic to the aspirations of equality but wary of quotas. Nevertheless, swayed by Brennan and others, he modified his original draft opinion denying any role to race in admission decisions to allow race to be a partial factor.[29]

In *Wygant*, Justice Marshall, this time writing for Brennan and Blackmun, again read the Constitution equitably, balancing the equities to reach toward equal concern for all parties. Without the new lay-off plan, the financial crisis in the district would have completely undone the effect of minority hiring plans. If the affirmative action hiring plans were a valid answer to prior discrimination in hiring, surely retention of teachers according to strict seniority amounted to a pernicious racial preference in layoffs: minorities went first. Indeed, the only reason minority teachers lacked seniority was that they were barred from getting positions until the affirmative action program was implemented. Even so, Marshall quoted one official of the teachers' union as saying that the development of the lay-off compromise was "the most difficult balancing of equities that he had ever encountered." While it is possible that the labor leader used the phrase "balancing of equities," it is more likely that Marshall paraphrased the witness's remark in terms of the equitable doctrine that he and Justices Brennan and Blackmun employed. For the community, striking down the lay-off plan would reverse a "hard-won" benefit of voluntary integration of its educational program. Such a great gain outweighed the genuine loss sustained by the layoff of more senior teachers.[30]

The significance of Marshall's dissent was not lost on the other justices. Justice White was willing to balance the equities, as he had in *Swann* and *Bakke*, but he agreed with Justice Powell that layoffs were not the same as educational quotas. The harms to the third parties were greater, and the balance of equity shifted.[31] Justice Stevens filed his own dissent in *Wygant*, making the vote to strike down the lay-off provisions a five-to-four decision. He judged the public purpose—the integration of teaching bodies—to be so worthy, and the process by which it was reached—union negotiation—to be so admirable, that it outweighed the harm to the laid-off teachers. Indeed, their firing was not a racial stigma but a response to economic conditions affecting the region. Even without the prominority lay-off provision in the contract, nonminority teachers might have lost their jobs.[32]

In *Richmond v. Croson* Justice Marshall, joined in part by Justices Brennan and Blackmun, returned to the themes of his dissent in *Wygant*. One reads both irony and anger in his references to the majority's indifference to the history of Richmond, so long a breakwater against the tide of civil rights.[33] He found the economic injustices of race pervasive in the history of Richmond and thought the Court's hidden quota "a myopic view of the factual predicate on which the Richmond City Council relied when it passed the Minority Business Utilization Plan." The city had "before it a rich trove of evidence that discrimination in the nation's construction industry had seriously impaired the competitive position of businesses owned by minority groups." Marshall's use of history was exactly what Justice O'Connor condemned, for he could no more demonstrate the harm to minority business people than the city could in arguing its case. Nevertheless, for him the very paucity of minority businesses was part of the evidence for discrimination—how could the city show that minority businessmen in large numbers were denied contracts when there were so few minority owners of businesses? Such circular ironies are common in civil rights cases. Marshall saw a compelling state interest in "preventing the city's own spending decisions from reinforcing and perpetuating the exclusionary effects of past discrimination."[34]

All modern public-question equity is prospective as well as retrospective; it requires assessment of the future effects of decrees. Balance of Equity is as concerned with the continuing impact of the chancellor's discretion on parties as with redress for past wrongs. Justice Marshall spoke in these terms when he concluded that "the majority [of the Court] is wrong to trivialize the continuing impact of government acceptance or use of private institutions once wrought by discrimination." The effects of unjust enrichment went on, even when the discrimination that occasioned the unjust enrichment had disappeared. Marshall sensed that the Court had set its face against the equitable enforcement mechanisms of the second Reconstruction, and he decried "the daunting standard [the majority] imposes upon states and localities."[35]

Justice Blackmun wrote a short dissent, though he had signed on to Marshall's opinion. Justice Marshall, Blackmun opened, "convincingly discloses the fallacy and the shallowness of [the majority's] approach. History is irrefutable." Blackmun lacked Marshall's personal experience with civil rights litigation against Richmond and took a more optimistic position on the second redemption of the equal protection clause: "So the Court today regresses. I am confident, however, that, given time, it one day again will do its best to fulfill the great promises of the Constitution's Preamble and of the guarantees embodied in the Bill of Rights—a fulfillment that would make this Nation very special."[36] Blackmun's hopes exceeded his fears, but subsequent majority decisions suggest that he was not the best of prognosticators.[37]

Does Justice Blackmun nevertheless have history "on his side?" A historian ought not to attempt to answer such a question, but, insofar as this book has made sense of the interrelationship of equity and constitutional thought in our past, Blackmun should take some comfort from history. Equitable constitutionalism—an equitable reading of our fundamental law—has firm foundations in our past and our future.[38]

CONCLUSION

And the end of all our exploring
Will be to arrive where we started
And know the place for the first time.
—T. S. Eliot, "Little Gidding," *Four Quartets*

In John Barth's historical novel *The Sot-Weed Factor*, the characters discover that history has the eyes of a snake—it sees only motion. Every historian will concede a momentous and thoroughgoing transformation in American social, economic, and political structures over the course of three centuries, a transformation to which law and law courts made major contributions. To say we have come far from those first tiny settlements on the shore of an uncharted sea is not to dismiss the great sacrifices, voluntary and involuntary, of twenty generations of working people. For them the law and its ways were often incomprehensible and inhospitable. Despite the gradual opening of the courts to the suffering of the least powerful among us, the legal process remains a chancy aid at the best of times to private individuals damaged by other private individuals. The record in public law seems more appealing. The right to vote, hold office, obtain a decent education, engage in political speech, worship, and move about freely—personal liberties and civil rights—are protected more firmly against state-sponsored discrimination than ever before.

In the long sweep of legal and constitutional history, equity was a visible force. It resisted the best efforts of some to reduce it to a dull science. Compressed into maxims, it expanded into new domains. Cabined by law, it insisted on innovation. Chided by rule makers, it remained a still, silent voice of conscience. As an assistant to the law courts, equity allowed and often encouraged the pleas of the less powerful party. It forgave mistakes in form. It permitted a bigger piece of social reality to come before the court. It concerned itself with substantial justice. It found new remedies. As a theory of relief it infiltrated and conquered law, converted or made cautious its critics, and established itself at the center of the legal process. In our day, it has proven itself capable of engineering judicial intervention into the institutional roots of harms, patiently but persistently demanding good-faith compliance from all parties. Merged into common-law pleading, equity remains the conscience of the law.

As the bearer of a vision of a more just society, equity can claim a few shining moments. Chancellors did not make the world whole, whatever the Jeffersons, O'Nealls, Brennans, and Warrens may have wanted in their heart of hearts. Even trial judges as skilled in the tools of equity and as committed to an egalitarian society as Frank Johnson and J. Skelly Wright regarded equitable intervention as a last resort thrust upon them by the recalcitrance of defendants.

True, there were extended moments in our history when lawmakers and lawgivers read our state and federal constitutions in an equitable way, fusing trusteeship, equality, and reality. In the inception of our republican system, the first Reconstruction and second Reconstruction, chancellors and lawyers using the language of equity significantly broadened the area of human equality, making republican government a trusteeship for all its beneficiaries. These moments were times of ferment in the law when revolutionaries, radicals, and reformers were tearing down old systems of authority and erecting new ones, but such moments of equitable constitutionalism were uncommon. The vast majority of the business of courts of equity remains now what it was in the past: highly technical, minutely detailed, and devoted to the private lawsuit. In such causes, chancellors do not regard themselves as the inheritors of John Lilburne but of Lord Eldon.

When Eric Foner subtitled his prize-winning volume on Reconstruction *The Unfinished Revolution*, surely an appropriate caption for the deferred dream of millions of black people, he captured a central theme of all our history. Revolutions of expectation are always unfinished. The civil rights movement did not complete Charles Sumner's program any more than the Civil Rights Act of 1866 was fulfilled by the Civil Rights Act of 1964. The fact remains that equity did play an important role in fashioning an ideology of trusteeship. That ideology was sufficiently plastic to absorb and give cohesion to increasingly capacious visions of political and social equality. Only Voltaire's Dr. Pangloss would find the ideal of equal justice realized in our own day. As we have seen, the goal of full racial justice remains elusive. The ideal lives as a "becoming," an unfulfilled vision of justice. Such visions are the stuff of American idealism, always unfolding—much like equity itself.

A NOTE ON THE SOURCES

The sources for *The Law's Conscience* were drawn from manuscript collections, court records, and published materials. The latter include law "reporters" (reports of cases) and law review articles. Although most of the citations in this book follow the *The Chicago Manual of Style*, 13th ed. (Chicago: University of Chicago Press, 1982), with a few minor variations, the Chicago style does not handle specifically legal materials as well as does *A Uniform System of Citation*, 14th ed. (Cambridge, Mass.: The Harvard Law Review Association, 1986), familiarly known as the "Blue Book." I have elected to use Blue Book style for the citation of cases and law review articles, with a few minor variations. In particular, I have not used as many parenthetical phrases after the case citations as the Blue Book requires, and I have deviated from the recommended punctuation for titles of law reviews.

Citations of cases in the Blue Book have the following form: plaintiff v. defendant, volume number of reporter, reporter name or designation (for example, Pa. is Pennsylvania Supreme Court and U.S. is the United States Supreme Court Reports), first page number on which the case appears, page number(s) cited or quoted, date of the case in parentheses, and any additional clarifying information. Subsequent references to the case, if no confusion will ensue, take the short form: volume number, reporter, "at" page number. Blue Book citations of law review articles take the form: author, title of article, volume number of the law journal, title of the journal, first page on which the article appears, page number(s) of citations or quotations, date of the article in parentheses. In proper Blue Book style, the title of the article is italicized, the title of the journal is not. I have put the title of the article in quotation marks and italicized the title of the journal.

A list of short titles for frequently cited sources follows.

Bailyn, *Ideological Origins*	Bernard Bailyn. *The Ideological Origins of the American Revolution*. Cambridge, Mass., 1967.
Blackstone, *Commentaries*	William Blackstone. *Commentaries on the Laws of England*. 4 vols. Oxford, 1765–69.
Boyd, ed., *Papers of Jefferson*	Julian P. Boyd et al., eds. *The Papers of Thomas Jefferson*. 26 vols. Princeton, N.J., 1950–.

Burbank, "Rules Enabling
   Act of 1934"   Stephen B. Burbank. "The Rules Enabling
                                          Act of 1934." 130 *University of Pennsylvania
                                          Law Review* 1015 (1982).

Federalist   Clinton Rossiter, ed. *The Federalist Papers.*
                                          New York, 1961.

Fed. R. Civ. P.   Federal Rules of Civil Procedure.

Fiss, *Civil Rights Injunction*   Owen Fiss. *The Civil Rights Injunction.*
                                          Bloomington, Ind., 1978.

Foner, *Reconstruction*   Eric Foner. *Reconstruction: America's
                                          Unfinished Revolution, 1863–1877.* New
                                          York, 1987.

Frankfurter and Greene, *The Labor
Injunction*   Felix Frankfurter and Nathan Greene. *The
                                          Labor Injunction.* New York, 1930.

Friedman, *History of American Law*   Lawrence Friedman. *A History of American
                                          Law.* 2d ed. New York, 1985.

Hoffer and Hull,
   Impeachment in America   Peter Charles Hoffer and N. E. H. Hull.
                                          Impeachment in America, 1635–1805. New
                                          Haven, Conn., 1984.

Holdsworth, *HEL*   William Holdsworth. *A History of English
                                          Law.* 18 vols. London, 1903–63.

Horwitz, *Transformation*   Morton J. Horwitz. *The Transformation of
                                          American Law, 1780–1860.* Cambridge,
                                          Mass., 1977.

Kelly, Harbison, and Belz,
   The American Constitution   Alfred H. Kelly, Wilfred A. Harbison, and
                                          Herman Belz. *The American Constitution: Its
                                          Origins and Development.* 6th ed. New York,
                                          1983.

Kluger, *Simple Justice*   Richard Kluger. *Simple Justice: The History of
                                          Brown v. Board of Education and Black
                                          America's Struggle for Equality.* New York,
                                          1976.

Kurland and Casper, eds.,
   Landmark Briefs   Philip Kurland and Gerhard Casper, eds.
                                          *Landmark Briefs and Arguments on the
                                          Supreme Court of the United States.* Arlington,
                                          Va., 1975–.

LW   *The United States Law Week.* Supreme Court
                                          Opinions.

Maitland, *Equity and the Forms of Action* Frederic William Maitland. *Equity and the
                                          Forms of Action.* London, 1909.

Newmyer, *Story*   R. Kent Newmyer. *Supreme Court Justice
                                          Joseph Story: Statesman of the Old Republic.*
                                          Chapel Hill, N.C., 1984.

Schwartz, *Unpublished Opinions*

Bernard Schwartz. *The Unpublished Opinions of the Warren Court*. New York, 1985.

Story, *Equity Jurisprudence*

Joseph Story. *Commentaries on Equity Jurisprudence*. 2 vols. Boston, 1836.

Subrin, "How Equity Conquered Common Law"

Steven Subrin. "How Equity Conquered Common Law: The Federal Rules of Civil Procedure in Historical Perspective." 135 *University of Pennsylvania Law Review* 909 (1987).

Swindler, ed., *Sources and Documents*

William F. Swindler, ed. *Sources and Documents of United States Constitutions*. 11 vols. Dobbs Ferry, N.Y., 1972–81.

Tushnet, *NAACP's Legal Strategy*

Mark V. Tushnet. *The NAACP's Legal Strategy against Segregated Education, 1925–1950*. Chapel Hill, N.C., 1987.

U.S.C.

United States Code.

U.S. Stats

Statutes at Large of the United States. Washington, D.C., 1845–. Note that the volume number of the *Stats* precedes the citation and the page number follows it.

Wolter, *The Burden of Brown*

Raymond Wolter. *The Burden of Brown: Thirty Years of School Desegregation*. Knoxville, Tenn., 1984.

Yeazell, *Class Action*

Stephen C. Yeazell. *From Medieval Group Litigation to the Modern Class Action*. New Haven, Conn., 1987.

NOTES

PREFACE

1 For one striking example, see Alfred Kelly's reminiscences of his service to the NAACP during the assault on segregated elementary schools. Kelly, "An Inside View of *Brown v. Board of Education*," talk to the American Historical Association, December 28, 1961, reported in *U.S. News and World Report*, February 5, 1962. Kelly concluded that highly selective use of history in the service of a greater justice was acceptable law. He did not find it acceptable scholarship. See also Kelly, "Clio and the Court: An Illicit Love Affair," *Supreme Court Review* (1965): 119–58.

2 "Historians Carrying More Weight in Court," *New York Times*, Friday, November 10, 1989, B6, col. 3. "Expert witnessing" by historians hired by one side or the other has become very controversial after the conflicting testimony offered by scholars Alice Kessler-Harris and Rosalind Rosenberg in the Sears, Roebuck and Co. gender discrimination suit. EEOC v. Sears, Roebuck and Co., 628 F. Supp. 1264 (N.D. Ill. 1986), *aff'd*, 839 F.2d 302 (7th Cir. 1988). For the ensuing debate, see Thomas Haskell and Sanford Levinson, "Academic Freedom and Expert Witnessing: Historians and the Sears Case," 66 *Texas Law Review* 1629 (1988), and Alice Kessler-Harris, "Academic Freedom and Expert Witnessing: A Response to Haskell and Levinson," 67 *Texas Law Review* 429 (1988). Special masters appointed by the court itself may also be historians. They do not represent any of the parties. See Federal Rules of Civil Procedure, Rule 53. The court accepts the master's findings as fact in non-jury actions. Fed. R. Civ. P. 53(c)2.

3 Wilcomb Washburn, "History Reconsidered: The Supreme Court's Use and Abuse of History," *Organization of American Historians Newsletter*, August 1983, 7–9, argues that Court opinions in Indian cases were flawed by reliance on out-of-date, biased, and flawed historical sources. A more sustained critique of the Court's use of history is Charles A. Miller, *The Supreme Court and the Uses of History* (Cambridge, Mass., 1969).

4 For example, in "originalism" the purposes of the framers of a legal rule, be it constitutional or statutory, become one guide to its interpretation. See, e.g., Robert Bork, "Neutral Principles and Some First Amendment Problems," 47 *Indiana Law Journal* 1 (1971); "The Impossibility of Finding Welfare Rights in the Constitution," 3 *Washington University Law Quarterly* 695 (1979); and a more moderate version of the doctrine in "The Constitution, Original Intent, and Economic Rights," 23 *San Diego Law Review* 823 (1986), allowing latitude for

interpretation of the broader purposes of the framers in economic questions—
e.g., a corporation's rights—than in social questions. Of course, history can be
used to attack the legitimacy of the doctrine of original intent; see Leonard W.
Levy, *Original Intent and the Framers' Constitution* (New York, 1988), 1–29.

5 E.g., see note 11 in Duncan v. Louisiana, 391 U.S. 145 (1973), arguing that
fundamental fairness, not strict precedent—i.e., a historical rule—governs extension of the Fifth and Sixth amendments to the states.

6 163 U.S. 537 (1896), stating that separate but equal facilities in interstate train
accommodations do not violate the Fourteenth Amendment to the U.S. Constitution.

7 347 U.S. 483 (1954), concluding that state-sponsored racial segregation of elementary schools is a violation of the Fourteenth Amendment guarantee of
equal protection of the law. Even *Brown* on its face did not overturn all of
Plessy, merely that portion of it that might have applied to education, yet the
Court knew where *Brown* would lead.

8 I have not fully identified the reefs upon which modern legal history may
founder. Others are nostalgia, antiquarianism dressed up as scholarship; mind-
less narration, reveling in unimportant details; teleological thinking, mapping
the deep structures of the historical terrain and ignoring human decisions,
failings, and wants; and old-fashioned "scientific" history, measuring each statute, case, and brief in terms of an underlying determinism. One answer may
be Peter Novick's assertion that "I don't think that the idea of historical objectivity is true or false, right or wrong: I find it not just essentially contested, but
essentially confused." Novick, *That Noble Dream: The "Objectivity Question" and
the American Historical Profession* (Cambridge, Mass., 1988), 6. Perhaps "fair-
mindedness" is all that any historian ought to ask of himself or herself.

9 Schwartz, *Unpublished Opinions*, 448, citing Warren's Memo to the Conference,
May 7, 1954, in Tom Clark Papers, University of Texas Law Library.

PROLOGUE

1 The Reconstruction amendments are the Thirteenth Amendment, abolishing
slavery or involuntary servitude except on conviction for a crime (1865); the
Fourteenth, declaring that all citizens of the United States are citizens of the
states in which they reside and that no citizen of the United States shall be
deprived of the privileges and immunities of such citizenship by any of the
states, nor may the states deny any person due process or equal protection of
the laws (1868); and the Fifteenth, stating that the right to vote shall not be
denied or abridged by the United States or any state on account of race (1870).

2 For a description of the events of that day in court and of the cases joined
under the leading citation of *Brown v. Board of Education of Topeka*, see Kluger,
Simple Justice, esp. 700–747.

3 347 U.S. 483, 491–92 (1954). After the first hearing of the suit in December
1952, Justice Felix Frankfurter asked his clerk, Alexander Bickel, to research
the history of the amendment with specific reference to education. Felix
Frankfurter Papers, box 72, Harvard Law School Library. Frankfurter circulated drafts of Bickel's massive effort in the Court and Bickel later published
the final version of the draft with his own comments on it in "The Original
Understanding and the Segregation Decision," 69 *Harvard Law Review* 1
(1955).

4 347 U.S. at 494. Later scholarship has singled out Professor Kenneth Clark's
research into the self-images of white and black schoolchildren. See Kluger,

Simple Justice, 315–45. The Court did not rely on these experiments or any other laboratory investigations. The footnotes, so vulnerable to critics' attacks on the decision, were not part of Chief Justice Warren's draft opinion for the Court. They were added (as was becoming customary in his chambers) by his clerks. See Schwartz, *Unpublished Opinions*, 449. While not window dressing, these supportive references were merely illustrative. Nevertheless, even so thoughtful a critique of the Court as Wolter's *The Burden of Brown*, 38, continues the attack on the Court's "sociological jurisprudence." A more neutral example of the same assumption appears in Herbert Hovenkamp, "Social Science and Segregation Before *Brown*," 1985 *Duke Law Journal* 624, 664.

5 This requirement is mandated in the U.S. Constitution, Art. III, sec. 2. Advisory opinions are not permitted.

6 On the practicality of the thinking of the LDF, see Tushnet, *NAACP's Legal Strategy*, 138–66.

7 The plea for declaratory relief appeared in the first complaint filed in the First District of Kansas Federal Court. See *Brown v. Board of Education* [1952], "Complaint" Plea for Relief, Legal File, 1940–55, NAACP Papers, box 138, Library of Congress. The plea followed the suit to the Supreme Court. *Brown v. Board of Education*, Brief for the Appellant on Reargument, October term 1953, in Kurland and Casper, eds., *Landmark Briefs*, 49:703–4.

8 According to the Declaratory Judgment Act of 1934, now part of the federal code, 28 *U.S.C.* 2201.

9 349 U.S. 294, 297 (1955).

10 Briggs v. Elliott (South Carolina); Davis v. County School Board of Prince Edward County (Virginia); Bolling v. Sharpe (Washington, D.C.); Gebhart v. Belton (Delaware). The first two, with *Brown*, had been decided against plaintiffs in district federal courts on the basis of *Plessy*. The third, in the District of Columbia, was joined to the others by suggestion of the chief justice. The fourth was determined by the Delaware Court of Chancery for the petitioners and upheld by the state supreme court. The school board appealed. Arguments by the appellants against segregation appear in Kurland and Casper, eds., *Landmark Briefs*, 49:36 et seq. Ultimately, *Bolling* was decided separately, under the Fifth rather than the Fourteenth Amendment, because the District of Columbia is not a state and therefore is not affected by the Fourteenth Amendment. The decision in *Bolling* came down the same day as *Brown*. See Bolling v. Sharpe, 347 U.S. 497 (1954).

11 Charles Black, Jr., *Decision According to Law* (New York, 1981), 12–13.

12 Ibid., 14–15; On Black, see Kluger, *Simple Justice*, 644–45.

13 Orlando Patterson, *Slavery and Social Death* (Cambridge, Mass., 1982), 6ff.

14 Numan V. Bartley, *The Rise of Massive Resistance: Race and Politics in the South during the 1950s* (Baton Rouge, La., 1969).

15 See, e.g., Charles Fairman, "The Attack on the Segregation Cases," 70 *Harvard Law Review* 83 (1955), and Paul Freund, "Storm over the American Supreme Court," 21 *Modern Law Review* 344 (1958). George Wharton Pepper, president of the American Law Institute, organized professional support for the Court: a carefully orchestrated and worded petition signed by one hundred leading lawyers. See Pepper to the signatories, October 23, 1956, George Wharton Pepper Papers, box 63, University of Pennsylvania Archives.

16 Two decades and more after *Brown* that criticism goes on, though its voice is increasingly muted. See, e.g., Lino Graglia, *Disaster by Decree* (Ithaca, N.Y., 1976), Richard E. Morgan, *Disabling America* (New York, 1984), and Christopher Wolfe, *The Rise of Modern Judicial Review from Constitutional Interpretation to*

Judge-Made Law (New York, 1986), all of which find that the Court violated the traditional proscription on judicial lawmaking. The critics are right to this extent: common-law courts traditionally denied that they were making law; they merely "discovered" it. Common law, of course, *is* judge-made law; the modern imposition of so much statutory regulation threatens to shove judges away from their traditional role as lawmakers, and the judges have replied by interpreting the statutes. See Guido Calabresi, *A Common Law for the Age of Statutes* (Cambridge, Mass., 1982), and Melvin Aaron Eisenberg, *The Nature of the Common Law* (Cambridge, Mass., 1988).

17   Fed. R. Civ. P. 52(a); Federal Rules of Appellate Practice 12 (filing record), 28 and 31 (briefs), and 30 (certification of the original record). If further factual determinations are needed for the appellate court to reach its decision, they are made by remanding the case to the trial court below. See 28 *U.S.C.* sec. 2106. Before the adoption of the Federal Rules of Civil Procedure (1938) amalgamating equity and common-law pleading, the Court heard all equity suits under the traditional regime of equity—that is, they could seek additional factual findings. Common-law appeals were heard on the record created in the trial court. After 1938 this distinction was supposedly abolished in favor of the common-law rule, but not everyone on the high court finds this to be so. See Wygant v. Jackson Board of Education, 476 U.S. 267, 278 n. 5 (Powell, J., criticizing the introduction of new evidence at the appellate level).

18   See Fiss, *The Civil Rights Injunction*, 5ff., and Tushnet, *NAACP's Legal Strategy*, 105–37.

19   The "trilogy" of Sipuel v. Oklahoma State Regents, 332 U.S. 631 (1948), McLaurin v. Oklahoma State Regents, 339 U.S. 637 (1950), and Sweatt v. Painter, 339 U.S. 629 (1950), all involved suits by black professional students against state universities. All ended with the Court ordering placement of the plaintiff in regular classes. The impact of these on graduate education is discussed in Dennis J. Hutchinson, "Unanimity and Desegregation: Decisionmaking in the Supreme Court, 1948–1958," 68 *Georgetown Law Journal* 1 (1979).

20   Brown v. Board of Education, 347 U.S. 492, 495 (1954), repeated the lower federal courts' certification of the cases as class actions. The class-action relief is available not only to the named plaintiff who brings the suit, but also to all "similarly situated" whom the named plaintiff represents in the court. Fed. R. Civ. P. 23 guides the formation of such a class. In 1954, the rule was fairly simple: If the members of a class were "so numerous as to make it impracticable to bring them all before the court," one of them "as will fairly insure the adequate representation of all" could sue on behalf of all. The object of the suit had to be "joint or common" to the class; the class had to seek a common remedy; and a common question of law or fact was to be involved. Fed. R. Civ. P. 23. The current formulation of the rule is more complex. If the court finds that the named plaintiff adequately represents the class, that is, that the issues pleaded by the former are common, typical, and will be fully pressed by the named plaintiff, and that others "similarly situated" are too numerous or otherwise unable to present themselves to the court, the judge may certify the class. In addition, the class must fit one of the 23(b) classifications to be certified: the common issue outweighs individual class members' differences; the members of the class are being distinguished and differentially treated by the defendants; or potential members of the class would lose their rights if they were not included. Fed. R. Civ. P. 23 (as amended, 1966).

21   I have relied on Hutchinson, "Unanimity," Bernard Schwartz, *Super Chief* (New York, 1983), 78–124, and Kluger, *Simple Justice*, for these conclusions, but Frankfurter spoke them clearly in the oral examination of counsel in *Briggs* on

December 9, 1952: "I think that nothing would be worse for this court—I am expressing my own opinion . . . than for this court to make an abstract declaration that segregation is bad and then have it evaded by tricks." Kurland and Casper, eds., *Landmark Briefs*, 49:321.

22   See, e.g., Giles v. Harris, 189 U.S. 475 (1903). Deliberation within chambers of both the Vinson Court and the Warren Court dwelt on the prospect of disobedience to any sweeping desegregation decree. See Hutchinson, "Unanimity," 37ff. The problem of compliance played into the consensus on the Court that unanimity was necessary. Kluger, *Simple Justice*, 543ff. The Supreme Court is still chary of ordering injunctive relief when that relief "would be so intrusive and unworkable." O'Shea v. Littleton, 414 U.S. 488 (1974).

23   It did cause him to give great weight to the suggestions of two members of the Court more versed in the mechanics of equity than he: Justices Frankfurter and William O. Douglas. It was the former who suggested the phrase "all deliberate speed" for the implementation guidelines and the latter who lobbied for decertifying the class action in *Brown* II. See the discussion in Chapter 7 on the two opinions in *Brown*.

24   Earl Warren, *A Republic, If You Can Keep It* (New York, 1972), 6, 52–53. It can also be argued that, from his first moments on the bench, Warren acted the role of chancellor in a very old-fashioned way—reminiscent of the premodern English chancellors discussed in Chapter 2. He did not stop with the traditional rationale for equity, that it was limited to particular cases of injustice. Systematic injustice, perpetuated by institutions whose purpose was illegal under the most principled reading of the Constitution, could not hide from such a chancellor under a cloak of local self-determination, behind a barrier of federalism, or in a fortress of precedent. See G. Edward White, *Earl Warren: A Public Life* (New York, 1982), 369. Schwartz, *Super Chief*, 171, does not find full deployment of Warren's expansive, socially egalitarian vision of equity until 1956.

25   Warren, "memorandum" in Schwartz, *Unpublished Opinions*, 454–55.

26   349 U.S. at 300. While the justices deliberated, law professors also pondered the question of remedy. On July 24, 1953, Frank Maloney, a University of Florida law professor and that year's chairman of the Association of American Law Schools' (AALS) roundtable discussion on equity, asked the dean emeritus of Harvard Law School, Roscoe Pound, if he would join in a discussion of "equity's role in the protection of civil rights." Maloney to Pound, Roscoe Pound Papers, box 127, folder 9, Harvard Law School Library. Pound had been a leading light on equity practice in America for a half century, but there is no evidence that he replied to Maloney's solicitation. At the December 1953 meeting of the AALS, the roundtable discussed injunctions against additions to buildings in violation of building codes and the utility of decrees against out-of-state defendants. *Handbook of the AALS* (Chicago, 1953), 193. Evidently, the professors had decided to let the justices lead the way on this occasion.

CHAPTER ONE

1   Aristotle, *Nichomachean Ethics*, ed. H. Rackham (Cambridge, Mass., 1934), 313–17.

2   Some modern American jurisprudents regard the Aristotelian formulation as the starting point for a treatment of "wrong results." When a law or rule produces a result in a particular case either at odds with the reasons behind the rule (a weak version of intentionality) or with the way in which the rule makers would have applied the rule to the case had they thought of it (a strong

intentionality), equity corrects the error. Such an equity is wholly particular, applying only to individual cases by reference to original intentions, and therefore is fully constrained by conventions of statutory construction. It cannot wander into the forest of new remedies. It is not communal or redistributive. On the literature of wrong results, see Frederick Shaver, "Book Review," 87 *Michigan Law Review* 847 (1987).

3   Of course, Aristotle is not precedent in American courts, but his formulation of equitable justice remains a persuasive reminder that settled law, merely because it is law, does not fully discharge the courts' duty to do justice. See, e.g., Simonds v. Simonds, 45 N.Y.2d 233 (Ct. of App. 1978), in which Chief Justice Charles Breitel cited Aristotle to explain why a divorcée was equitably entitled to the property her deceased husband promised her even though he had remarried and left his first wife out of the new will in favor of his second wife.

4   Cicero, *De Officiis*, ed. Harry G. Edinger (Indianapolis, 1974), 152–53; Peter Stein, *The Character and Influence of the Roman Law* (London, 1988), 19–36.

5   See H. F. Jolowicz, *Historical Introduction to the Study of Roman Law* (Cambridge, 1952), 423, 520.

6   Cicero, *De Officiis*, 153.

7   Walter Ullmann, *The Medieval Idea of Law, as Represented by Lucas de Penna: A Study in Fourteenth-Century Legal Scholarship* (New York, 1946), 185.

8   Hugo Grotius, *De Jure Belli ac Pacis*, book 2, chaps. 12–16.

9   Christopher St. German, *St. German's Doctor and Student*, ed. T. F. T. Plucknett and J. L. Barton, Selden Society Proceedings (London, 1974), 91:95–97, 117.

10 Edward Hake, *Epieikeia*, ed. D. E. C. Yale (New Haven, Conn., 1953), 10.

11 Henry Home, Lord Kames, *Principles of Equity*, 4th ed. (Edinburgh, 1800), 5.

12 Roscoe Pound has demonstrated that Francis took many shortcuts to pull together his list of maxims. Some of his rules were not even well established when he wrote. "On Certain Maxims of Equity," in *Cambridge Legal Essays in Honor of Bond, Buckland, and Kenney* (Cambridge, Mass., 1926), 267 et seq. On the use and force of "maxims," see Peter Stein, *Regulae Juris: From Juristic Rules to Legal Maxims* (Edinburgh, 1966).

13 Richard Francis, *Maxims of Equity* (London, 1726), iii–iv.

14 Blackstone, *Commentaries*, 1:59. Blackstone was not a neutral, objective reporter. He wished to curb courts of equity. His successor as Vinerian Professor at Oxford, Robert Chambers, respectfully and subtly opined that the chancellor was not so constrained as Blackstone had insisted. See Chambers, *A Course of Lectures on the English Law, 1767–1773*, ed. Thomas M. Curley (Madison, Wis., 1986), 2:232–33, 241, 243.

15 Maitland, *Equity and the Forms of Action*, 3–19. Maitland did not believe that there was, by nature, any separate subject matter or approach that could be called equitable.

16 Story, *Equity Jurisprudence*, 1:8–19.

17 See, e.g., Gary McDowell, *Equity and the Constitution* (Chicago, 1982), and, more recently, Wolter, *The Burden of Brown*.

18 In 1791, Chief Justice John Jay made this decision. 5 U.S. (1 Cranch) xvii (Rules of Court) (1801), *aff'd*, Robinson v. Campbell, 16 U.S. (3 Wheaton) 212, 222–23 (1818).

19 Fed. R. Civ. P. 26.

20 Fed. R. Civ. P. 18–23. *In re* Agent Orange Products Liability Litigation, 597 F. Supp. 740 (E.D. N.Y. 1984), is discussed in "Mass Torts after Agent Orange," 52 *Brooklyn Law Review* 329 (1986). The chancellor's early jurisdiction in suits with multiple parties grew out of a corporate, communal society. See Yeazell,

Class Action, 122–23, 154. Did all the parties have to deal directly with each other ("privity")? See Robert Bone, "Mapping the Boundaries of a Dispute: Conceptions of Ideal Lawsuit Structure from the Field Code to the Federal Rules," 89 *Columbia Law Review* 1011, 1029 et seq. (1989).

21 On injunctions, see Douglas Rundleman and Owen Fiss, *Injunctions*, 3d ed. (Mineola, N.Y., 1985).

22 Fed. R. Civ. P. 53 (masters) and 66 (receivers).

23 The process of incorporation was not entirely smooth. Scholarly authors of treatises on equity disputed the boundary between law and equity throughout the last century.

24 The essence of the equitable rule is that those who have benefited must make restitution. In practice, this results in an accounting of the defendant's profits and an apportionment of those profits with the plaintiff. See Sheldon v. Metro-Goldwyn Pictures Corp., 309 U.S. 390 (1939). The American Law Institute's *Restatement of Restitution* (Philadelphia, 1937) remains the foremost scholarly examination of this equitable principle.

25 See, e.g., Zechariah Chafee, "Does Equity Follow the Law of Torts?" 75 *University of Pennsylvania Law Review* 1 (1926).

26 See Beatty v. Guggenheim Exploration Company, 225 N.Y. 380, 386 (1919), wherein Chief Justice Benjamin Cardozo explained that the agent of a mining conglomerate who turns on-the-job explorations to personal gain will be made a constructive trustee by the court, with the employer as beneficiary.

27 Jack B. Weinstein, "Justice and Mercy—Law and Equity," 27 *New York Law School Law Review* 817, 819 (1984).

28 The restrictions on the traditional role of the judge as here presented are exaggerated, but for a summary see Abram Chayes, "The Role of the Judge in Public-Law Litigation," 89 *Harvard Law Review* 1281 (1976), and Owen Fiss, "The Forms of Justice," 91 *Harvard Law Review* 1 (1978). Throughout the history of Anglo-American law there have been common-law judges who extended, interpreted, and remade law to fit a particular case which, according to contemporary rules, could have been decided some other way. The common law itself is a monument to judge-made law. After Judge Oliver Wendell Holmes, Jr.'s celebrated article, "The Path of the Law," 10 *Harvard Law Review* 457 (1897), and New York Chief Justice Benjamin Cardozo's seminal essay, *The Nature of the Judicial Process* (New Haven, Conn., 1921), let the cat out of the bag, it has been almost impossible for jurists to argue that judges merely discover and apply law. See, e.g., Frank Coffin, *The Ways of a Judge* (Boston, 1980), 195–96, arguing that the great judge is a craftsman.

29 "According to orthodox ideology, the Supreme Court's function in the constitutional process is essentially noncreative." That is, courts do not change the Constitution but merely apply it. Jeffrey M. Shaman, "The Constitution, the Supreme Court, and Creativity," 9 *Hastings Constitutional Law Quarterly* 257 (1982). Shaman does not subscribe to this view. A similar thesis is emphasized in Lawrence Tribe, *Constitutional Choices* (Cambridge, Mass., 1986). I have overdrawn the distinction between fairness in law and fairness in equity to emphasize the potential of the latter. For a corrective, see Richard H. Helmholz, "Damages in Actions for Slander at Common Law," 103 *Law Quarterly Review* 624 (1987), arguing that judges in early modern English courts could instruct the jury concerning damage awards in slander suits or, in the alternative, reduce the awards with a *remittitur*. The practice ended by 1622, but under it judges exercised a discretion similar to chancellors' in the interest of fairness to all parties.

30 John Selden, *Table Talk of John Selden*, ed. Frederick Pollock (London, 1927),

43. Shortly before he uttered his famous rebuke of the chancellor's jurisprudence, Selden had faced the wrath of James I. See David Sandler Berkowitz,
*John Selden's Formative Years: Politics and Society in Early Seventeenth-Century En-
gland* (Washington, D.C., 1988), 57–67.

31   Blackstone, *Commentaries*, 3:432.

32   Gee v. Pritchard, 2 Swans 413, 36 Eng. Rep. 674 (1818). Lord Eldon's footnote
at the end of the passage cited Selden. 36 Eng. Rep. at 679.

33   Raymond B. Marcin, "Epieikeia: Equitable Lawmaking in the Construction of
Statutes," 10 *Connecticut Law Review* 377, 388 (1978), reminds us that equitable
construction of statutes is inevitable and worthwhile.

34   Henry M. Hart, Jr., and Albert M. Sacks, *The Legal Process: Basic Problems in the
Making and Application of Law*, tentative ed. (Cambridge, Mass., 1958), chap. 7:
"The Role of the Courts in the Interpretation of Statutes"; Guido Calabresi, *A
Common Law for the Age of Statutes* (Cambridge, Mass., 1982).

35   See Owen Fiss, "Objectivity and Interpretation," 34 *Stanford Law Review* 739,
744 (1982), for a brilliant survey of these restraints, which concludes with a
plea for their flexibility.

36   Thomas C. Grey, "Langdell's Orthodoxy," 45 *University of Pittsburgh Law Review*
1 (1983).

37   G. Edward White, "From Sociological Jurisprudence to Legal Realism," 58 *Virginia Law Review* 999 (1972); N. E. H. Hull, "Some Realism about the Llewel-
lyn-Pound Exchange over Realism: The Newly Uncovered Private Correspondence, 1927–1931," 1987 *Wisconsin Law Review* 921.

38   See, e.g., Charles Wyzanski, *A Trial Judge's Freedom and Responsibility* (New York,
1952).

39   Subrin, "How Equity Conquered Common Law"; Burbank, "Rules Enabling
Act of 1934," 1195; Judith Resnik, "Managerial Judges," 96 *Harvard Law Review* 376 (1982), and "Failing Faith: Adjudicatory Procedure in Decline," 53
Chicago Law Review 494 (1986); but see, for a rebuttal, Steven Flanders, "Blind
Umpires—A Response to Professor Resnik," 35 *Hastings Law Journal* 505
(1984). An objection to overbroad joinder appears in Lon L. Fuller, "The
Forms and Limits of Adjudication," 92 *Harvard Law Review* 353 (1978). Fuller
adhered to a "Rule-of-Law" approach to adjudication: limit discretion, expand
rules. See also Theodore Lowi, *The End of Liberalism*, 2d ed. (New York, 1979).

40   Raoul Berger, *Government by Judiciary* (Cambridge, Mass., 1977), 23 et seq.;
Herbert Wechsler, "Neutral Principles," 73 *Harvard Law Review* 1 (1959); Robert Bork, *The Tempting of America: The Political Seduction of the Law* (New York,
1989); Gary L. McDowell, *Curbing the Courts: The Constitution and the Limits of
Judicial Power* (Baton Rouge, La., 1988).

41   See, e.g., Frankfurter and Greene, *The Labor Injunction*.

42   Giles v. Harris, 189 U.S. 475 (1903). Holmes refused to admit as much, however, and engaged in a perverse subterfuge: if the system was corrupt, then
the petitioner could not seek the aid of the chancellor in participating (i.e.,
voting) in it.

43   For example, in the nuisance case, if his intervention was not necessary to
prevent irreparable harm the chancellor would wait for proof of real harm.
The chancellor always had a principled reason for refusal to intervene, however. He could not cite an unrestrained discretion to refuse aid. See the discussion in Chapter 6.

44   J. G. A. Pocock, "The State of the Art," in Pocock, *Virtue, Commerce, and History*
(Cambridge, 1985), 14–17. Pocock's is a theoretical model about the function
of texts, how they are passed from user to user, how they are transformed in
the minds of listeners and future users, and how they pass from one genera-

tion to another. A splendid application of this theory, independently formulated, to the language of the law is Alan Watson's *Failures of the Legal Imagination* (Philadelphia, 1988), 20. Courts are aware of this cross-fertilization of ideal and technique, of internal and external stimuli. See, e.g., Cuyahoga County, Ohio v. United States, 294 F.2d 775, 781 (Ct. Cl. 1961), ruling that the U.S. government was equitably bound to reimburse a county for lost real estate taxes when the federal government took land from a private owner.

45   "A discourse carried on predominantly in verbal form among disputants who were essentially peers, who were cognizant of each other's views, and who shared both a language and what we would loosely call . . . a national culture." David A. Hollinger, "Historians and the Discourse of Intellectuals," in Hollinger, *In the American Province: Studies in the History and Historiography of Ideas*, 2d ed. (Baltimore, 1985), 137. Hollinger's marvelous essay, first published in 1979, does not mention jurists or lawyers, but their "discourse" surely fits his definition.

PART ONE

1   Such a moment may last for an entire generation in historical time. I have borrowed the metaphor from J. G. A. Pocock, *The Machiavellian Moment: Florentine Political Thought and the Atlantic Republican Tradition* (Princeton, N.J., 1975), viii.

CHAPTER TWO

1   The petition to the Crown for redress of grievance is as close to a natural phenomenon of political life as human affairs ever have demonstrated. Every civilization for which we have written records left evidence of such petitions.

2   Bertie Wilkinson, "The Chancery," in *The English Government at Work, 1327–1336*, vol. 1: *Central and Prerogative Administration*, ed. William A. Morris (1940), 189–95. Wilkinson believes that the separate court of equity emerged only late in the fourteenth century. S. F. C. Milsom, *The Historical Foundations of the Common Law*, 2d ed. (London, 1981), 82–88, makes a similar point, as does J. H. Baker, *An Introduction to English Legal History*, 2d ed. (London, 1979), 87.

3   That is, the petition came into the Council as well as to the king or arose out of some action of the Council. The chancellor was also the source of writs necessary to begin any action in the king's own courts. See James F. Baldwin, *The King's Council in England during the Middle Ages* (Oxford, 1913), 241; Holdsworth, *HEL*, 1:457ff. The copyhold was a customary tenure, proof of which lay in the records of the manor. In effect, the freeman holding tenure by a copyright was asking the chancellor to force the lord of the manor to provide an account of the tenure. The issues were more complicated than this summary, but chancellors willingly disentangled them on behalf of petitioners. See Charles M. Grey, *Copyhold, Equity, and the Common Law* (Cambridge, Mass., 1963), 14–36. The medieval "use" was a device to avoid royal fees by giving legal title of land or goods to another with interest or other fruits to be returned to one's own use. The use also contained instructions that the recipient was to continue the arrangement for the benefit of anyone the donor might name. The most common example would be the beneficiary of the donor's will. Holdsworth, *HEL*, 4:460–67; Baker, *Introduction*, 210–19.

4   Milsom, *Foundations*, 85.

5   Holdsworth, *HEL*, 4:279–83; Charles Grey, "The Boundaries of the Equitable Function," *American Journal of Legal History* 20 (1976): 192–226.

6   Christopher St. German, *St. German's Doctor and Student*, ed. T. F. T. Plucknett and J. L. Barton, Selden Society Proceedings (London, 1974), 91:48–49.

7   Holdsworth, *HEL*, 1:470, finds that internecine judicial rivalries extended from the middle of the sixteenth century through the middle of the seventeenth. Grey, "Boundaries," finds that a more generous spirit marked relations, though there were moments of real contention.

8   Holdsworth, *HEL*, 5:222. Wolsey aided petitioners in their efforts to obtain information on their deeds. See Edith G. Henderson, "Legal Rights to Land in Early Chancery," *American Journal of Legal History* 26 (1982): 102–3. On Wolsey, see Jasper Ridley, *The Statesman and the Fanatic: Thomas Wolsey and Thomas More* (London, 1982), 250; Charles W. Ferguson, *Naked to Mine Enemies: The Life of Cardinal Wolsey* (Boston, 1958), 150; and J. A. Guy, *The Cardinal's Court: The Impact of Thomas Wolsey in Star Chamber* (Hassocks, Eng., 1977), 130–31.

9   Richard Marius, *Thomas More: A Biography* (New York, 1985), 377; Holdsworth, *HEL*, 5:223.

10 J. R. Tanner, *Tudor Constitutional Documents, A.D. 1485–1603* (Cambridge, 1940), 301–2; I. S. Leadam, *Select Cases in the Court of Requests, A.D. 1496–1569* (London, 1898), xx. The Court of Requests was a "court of conscience" and thus drew upon the same springs for its jurisprudence as the chancellor's court.

11 W. H. Bryson, *The Equity Side of the Exchequer: Its Jurisdiction, Administration, Procedures, and Records* (Cambridge, 1975), 9–32.

12 See, e.g., G. R. Elton, *Studies in Tudor and Stuart Politics and Government* (Cambridge, 1973), 120–21. The extent of the Tudors' use of decrees and other executive instruments to rule is a matter of some controversy. The influence of the king and his Council on the jurisdiction of the courts cannot be doubted.

13 C. W. Brooks, *Pettifoggers and Vipers of the Commonwealth: The "Lower Branch" of the Legal Profession in Early Modern England* (Cambridge, 1986), 54–55; Louis Knafla, *Law and Politics in Jacobean England: The Tracts of Lord Chancellor Ellesmere* (Cambridge, 1977), 163; W. J. Jones, *The Elizabethan Court of Chancery* (Oxford, 1967), 16–17.

14 The attack on chancery is discussed in Donald Veall, *The Popular Movement for Law Reform, 1640–1660* (Oxford, 1970), 34 et seq.; Stuart E. Prall, *The Agitation for Law Reform during the Puritan Revolution, 1640–1660* (The Hague, 1966), 28 et seq.; Austin Woolrych, *Commonwealth to Protectorate* (Oxford, 1982), 264 et seq.; and Nancy L. Matthews, *William Sheppard: Cromwell's Law Reformer* (Cambridge, 1984), 110 et seq. Both the rump parliament and the bare bones parliament had before them bills to abolish or reform the central equity court. Under Oliver Cromwell, the Lord Protector, William Sheppard, a superb legal innovator, fashioned an ordinance to merge equity and legal pleading, anticipating the merger that actually took place in 1873 in England. He failed to get the assent of Parliament in 1657, despite the support of Cromwell. Resistance seems to have come from the bar itself, although the politics of the last years of the Protectorate were so complex that any sweeping reform had little chance of success. To the political obstacles to reform, internal disagreement among members of the various committees charged by Parliament with reforming chancery added more confusion. Some wanted an end to equity jurisdiction altogether. Others wanted the very ends that Ellesmere had set out to produce: an efficient and expeditious court. There is no question that the commissioners of the seal, later the Lords Commissioners, acted as a court of equity. See, e.g., *Pye v. Milton* (1646) in J. Milton French, *Milton in Chancery* (New York, 1939), 297–301.

15 The work of Lord Chancellor Nottingham is discussed fully in the two vol-

umes of D. E. C. Yale, ed., *Lord Nottingham's Chancery Cases* (London, 1957–61).

16 Baker, *Introduction*, 94. But see Roscoe Pound, "The Progress of the Law, 1918–1919—Equity," 33 *Harvard Law Review* 929, 941–43 (1920), arguing that eighteenth-century chancellors found ways to avoid the Statute of Frauds and statutes of limitations when these did injustice in particular cases. H. G. Hanbury, "Field of Modern Equity," 45 *Law Quarterly Review* 196, 203–7 (1929), also insisted that conscience remained the root of English equity in the eighteenth century. It is still alive and well, for example, in the thinking of Lord Denning, former master of the rolls and judge of the court of appeals. See Alfred Thompson, Lord Denning, *The Discipline of Law* (London, 1979), 51, citing his own opinion in Appleton v. Appleton, 1 WLR 25 (1965), and Denning, *The Due Process of Law* (London, 1980), 245. On the similarities between Denning and Nottingham, see George W. Keeton, *English Law: The Judicial Contribution* (Newton Abbot, Devon, Eng., 1974), 114–21.

17 The Supreme Court of Judicature Act, 36 and 37 Vict. c. 66 (1873), and the Supreme Court of Judicature Act, 38 and 39 Vict. c. 77 (1875), first merged pleading in the courts and then abolished the separate court of chancery, replacing it and the other old royal courts with a single court of appeals. The acts were the cumulative expression of a series of nineteenth-century reforms allowing the common-law courts certain powers once reserved to chancery (e.g., injunctions) and abolishing many of the dilatory and corrupting features of chancery (e.g., the fee system). These were the official answer to complaints against chancery like those in Dickens's *Bleak House*. See William Holdsworth, *Charles Dickens as a Legal Historian* (New Haven, Conn., 1928), 114–15.

18 The point is that the chancellor protected the rights of the beneficiary, not the trustee, because in good conscience the trustee had agreed to hold and use the land for the beneficiary. If the trustee wasted the estate, appropriated it, or neglected it, he was not acting in good faith. By 1400 the chancellor was fully engaged in protecting this new form of property. Margaret G. Avery, "The History of the Equity Jurisdiction of Chancery before 1460," *Bulletin of the Institute of Historical Research* 42 (1969): 132; Maitland, *Equity and the Forms of Action*, 30–31.

19 Milsom, *Historical Foundations*, 87. Holdsworth, *HEL*, 4:460–67, 5:304–6. It has been argued that the chancellor assumed jurisdiction over the use jointly with the church's own courts, the latter bowing out after 1465. See Richard H. Helmholz, "Early Enforcement of Uses," 79 *Columbia Law Review*, 1503, 1511 (1979), and Stephen W. DeVine, "Ecclesiastical Antecedents to Secular Jurisdiction over the Feoffment to the Uses to Be Declared in Testamentary Instructions," *American Journal of Legal History* 39 (1986): 295–96. This dating is questioned in J. A. Guy, "The Development of Equitable Jurisdictions, 1450–1550," in E. W. Ives and A. H. Manchester, eds., *Law, Litigants, and the Legal Profession* (London, 1983), 81–84.

20 The chancellor allowed testators to keep their estates intact, despite the law against "perpetuities," by making executors into trustees. The common-law judges were better disposed to the easy sale of property by inheritors. "The [trust's] main innovation was creating the remainder in favor of trustees during the life tenant's life rather [than] creating it directly in favor of the intended beneficiary." Gregory S. Alexander, "The Transformation of Trusts as a Legal Category, 1800–1914," *Law and History Review* 5 (1985): 319.

21 Yale, ed., *Nottingham's Cases*, 2:100.

22 See, e.g., Dyer v. Dyer, 2 Cox 91 (1788).

23 The constructive trustee was not ordered to manage the assets for the beneficiary, merely to give account and restore what he owed. The first case of this

type is Holt v. Holt, 1 Ch. Cas. 190, 22 Eng. Rep. 756 (1670), wherein the keeper of the rolls enforced a constructive trust on the executors (who were also the male heirs) to an estate for the benefit of the daughters of the descendant. Keech v. Sanford, 2 Eq. Cas. 741 (1728), formalized the power of the chancellor to create such a trust based on the doctrine of unjust enrichment.

24 Grey, "Boundaries," 200–202.

25 Ibid., 208.

26 Cro. Jac. 344; 79 Eng. Rep. 294 (1616). See Knafla, *Law and Politics*, 170, and J. H. Baker, *The Legal Profession and the Common Law* (London, 1986), 205–30.

27 Common-law judges were fully entitled to use the precepts of equity in their court, although they could not deliver the remedies that the chancellor could. So, too, the chancellor could cite the common law in his court, for example, if he wished to dismiss a suit because the petitioner had a perfectly adequate remedy at law. To this extent only the two sets of courts were fungible.

28 Parliament, in addition to its legislative duties, was also the highest court in the land. It derived that office, as it had its legislative power, from its origin as the king's Great Council. Thus there was appeal to Parliament from the common-law courts, but only because Parliament was a higher court.

29 Magdalen College Case, 11 Co. Rep. 66b, 77 Eng. Rep. 1235 (1616), and Sir Anthony Mildmay's Case, 6 Co. Rep. 40a, 77 Eng. Rep. 311 (1606).

30 Magdalen College Case, 11 Co. Rep. at 72b, 77 Eng. Rep. at 1244.

31 Earl of Oxford's Case, 1 Ch. Rep. 5, 9, 21 Eng. Rep. 485, 486 (1615).

32 Holdsworth, *HEL*, 1:463; Knafla, *Law and Politics*, 175–81.

33 Grey, "Boundaries," generally argues that the prohibition against equity meddling in certain types of cases was merely an attempt to determine the proper boundary of respective jurisdictions.

34 D. E. C. Yale, ed., *Lord Nottingham's "Manual of Chancery Practice" and "Prolegomena of Chancery and Equity"* (Cambridge, 1965), 189.

35 T. B. Howell, *A Complete Collection of State Trials* (London, 1816–26), 3:864. Thus, by implication, the king's ministry was abusing its public trust by misguiding the king—inducing him to order collection of the taxes at the ports. Forced to pay taxes that Charles I levied without consent of Parliament, resisters like Hampden were tried and convicted in the royal courts. See Barry Coward, *The Stuart Age* (London, 1980), 139, 143–44.

36 John Gough, *Fundamental Law in English Constitutional History* (Oxford, 1955), 39ff. This was the Edward Coke who resented royal intrusion into the courts and lost favor for his outspoken defense of common-law reasoning, not the Coke who, years before, had been the Crown's most energetic supporter. See Samuel E. Thorne, *Sir Edward Coke, 1552–1952* (London, 1957).

37 Dr. Bonham's Case, 8 Co. Rep. 107a, 113b; 77 Eng. Rep. 652 (1610). Coke was not challenging the judicial side of Parliament. Gough, *Fundamental Law*, 41–42. Coke may have been reaching for the doctrine we call judicial review, though the cases he cited did not in the main prove that the king's courts had ever overturned a statute of Parliament. See S. E. Thorne, "Bonham's Case and Judicial Review," 40 *Harvard Law Review* 30, 49–50 (1926–27). What Coke was probably doing in this case was the far less ambitious and more common "construction" of the meaning of a statute. That part of the statute that allowed the Guild of Physicians to both condemn and fine its rivals was "repugnant" to reason, that is, to the well-established maxim of construction that no judge or authority may directly benefit from its own jurisdiction.

38 Holdsworth, *HEL*, 5:478. With a few exceptions, judges in Anglo-American courts have to wait for a case to be brought to their court before they are able

to give an opinion on the legal issues in it. Ellesmere quite properly waited for a suitable occasion to reply to Coke.

39   J. G. A. Pocock, *The Ancient Constitution and the Feudal Law* (Cambridge, 1957), 35–45.

40   Grey, "Boundaries," 203 et seq.

41   Matthew Hale, *The History of the Common Law of England* [1713], ed. Charles M. Grey (Chicago, 1971), 30–31.

42   Lord Campbell, *Lives of the Lord Chancellors and the Keepers of the Great Seal of England*, ed. John Allan Mallory (Boston, 1874), 3:56–95. Having called for a broad inquiry into the conduct of the king's ministers, Coke did not say much about Bacon. See Stephen D. White, *Sir Edward Coke and the Grievances of the Commonwealth* (Manchester, Eng., 1979), 153.

43   Howell, *State Trials*, 2:1119.

44   *Commons Journal*, 3:574 (March 26, 1621).

45   Bacon to the Lords, April 17, 1621, quoted in Campbell, *Lives*, 87.

46   *Lords Journal*, 3:84 (April 24, 1621). Bacon, "Of Great Place" [1612], in J. Max Patrick, ed., *Selected Essays of Francis Bacon* (New York, 1948), 20.

47   On the English impeachments, see Hoffer and Hull, *Impeachment in America*, 3–10. Many of these impeachments were politically motivated, but the Lords' respect for the trial they were to perform often limited the license of the Commons. Nevertheless, anyone could be impeached for any offense with any penalty after conviction, so that impeachment and trial were not limited in theory or practice to officials. In the Restoration, private citizens who published criticism of the government were defendants. In general, however, these post–Civil War impeachments were carefully controlled assaults on entrenched ministers who used their power to line their own pockets or to subvert parliamentary policy. The vast majority of cases never even went to trial. The end result of all but one of them was, in effect, removal from office and a fine or banishment for a time.

48   William Sheppard, *England's Balme* . . . (London, 1657), 21, 64–65, 83–84, 99.

49   Henry Parker, *Observations upon Some of His Majesties Late Answers and Expresses* [1642], in William Haller, ed., *Tracts on Liberty in the Puritan Revolution, 1638–1647* (New York, 1965), 2:174. Parker's idea of trust ended in the right of rebellion against a tyrant. As such it looked back to the tradition of legitimate rebellion developed in Scotland by George Buchanan, in France by the Huguenots, and in Germany by some of Luther's disciples, notably Melanchthon. See Quentin Skinner, *The Foundations of Modern Political Thought*, vol. 2: *The Age of Reformation* (Cambridge, 1978), 330 et seq.

50   William Ball, *Tratatus de Jure Regnandi* [1644], quoted in Richard Tuck, *Natural Rights Theories: Their Origin and Development* (Cambridge, 1979), 148.

51   A multitude of examples are marshaled in John Gough, "Political Trusteeship," in Gough, *John Locke's Political Philosophy: Eight Studies* (Oxford, 1950), 132–61.

52   Tuck, *Natural Rights Theories*, 148.

53   A group biography of the three principal levellers, John Lilburne, William Walwyn, and Richard Overton, is H. N. Brailsford, *The Levellers and the English Revolution*, ed. Christopher Hill (Stanford, Calif., 1961). Mark Kishlansky, *The Rise of the New Model Army* (Cambridge, 1979), 206, judges the levellers to be merely an irritant. Christopher Hill, *The World Turned Upside Down* (London, 1972), thinks they were very important indeed. In the realm of armies and parliaments, they were not in a position, save for their brief sway over the passions of some officers and men in the New Model Army, to force the issue.

When this forum was denied them, they lost whatever chance they might have had to play the game of politics at the high-stakes table. See David Underdown, "Honest Radicals in the Counties, 1642–1649," in Donald Pennington and Keith Thomas, eds., *Puritans and Revolutionaries* (Oxford, 1978), 199–200. Leveller ideas did influence many in the City of London, however, and were radical enough in implication to worry the more conservative leaders of the army. When the army, rid of leveller influence, moved to suppress radicalism in the City, the City capitulated.

54 John Lilburne, *A Remonstrance of Many Thousand Peoples* [1646], in Haller, ed., *Tracts*, 3:353.

55 Ibid., 356: should people be contented with "such unworthy returns of our trust and love?"

56 Richard Overton, *An Appeale from the Degenerate Representative Body of the Commons of England Assembled at Westminster* [1647], in Don M. Wolfe, ed., *Leveller Manifestoes of the Puritan Revolution* (New York, 1944), 161.

57 Edward Hake, *Epieikeia*, ed. D. E. C. Yale (New Haven, Conn., 1953), 85–118. The conventions of construction of statutes are not unique to equity. Common-law courts construe statutes all the time. Thus, strictly speaking, the doctrine of "equity of the statute" is a cousin once removed to equitable jurisprudence. It often implies a liberal reading of remedial statutes if their language seems to obstruct the purpose behind their passage. See William S. Blatt, "The History of Statutory Interpretation: A Study in Form and Substance," 6 *Cardozo Law Review* 799 (1985).

58 But Overton was not the first reformer to use this line of argument. In 1643, an anonymous author defended parliamentary resistance against the Crown by proposing, "There is in Laws an equitable, and a literal sense." If the king's party sought obedience to the letter of the law "against the *equity* of it . . . [the subject may] refuse *obedience* to the Letter for the Law taken abstract from its original reason and end, is made a shell without a kernell." *A Question Answered: How Laws Are to Be Understood, and Obedience Yielded* [1643], quoted in Ernest Sirluck, ed., *The Complete Prose Works of John Milton*, vol. 2: *1643–1648* (New Haven, Conn., 1959), 18–19. Henry Parker, whose 1642 pamphlet had acknowledged the parallel between public trust and private trusts, also assayed an "equitie" that arose from natural law and superseded all statute. Parker, *Animadversions Animadverted* (London, 1642), 3.

59 Overton, *An Appeale*, 162.

60 [John Lilburne et al.], *An Agreement of the People* [1648], in Wolfe, ed., *Leveller Manifestoes*, 300.

61 To be sure, the levellers were not unique in this commitment to law, nor was the language of equity. See Howard Nenner, *By Color of Law: Legal Culture and Constitutional Politics in England, 1660–1689* (Chicago, 1977), arguing that the common law was also a source of metaphor for political reformers.

62 See, e.g., Harrington, *The Commonwealth of Oceana*, in J. G. A. Pocock, ed., *The Political Works of James Harrington* (Cambridge, 1977), 174. The close ties between Florentine civic humanism and Harrington's ideal republic are traced in J. G. A. Pocock, *The Machiavellian Moment* (Princeton, N.J., 1975), 386ff.

63 Harrington, *A System of Politics*, in Pocock, ed., *Political Works of James Harrington*, 848–49.

64 Caroline Robbins, "Algernon Sidney's 'Discourses concerning Government,'" in Robbins, *Absolute Liberty*, ed. Barbara Taft (Hamden, Conn., 1982), 277.

65 *The Instrument of Government* [1653] appears in S. R. Gardiner, ed., *The Constitutional Documents of the Puritan Revolution, 1625–1660* (Oxford, 1906), 412–17.

66 Mary Maples Dunn, *William Penn: Politics and Conscience* (Princeton, N.J.,

1967), 81–83. Penn allowed courts of equity to function in his colony from its founding. See Chapter 3.

67 The Third Earl of Shaftesbury to Jean LeClerc, February 8, 1706, quoted in Maurice Cranston, *John Locke: A Biography* (London, 1957), 114.

68 Peter Laslett, ed., *John Locke's Two Treatises of Government*, 2d ed. (Cambridge, 1967), 59–66. The movement to exclude James II from the throne occupied much of Shaftesbury's circle in the 1670s. Locke was an active conspirator before and after his exile. See Richard Ashcraft, *Revolutionary Politics and Locke's Two Treatises of Government* (Princeton, N.J., 1986), 338–466.

69 Cranston, *Locke*, 208–13. On the importance of this refutation of Filmer and Hobbes to the structure of Locke's argument, see John Dunn, "The Politics of Locke in England and America in the Eighteenth Century," in John W. Yolton, ed., *John Locke: Problems and Perspectives* (Cambridge, 1969), 47–56. One might note that Hobbes was a defender of equity in a state of nature but saw "trust" as a relationship between masters and servants, lords and subjects—an asymmetry, not a doctrine promoting equality. See Thomas Hobbes, *De Cive* [English version, 1651], ed. Howard Warrender (Oxford, 1983), 68–70, 118–20, and Hobbes, *The Elements of Law: Natural and Politic* [1640], ed. Ferdinand Tonnies (New York, 1969), 168–84.

70 Laslett, ed., *Locke's Two Treatises, Second Treatise*, 392–93, 395–96. Discretion here included a power "to mitigate the severity of the law" analogous to that of a chancellor.

71 Ibid., 430–31, 444–45.

72 Laslett, Introduction, *Locke's Two Treatises*, 112. Gough, "Political Trusteeship," 163, agrees that Locke did nothing more than "receive and transmit" the concept of political trusteeship.

73 K. H. D. Haley, *The First Earl of Shaftesbury* (Oxford, 1968), 309–12; Holdsworth, *HEL*, 6:525–27, 614–15. Lord Campbell, *Lives of the Chancellors*, 4:126, regards Shaftesbury as an honest and well-meaning but ignorant, pompous, and ineffectual chancellor. In the end, it is hard to render judgment on so short-lived an incumbent.

74 J. R. Pole, *Political Representation in England and the Origins of the American Republic* (Berkeley, Calif., 1966), 431; Gough, "Political Trusteeship," 164–65. In the context of his efforts to mediate between parliamentary aims and William of Orange's understanding of monarchy, Locke may himself have given credence to the later pro-parliamentary gloss on the *Second Treatise*. See Ashcraft, *Two Treatises*, 548–49.

75 Viscount Bolingbroke, a discredited Tory politician from Queen Anne's cabinet who escaped punishment after impeachment in 1714 by fleeing to France, argued in his *Idea of a Patriot King* (1738) that the corruption of Parliament proved that only a perfect Christian magistrate could and ought to rule England. Locke's idea of popular rule could not be farther from Bolingbroke's in substance, but in Locke's *Second Treatise*, as in the Tory former minister's essays, one could discern a thread of uncompromising moral anarchism. See Dunn, "The Politics of Locke," 53. One cannot find nearly as many references to Milton or Harrington in the commonwealthmen's writings as to Locke and the "agitators" (the radical reformers at Putney Green in the fall of 1647), among whom were the levellers themselves.

76 The term was contemporary, and it was recovered in Caroline Robbins's encyclopedic *Eighteenth-Century Commonwealthman* (Cambridge, Mass., 1961), 3.

77 James Burgh, *Political Disquisitions* (London, 1774), 1:4, 23, 48. The rotten boroughs were medieval voting franchises granted for service, many of which had by 1774 only a handful of voters but sent a representative to Parliament

nonetheless. Such seats could be and were regularly purchased by a powerful party leader or by the Crown and given to loyal supporters.
78 Ibid., 1:62, 72, 237, 123, 126, 401, 186, 196–97, 209. There was only one trial upon an impeachment for corruption in government between 1715 and Warren Hastings's trial in 1795, that of Lord Chancellor Macclesfield in 1725. The leaders of the Scottish rebellion were impeached and tried in 1745, but not for corruption.
79 Bailyn, *Ideological Origins*, 41.
80 Catherine Macaulay, *The History of England from the Accession of James I to the Elevation of the House of Hanover* (London, 1769), 1:404. Macaulay cited Locke in her support as well—the same section 240 of the *Second Treatise* cited above in the text.
81 John Wilkes, *North Briton No. 19*, in *The North Briton* (London, 1763), 115. Wilkes and his followers made "accountability" a central theme of their campaign. See John Brewer, "The Wilkesites and the Law, 1763–1764: A Study of Radical Notions of Governance," in Brewer and John Styles, eds., *An Ungovernable People: The English and Their Laws in the Seventeenth and Eighteenth Centuries* (New Brunswick, N.J., 1980), 131–32, 136, 142.
82 [John Almon], *A Letter to the Right Honorable Charles Jenkinson* (London, 1781), 16.
83 Bailyn, *Ideological Origins*, 52ff.

CHAPTER THREE

1 The origin of colonial legal ideas remains a controversial historical issue folded within the broader dispute over how "English" the settlers were. Compare David Grayson Allen, *In English Ways* (Chapel Hill, N.C., 1982), 16: "Indeed, it is striking that the old local English ways persisted [in Massachusetts towns] after the economic and social reasons for them had vanished on the American continent," with Bernard Bailyn, *Education in the Forming of American Society* (Chapel Hill, N.C., 1960), 22: "Disruption and transplantation in alien soil transformed the character of traditional English family life. Severe pressures were felt from the first."
2 See, e.g., David T. Konig, "Dale's Laws and the Non-Common Law Origin of Criminal Justice in Virginia," *American Journal Legal of History* 26 (1982): 338–66.
3 Bernard Bailyn, *Voyagers to the West* (New York, 1987), 127ff.
4 G. B. Warden, "Law Reform in England and America, 1620 to 1660," *William and Mary Quarterly*, 3d ser., 35 (1978): 672–80.
5 Bradley Chapin, *Criminal Justice in Colonial America, 1606–1660* (Athens, Ga., 1982), 9.
6 See, e.g., John M. Murrin, "The Legal Transformation of the Bench and Bar of Colonial Massachusetts," in Stanley N. Katz, ed., *Colonial America* (Boston, 1971), 415–49.
7 Many of these divergences are discussed in Peter Charles Hoffer, *Law and People in Colonial America* (forthcoming).
8 John Philip Reid, *Constitutional History of the American Revolution*, vol. 2: *The Authority to Tax* (Madison, Wis., 1987), 10–11ff., argues that there was a *British* constitution which Americans, at least in the 1760s, regarded as their own. Surely such a conception of shared sovereignty violated the central axiom of the English constitution—the supremacy of Parliament.
9 Maryland Charter of 1632, in Swindler, ed., *Sources and Documents*, 4:361. The same term for equity and equitable judgment appears in William Lambard,

Archeion, ed. Charles L. McIlwaine and Paul L. Ward (Cambridge, Mass., 1957), 450, and in later English manuals. See David Yale, "A Trichotomy of Equity," *Journal of Legal History* 6 (1985): 197.

10 J. Hall Pleasants, ed., *Proceedings of the Court of Chancery of Maryland, 1669–1679*, Archives of Maryland (Baltimore, 1935), 51:xxxiii–xxxiv. The manuscript records of the court of chancery of Maryland for 1669–1779 are preserved in bound ledgers at the Maryland Hall of Records, Annapolis; see Peter Charles Hoffer, "Their Trustees and Servants: Colonial Maryland Lawyers and the Constitutional Implications of Equity Precepts," *Maryland Historical Magazine* 82 (1987): 142.

11 William W. Hening, ed., *Statutes at Large of Virginia* (Richmond, 1812), 1:303 (1645), amended Hening, *Statutes at Large*, 3:291 (1705); Thomas Jefferson, ed., *Reports of Cases Determined in the General Court of Virginia* (Richmond, 1829); Frank L. Dewey, "New Light on the General Court of Colonial Virginia," 21 *William and Mary Law Review* 4 (1979).

12 North Carolina Charter [1663], in Swindler, ed., *Sources and Documents*, 7:359; Fundamental Constitutions [1669], in Swindler, ed., *Sources and Documents*, 7:360. There is no evidence that Locke's plan was ever put into effect. For printed dockets, see Mattie E. E. Parker, ed., *North Carolina Higher-Court Records, 1670–1696* (Raleigh, 1968); William Price, ed., *Colonial Records of North Carolina*, vol. 5: *North Carolina Higher-Court Minutes, 1709–1723* (Raleigh, 1974); and Robert J. Cain, ed., *Colonial Records of North Carolina*, vol. 6: *North Carolina Higher-Court Minutes, 1723–1735* (Raleigh, 1981). File papers for the period 1739–75 are available in the Secretary of State Papers, S.S. 309, North Carolina Division of Archives and History, Raleigh.

13 J. Nelson Frierson, Introduction to *Records of the Court of Chancery of South Carolina, 1671–1779*, ed. Anne King Gregorie (Washington, D.C., 1950), 5, 7. The royal colony of South Carolina continued the practice of its proprietary predecessor. "An Act for Establishing a Court of Chancery in . . . South Carolina," in *Earliest Printed Laws of South Carolina, 1692–1734* (1978), 369–71; Marylynn Salmon, "Women and Property in South Carolina," *William and Mary Quarterly*, 3d ser., 39 (1982): 655–85.

14 Georgia Charter of 1732, in Swindler, ed., *Sources and Documents*, 2:434. The land was "in trust" for the benefit of the settlers. Ibid., 439; Lords of Trade to Governor Henry Ellis, December 13, 1759, Colonial Office Files 5/673, Public Record Office, London. The court first met in November 1761. Kenneth Coleman and Milton Ready, eds., *Colonial Records of the State of Georgia*, vol. 28, part 2 (Athens, Ga., 1979), 194.

15 Pennsylvania Charter of 1683, in Swindler, ed., *Sources and Documents*, 8:257, 260–61; *Colonial Records of Pennsylvania*, 1:47 (1684); Pennsylvania Frame of Government of 1696, in Swindler, ed., *Sources and Documents*, 8:272; Spencer R. Liverant and Walter H. Hitchler, "A History of Equity in Pennsylvania," 37 *Dickinson Law Review* 156 (1933). *Votes and Proceedings of the Province of Pennsylvania*, 2:273 (1720), reprints the enabling statute. Gary B. Nash, *Quakers and Politics: Pennsylvania, 1681–1726* (Princeton, N.J., 1968), 265–67, describes the fiasco of 1706. *Registrar's Book of Governor Keith's Court of Chancery* (Philadelphia, 1941) records the dockets and minutes of the ill-starred court from 1720 to 1735. On the county courts, see Marylynn Salmon, "The Court Records of Pennsylvania in the Seventeenth and Eighteenth Centuries," *Pennsylvania Magazine of History and Biography* 107 (1983): 252, and "An Act Establishing Courts of Law and Equity within this Government," in *Laws of the Government of New Castle, Kent, and Sussex upon Delaware* (1741), 42. Arthur T. Cowan, "Legislative Equity in Pennsylvania," 4 *University of Pittsburgh Law Review* 1 (1937), traces

the assembly's equity powers. The seven-hundred-case figure is for the years 1700 to 1837.

16 Preston W. Edsall, ed., *Journal of the Courts of Common Right and Chancery of East New Jersey, 1683–1702* (Philadelphia, 1937); H. Clay Read and George L. Miller, eds., *The Burlington Court Book: A Record of Equity Jurisprudence in West New Jersey, 1680–1709* (Washington, D.C., 1944); Richard S. Fields, "The Provincial Courts of New Jersey," *Collections of the New Jersey Historical Society* 9 (1849): 108; James Alexander Papers, boxes 3, 37–38, New-York Historical Society. Other scattered surviving file papers and decrees of the court have been carefully preserved in boxes and bound ledgers in the New Jersey State Archives, under the State House, in Trenton. On Alexander, see Henry N. MacCracken, *Prologue to Independence: The Trials of James Alexander, American, 1715–1756* (New York, 1964). Some colonial governors refused to act as chancellors, however. See William Paterson, "Political Essays" (1798), quoted in John E. O'Connor, *William Paterson* (New Brunswick, N.J., 1979), 217.

17 "An Ordinance for Erecting and Establishing a High Court of Chancery in the Province of New York" [1701], in *Colonial Laws of New York* (1894), 1:125. See also Joseph H. Smith, "Adolph Philipse and the Chancery Resolves of 1727," in *Courts and Law in Early New York*, ed. Leo Hershkowitz and Milton Klein (Port Washington, N.Y., 1978), 30–32. The colonial records of the court have been once again assembled in the New York State Library in Albany. The Orders in Chancery, Records, Bound Petitions, and Docket Books for 1701–75, with gaps, in the New York State Library demonstrate that the court was a relatively busy one, with half a dozen or more cases on its docket at any given time. The Mayor's Court of the City of New York, the English successor to the Dutch court of the city, also had equitable powers. See Richard B. Morris, ed., *Select Cases of the Mayor's Court of New York City* (Washington, D.C., 1935), 35–49.

18 The first equity courts are described in Barbara Black, "The Judicial Power and the General Court in Early Massachusetts" (Ph.D. diss., Yale University, 1975), 151–311; David Thomas Konig, *Law and Society in Puritan Massachusetts, Essex County, 1629–1692* (Chapel Hill, N.C., 1979), 159–60; *Massachusetts Colonial Laws*, chap. 31, sec. 18 (1685); *Colonial Laws . . . of Massachusetts Bay* (1814), 93–94; Zechariah Chafee, ed., *Suffolk County Court Records Publications of the Colonial Society of Massachusetts: No. 29* (Boston, 1933), 1:l–liii. The commission to Sir Edmund Andros appears in Swindler, ed., *Sources and Documents*, 5:68–70. Later efforts to establish a court of equity are traced in Province Laws 1691/3, chap. 33, sec. 14, *Acts and Resolves, Public and Private, of the Province of Massachusetts Bay* (Boston, 1861), 1:75–76; Province Laws, 1693/4, chap. 12, *Acts and Resolves*, 1:144–45. The disallowance in England is noted in Province Laws, 1693/4. The reason for the disallowance was that the judges of the court were to be selected by the assembly rather than by the Crown. See Edwin H. Woodruff, "Chancery in Massachusetts," 20 *Law Quarterly Review* 374, 376 (1880).

19 Commission to Sir Edward Cranfield, Governor of New Hampshire, 1682, in Swindler, ed., *Sources and Documents*, 6:335; David S. Lovejoy, *The Glorious Revolution in America* (Chapel Hill, N.C., 1972), 151; William F. Walsh, "The Growing Function of Equity in the Development of the Law," in *Law: A Century of Progress* (New York, 1937), 147–48.

20 Charles J. Hoadley, ed., *Connecticut Colonial Records* (Hartford, 1883), 14:79 (1773); Zephaniah Swift, *A Digest of the Laws of the State of Connecticut* (Hartford, 1823), 2:14. Bruce Mann, *Neighbors and Strangers: Law and Community in Early Connecticut* (Chapel Hill, N.C., 1987), 155–61, notes that two evanescent efforts were made to erect a separate court of equity in the colony in 1681 or

1682 and 1715. For later changes, see Supreme Court Records, 1774–96; Chancery Cases, Connecticut State Library, Hartford; and John T. Farrell, ed., *The Superior Court Diary of William Samuel Johnson* (Washington, D.C., 1942), xix.

21 Providence Plantations Agreement [1640], in Swindler, ed., *Sources and Documents*, 8:353; Rhode Island Charter [1663], in Swindler, ed., *Sources and Documents*, 8:368. Williams sought royal ratification of a charter earlier granted by the Lord Protector. Walsh, "Equity," 148.

22 See, e.g., Thomas Pownall's *Administration of the Colonies* (London, 1768), 81–82. Pownall had preceded Bernard and Hutchinson as governor of Massachusetts. For a governor to ask for a court of his own may seem anything but neutral. Nevertheless, Pownall was a sincere friend to the colonies and probably did not seek personal aggrandizement. In any case, when he wrote he had been out of the governorship for almost a decade.

23 In Massachusetts, for example, efforts by the General Court to set up its own high court of equity (i.e., with a bench chosen in the colony) failed to gain Privy Council approval. See William J. Curran, "The Struggle for Equity Jurisdiction in Massachusetts," 31 *Boston Law Review* 172 (1951), and Woodruff, "Chancery in Massachusetts," 374.

24 Local opposition to equity practice came from many directions. Nonlawyers found it dangerously arbitrary; see, e.g., William Douglass, *Summary View of the First Planting of the British Settlements in North America* (Boston, 1747), 2:33, 49. Some lawyers found its discretion overbroad and unconstrained; see John Dickinson to his father, August 2, 1756, cited in Gordon Wood, *The Creation of the American Republic* (Chapel Hill, N.C., 1969), 198.

25 See, e.g., Albert Batchellor, ed., *Laws of New Hampshire* (Concord, 1904), 2:377–79 (1724) (equity of redemption); *Acts and Resolves of . . . Massachusetts Bay*, 1:356 (1698) (chancering of penalty bond); J. H. Trumbull and Charles J. Hoadley, eds., *Colonial Records of Connecticut* (Hartford, 1873), 7:515–16 (1734) (restraints on interest payments).

26 Richmond County, Va., Court Order Book no. 6, May 5, 1712, Virginia State Library, Richmond, for example, opens the long-running suit of *Metcalfe v. Barrow* over an estate disputed by two of the great families of the county. The county court, sitting in equity, convinced both parties to agree to submit account books to commissioners. Eight other suits at equity were commenced the same year. Shortly thereafter, Barrow refused to cooperate with the consent order and had to be warned by the court to comply or he would lose the suit (June 6, 1713, Richmond County Court Order Book no. 6, p. 106). The court finally apportioned one-eighth of the estate to the plaintiff, the daughter of the deceased. The rest went to his widow. In 1753, the justices heard nineteen chancery cases, of which five were new; the rest were continuations of older suits or reports of commissioners. Richmond County Court Order Book no. 13.

27 Anne King Gregorie, ed., *Court of Chancery of South Carolina, 1671–1779* (Washington, D.C., 1950), has assembled all the extant dockets.

28 Parker, ed., *North Carolina Higher-Court Records*, 1:89 et seq.; vols. 2–4 carry the dockets through 1708. Price, ed., *North Carolina Higher-Court Minutes*, and Cain, ed., *North Carolina Higher-Court Minutes*, provide dockets through 1728. For the 1760s, see Court of Chancery file papers, 1739–75, Secretary of State Papers, S.S. 309, North Carolina Division of Archives and History, Raleigh.

29 Chancery Records, Maryland Hall of Records, Annapolis. The dockets have been preserved in oversize ledgers, wherein they were originally recorded by the clerk of the court. In a typical suit, decided in the February 1739 session of

the court, the complainant, a youth (a special object of the chancellor's concern), came into court, represented by Daniel Dulany the Elder. The first issue was the value of the estate the youth inherited and the way in which it was
to have been distributed. There were assets of £600–800. There was some
"doubt concerning the construction of the true interest and meaning" of the
will. Tangled with this large question was the more pressing allegation by the
complainant that he had been defrauded in the sale of slaves belonging to the
estate. The complainant later discovered that he had received an unfair price
for the slaves and sought an adjustment of the payment. The chancellor could
do this by reforming the contract (the "indenture"), ordering restitution and
resale, or decreeing some other arrangement. On fair market price, see Horwitz, *Transformation*, 161–67 (eighteenth-century courts still clung to medieval
canonist conceptions of warranties of quality in the sale of goods). Horwitz's
theory has been challenged by A. W. B. Simpson, "The Horwitz Thesis and the
History of Contracts," 46 *University of Chicago Law Review* 533, 543 (1979), but
in the sale of slaves warranties of quality were enforced by courts into the
nineteenth century. See Chapter 5, n. 17, below. The defendant answered that
the youth mistook the value of his slaves. The court appointed commissioners
to take depositions from fifteen witnesses. These were turned over to a court-
appointed master, who made a report recommending a redivision of the
goods. The defense took exception to this report, and counsel debated the
issue in front of the chancellor. In this case, the chancellor overrode the exceptions and issued a final decree for the complainant. The entire case, *Parker v.
Mackall*, took four and a half years to resolve.

30 Jefferson, ed., *Reports of Cases*. Two of the four early equity cases, typically of
southern equity courts' business, involved disputed possession of slaves.

31 James Alexander Papers, boxes 37–38, New-York Historical Society; Chancery
Court Cases, 1743, 1773–74, New Jersey State Archives, Trenton. There are
bits and pieces here that indicate extensive equity litigation over land titles, but
a substantial minority of the business concerned agency, fraud in sales, and
other commercial transactions.

32 Orders in Chancery, 1701, 1705–8, 1720–35, New York State Archives, Albany. Mixed with the usual batch of disputed land titles, claims of fraud, trusteeship business, and mortgages are a number of disputed boundary cases. The
greatest of these grew out of the Connecticut–New York boundary dispute
over the "Oblong." See n. 54 below.

33 *Register Book of Governor Keith's Court of Equity*, 64–73. These cases included the
usual procedural issues—requests for stays of execution, injunctions, subpoenas for evidence, and rules that a litigant might not exit the province (*ne exeat
regno*)—as well as some substantive matters under the control of equity—part-
nership and mortgage, for example.

34 *Middleton v. Cole and Jenkins* (1743), a case originating in 1739, in which the
renters were able to sustain their right to remain on the land against a fraudulent claim by the planter. Mixed in the case was a quarrel that the proprietor
had with defendants. The chancellor could compel the greatest planter to
come to court to answer a suit by the least important citizen in the colony. Such
power was immense and provides a potential exception to the asymmetries of
law and "rank" hypothesized in Donald Black, *The Behavior of Law* (New York,
1976), 13–18. Of course, these chancellors were undoubtedly more sympathetic to the claims of upper-class litigants than to the claims of their servants.
Eighteenth-century colonists lived in a deferential culture, wherein rank mattered everywhere, even in court. The point is that one finds all manner of
suitors in the Maryland court bringing complaints against the magnates of the

colony. See, e.g., Stone v. Lane (1669), *Maryland Archives*, 51:14–15.

35   The outlines of the "English bill" in chancery came to the colonies long before any "books of forms" were imported. Thomas Letchford wrote bills in equity for suits in the Massachusetts Court of Assistants in 1638. See Thomas G. Barnes, "Thomas Letchford and the Earliest Lawyering in Massachusetts, 1638–1641," in *Law in Colonial Massachusetts, 1630–1800*, Publications of the Colonial Society of Massachusetts, no. 62 (1984), 25–36.

36   See, e.g., Carroll v. Warren (1739), Maryland Chancery Records, Annapolis.

37   Land title disputes often produced interminable paperwork. See the "Answer of the Proprietors of the Equivalent Lands [the "Oblong"] to the Attorney Generals Bill, in Chancery before [New York] Governor Cosby," prepared in 1735 by William Smith, Sr., and James Alexander, among others, a defense to a complaint that ran ninety-six longhand pages. In *Medina v. Het*, the king of Spain sought to regain possession of 1,998 bags of snuff and 108 casks of tobacco seized by a British privateer in 1718 and aging in a New York City merchant's warehouse. The latter, Rene Het, had purchased the goods as contraband of war from the privateer. The court decided that snuff and tobacco were not articles of war, but Het countered that he should be paid for storing the goods. He got 5 percent of their value. See Het v. Medina (N.Y. Ch. 1718), James Alexander Papers, box 3, New-York Historical Society.

38   Not all suitors were cooperative. Typical of the frustrations some chancellors faced is Bassett et al. v. Williamson et al. (1722–24), a South Carolina case that seemed to end with agreement of the parties to a distribution of assets under the supervision of the court, but it came unglued as both parties delayed, seeking a better financial position. Gregorie, ed., *Court of Chancery of South Carolina*, 277, 281, 286, 289–90, 303, 305–6, 311.

39   See, e.g., Thomas Jefferson, *Notes on the State of Virginia* [1781], ed. William Peden (Chapel Hill, N.C., 1955), 130–31. When Jefferson drafted the act that created the state's first high court of chancery, in November 1776, he tried to introduce trial by jury of matters of fact. Boyd, ed., *Papers of Jefferson*, 1:330. This innovation was modified by the House of Assembly to allow juries if both parties so desired. *Papers of Jefferson*, 2:433. Jefferson later recalled that this modification of his plan disappointed him but did not dampen his respect for equity courts. Dumas Malone, ed., *Autobiography of Thomas Jefferson* [1821] (New York, 1959), 15.

40   See, e.g., Glaister v. Palin (1717), *North Carolina Colonial Records, 2d Ser.*, 5:506.

41   [William Henry Drayton], "A Letter from a 'Freeman' of South Carolina to the Deputies of North America, assembled in the High Court of Congress at Philadelphia" [1776], in R. W. Gibbes, ed., *Documentary History of the American Revolution* (New York, 1855), 1:17.

42   Joseph H. Smith, *Appeals to the Privy Council from the American Plantations* (New York, 1950), 236–40. Appeals were rare, but the power of the high court of chancery as an adjudicator was immense when invoked. In Penn v. Baltimore, 1 Ves. Sen. 444 (1750), Lord Chancellor Hardwicke determined the boundary between Maryland and Pennsylvania—a decree affecting the lives and fortunes of thousands of settlers.

43   On the relative weakness of American lawyers' formal education in the law, see, e.g., Hiller B. Zobel and Kinvin Wroth, eds., *The Legal Papers of John Adams* (Cambridge, Mass., 1965), 1:iv, and Julius W. Goebel, Jr., ed., *The Law Practice of Alexander Hamilton* (New York, 1964), 1:47–53. Equity was, for many Americans, an even more arcane branch of legal practice than common-law pleading.

44   [William Livingston], *The Independent Reflector No. XXVIII* [June 7, 1753], *The*

Independent Reflector, ed. Milton M. Klein (Cambridge, Mass., 1963), 254.

45 William L. Saunders, ed., *The Colonial Records of North Carolina* (Raleigh, 1886), 4:237, 239, 824, 926.

46 Richard L. Bushman, *King and People in Provincial Massachusetts* (Chapel Hill, N.C., 1985), 91ff.; Allison Gilbert Olson, *Anglo-American Politics, 1660–1775* (Oxford, 1973), 40–41; Bernard Bailyn, *The Origins of American Politics* (New York, 1970), 66–70; Hoffer and Hull, *Impeachment in America,* 11–12; Jack P. Greene, "An Uneasy Connection: An Analysis of the Preconditions of the American Revolution," in Stephen G. Kurtz and James H. Hutson, eds., *Essays on the American Revolution* (Chapel Hill, N.C., 1973), 32–80; Pauline Maier, *From Resistance to Revolution: Colonial Radicals and the Development of an American Resistance to Great Britain, 1765–1776* (New York, 1973), 3–26.

47 John Philip Reid, *In Defiance of the Law: The Standing Army Controversy, the Two Constitutions, and the Coming of the American Revolution* (Chapel Hill, N.C., 1981), 8; Reid, *In a Rebellious Spirit: The Arguments of Facts, the Liberty Riots, and the Coming of the American Revolution* (University Park, Pa., 1979), 43; and generally Reid, *Constitutional History of the American Revolution,* vol. 1: *The Authority of Rights* (Madison, Wis., 1986).

48 See, e.g., George Dargo, *Roots of the Republic: A New Perspective on Early American Constitutionalism* (New York, 1974), 53–76; Milton M. Klein, "Prelude to Revolution in New York: Jury Trials and Judicial Tenure," *William and Mary Quarterly,* 3d ser., 17 (1960): 436–62; Lawrence Henry Gipson, *The Coming of the Revolution, 1763–1775* (New York, 1957), 28–54; Hoffer and Hull, *Impeachment in America,* 52–55. David Konig has noted that all of these examples are criminal cases, that is, involving political crimes or crimes with political overtones. Traditionally, chancellors refused to intervene in criminal prosecutions, but there were some exceptions.

49 See, e.g., Dumas Malone, *Jefferson the Virginian: Jefferson and His Time* (Boston, 1948), 1:173; Page Smith, *John Adams* (Garden City, N.Y., 1962), 1:102–62.

50 For example, a dispute over the return of the writ of habeas corpus against imprisonment by the assembly led to a full-scale constitutional crisis in Pennsylvania. See Peter C. Hoffer, "Law and Liberty: In the Matter of Provost William Smith of Philadelphia, 1758," *William and Mary Quarterly,* 3d ser., 38 (1981): 681–701. So, too, disputes over the burden of proof each side had to carry in seditious libel cases led to the explosive outcome of the John Peter Zenger trial. See Stanley Nider Katz, ed., *A Brief Narrative of the Case and Trial of John Peter Zenger—By James Alexander,* 2d ed. (Cambridge, Mass., 1972), 1–35.

51 Smith, "Adolph Philipse and the Chancery Resolves of 1727," 30–45; Joseph H. Smith and Leo Hershkowitz, "Courts of Equity in the Province of New York: The Cosby Controversy, 1732–1736," *American Journal of Legal History* 16 (1972): 7–9.

52 The Cosby episode is well told in Stanley N. Katz, "The Politics of Law in Colonial America: Controversies over Chancery Courts and Equity Law in the Eighteenth-Century," *Perspectives in American History* 5 (1971): 257–84, and Smith and Hershkowitz, "The Cosby Controversy," 1–50.

53 "The Opinion and Argument of Lewis Morris to Governor William Cosby, 1733," *Proceedings of the New Jersey Historical Society* 55 (1937): 87–116. On Morris in New Jersey, see Thomas L. Purvis, *Proprietors, Patronage, and Paper Money: Legislative Politics in New Jersey, 1703–1776* (New Brunswick, N.J., 1986), 121ff.

54 The "Oblong" was a parcel of land stretching along the New York–Connecticut border, which, by 1732, both colonies had disputed for fifty years. See Philip J.

Schwarz, *The Jarring Interests: New York's Boundary Makers, 1664–1776* (Albany, 1974), esp. 60–73.

55 Katz, ed., *Trial of Zenger*, 101.

56 The two Dulanys, Charles Carroll of Carrollton, William Paca, and Samuel Chase practiced in the equity court; one finds their signatures on documents throughout the equity court's files in Annapolis.

57 Aubrey C. Land, *The Dulanys of Maryland* (Baltimore, 1955), 1–61.

58 St. George L. Sioussat, *The English Statutes in Maryland* (Baltimore, 1903), 30–60.

59 Land, *Dulanys*, 82–83.

60 Daniel Dulany, Sr., *The Right of Inhabitants of Maryland to the Benefit of the English Laws* (Annapolis, 1728), 10, 12–13, 19, 30.

61 Land, *Dulanys*, 213–70; Bernard Bailyn, ed., *Pamphlets of the American Revolution, 1750–1776* (Cambridge, Mass., 1965), 599–606.

62 Daniel Dulany, Jr., *Considerations on the Propriety of Imposing Taxes in the British Colonies* [1765], Bailyn, ed., *Pamphlets*, 620.

63 Ibid., 612, 617, 630.

64 Ibid., 626–27.

65 Ibid., 627–28, 630.

66 Peter S. Onuf, ed., *Maryland and the Empire, 1773: The Antilon-First Citizen Letters* (Baltimore, 1974), 13–16.

67 Ibid., 37, 64–65, 57, 71, 95, 156, 220.

68 Richard D. Brown, *Revolutionary Politics in Massachusetts* (Cambridge, Mass., 1970), 164–236.

69 One-half of the members of the Continental Congress were lawyers (though not all of them practiced law), and legal concepts appeared everywhere in the debates and proclamations of that body. As an occupational group, lawyers were four times as numerous among the revolutionaries as any other profession and constituted one-third of the revolutionary leadership. Harry J. Lambeth, "The Lawyers Who Signed the Declaration of Independence," 62 *American Bar Association Journal* 869–70 (1976); James Kirby Martin, *Men in Rebellion: Higher Government Leaders and the Coming of the Revolution* (New Brunswick, N.J., 1973), 66, 68.

70 Hoffer and Hull, *Impeachment in America*, 11–12, 31, 45.

71 Stanley N. Katz, "The American Constitution: A Revolutionary Interpretation," in Richard Beeman, Stephen Botein, and Edward C. Carter II, eds., *Beyond Confederation: Origins of the Constitution and American National Identity* (Chapel Hill, N.C., 1987), 25.

72 See Bailyn, *Ideological Origins*, 28–31, arguing that philosophy, including legal philosophy, did not have a decisive influence on revolutionary thought.

73 The revolutionaries were certainly aware of earlier parliamentary petitions to the Crown to declare rights (Garry Wills, *Inventing America* [New York, 1978], 54–59), but the precedent was not suitable. Parliament, as a court of law, asked the king to declare rights because, as a court itself, Parliament was entitled to seek (or, in the actual case, to force) a statement from him. On the Congress's understanding of its own limitations, see Jerrilyn Greene Marston, *King and Congress* (Princeton, N.J., 1987), 87–99.

74 Early English bills of peace are discussed in Yeazell, *Class Action*, chap. 1. Slightly more farfetched, but just as soundly grounded in equity, is the argument that the colonists had rights because they had *relied* on the assurances of the Crown and added to the value of the colonies. This is the doctrine of equitable reliance and modifies the common-law notion of contract formation. See Reid, *Authority of Rights*, 142–45, for a similar argument.

75 On Dickinson's career as a pamphleteer and congressman, see Milton E. Flowers, *John Dickinson: Conservative Revolutionary* (Charlottesville, Va., 1983), 125–67, and Bailyn, ed., *Pamphlets*, 1:660–67.

76 John Dickinson, "Draft Memorial to the Inhabitants of the Colonies" [October 19–21? 1774], in Paul H. Smith, ed., *Letters of the Delegates to Congress* (Washington, D.C. 1976–), 1:207, 211, 216.

77 Dickinson, "Second Petition from Congress to the King" [July 8, 1775], in Boyd, ed., *Papers of Jefferson*, 1:220.

78 Dickinson, "Draft Address to the Inhabitants of America" [January 24? 1776], in Smith, ed., *Letters of the Delegates*, 3:139.

79 Dickinson, "Notes for a Speech in Congress" [January 24, 1776], in Smith, ed., *Letters of the Delegates*, 3:133.

80 Dickinson may have faltered, but his cause has been taken up with vigor and brilliance two centuries later by Reid, *Authority of Rights*, 28ff.; Barbara Black, "The Constitution of the Empire: The Case for the Colonists," 124 *University of Pennsylvania Law Review* 1203 (1976); and Jack P. Greene, "From the Perspective of Law: Context and Legitimacy in the Origins of the American Revolution," *South Atlantic Quarterly* 85 (1986): 56–77.

81 On Jefferson's legal education, see Edward Dumbauld, *Thomas Jefferson and the Law* (Norman, Okla., 1978), 3–17, and Frank L. Dewey, *Thomas Jefferson: Lawyer* (Charlottesville, Va., 1986), 9–17. Henry Ballow's *Treatise in Equity* (London, 1737) [often cited under the editor's name, John Fonblanque] and Richard Francis's *Maxims of Equity*, 2d ed. (London, 1739), were in Jefferson's first library; see Herbert A. Johnson, *Imported Eighteenth-Century Law Treatises in American Libraries, 1700–1799* (Knoxville, Tenn., 1978), 4, 21. On Wythe, see Robert B. Kirtland, "George Wythe: Lawyer, Revolutionary, Judge" (Ph.D. diss., University of Michigan, 1983). On Jefferson and Wythe, see Malone, *Jefferson the Virginian*, 65–74.

82 Thomas Jefferson, Bound Ledger of Cases, 1767–74, Huntington Library, San Marino, Calif. When Jefferson briefly resumed his legal career as a consultant during his wife's last illness, he was approached for opinions in equity cases once again; see Boyd, ed., *Papers of Jefferson*, 6:145–46, 151–54, 180–82, and John Cook Wyllie, "The Second Mrs. Wayland: An Unpublished Jefferson Opinion on a Case in Equity," *American Journal of Legal History* 6 (1965): 64–68.

83 Bolling v. Bolling (Va. Ch. 1770), Jefferson Case Book #489; Bolling v. Bolling, Argument for the Plaintiff, and Argument for the Defendant, BR 2, Huntington Library, San Marino, Calif.

84 Jefferson, Equity Commonplace Book, entry #1077 [p. 146], Huntington Library, San Marino, Calif. The entry can be dated as 1767 or 1768; see Douglas L. Wilson, "Thomas Jefferson's Early Notebooks," *William and Mary Quarterly*, 3d ser., 42 (1985): 449–51. The question of whether the actual practice of equity in Virginia courts lived up to the promise in these manuals that equity embodied natural justice is not the most relevant question. Instead, it is whether Jefferson believed equity could live up to this promise. I am grateful to Wythe Holt for insisting I make this point.

85 Lord Kames, *Principles of Equity*, 4th ed. (Edinburgh, 1800), 9.

86 As the following pages reveal, I believe that Jefferson's training in the law, his practice as a lawyer, and his approach to subsequent political questions were indissolubly linked. But see A. G. Roeber, *Faithful Magistrates and Republican Lawyers: Creators of Virginia Legal Culture, 1680–1810* (Chapel Hill, N.C., 1981), 164–65, and Thomas C. Grey, "Origins of the Unwritten Constitution: Fundamental Law in American Revolutionary Thought," 30 *Stanford Law Review* 843

(1978), both of which regard Jefferson as a political philosopher rather than a legal advocate. My position is far closer to John Phillip Reid, "The Irrelevance of the Declaration," in Hendrik Hartog, ed., *Law in the American Revolution and the Revolution in the Law* (New York, 1981), 46–89.

87   Howell v. Netherland, Jefferson, ed., *Reports of Cases*, 90, 92, 96 (1770). The Jefferson Case Book lists *Howell v. Netherland* as an action for assault and battery commencing on October 18, 1769. The case actually turned on a matter of statutory construction; Jefferson's foray into trust theory was brilliant but not quite "on point." Moreover, Jefferson may have adopted the constructive trust argument from counsel arguing a similar point for the appellant in *Gwinn v. Bugg*; see Jefferson, ed., *Reports of Cases*, 87, 89 (1769). Note that the date in Jefferson's *Reports* is one year before *Howell*. Appellant in *Gwinn* lost on appeal.

88   "Resolution of the Freeholders of Albemarle County, July 26, 1774," in Thomas P. Abernathy, ed. [Thomas Jefferson], *A Summary View of the Rights of British America* (New York, 1943), iv.

89   Abernathy, *Summary View*, vii; Charles M. Wiltse, *The Jeffersonian Tradition in American Democracy*, rev. ed. (New York, 1960), 158. Modern contract law thinks in terms of "offer" and "acceptance." In Jefferson's day, contract theory concerned exchanges of promises.

90   Manuscript text of *Summary View* in Boyd, ed., *Papers of Jefferson*, 1:121–22, 125, 128, 134. "The violation of our rights"—a violation of legal rights and natural rights—was conjoined throughout Jefferson's argument. The list of oppressive acts on p. 126 reinforced the proposition that legal rights were at stake.

91   Julian P. Boyd, "The Declaration of Independence: The Author and the People Who Produced It," in *Political Separation and Legal Continuity*, ed. Harry W. Jones (Chicago, 1976), 76.

92   Ed. Note, "Declaration of the Causes and Necessity for Taking Up Arms," in Boyd, ed., *Papers of Jefferson*, 1:187–92; Jefferson, "Draft Resolutions for Congress on Lord North's Conciliation Proposal" [July 25, 1775], in Boyd, ed., *Papers of Jefferson*, 1:225.

93   Jefferson, "Draft Resolutions," 1:225–29.

94   Jefferson owned a copy of William Brown's *Praxis Almae Curiae Cancellariae: Being a collection of precedents, by bill and answer, plea and demurrer, in causes of greatest moment (wherein equity hath been allowed) which have been commenced in the High Court of Chancery for more than 30 years last past*, 3d ed. (London, 1714). See Johnson, *Imported Treatises*, 10. When John Mitford [Lord Redesdale], *A Treatise of the Pleading in Suits in the Court of Chancery by English Bill* (London, 1780), was published, Jefferson obtained a copy of it. Johnson, *Imported Treatises*, 47.

95   Throughout the discussion of the Declaration, I have used the text of Jefferson's draft in Boyd, ed., *Papers of Jefferson*, 1:315–19.

96   Ronald Hamowy, "Jefferson and the Scottish Enlightenment: A Critique of Garry Wills's *Inventing America: Jefferson's Declaration of Independence*," *William and Mary Quarterly*, 3d ser., 36 (October 1979): 504–23. See also John Dunn, "The Politics of Locke in England and America in the Eighteenth Century," in John W. Yolton, ed., *John Locke: Problems and Perspectives* (Cambridge, 1969), 53–54.

97   Peter Laslett, ed., *John Locke's Two Treatises of Government*, 2d ed. (Cambridge, 1967), Introduction, 112, 114.

98   Maitland, *Equity and the Forms of Action*, 44.

99   Wood, *Creation of the American Republic*, 91–124.

100 [Drayton], "Letter from a 'Freeman,'" 15. On the Congress' sovereignty, see Richard B. Morris, *The Forging of the Union, 1781–1789* (New York, 1987), 55–79.

101 See Marston, *King and Congress*, 100–150, 294–304, arguing that the Congress's authority and legitimacy lay in executive action.

102 See, e.g., Joseph Story, *Commentaries on the Constitution of the United States* (Boston, 1833), 1:198–99, 200–201, 203. The extent to which the content of the Declaration was incorporated in the federal Constitution would become by 1840 a more troubling question.

103 Dumas Malone, *Jefferson: Sage of Monticello*, vol. 6: *Jefferson and His Time* (Boston, 1981), 432–34; Peter Charles Hoffer, *Revolution and Regeneration: Life Cycle and the Historical Vision of the Generation of 1776* (Athens, Ga., 1983), 125–26.

104 Malone, ed., *Autobiography of Thomas Jefferson*, 25, 29–36; Ed. Note, "Notes of Proceedings," in Boyd, ed., *Papers of Jefferson*, 1:299–308.

105 Robert A. Rutland, ed., *The Papers of George Mason, 1725–1792* (Chapel Hill, N.C., 1970), 1:277 and Ed. Note, 174–76. The same passage appears in the final version of the Virginia Declaration of Rights (Swindler, ed., *Sources and Documents*, 10:49) without the reference to "god and nature."

106 Pennsylvania Declaration of Rights [1776], in Swindler, ed., *Sources and Documents*, 8:278.

107 Maryland Declaration of Rights [1776], in Swindler, ed., *Sources and Documents*, 4:372

108 In their treatment of the loyalists, for example, state authorities violated much of the Declaration of Rights of Virginia, Pennsylvania, and Maryland. See Wallace Brown, *The Good Americans: The Loyalists in the American Revolution* (New York, 1969), 126–46.

109 Hoffer and Hull, *Impeachment in America*, 68–71, 78–95.

110 John C. Rainbolt, "A Note on the Maryland Declaration of Rights and Constitution of 1776," *Maryland Historical Magazine* 66 (1971): 420–35, explains the revision of the first draft (a conservative document written by Charles Carroll) in the direction of democracy.

111 Melvin Yazawa, ed., *Representative Government and the Revolution: The Maryland Constitutional Crisis of 1787* (Baltimore, 1975), 3–28. On Paca's and Chase's apprenticeships as spokesmen for the popular party, see Anne Y. Zimmer, "The 'Paper-War' in Maryland, 1772–73: The Paca-Chase Political Philosophy Tested," *Maryland Historical Magazine* 66 (1971): 177–93.

112 William Paca, "To the Citizens" [February 15, 1787], in Yazawa, ed., *Representative Government*, 66.

113 Amendments [to the Constitution] Proposed by the Virginia Convention, June 27, 1788, in Charlene Bangs Bickford and Helen E. Veit, eds., *Documentary History of the First Federal Congress of the United States of America*, vol. 4: *Legislative Histories* (Baltimore, 1986), 15.

114 Alexander Hamilton, "Report on the Public Credit" [1790], in Harold C. Syrett, ed., *The Papers of Alexander Hamilton* (New York, 1960–82), 6:82–83.

PART TWO

1 Joseph Story, *Commentaries on the Constitution of the United States* (Boston, 1833), 3:539.

2 Paul C. Nagel, *This Sacred Trust: American Nationality, 1798–1898* (New York, 1971), 7–11, 50–60, 131–38.

3 See State v. Mann, 13 N.C. (2 Devereaux) 263 (1829).

4 See Wood v. Davis, 11 U.S. (7 Cranch) 271 (1812).

5   W. W. Hening, ed., *Statutes at Large of Virginia* (Richmond, 1809–23), 9:389 (1777).

6   Erastus Washington, *An Essay on the Establishment of a Chancery Jurisdiction in Massachusetts* (Boston, 1812), 87.

7   Frederick Brightly, *A Treatise on the Equitable Jurisdiction of the Courts of Pennsylvania* (Philadelphia, 1855), 26–27.

8   Story, *Equity Jurisprudence*, 1:13–19.

9   Bailyn, *Ideological Origins*, 246–72; Richard B. Morris, *The Forging of the Union, 1781–1789* (New York, 1987), 162–93; Ralph Lerner and Philip Kurland, eds., *The Founders' Constitution* (Chicago, 1987), 1:500; Arthur Zilversmit, *The First Emancipation: The Abolition of Slavery in the North* (New York, 1967).

10 Robert H. Wiebe, *The Opening of American Society* (New York, 1984), 131–42, 257–64; Daniel Walker Howe, *The Political Culture of the American Whigs* (Chicago, 1979), 210–37.

11 James Willard Hurst, *Law and the Conditions of Freedom in the Nineteenth-Century United States* (Madison, Wis., 1956), 1–39; L. Ray Gunn, *The Decline of Authority, Public Economic Policy, and Political Development in New York, 1800–1860* (Ithaca, N.Y., 1988); Harry N. Scheiber, *Ohio Canal Era: A Case Study of Government and Economy, 1820–1861* (Athens, Ohio, 1969).

CHAPTER FOUR

1   An argument familiar to all legal scholars, if not before, then after Henry M. Hart, Jr., and Herbert Wechsler, *The Federal Courts and the Federal System* (Brooklyn, N.Y., 1953), 312–40. The classic modern case is Hanna v. Plumer, 380 U.S. 460 (1965), in which Chief Justice Earl Warren and Associate Justice John Marshall Harlan disputed the boundary line between a state's substantive law and the applicable Federal Rules of Civil Procedure. The classic earlier case was Erie Railroad Co. v. Tompkins, 304 U.S. 64 (1938).

2   Frances R. Aumann, "The Influence of English and Civil Law Principles upon the American Legal System during the Critical Post-Revolutionary Period," 12 *University of Cincinnati Law Review* 289, 293–95 (1938). Friedman, *History of American Law*, 109, notes: "In hindsight, the common law had little to fear." Perry Miller, *The Life of the Mind in America* (New York, 1968), 174, argued that equity became acceptable to Americans only in the early nineteenth century. Miller erred by relying on pamphlet and tract literature. Greater attention to statutes and court records would have demonstrated to him a much readier reception of equity. To be sure, equity was not universally appreciated. Initial efforts to give territorial courts "chancery jurisdiction" were defeated by Massachusetts land speculators' fears of territorial judges' discretion. See Nathan Dane, *A General Abridgement and Digest of American Law* (Boston, 1824), 8:518, and William W. Blume, "Chancery Practice on the American Frontier," 59 *Michigan Law Review* 49, 50–54 (1960).

3   Anne King Gregorie, ed., *Records of the Court of Chancery of South Carolina, 1671–1779* (Washington, D.C., 1950), 8; No. 1323, *Public Laws of South Carolina* (Charleston, 1784), 337–39. This bench was replaced by circuit courts of chancery in 1791, a central court of equity in 1822, and circuit courts of equity in the 1830s.

4   Walter Clark, ed., *State Records of North Carolina* (Raleigh, 1895), 12:175–76, 212, 334, 402–3, 593 (assembly journal, 1777–78): lower house passes bills for a central equity tribunal; *State Records* (1896), 13:609 (assembly journal, 1784): another effort to establish a central court of equity comes to naught. Resistance to such a court may have come from the memory of late colonial gover-

nor William Johnston's refusal to hold court in any place other than his family home. Typical caseloads of half a dozen cases per session are recorded in the Halifax District Court Bills and Answers in Equity, August 1782; Fayetteville District Court, Equity Minutes Docket, December 1788; Hillsborough Judicial District Equity Docket Book A, April 1788, all in the North Carolina Division of Archives and History, Raleigh. These manuscript court records demonstrate that the superior courts did hear and determine equity suits. It is not clear whether juries made determinations of facts in these courts.

5   "An Act for Establishing a High Court of Chancery," in W. W. Hening, ed., *Statutes at Large of Virginia* (Richmond, 1809–23), 9:389–99 (1777); Boyd, ed., *Papers of Thomas Jefferson*, 1:610–19; Hening, *Statutes at Large*, 11:342–44 (1783): a single chancellor replaced the bench of three chancellors, with appeal to a supreme court of appeals, and 12:464–67 (1788): changes in default judgments on non-appearance. Later reforms included the creation of a second equity court, hearing cases in the western portion of the state. Behind these reforms was the increasing number of cases on the court's docket and its growing backlog of pending suits.

6   "Act for Opening and Regulating the Superior Courts in the Several Counties," *Digest of the Laws of the State of Georgia . . . to the Year 1798* (1800): 220–21.

7   Constitution of Delaware, Art. VI, sec. a.

8   Pollard v. Schaffer, 1 Dallas 210, 211, 213, 215 (Pa. Sup. Ct. 1787). See also Wharton et al. v. Morris et al., 1 Dallas 124 (Phila. Com. Pl. 1785).

9   New York State Constitution of 1777, Arts. 24, 25, 27, in Swindler, ed., *Sources and Documents*, 7:116–17. The chancery register for the sessions of the court in Albany and New York City from 1780 through 1848 (when the court was abolished and equity pleading was heard in the regular courts of law) is available at the New York State Library, Albany. The registers were logs of clerks' fees and they show a busy chancery. Subsequent statutory amendments to the procedures appeared at regular intervals. See, e.g., 1 *Laws of the State of New York*, chap. 11, sec. 9 (1784): appeals from chancery; 2 *Laws of the State of New York*, chaps. 16–22 (1792): process revisions. On New Jersey, see New Jersey Court of Chancery Register, 1781–94, New Jersey State Archives, Trenton. The average caseload in the latter years of the register was three or four per session.

10   Massachusetts' General Court did create a commission to study court reform ("Resolve Commissioning the Committee Appointed to Revise the Law," chap. 98 [November 30, 1789], 1 *Acts and Laws . . . of Massachusetts* [1890], 187), but nothing concrete resulted. The state's first common-law courts continued to hear a limited range of equity suits. See, e.g., "An Act Directing . . . Executions," sec. 3, 1 *Acts and Laws of . . . Massachusetts* 170 (1784): equity of redemption; "An Act . . . for Giving Remedies in Equity," 1 *Laws of . . . Massachusetts* 251 (Boston, 1785).

11   "An Act for Constituting and Regulating Courts," secs. 19, 25 (1796), *Acts and Laws of the State of Connecticut* (Hartford, 1850), 127–28.

12   That is, courts had an equity side and a law side. See James W. Ely, Jr., and Theodore Brown, Jr., eds., *The Legal Papers of Andrew Jackson* (Knoxville, Tenn., 1987), lii–liii.

13   William Henry DeSaussure, Introduction to *Reports of Cases Argued and Determined in the Court of Chancery of the State of South Carolina* (Charleston, 1817), 1:xxxvii–liii. DeSaussure was one of the chancellors. An entirely different approach might have served the same ends. See Zephaniah Swift, *A System of the Laws of the State of Connecticut* (Hartford 1796), 2:419: "It is evident that courts of law might have assumed, and that the legislature might now transfer to

them, the whole business of courts of equity, and that there is no necessity for two distinct tribunals, to administer justice between man and man."

14 Wilson, "Lectures on the Law," in Robert Green McCloskey, ed., *The Works of James Wilson* (Cambridge, Mass., 1967), 2:492.

15 In Leith v. Hite et al. (Va. Ch. 1786–90), Marshall represented claimants in suits disputing titles to the "Northern Neck" between the Rappahannock and Potomac rivers. Charles F. Hobson, ed., *Papers of John Marshall* (Charlottesville, Va., 1987), 5:62–71. In Turpin et al. v. Locket et al. (Va. Ch. 1802), Randolph represented petitioners against an incumbent minister. See John J. Reardon, *Edmund Randolph: A Biography* (1979), 349–50.

16 Throughout the 1790s, St. George Tucker and other Virginia lawyer-legislators tried to relieve the burden on the Richmond equity court and on potential petitioners and defendants from elsewhere in the state by creating district courts of equity. See Charles T. Cullen, "St. George Tucker and the Law in Virginia, 1772–1804" (Ph.D. diss., University of Virginia, 1971), 47; Reardon, *Randolph*, 349. On the Livingstons, see William Livingston to William Livingston, Jr., January 19, 1781, Livingston Papers, New Jersey State Archives, Trenton.

17 Legislative control of courts' procedure and jurisdiction began with the Revolution and goes on today. Under Article III, the U.S. Congress has the authority to prescribe the jurisdiction and rules of practice for the federal courts, but it has shared that authority, by statute, with the Supreme Court. Over the past three decades that compromise has come partially unraveled. See Burbank, "Rules Enabling Act of 1934," 1020–21.

18 Title 19 (Courts), *Public Statute Laws of the State of Connecticut* (Hartford, 1824), sec. 10 (superior courts), sec. 19 (county courts), 82–83 (1821); Title 29, 142–44 (1821); Title 30, *Public Laws of Connecticut* (Hartford, 1835), 190–91, 181–93; Title 12, sec. 16, *The Revised Statutes of the State of Connecticut* (Hartford, 1849), 338; sec. 21, 339. On the merger of law and equity in Connecticut, see Charles E. Clark, *Handbook of the Law of Code Pleading*, 2d ed. (St. Paul, Minn., 1947), 24.

19 *Laws of the Commonwealth of Massachusetts*: Act of November 4, 1784 (Boston, 1807), 2:853, Act of March 1, 1799, sec. 4, 854; sec. 6, 855; Act of February 18, 1819 (Boston, 1822), 3:149; Act of February 21, 1827, sec. 1 (Boston, 1825), 9:399; sec. 2, 399–400; Act of March 5, 1827, sec. 4 (Boston, 1828), 10:497; Act of February 28, 1828, 739–40. *The Revised Statutes of the Commonwealth of Massachusetts*: Chap. 44, sec. 9, and Chap. 69, sec. 12 (Boston, 1828), 364, 445; Chap. 70, sec. 35, 451; Chap. 81, sec. 8, 500. *Acts and Resolves . . . of Massachusetts*: Chap. 129, sec. 1 (Boston, 1839), 406; Chap. 71 (Boston, 1843), 34; Chap. 14, sec. 2 (Boston, 1849), 568; Chap. 214 (Boston, 1857), 548. *The General Statutes of . . . Massachusetts*: Chap. 113, sec. 26 (Boston, 1860), 561.

20 Kent was a controversial figure in the contemporary legal arena; see John T. Horton, *James Kent: A Study in Conservatism, 1763–1847* (New York, 1939), 247–49, 254–58. His impact on equity was undeniable; see ibid., 197–231, and R. Kent Newmyer, *Supreme Court Justice Joseph Story: Statesman of the Old Republic* (Chapel Hill, N.C., 1984), 286–87.

21 Constitution of the State of New York, 1821, Art. V, sec. 5; Daun Van Ee, *David Dudley Field and the Reconstruction of the Law* (New York, 1986), 27–28; Norma Basch, *In the Eyes of the Law: Women, Marriage, and Property in Nineteenth-Century New York* (Ithaca, N.Y., 1982), 70–71. If the legislature did not intrude very far into process, it did take great bites out of the substantive jurisdiction of its chancery court, particularly in the area of trusts. See Stanley N. Katz, Barry

Sullivan, and C. Paul Beach, "Legal Change and Legal Autonomy: Charitable Trusts in New York, 1777–1893," *Law and History Review* 3 (1985): 64–67.

22 In 1806, Chancellor John Lansing, Jr., ordered publication of the *Rules and Orders of the Court of Chancery* (New York, 1806). He repeated the rules given by the enabling act of 1784, to which he added his own rules. These were restated, amended, and enlarged by Kent in his *Rules and Orders of the Court of Chancery of the State of New York, Revised and Digested by the Present Chancellor* (New York, 1815). Both men were wont to hand down new rules and revise old ones while their court was in session. For example, Lansing decided that the four days allowed for opposing counsel to examine the proposed "interrogatories" (lists of questions) before they were put to witnesses was too short a time, so he enlarged it to six days. Cf. Lansing, *Rules* #26, 15 (four days), and Kent's *Rules* reporting Lansing's change, #68, 40–41, which Lansing had handed down from the bench on July 15, 1808.

23 Constitution of New York, Art. XIV, sec. 8 (1846). The jurisdiction of the old court of chancery was given to the state supreme court. Behind the move were twenty years of organized lobbying against the delay and inefficiency of the dual system. See Alison Reppy, "The Field Codification Concept," in Reppy, ed., *David Dudley Field: Centenary Essays* (New York, 1949), 32; Charles M. Cook, *The American Codification Movement: A Study of Antebellum Legal Reform* (Westport, Conn., 1981), 185–91; and Katz, Sullivan, and Beach, "Charitable Trusts in New York," 69. Cook argues that the constitutional demolition of the chancery court made some reform of pleading a necessity. Katz finds less a direct relationship between the abolition of chancery and substantive reform than an ironic series of wavelike transformations in the latter following the upheaval in the former.

24 Chap. 379, "An Act to Simplify and Abridge the Practice, Pleadings, and Proceedings of the Courts of This State," Part I, Title I, *Laws of the State of New York* . . . (Albany, 1848), 497; Part II, Title VI, chap. 1, sec. 120, 521; Part II, Title I, 510; Part II, Title VI, chap. 4, sec. 136, 524.

25 On Field's life and early career, see Van Ee, *Field*, 3–112.

26 Field, "Free Soil, Free Speech, Free Men," speech to the Democratic Republican State Convention, Syracuse, N.Y., July 24, 1856, in *Speeches, Arguments, and Miscellaneous Papers of David Dudley Field*, ed. Titus M. Coan (New York, 1890), 3:32–42.

27 Van Ee, *Field*, 162, 206–11, 145–47.

28 Field, "What Shall Be Done with the Practice of the Courts? Questions Addressed to Lawyers, January 1, 1847," in *Speeches of . . . Field*, ed. A. P. Sprague (New York, 1884), 1:227, 231, 251. Though Field did not say as much to his legal audience, his very limited provision for judicial discretion under the code of pleading was in perfect accord with Jacksonian Democracy's fear of discretion anywhere in government. The Jacksonians campaigned for narrowly framed charters of incorporation for banks, an elective judiciary, and other limitations on the powers of government to intrude into private life.

29 For example, despite Jefferson's effort to reduce the influence of English common law, an effort encouraged by the General Assembly, and Madison's attack on the common-law basis for the Seditious Libel Law of 1798 in the "Address of the General Assembly" (Gaillard Hunt, ed., *The Writings of James Madison* [New York, 1900–1910], 6:338), there was no wholesale rejection of common law by the Virginia legislature.

30 Miller, *The Life of the Mind in America*, 251–65.

31 Cook, *Codification*, 158–81. Stephen N. Subrin, "David Dudley Field and the

Field Code: A Historical Analysis of an Earlier Procedural Vision," 6 *Law and History Review* 311 (1988), defends Field and his program.

32   Cook, *Codification*, 169–80. On Story and codification, see Newmyer, *Story*, 272–81. On Choate, see Miller, *The Life of the Mind in America*, 142–43.

33   Theodore Sedgwick, *A Treatise on the Rules which Govern the Interpretation and Application of Statutory and Constitutional Law* [1857], quoted in Perry Miller, ed., *The Legal Mind in America* (New York, 1969), 305–6.

34   See Ralph E. Kharas, "A Century of Law-Equity Merger in New York," 1 *Syracuse Law Review* 186 (1949), and Basch, *In the Eyes of the Law*, 200–232.

35   Despite the fact that the phrase "and equity" only precedes federal question jurisdiction, the equitable powers of the Supreme Court have been taken to extend to all matters before it that entail equity. I am grateful to William E. Nelson for prompting me to clarify this point. All of these grants of jurisdiction have constitutional and statutory expression. The question lurking behind the plain text is whether the constitutional language is a limit or an invitation. For the present congressional definition of federal jurisdiction, see 28 *U.S.C.* chaps. 81, 83, 85. Any standard constitutional treatise or casebook will provide line and verse on the constitutional question of jurisdiction. See, e.g., Gerald Gunther, *Cases and Materials on Constitutional Law*, 5th ed. (Mineola, N.Y., 1982), 48–60 (congressional authority to regulate jurisdiction) and 1604–1716 (self-denying decrees by the Supreme Court). Similarly, any casebook on civil procedure will trace venue, federal questions, and diversity jurisdiction. See, e.g., Richard H. Field, Benjamin Kaplan, and Kevin M. Clermont, *Materials for a Basic Course in Civil Procedure*, 5th ed. (Mineola, N.Y., 1984), 712–956.

36   The constitutional authority appears in the U.S. Constitution, Art. I, sec. 8, cl. 9. The first regulatory act was the Judiciary Act of 1789, 1 *U.S. Stats* 79 (1789). On it, see Charles Warren, "New Light on the History of the Federal Judiciary Act of 1789," 37 *Harvard Law Review* 49 (1923); Julius Goebel, Jr., *History of the Supreme Court of the United States*, vol. 1: *Antecedents and Beginnings to 1801* (New York, 1971), 458–501; and Wythe Holt, "'Federal Courts as the Asylum to Federal Interests' . . .," 36 *Buffalo Law Review* 341 (1988).

37   In the first place, the judiciary was discussed far less often than the legislative and executive branches. In the second place, the provisions for the judiciary were far less specific and certainly less voluminous than the provisions for the other branches. Finally, much more of the structural and substantive detail of the judiciary was left to another branch, Congress, than was true of provisions for the legislative or executive branches. The phrase "least dangerous branch" is Hamilton's; see *Federalist* No. 78 in *Federalist*, 465.

38   Max Farrand, ed., *Records of the Federal Convention*, rev. ed. (New Haven, Conn., 1964), 2:422, 425, 428 (hereafter cited as Farrand).

39   Ibid., 2:428. Blair's draft was found by Farrand in the George Mason Papers. Ibid., 4:54. The proposal never reached the floor, however. Ibid., 2:432. Blair was a leading equity lawyer in Virginia, which like Maryland and Delaware had a separate court of equity. These lines of argument are an example of the influence of state experience on the drafts.

40   Ibid., 2:428, 600, 602, 621.

41   Despite the efforts of William Samuel Johnson and James Paterson to do just this in the Judiciary Act, a compromise prevailed in the Senate. Equity claims were barred when a clear, complete, and adequate remedy was available in law. See Goebel, Jr., *Antecedents*, 499–501.

42   "Centinel, No. 2" (1787), in Herbert J. Storing, ed., *The Complete Anti-Federalist* (Chicago, 1981), 2:147. See also "Federal Farmer, No. 3" (1787), in *The Com-*

plete Anti-Federalist, 2:43, a diatribe against merger, "for if the law restrain [the judge], he is only to step into his shoes of equity." John Selden's witticism about chancellors' feet marched on.

43   "Democratic Federalist" (Pennsylvania, 1787), in Storing, ed., *The Complete Anti-Federalist*, 3:60.

44   Hamilton, *Federalist* No. 80 in *Federalist*, 480.

45   How important were juries as checks on judicial discretion in this era? William E. Nelson, *The Americanization of the Common Law* (Cambridge, Mass., 1975), 20, argued that eighteenth-century juries not only found facts but also had some scope to make law. In the nineteenth century, this capacity was crushed by judges. Ibid., 165–71. Morton Horwitz, *Transformation*, 28–29, agreed that eighteenth-century juries had some lawmaking capacity, which nineteenth-century judges sharply curbed. Whether or not this was so, anti-federalists perceived the jury to be a genuine check on the judge's discretion. The swift adoption of the Seventh Amendment to the Constitution, in 1791, guaranteeing jury trial in federal courts in suits at common law was a triumph for the anti-federalists' general critique, but the equity exception was left undisturbed. In modern Federal Rules pleading, the controversy over the right to jury trial goes on. See Note, "The Right to a Jury Trial in Complex Civil Litigation," 91 *Harvard Law Review* 898 (1979).

46   Hamilton, *Federalist* No. 83 in *Federalist*, 502. At the New York State ratification convention, Hamilton replied to Robert Lansing's proposed amendment requiring jury trial in all federal courts by reminding Lansing, a lawyer and a future state chancellor, that admiralty and equity proceedings never had juries, implying that the alternative was simply unthinkable. Hamilton, Second Speech to the Convention, July 19, 1788, in Harold C. Syrett, ed., *The Papers of Alexander Hamilton* (New York, 1960–82), 5:179.

47   On Hamilton's career in the New York Court of Chancery, see Julius Goebel, Jr., ed., *The Law Practice of Alexander Hamilton* (New York, 1964), 1:167–72ff. One hesitates to second-guess such an experienced litigator, but Hamilton might have argued more directly that juries were simply incompetent to determine facts in some areas of equity. For example, in copyright and patent cases, the jury would not have the expertise to sort out the factual claims, which a special master could easily do. This was English practice in the era of the framing of the Constitution. See Lord Devlin, "Jury Trial of Complex Cases: English Practice at the Time of the Seventh Amendment," 80 *Columbia Law Review* 43 (1980). Modern antitrust suits raise a similar question of jury competence. See *In re* Japanese Electronic Products Antitrust Litigation, 631 F.2d 1069 (3d Cir. 1980), a suit by an American manufacturer of electronic parts against Japanese competitors that the court found to be too complex for a jury to decide properly.

48   The term "publian" appears in Bruce Ackerman, "The Storrs Lectures: Discovering the Constitution," 93 *Yale Law Journal* 1013 (1985). Ackerman is applying the "civic humanism" thesis, propounded by J. G. A. Pocock and others, to the Federalists.

49   Elizabeth McCaughey, *From Loyalist to Founding Father: The Political Odyssey of William Samuel Johnson* (New York, 1980), 148–90, 219–22; George C. Croce, Jr., *William Samuel Johnson* (New York, 1937), 142–49.

50   This is only to say that the delegates tended to reflect certain economic interests more faithfully than others.

51   John T. Farrell, ed., *The Superior Court Diary of William Samuel Johnson* (Washington, D.C., 1942), xlii. The colony had superior courts, which held sessions in each county. Johnson followed the court until 1772, when he was appointed

to its bench. He held this position for a year, after which he resigned to return to his law practice. Ibid., xlix. Typical of Johnson's equity suits was Marston v. Hawley, Fairfield County Superior Court (1768), Johnson Docket Book No. 9, William Samuel Johnson Letterbook, Connecticut Historical Society, Hartford (hereafter cited as Johnson mss.). There were seven other cases involving Marston. All were labeled "in chanc." The terse entries in these memoranda books are explained in Johnson to Nathaniel Marston, November 3, 1763, Johnson mss. Marston was a New York merchant trying to collect from his Connecticut correspondents, all of whom evidently raised equitable defenses.

52   The Susquehannah Company was a major force in Connecticut colonial politics after its charter. Composed of land speculators and merchants, it sought to capitalize on the growing density of population in Connecticut and the ease with which tracts of land on the New York–Pennsylvania border could be obtained from the Indians. See Robert J. Taylor, ed., *The Susquehannah Company Papers* (Ithaca, N.Y., 1969), 7:144–235.

53   Robert J. Taylor, "Trial at Trenton," *William and Mary Quarterly*, 3d ser., 26 (1969): 521–47. Of the five commissioners eventually chosen (for both sides in the dispute could strike potential commissioners, and two of those agreeable to both sides refused to serve), all five had legal training and two of them were judges. The commission was not, however, composed of outstanding jurists. Article IX of the Articles of Confederation had provided for compulsory arbitration of disputes between states, each of which, under the Articles, retained its full sovereignty. It was an unwieldy process and only was employed with any success in the Connecticut/Pennsylvania case. William F. Swindler, "Seedtime of the American Judiciary: From Independence to the Constitution," 17 *William and Mary Law Review* 503, 514–17 (1976).

54   See Taylor, ed., *Susquehannah Company Papers*, 7:199–200, 202–3, for Johnson's presentation to the commissioners at Trenton in November 1782.

55   The doctrine is still good. See, e.g., Holbrook v. Taylor, 532 S.W.2d 763 (Ky. 1976), reiterating that long use of roadway across another's property without the latter's objection creates a right of use. Use, of course, is not title.

56   Johnson, "Autobiography," Johnson mss.

57   Bruce Mann, *Neighbors and Strangers: Law and Community in Early Connecticut* (Chapel Hill, N.C., 1987), 47–66, Richard Bushman, *From Puritan to Yankee* (Cambridge, Mass., 1972), 107–21, and Christopher Collier, *Roger Sherman's Connecticut* (Middletown, Conn., 1971), 37–40, outline the rise of Connecticut commerce, and Merrill Jensen, *The New Nation* (New York, 1950), 170–258, discusses the trade war among the states.

58   The historiographic dispute over the extent and consequences of this interstate rivalry remains acute. There is no question that the Congress created by the Articles of Confederation did resolve many of these disputes. The critical shortages of capital and spiraling inflation staggering the national economy were as much the result of massive importation of consumer goods from Great Britain and the devastation caused by the War for Independence as they were by-products of weak central government. At the same time, critical sectors of the commercial establishment, particularly overseas traders, bankers, manufacturers, and large agricultural producers, welcomed a strengthening of central government. These groups' clamor for reform, added to speculator-creditors' desire to obtain a return on their financial dealings, fed into the federalist movement.

59   Peter Onuf, *The Origins of the Federal Republic: Jurisdictional Controversies in the United States, 1775–1787* (Philadelphia, 1983), 49–102.

60   See, e.g., New York v. Connecticut, 3 U.S. (3 Dallas) 411 (1799), in which the

U.S. Supreme Court heard the last shots fired in the "Oblong" suit.

61 Ordinarily, in an ongoing system like ours authority arises from a "rule of recognition," that is, that a law or opinion is consistent with prior, superior laws or judges' opinions in the highest courts (e.g., constitutions and appellate court opinions). In our constitutional "moment," this rule could not apply.

62 The delegates to the Philadelphia convention were charged with fashioning amendments to the Articles of Confederation. Resolution of [Continental] Congress, February 21, 1787, in Farrand, 2:13–14. The actual course of events was anticipated by some at the Congress, of course. See Jack Rakove, *The Origins of National Politics* (New York, 1982), 389–99. The decision to write a distinct constitution, creating a wholly new fabric of government, was the delegates' idea. See, e.g., George Mason to George Mason, Jr., May 20, 1787, in Farrand, 2:23.

63 Edgar S. Maclay, ed., *The Journal of William Maclay: U.S. Senator from Pennsylvania, 1789–1791* (New York, 1927), 93; Hamilton, *Federalist* No. 83 in *Federalist*, 503. There was some precedent for juries in the chancellor's court. See Harold Chesnin and Geoffrey Hazard, "Chancery Procedure and the Seventh Amendment: Jury Trial of Issues in Equity Cases before 1791," 83 *Yale Law Journal* 999 (1974), finding that chancellors directed feigned trials of issues before juries to get findings of facts. John H. Langbein's reply, in 83 *Yale Law Journal* 1620 (1974), demonstrates that chancellors determined facts on their own except when their courts had no subject-matter jurisdiction; then and only then they might call on an advisory jury. Even if a chancellor sought advice from a jury that report was advisory, not binding.

64 Joseph Story, *Commentaries on the Constitution of the United States* (Boston, 1833), 3:518.

65 See Hoffer and Hull, *Impeachment in America*, 96–97. "Corresponding power," the term used there, denoted those functions or structures of state government that the federal government adopted. The process is evidence of the conscious and widespread reliance of the framers at Philadelphia on the experience of the states in general, and the particular effectiveness of certain state laws and constitutional provisions. Ibid., 269–70.

66 Jefferson to Philip Mazzei, November 18, 1785, in Boyd, ed., *Papers of Jefferson*, 9:70–71. Jefferson, the author of the Virginia Chancery Court Act of 1776, had a personal stake in the separation of law and equity.

67 Iredell, speaking at the North Carolina ratification convention, *Debates in the Various State Conventions on the Adoption of the Constitution*, ed. Jonathan Elliot (Washington, D.C., 1836), 4:145; Hamilton, *Federalist* No. 80 in *Federalist*, 480–81. DeSaussure, *Reports*, 1:liii, understood Hamilton to be concerned about efficiency.

68 Over the past three decades, the "law and economics" school has come close to arguing that economic or allocative efficiency is a legitimate source of authority for law courts. See, e.g., Richard Posner, *Economic Analysis of Law*, 3d ed. (Boston, 1986).

69 Farrell, ed., *Johnson*, xlix; Johnson, Court Docket Book No. 9, Johnson mss.

70 Swift, *Connecticut*, 2:420. On the efficiency of two courts of law and equity, see Barbara Black's magnificent re-creation of Blasgrove v. Blyfield (Mass. Superior Court of Judicature, 1698–1708?) in Black, "Nathaniel Blyfield, 1653–1733," in *Law in Colonial Massachusetts, 1630–1800*, Publications of the Colonial Society of Massachusetts, no. 62 (1984), 81–105.

71 Wilson, "Lectures on Law," in *The Works of James Wilson*, ed. McCloskey, 2:486–87.

72 Madison, *Federalist* No. 37 in *Federalist*, 228. See also Lawrence E. Mitchell,

"The Ninth Amendment and the 'Jurisprudence of Original Intention,'" 74 *Georgetown Law Journal* 1719 (1986); H. Jefferson Powell, "The Original Understanding of Original Intent," 98 *Harvard Law Review* 885 (1985); and James Willard Hurst, *Dealing with Statutes* (New York, 1982), 10.

73 D. E. C. Yale, ed., *Lord Nottingham's Chancery Cases* (London, 1957), 1:270.

74 Swift, *Connecticut*, 2:418; DeSaussure, *Reports*, 1:xxiv. Nevertheless, the question of discretion was a dragon in a cave, for a chancellor like George Wythe might rely less on precedent and more on his own ideal of equality than his peers preferred.

75 Judiciary Act of 1789, 1 *U.S. Stats* 79. Modern federal courts follow state law—that is, the substance of state law—for the jurisdiction in which the courts sit when the basis of federal jurisdiction is the diverse state residence of the parties.

76 See Goebel, Jr., *Antecedents*, 500–501. Goebel argued that William Paterson, who had represented New Jersey on the drafting committee and was soon to leave the Senate to assume the governorship (and the chancellor's office) of New Jersey, favored such a broad grant, but an unpublished draft of Paterson's speech to the Senate on federal equity indicates that he preferred common-law rules over equitable ones in some cases. For example, he opposed the use of pre-trial depositions in federal court, opting for testimony at trial instead. Here, he feared, "Equity has swallowed up the common law—overleaped her bounds." Speech on July 14–17, 1789, William Paterson Papers, Bancroft Transcript, New York Public Library. Ten years later, in his proposed revision of New Jersey equity procedure, he argued that the rules of court ought to be left to the judges. John E. O'Connor, *William Paterson* (New Brunswick, N.J., 1979), 216–17. It seems clear that his advocacy of a broad grant of jurisdiction to the federal judges bespoke a preference for judge-made rules of court rather than for an unrestrained equitable discretion in case after case.

77 Judiciary Act of 1789, 1 *U.S. Stats* 82. The Process Regulation Act of 1789, 1 *U.S. Stats* 94, sec. 2(b), provided that "The forms and modes of proceedings in causes in equity . . . shall be according to the course of civil law." When Richard Peters, reporter for the Supreme Court until 1842, undertook publication of the U.S. Statutes in 1845, he appended "note (a)" to the above section. It read: "this has been generally understood to adopt the principles, rules, and usages of the court of chancery in England." 1 *U.S. Stats* 94. This was not strictly true, for the body of the 1789 act mixed English usages with state equity rules (e.g., the rule for discovery of documents was taken from the New York Court of Chancery). See Goebel, Jr., *Antecedents*, 483–84.

78 Process Regulation Act of 1792, 1 *U.S. Stats* 276. Congress added that courts might use their "discretion" to direct "such alterations and additions" as they might deem "expedient" and the Supreme Court could issue "regulations—by rule" to lower courts. This internal rule-making power was reiterated in 1842, 5 *U.S. Stats* 516. Congress had good reason to fear conflict between state and federal courts. See Wythe Holt and James R. Perry, "Writs and Rights 'Clashing and Animosities': The First Confrontation between Federal and State Jurisdictions," *Law and History Review* 7 (1789): 89 et seq.

79 Among state chancellors, William Henry DeSaussure of South Carolina, William Livingston of New Jersey, and George Wythe of Virginia had well-established reputations as jurists. Nevertheless, official reports of American equity cases did not appear until the end of the eighteenth century and after. William Henry DeSaussure's *South Carolina Reports* (1817) and Alexander James Dallas's first volumes on federal cases (1798) came after Wythe's reports of his own cases, in 1795, and were followed by William Johnson's New York *Chancery*

Reports in 1816. In the new states and territories, judges relied on a combination of English and American reports and treatises as sources of authority. By 1836, more American reports were used than English reports, but English treatises still predominated. See Blume, "Chancery Practice on the American Frontier," 89–93. The latter state of affairs ended with publication of Story's *Commentaries* on equity in 1836 and 1838. They swept the field.

80   U.S. Supreme Court Justice James Iredell, on circuit in South Carolina, decreed that he would use the equity rules of that state. See Goebel, Jr., *Antecedents*, 580–81.

81   The question of the boundary dividing the sovereignty of the state from that of the federal government was not resolved by the supremacy clause (U.S. Const. Art. VI, cl. 2), nor by the series of debates over interposition and nullification engaging jurists and politicians in the antebellum era, any more than by the invocation of "new federalism" in our own time. Nevertheless, Hamilton, in *Federalist* No. 32, stated that only the enumerated powers restricted the states in the exercise of their sovereignty. See *Federalist*, 201.

82   See Leonard Levy, *The Emergence of a Free Press* (New York, 1985), 220–349.

83   5 U.S. (1 Cranch) xvii (Rules of Court) (1801). It is not clear how influential this rule was, however, particularly at the district or circuit court level. See Goebel, Jr., *Antecedents*, 583.

84   See, e.g., Swift, *Connecticut*, 2:417; DeSaussure, *South Carolina Equity*, 1:li. For much of the revolutionary crisis (1766–70), Lord Camden was chancellor, and he had been a friend to the American cause.

85   16 U.S. (3 Wheaton) 212, 221–22 (1818).

86   31 U.S. (6 Peters) 648, 657–58 (1832). Congress did not forget altogether its primacy in assigning jurisdiction and making rules for federal courts. Enjoying the land rush after the depression of 1819, Congress balked at the Supreme Court's imposition of uniform equity pleading on states in Wayman v. Southard, 23 U.S. (10 Wheaton) 1 (1825). In the Process Act of May 19, 1828, 4 *U.S. Stats* 278, Congress allowed states to use their own forms of equity pleading, reserving to the federal courts their established authority to select equitable rules.

87   Note, "The Remedial Rights Doctrine: Past and Present," 67 *Harvard Law Review* 826, 828 (1954), suggests that adoption of English rules was dictum, that is, the Supreme Court speaking outside of its holding in the case. There certainly was a vacuum as far as the Court was concerned. Had the justices overlooked an emerging American body of equity rules, which might, in their own hands, have come to supplant the English rules? Story left the way open for this in the last sentence of his opinion in *Boyle*, but it was only a door left ajar. One may argue that the Court fully opened and stepped through that door with *Brown* and its sister cases.

88   Rules of Practice for the Courts of Equity of the United States, Rule 32, 20 U.S. (7 Wheaton) xvii, xxi (1822). Later revisions of the Rules of Procedure came in 1841 and 1912. See 226 U.S. 649 (1913). Equity procedure was merged with common-law pleading in the 1938 Federal Rules of Civil Procedure and remains so. Equitable relief available from federal courts was determined by those courts, not by the case law or statutes of the states in which the federal court sits. See Guffey v. Smith, 237 U.S. 101 (1915), and Guaranty Trust Co. v. York, 326 U.S. 99, 112 (1945) (Rutledge, J., dissenting) (federal equity procedure should still be tied to the great maxims of equity, not limited). Did *Brown* II track Rutledge's dissent?

89   Blackstone, *Commentaries*, 3:429–31, insisted that equity was an auxiliary to law and wholly constrained by prior decisions, rules, and statutes. See Story to

William Scott, May 20, 1820, in William W. Story, *The Life and Letters of Joseph Story* (Boston, 1851), 1:327, on Story's high regard for Lord Eldon.

90 Story, *Equity Jurisprudence*, 1:12–13, 19, 54. The full deployment of English equity was not just Story's idea. James Kent, Chancellor of New York, and Nathan Dane, creator of the chair at Harvard Law School that Story occupied, had the same high opinion and attachment to English equity. See Story, *Equity Jurisprudence*, 1:53; Kent, *Commentaries on American Law* (New York, 1827–30), 4:295–308, wherein the law of trusts is lifted literally from English equity cases; and Nathan Dane, *A General Abridgement and Digest of American Law* (Boston, 1824), 7:516. The same view was widely shared in antebellum state courts of equity, particularly in the South. See "The Chancellor's Case," in *Reports of Cases Decided in the High Court of Chancery [Maryland]*, ed. Theodorick Bland (chanc.) (Annapolis, 1836), 1:648, which found Bland arguing against a diminution of his own salary by the lower house.

91 Newmyer, *Story*, 295.

92 The fact is that very little equity business came the federal courts' way in the antebellum period. Most of it arrived in the circuit courts because plaintiff and defendant resided in different states and the federal court was deemed by Congress a neutral forum. This is called "diversity" jurisdiction. See U.S. Const. Art. III, sec. 2; Judiciary Act of 1789, sec. 35: if plaintiff and defendant were from different states, either the plaintiff could bring the suit in federal court or the defendant could remove it there; now 28 *U.S.C.* sec. 1332. A count of equity suits in William Branch's reports of cases from the Circuit Court for the District of Columbia (1–30 F. Cas.) shows more than 150 cases in the years 1800 to 1840. Almost all concerned traditional equity practice, i.e., mistake in contracts, dower rights, construction of wills, etc., as opposed to other federal courts' equity dockets' increasing load of patent and receivership suits. In the southern district of New York, the suits were more commercial in nature. See "Equity Case Files," U.S. Circuit Court for the Southern District of New York, 1791–1846, R.G. 21, National Archives. In Kentucky, whose federal district court had the powers of a circuit court as well, equity suits were often disputes over federal land grants and surveys. See Mary K. Bonsteel Tachau, *Federal Courts in the Early Republic: Kentucky, 1789–1816* (Princeton, N.J., 1978), 82–85, 179–83. The Supreme Court had little equity business brought to its doors in its first three decades. Maeva Marcus et al., eds., *The Documentary History of the Supreme Court of the United States, 1789–1800* (Washington, D.C., 1985), list *Oswald v. New York* (1792), *Telfair v. Brailsford* (1792–94), *Chisholm v. Georgia* (1792), *South Carolina v. The French Republic* (1792), and *New York v. Connecticut* (1799) on the Court's docket. George L. Haskins and Herbert A. Johnson, *History of the Supreme Court of the United States*, vol. 2: *Foundations of Power: John Marshall, 1801–1815* (New York, 1981), find very little equity business in these years. What is more, the justices took a very narrow view of their powers in equity, despite their insistence on the independence of federal equity procedure. See, e.g., Geyger's Lessee v. Geyger, 2 U.S. (2 Dallas) 332 (1795): no need to go to equity to get discovery in federal court; and New York v. Connecticut II, 4 U.S. (4 Dallas) 1, 3 (1799): the Court does not regard the states themselves as parties and will not enjoin either of them. The Court's policy of not using equitable injunctions to direct the actions of state courts was firmly entrenched by the 1810s. See Haskins and Johnson, *Foundations*, 632–33.

CHAPTER FIVE

1 See, e.g., Harry N. Scheiber, "Property Law, Expropriation, and Resource Allocation by Government," *Journal of Economic History* 33 (1973): 232–51.

2 Horwitz, *Transformation*, 161–210. But see A. W. B. Simpson, "The Horwitz Thesis and the History of Contracts," 46 *University of Chicago Law Review* 533 (1979), and Philip A. Hamburger, "The Development of the Nineteenth-Century Consensus Theory of Contract," *Law and History Review* 7 (1989): 248–54.

3 See Peter Charles Hoffer, "Principled Discretion: Contracts, Conscience, and Chancellors in Antebellum America," ms. in author's possession.

4 6 N.H. 481 (1834). For analogous contemporary cases, borrowing equity for use in admiralty suits by sailors, see Story's opinion in Cloutman v. Tunison, 5 F. Cas. 1091 (C.C.D. Me. 1833), and Newmyer, *Story*, 152. The gradual acceptance of *Britton* is traced in Lancellotti v. Thomas, 341 Pa. Super. Ct. 1 (1985).

5 See, e.g., Erastus Washington, *An Essay on the Establishment of a Chancery Jurisdiction in Massachusetts* (Boston, 1812), 50. The equitable doctrine was simple— for part performance, part payment. The concept has made a comeback in modern contract theory. See, e.g., Ian R. Macneil, "Contracts: Adjustment of Long-term Economic Relations under Classical, Neo-classical, and Relational Contract Law," 72 *Northwestern University Law Review* 854 (1978). The "relational" contract returns to equitable mutuality and fairness as a standard.

6 Parker, a man of conservative principles, was a traditionalist in law as well as politics. He defended equitable discretion and convinced his state's legislature to confer it on the Supreme Court. See Philip Paludan, *A Covenant with Death: The Constitution, Law, and Equality in the Civil War Era* (Urbana, Ill., 1975), 115– 16. On the "grand style," see Karl Llewellyn, *The Common Law Tradition—Deciding Appeals* (Boston, 1960), 37–38.

7 Nathan Dane, *A General Abridgement and Digest of American Law* (Boston, 1829), 9:696.

8 6 Johns Ch. 222, 224, 233–34 (N.Y. Ch. 1822); 3 Cowen 446 (N.Y. Ct. of Errors, 1824). See, in accord, Kent's opinion in Reigal v. Wood, 1 Johns Ch. 401 (1815). An Indiana chancellor reached the same conclusions in a similar set of facts in Marshall v. Billingsley, 7 Ind. 250 (1855).

9 Exactly what James Duer, for the plaintiff-appellant, said on appeal to the Supreme Court of Errors. 3 Cowen at 446–51.

10 James Kent, *Commentaries on American Law* (New York, 1827–30), 4:302.

11 3 Cowen at 521, 528, 535, 451. Sudam also noted how vital such contracts for land sales were in the commercial development of the state.

12 6 Johns Ch. at 232. Kent never acceded to the "authority" of the court of errors' reversal of his decree. See Kent, *Commentaries on American Law*, 2:383. U.S. Supreme Court Justice Stephen J. Field agreed with Kent, writing for the Court in Willard v. Tayloe, 75 U.S. (8 Wallace) 557, 566 (1868).

13 Kent, *Commentaries on American Law*, 2:328, 330. Kent was very receptive to the needs of turnpike and canal corporations, bowing to their incursions upon others' quiet enjoyment of land. See John T. Horton, *James Kent: A Study in Conservatism, 1763–1847* (New York, 1939), 220.

14 Gardner v. Village of Newburgh, 2 Johns Ch. 162, 166 (N.Y. 1816).

15 Beekman v. Saratoga and Schenectady Railroad, 3 Paige Ch. 44 (N.Y. 1831). Even after the chancellor was banished by the New York Code of Civil Pleading (the Field Code), the court protected the railroads. See, e.g., Hentz v. Long Island R.R., 13 Barbour 646, 658 (1852). Meanwhile, the state legislature had also bowed to the majesty of the railroads. After 1852 the farmer had to prove that he was entitled to compensation; statute did not automatically require it.

See L. Ray Gunn, *The Decline of Authority: Public Economic Policy and Political Development in New York, 1800–1860* (Ithaca, N.Y., 1989), 236–39. The brakes were applied to this doctrine in Pumpelly v. Green Bay and Mississippi Canal Co., 80 U.S. (13 Wallace) 166 (1872).

16 Doggett v. Emerson, 7 F. Cas. 804, 816 (C.C.D. Me. 1845). See also Warner v. Daniels et al., 29 F. Cas. 246 (C.C.D. Mass. 1845). Story's insistence on good faith was recovered by the drafters of the Uniform Commercial Code. See U.C.C. secs. 1–203, "obligation of good faith."

17 Story, *Equity Jurisprudence*, 1:241. See also Horwitz, *Transformation*, 198. But see Friedman, *History of American Law*, 264–65, on the limits of adoption of *caveat emptor*. In the South, particularly South Carolina, *caveat emptor* did not apply to sales of slaves. Andrew Fede, "Legal Protection for Slave Buyers in the United States South: A Caveat concerning Caveat Emptor," 31 *American Journal of Legal History* 322, 327 (1987). Fede notes that all slave sales had an implied warranty of merchantability, subject to review by the courts. The doctrine of "sound" or fair price persisted here. See, e.g., Grant v. Bontz, 10 F. Cas. 977 (C.C.D.C. 1819).

18 Chancellors, all of whom were drawn from the "better sort," did not interpose themselves into business relationships unless the law was inadequate and equity offered a remedy. When one businessman sued another, the chancellors often favored the more productive entrepreneur. For example, in Eason v. Perkins, 2 Devereaux Eq. 38 (1831), Justice Thomas Ruffin of the North Carolina Supreme Court denied a farmer's request for an injunction to prevent a mill from reopening next to his land. Though the millpond might have caused a health problem for the petitioner and his family, Ruffin asserted that "our views can not be thus limited in the case before us. Mills are necessary public conveniences, and water mills the ordinary and almost the universal kind in this state. It is a maxim that private right must yield to public convenience, upon adequate compensation." That the mill was privately owned and the contest was not between the public per se and a private complainant did not deter Ruffin from an analogy to public use: "There is nothing in this case but the interest of a single individual, to weight against public utility." In between the two assertions of the public utility of mills, Ruffin admitted that if "the pond of an insignificant mill [were] throwing off vapours destructive to the healthfulness of a large landed estate," the court might act to enjoin the nuisance. Id. at 40. Ruffin, one should add, came from one of the best families in the state.

Sometimes the chancellor had to decide between two major commercial enterprises. Indeed, the grandest of all the antebellum nuisance suits (it was litigated for nearly a decade, involved dozens of petitions from merchants and builders to state and federal authorities, and ended with a series of bills in Congress as well as four Supreme Court cases), Pennsylvania v. Wheeling and Belmont Bridge Company, 50 U.S. (9 Howard) 647 (1852), featured the temporary closing of the longest suspension bridge in the country. The suit pit Virginia politicians and promoters against Pennsylvania legislators and entrepreneurs, and advocates of land and road traffic against defenders of riverboats. The Court's initial, divided decision to force the bridge company to raise its span to accommodate the smokestacks of Ohio riverboats was based in large measure on the report of a specially appointed master, retired New York Chancellor Reuben Walworth. Walworth produced a 770-page monograph on river travel and road-bound commerce which convinced a majority of the Court, led by Ohio's John McLean, that the bridge was a nuisance. Dissenters were led by Virginia's Peter V. Daniel. The clash of regional interests (Ohio gained greatly from downriver traffic, Virginia from the road and the bridge) apparently had found its way into the Court, though the alignment of the justices may have been purely accidental. In the end, Congress designated the bridge a postal and military roadway, and the Court acceded. The bridge became a rail crossing as well as a roadway. On the clash of interests, see Elizabeth B. Monroe, "Spanning the Commerce Clause: The Wheeling Bridge Case, 1850–1856," *American Journal of Legal History* 32 (1988): 265 et seq.

19 For example, Mark V. Tushnet, *The American Law of Slavery, 1815–1860* (Princeton, N.J., 1980), 3–15, finds slaves simultaneously were viewed as a form of property in the stream of commerce and important members of the human community.

20 Story, *Equity Jurisprudence*, 1:21. Under the equity doctrine of *cy pres*, the court was to determine and carry out the intentions of the testator. The exception was that state statutes forbidding the testator to do something barred that part of his will from operating. One case in point, Ross v. Vertner, 6 Miss. 305 (1840), affirmed that equitable power. The chancellor of Mississippi denied the heirs' challenge to a will providing for the testator's slaves to be transported to Liberia and there freed. Mississippi prohibited manumission of slaves within its borders, but Captain Isaac Ross had anticipated that problem and ordered his executors to transport the slaves before freeing them. The heir departed the courtroom without the slaves.

21 1 Bay 260 (S.C. 1792). In upholding the right of a slave to purchase the freedom of another slave with funds the master allowed the purchaser to earn for herself, Rutledge instructed a jury that it should ignore the Roman law precept that everything a slave had belonged automatically to the master: the jury "were too humane and upright, he hoped, to do such manifest violence to so singular and extraordinary an act of benevolence." The jury allowed the purchased slave to retain her freedom. 1 Bay at 262–63.

22 2 Call 319 (Va. 1799). Wythe was an innovative chancellor who believed in the principle of discretionary reform where statute was silent and injustice was manifest and used his office aggressively to argue for these positions. See Robert B. Kirtland, "George Wythe: Lawyer, Revolutionary, Judge" (Ph.D. diss., University of Michigan, 1983), 220–24. Among these precepts was that American law should move toward greater equality of status for persons.

23 For Virginia cases protecting trusts for slaves, see Dawson v. Thurston, 2 Hen. and Mun. 132 (Va. 1808); Wilson v. Butler, 3 Mun. 559 (Va. 1813); Dawson v. Dawson, 10 Leigh 602 (Va. 1840); and Osborne v. Taylor, 12 Grattan 117 (Va. 1855). On Wythe's personal aversion to slavery and willingness to use equity to lean in favor of freedom, see Hudgins v. Wrights, 1 Hen. and Mun. 134 (Va. 1806).

24 The lead cases in South Carolina were Bynum v. Bostick, 4 DeSaussure 266 (S.C. Ch. 1812), in which Chancellor DeSaussure ruled that a bequest of slaves to a trustee in order that they be freed at a future time was an attempt to evade the statute barring domestic manumission, and so void; Frazier v. Frazier, 2 Hill 304 (S.C. 1835), in which Chief Justice John Belton O'Neall overturned *Bynum* by finding that the statute of 1800 which forbade domestic manumission did not prohibit the freeing of slaves if they were taken out of the state for that purpose; and Blackman v. Gordon, 2 Richardson 43 (S.C. 1845), reversing *Frazier*, in part because the statute of 1841 forbade trusts made with the intent of freeing slaves.

25 See T. R. R. Cobb, *An Inquiry into the Law of Negro Slavery in the United States* (Philadelphia, 1858), 291–92, noting that Georgia, North Carolina, and South Carolina all had such laws. What is striking is the persistence of efforts to

create trusts for slaves even after the statute of 1841 in South Carolina forbade executory trusts for emancipation without explicit language directing when and where (outside of the state) the emancipation was to occur. These trusts confuted the not quite monolithic but certainly imposing determination on the bench that wills not conforming to every particular of the statute were to be construed against liberality (and the testator's intent). See, e.g., Gordon v. Blackman, 1 Richardson 61 (S.C. 1844), aff'd, 2 Richardson 43 (S.C. 1845); Morton v. Thompson, 4 Richardson 370 (S.C. 1854); Ford v. Dangerfield, 8 Richardson 95 (S.C. 1856); and Belcher v. Belcher, 11 Richardson 9 (S.C. 1859). There were a few exceptions, all involving John Belton O'Neall. The same pattern of equitable dissolution of wills creating trusts for slaves developed in North Carolina; so long as no provision was made to remove the slave beneficiary of the trust from the state, the trust was void *ab initio*. See Gossett v. Weatherly, 5 Jones Eq. 46 (N.C. 1860).

26   Bennahan v. Norwood, 5 Iredell Eq. 106, 107 (N.C. 1847). A tantalizing note: women may have been more likely to pursue this course than men. See Suzanne Lebsock, *The Free Women of Petersburg: Status and Culture in a Southern Town, 1784–1860* (New York, 1984), 136–41. A collateral observation: one strand of modern jurisprudence, sometimes labeled "feminist jurisprudence," appears to me to closely resemble the ideal of equity set forth in the introduction to this book and exemplified in the slave trust cases.

27   Cobb, *Law of Slavery*, 23–52, argued that blacks were by nature mentally sluggish, lascivious, and amoral.

28   Ibid., 303.

29   O'Neall, *The Negro Law of South Carolina* (Columbia, 1848), 1:35. In Ford v. Porter, 11 Richardson 128 (S.C. 1860), O'Neall upheld a bequest to slaves from a will that explicitly disavowed any attempt to make a secret trust for their freedom. On O'Neall, see A. E. Keir Nash, "Negro Rights, Unionism, and Greatness on the South Carolina Court of Appeals: The Extraordinary Chief Justice John Belton O'Neall," 21 *South Carolina Law Review* 141, 154–66 (1969). Surely part of O'Neall's greatness lay in his ability to avoid controversy off the bench. See, e.g., his eulogy on George Washington Dargin in *Biographical Sketches of the Bench and Bar of South Carolina* (Charleston, S.C., 1859), 1:288.

30   35 Miss. 246 (1858). On comity, see the discussion in Paul Finkelman, *An Imperfect Union: Slavery, Federalism, and Comity* (Chapel Hill, N.C., 1981), 231–34. Mississippi courts had approved the trust to free a slave out of state in Ross v. Vertner, 5 How. 305, 359 (Miss. 1840), but in 1842 the state legislature forbade such manumissions.

31   See, e.g., Elias et al. v. Smith et al., 25 Tenn. 18 (1845). The cases are discussed in Arthur F. Howington, *What Sayeth the Laws: The Treatment of Slaves and Free Blacks in the State and Local Courts of Tennessee* (New York, 1986), 3–24, and A. E. Keir Nash, "Reason of Slavery: Understanding the Judicial Role in the Peculiar Institution," 32 *Vanderbilt Law Review*, 7, 98–103 (1979).

32   Cooper v. Blakely, 10 Ga. 263 (1851). See also Cleland v. Waters, 16 Ga. 496 (1854), in which Chief Justice Joseph Henry Lumpkin construed a testator's intent to be to free all his slaves, rather than just the parents, under a trust providing for foreign manumission.

33   Cox v. Williams, 4 Iredell Eq. 15, 18–19 (N.C. 1845). Ruffin was not immune to the claims of sentiment, however, and in Waddill v. Martin, 3 Iredell Eq. 562 (1845), rebuked an heir at law who tried to seize a postmortem gift to a slave. See also Wade v. Executor of Isaac Ross, 7 Smedes and Marshall 663 (Miss. 1846), in which the Mississippi Supreme Court effectuated a testator's wish to

give a slave to the American Colonization Society.

34   Carmille v. Carmille's Administrator, 2 McMul. 454, 470 (S.C. 1842). This is clear proof that South Carolina judges were fully aware of abolitionist attacks on the law of slavery.

35   37 Miss. 235, 285 (1859), finding that a former slave cannot inherit in Mississippi under its laws.

36   See the discussion of precedents in favor of trusts in Nash, "Reason of Slavery," 95–104. The law (and equity) favoring slavery was rehearsed at length in Cobb, *Law of Slavery*, 278–305.

37   2 Hill Eq. at 304.

38   Gordon v. Blackman, 1 Richardson 61 (S.C. 1844), in which a Johnson circuit court chancellor, affirmed by Chancellor William Harper on appeal, found that O'Neall's opinion in *Frazier* had no weight after the 1841 statute.

39   Morton v. Thompson, 6 Richardson 370, 372 (S.C. 1854). Out-of-doors, these chancellors were more avid still in their view of the propriety of slavery. See, e.g., Harper's posthumously published *Memoir on Slavery* (Charleston, S.C., 1852), 3: "perhaps nothing can be more evident than that [slavery] is the sole cause of civilization."

40   E.g., Bell v. Hogan, 3 F. Cas. 107 (C.C.D.C. 1811); Bell v. McCormick, 3 F. Cas. 107 (C.C.D.C. 1838); Brown v. Wingard, 4 F. Cas. 438 (C.C.D.C. 1822); Bell v. Greenfield, 3 F. Cas. 103 (C.C.D.C. 1840).

41   Alice v. Morte, 1 F. Cas. 408 (C.C.D.C. 1824).

42   Brown v. Wingard, 4 F. Cas. at 439. On Key's views, see Edward S. Delaplaine, *Francis Scott Key: Life and Times* (New York, 1938), 441–58.

43   Fountain v. Ravenal, 58 U.S. (17 Howard) 369, 392–94 (1854) (Taney, C.J., dissenting in part). In Dred Scott v. Sanford, 57 U.S. (10 Howard) 393 (1857), Taney used trust terminology to defend slavery: Congress regulated the territories as a trust for American citizens and violated its duties as a trustee when it barred slave owners from full enjoyment of their property. 57 U.S. at 448. See also Carl B. Swisher, *History of the Supreme Court of the United States*, vol. 5: *The Taney Period, 1836–64* (New York, 1974), 534ff.; Harold M. Hyman and William M. Wiecek, *Equal Justice under Law: Constitutional Development, 1835–1875* (New York, 1982), 101ff.

44   William E. Nelson, *The Roots of American Bureaucracy, 1830–1900* (Cambridge, Mass., 1982), 41–61; George Edward Carter, "The Use of Higher Law in the American Anti-Slavery Crusade, 1830–1860" (Ph.D. diss., University of Oregon, 1970); William Wiecek, *The Sources of Antislavery Constitutionalism in America, 1760–1848* (Ithaca, N.Y., 1977), 202–27.

One may ask if the Declaration of Independence was in any way "received" into the Constitution. Following Justice William Paterson's draft opinion on the constitutionality of the Alien and Sedition Acts (an unused opinion as well, since the case was never brought to court), one might argue that the Constitution gave to the federal courts the power to create a federal common law based on the founding conceptions of the new nation. See Paterson, "Opinions on the Bench," William Paterson Papers, Bancroft Transcript, New York Public Library, 535–69. This conception underlay the thinking of some of the justices in the dispute over the existence of a federal common law of crime. See G. Edward White, *History of the Supreme Court*, vol. 3: *The Marshall Court and Cultural Change, 1815–1835* (New York, 1988), 118–25. To this could be added Story's later view that the national government originated with the Declaration (see n. 102, Chapter 3 above), making the Declaration the first law of the new nation. One conclusion from the confluence of these two theories (a conclusion quite likely opposite to that Paterson and Story might draw) was that the Constitution could not be construed to sanction slavery. For a parallel argument, see Timothy Farrar, *Manual of the Constitution of the United States of America* (Boston, 1867), 53–62.

45 This was particularly true when Southern domestic law was not the rule of reference, as in admiralty cases involving salvaged ships with slaves aboard. See, e.g., The Marianna Flora, 24 U.S. (11 Wheaton) 1 (1826), and The Armistad, 40 U.S. (15 Peters) 518 (1841), during Taney's tenure.

46 See, e.g., Wood v. Davis, 11 U.S. (7 Cranch) 271 (1812), ruling that a purchaser who did not know that the mother of the black children he bought was free could hold the children in bondage nonetheless; Mima Queen v. Hepburn, 27 U.S. (2 Peters) 151 (1828), determining that hearsay evidence was not acceptable in court to prove freedom of petitioner; and after Taney replaced Marshall, a series of cases allowing recapture of suspected runaways under the Fugitive Slave laws of 1793 and 1850, ending in *Dred Scott*.

47 30 U.S. (5 Peters) 1 (1831). Marshall, for the Court, denied that the Cherokee had standing to bring the suit in federal court because they were not a foreign nation at all, and only a foreign nation or its agents might sue a state under the restrictions of the Eleventh Amendment.

48 Act of March 30, 1802, 2 *U.S. Stats* 139. The sordid episode of the federal government's inability (in President Andrew Jackson's case, unwillingness) to protect the treaty rights of the Indians against state avarice and force is recounted in Ronald N. Satz, *American Indian Policy in the Jacksonian Era* (Lincoln, Nebr., 1975).

49 Worcester v. Georgia, 31 U.S. (6 Peters) 515 (1832).

50 Newmyer, *Story*, 155–95.

51 See, e.g., U.S. v. Coolidge, 25 F. Cas. 619 (C.C.D. Mass. 1813); Swift v. Tyson, 41 U.S. (16 Peters) 1 (1842).

52 See, e.g., Story's opinion for the Court in Vidal et al. v. Girard's Executors, 43 U.S. (2 Howard) 127 (1844). On Story and slavery, see Newmyer, *Story*, 365–79. The metaphor (with its biblical overtones) was Jefferson's when discussing slavery and the Missouri controversy. Jefferson to John Holmes, April 22, 1820, quoted in Dumas Malone, *Jefferson: Sage of Monticello*, vol. 6: *Jefferson and His Times* (Boston, 1981), 325.

53 The Fugitive Slave Law of 1793, 1 *U.S. Stats* 302, passed to provide an enforcement mechanism for Art. IV, sec. 2, cl. 3, of the Constitution, provided for summary hearings before federal or state authorities before the putative fugitive was given to the custody of her master or her master's agent.

54 Thomas Morris, *Free Men All: The Personal Liberty Laws of the North, 1780–1861* (Baltimore, 1974), traces this movement.

55 See Prigg v. Pennsylvania, 41 U.S. (16 Peters) 539 (1842). Story, writing for the Court, struck down a Pennsylvania antikidnapping law as an unconstitutional restraint on the Fugitive Slave Law of 1793. Story's dilemma was a common one for Northern jurists who abhorred slavery but refused to find it illegal. See Robert Cover, *Justice Accused* (New Haven, Conn., 1975), 131ff.

56 The full faith and credit clause of the Constitution, Art. IV, sec. 1, mandating that one state enforce the judicial holdings of another, was conflated during the Civil War with the privileges and immunities clause, Art. IV, sec. 2, stating that the citizens of one state were entitled to the privileges and immunities of citizens in all states. See [Rev.] George B. Cheever et al., *Petition and Memorial . . . November 30, 1865* (New York, 1865), insisting that the privileges and immunities clause mandated equal treatment of blacks and whites in readmitted

Confederate states, and John Bingham, an Ohio Republican, Speech to the House of Representatives, *Congressional Globe*, 39th Cong., 1st sess. (January 9, 1866), 157–58.

57   By the 1850s, Northern courts, led by Massachusetts and New York, regarded slaves *domiciled* in the state, even in service to citizens of other states, as free. See Finkelman, *Imperfect Union*, 101–45.

58   E.g., *In re* Booth, 3 Wis. 1 (1854), upholding a state writ of habeas corpus that freed an abettor of a runaway from federal detention; Lemmon v. People, 20 N.Y. 562 (1860), deciding that even a sojourner's slaves were freed the moment they came in contact with free soil, a clear disavowal of *Dred Scott*.

59   Cover, *Justice Accused*, 201.

60   12 Wendell 311 (N.Y. 1834).

61   14 Wendell 507, 524 (N.Y. 1835).

62   Abraham Lincoln, First Inaugural Address, March 4, 1861, reprinted in Richard Hofstadter, ed., *Great Issues in American History: A Documentary Record* (New York, 1959), 1:394.

63   Jefferson Davis, Message to the Confederate Congress, April 29, 1861, reprinted in Hofstadter, ed., *Great Issues*, 1:399.

64   The conservatism of many Republicans in the first six months of the Civil War is documented in Herman Belz, *Reconstructing the Union* (Ithaca, N.Y., 1969), 1–39. Precedent for the decision not to return runaway slaves came from General Benjamin Butler's command at Fort Monroe, Va. Deluged with fleeing slaves in the first months of the war, he ordered them protected as contraband of war. On the proclamation, see Hyman and Wiecek, *Equal Justice under Law*, 252–55; Mary F. Berry, *Military Necessity and Civil Rights Policy* (Port Washington, N.Y., 1977), 45ff.; James M. McPherson, *The Struggle for Equality: Abolitionists and the Negro in the Civil War and Reconstruction* (Princeton, N.J., 1964), 99–133.

65   A number of theories were proposed to justify the confiscation of private property without due process. The first and most durable was the "grasp-of-war" theory, whose inner machinery worked on the principle that the rebel South was a belligerent without rights. A second theory, of "state suicide," posited that the seceding states were no more than territories once again, and that their laws (including those laws enslaving blacks) were again subject to federal approval. The issue was resolved, in law if not in fact, by the Thirteenth Amendment to the Constitution. Michael Les Benedict, *A Compromise of Principle: Congressional Republicans and Reconstruction, 1863–1869* (New York, 1974), 122–26, 134ff. On Johnson, see Benedict, *The Impeachment of Andrew Johnson* (New York, 1973), 6–7ff. On the lasting conservatism of many in the Republican camp, see Earl M. Maltz, "Reconstruction without Revolution: Republican Civil Rights Theory in the Era of the Fourteenth Amendment," 24 *Houston Law Review* 221 (1986).

66   George Washington Julian, January 14, 1862, Speech to the House of Representatives, in Julian, *Speeches on Political Questions* (New York, 1872), 155; Patrick W. Riddleberger, *George Washington Julian: Radical Republican* (Indianapolis, 1966), 95.

67   Rev. Samuel Spears, Sermon, October 19, 1862, in Harold Hyman, ed., *The Radical Republicans and Reconstruction, 1861–1870* (Indianapolis, 1967), 74; Hans L. Trefousse, *Benjamin Franklin Wade: Radical Republican from Ohio* (New York, 1963), 236–37; Fawn M. Brodie, *Thaddeus Stevens: Scourge of the South* (New York, 1966), 154–68, 203–4; David Donald, *Charles Sumner and the Rights of Man* (New York, 1970), 152.

68   McPherson, *The Struggle for Equality*, 181–84. The dispute was not over the

need for federal assistance but over full freedom for the former slave. "Guardianship" in these proposals implied that freedmen and women were to be denied the rights of citizens (the definition of which, admittedly, was hardly settled). If guardianship meant that former slaves would be the nation's stepchildren, it would be a badge of continuing, legalized inferiority. Trusteeship, by contrast, implied no such legal debilities in the beneficiary, nor did it deny the beneficiary any legal rights.

69 The story of Secretary of State William Seward's brokerage of a coalition of Union Democrats and conservative Republicans to support the Radicals is told in John Cox and LaWanda Cox, *Politics, Principles, and Prejudice, 1865–1866* (Toronto, 1963), 1–30.

70 Herman Belz, *A New Birth of Freedom: The Republican Party and Freedman's Rights, 1861 to 1866* (Westport, Conn., 1976), 43–44, 46, 56, 59, 64, 70–71, 73. Earl M. Maltz, "Fourteenth Amendment Concepts in the Antebellum Era," *American Journal of Legal History* 32 (1988): 305ff., argues that "equal protection" only meant inclusion of slaves and former slaves as persons under law. This is not what the Republican Radicals meant, however.

71 Roberts v. City of Boston, 59 Mass. 198 (1850); J. Morgan Kousser, *Dead End: The Development of Litigation on Racial Discrimination in Schools in Nineteenth-Century America* (Oxford, 1986); Kousser, " 'The Supremacy of Equal Rights': The Struggle against Racial Discrimination in Antebellum Massachusetts and Foundations of the Fourteenth Amendment," 82 *Northwestern University Law Review* 941 (1988); Leonard W. Levy and Harlan B. Phillips, "The *Roberts* Case: Source of the Separate but Equal Doctrine," *American Historical Review* 66 (1956): 510–18. Sumner continued to add provisions for integration of schools to congressional acts until the day he died.

72 Allan G. Bogue, *The Earnest Men: Republicans of the Civil War Senate* (Ithaca, N.Y., 1981), 204; William E. Nelson, *The Fourteenth Amendment* (Cambridge, Mass., 1988), 72–73. Equality was not a self-actualizing concept, however; its enforcement called for more than exhortation to the fallen rebels—or to recalcitrant unionists for that matter.

73 The Wade-Davis draft bill provided for removal of freedmen and women from state custody upon writs of habeas corpus to federal judges and required that newly reconstructed states offer to freedmen and women all the procedural guarantees enjoyed by whites. The new states had also to abolish all of their slave codes. Lincoln pocket vetoed the bill, then repeated the essence of its provisions in a presidential proclamation.

74 Whittlesey to Oliver Otis Howard, December 1, 1865, quoted in Howard, *Autobiography of Oliver Otis Howard* (New York, 1907), 2:279–80.

75 See Kousser, "Supremacy," 960–80; Roberts v. Boston, 59 Mass. at 200–201.

76 Cox and Cox, *Politics, Principle, and Prejudice*, 1–30; William S. McFeely, *Yankee Stepfather: O. O. Howard and the Freedmen's Bureau* (New Haven, Conn., 1968), 45–64; Willie Lee Rose, *Rehearsal for Reconstruction: The Port Royal Experiment* (Indianapolis, 1964).

77 It was recognized as such even by Republican moderates like Lyman Trumbull of Illinois. Leading the Senate effort to repass the bureau bill over the veto of President Johnson, Trumbull insisted that "we never before were in such a state as now . . . never before in the history of this government have nearly four million people been emancipated from the most abject and degrading slavery ever imposed upon human beings; never before has the occasion arisen when it was necessary to provide for such large numbers of people thrown upon the bounty of the government, unprotected and unprovided for." *Congressional Globe*, 39th Cong., 1st sess. (February 20, 1866), 318.

78 Howard, *Autobiography*, 176, 178–79, 199, 203, 221–22, 230, 234. Confiscation was authorized by Congress in 1862. Foner, *Reconstruction*, 158. The policy was a wartime expedient, however, and its future after the war was uncertain. Lyman Trumbull's plan for the renewal of the Freedmen's Bureau, authorizing the grant of public lands to the freedmen and women, was passed by Congress but vetoed by President Andrew Johnson in February 1866. The Freedmen's Bureau was continued in operation by a revised act, passed in July 1866, without the controversial land grant provisions for the former slaves. The proposed land grant appears in section 4 of the bill. *Congressional Globe*, 39th Cong., 1st sess. (1866), 209.

79 James Speed to O. O. Howard, June 22, 1865, quoted in McFeely, *Yankee Stepfather*, 99.

80 Julian, Speech of February 1864, quoted in Riddleberger, *Julian*, 191. A year before, Julian had told the House that he favored "an equitable homestead policy" including land for the freedman. Here "equitable" had a force that reached upward toward the "other equity" of communal, mutual, rather than merely remedial, fairness. *Congressional Globe*, 37th Cong., 3d sess. (1863), 1069.

81 See, e.g., Texas v. Hardenberg, 77 U.S. (10 Wallace) 68 (1869), in which the court found that the holder of U.S. securities issued to the state of Texas before the war must surrender them to Texas, as they had been illegally mishandled, and he had or should have taken notice of the defect in them before he bought them on the New York money market. Lincoln had begun to restore to some former Confederates their rights and their land after they had subscribed to a loyalty oath. Was this adequate notice to the freedmen and women of a potential defect in their promised title to abandoned lands, defeating any equitable right they might have had in those lands? On Lincoln's first efforts at Reconstruction, see Belz, *Reconstructing the Union*, 143–67.

82 Howard, *Autobiography*, 238–39. What if the army or the bureau had been unhindered by President Johnson in its redistribution of confiscated or abandoned lands? Even assuming the pool of available land would eventually exceed the 850,000 acres on hand in 1865, would the lot of the freedmen and women thereby have risen above the poverty line? Sharpies, scalpers, and confidence men stood ready to join former planters and rebels to deny the freedman and woman whatever federal care bestowed. One scenario of this sort is proposed in C. Vann Woodward, "Unfinished Business," *New York Review of Books*, May 12, 1988, 27, though his parallel between the freedmen of the South and the homesteaders of the Great Plains is hardly exact. True, equity courts will not decree the impossible—that is another maxim of equity. Raising all the former slaves above subsistence may have been impossible, but granting homesteads to freedmen and women was not impossible.

83 See, e.g., House v. Jackson, 24 Oregon 89 (1893), in which an agreement to sell to lessor and assignees for a fixed price within a fixed period of time was construed to convey equitable title to the assignee of the lessor. Under the English Statute of Frauds (1672), widely adopted in the states, verbal contracts to sell land were not enforceable. Thus, freedmen and women promised land could not sue for specific performance unless the promise was in writing. Did army orders such as General William Sherman's Special Field Order of January 16, 1865, constitute such a writing?

84 See Paul Wallace Gates, "Federal Land Policy in the South," *Journal of Southern History* 6 (1940): 303–30. The "Great Compromise" entailed Republican Rutherford B. Hayes's dismantling of the last vestiges of Reconstruction (and other favors) in return for southern congressional support in the disputed presiden-

tial electoral count of 1876–77. Foner, *Reconstruction*, 581.

85   Gregory S. Alexander, "The Transformation of Trusts as Legal Category, 1800–1914," *Law and History Review* 5 (1985): 322ff.; Stanley N. Katz, Barry Sullivan, and C. Paul Beach, "Legal Change and Legal Autonomy: Charitable Trust Law in New York, 1777–1893," *Law and History Review* 3 (1985): 72–85.

86   Patrick W. Riddleberger, *1866: The Critical Year* (Carbondale, Ill., 1976), 63–64; Foner, *Reconstruction*, 144–48. On the importance of education in the legal strategy of a later generation of black leaders, see Tushnet, *NAACP's Legal Strategy*, 34ff., arguing that the NAACP's staff targeted education because education prepared blacks for later life, and segregation in education was symbolic of all other kinds of segregation.

87   Report of the Joint Committee on Reconstruction, 39th Cong., 1st sess. (1865), part ii, pp. 5, 13, 54–55, 83, 130, 210, 226–27, 234, 243, offers some examples of this collusive conduct. I am grateful to Robert Kaczorowski for calling this evidence to my attention. See also Donald Nieman, *To Set the Law in Motion* (Millwood, N.Y., 1979).

88   The task system was a product of lowland agriculture. It originated in the South Carolina rice plantations and involved a fixed task for each day. When that was done, the slave's time was his or her own. See Philip D. Morgan, "Work and Culture: The Task System and the World of Lowcountry Blacks, 1700–1880," *William and Mary Quarterly*, 3d ser., 39 (1982), 563–99.

89   Nieman, *To Set the Law in Motion*, 53–66, 172–90, argues that the bureau readily forced freedmen to perform their tasks. In contrast, one of the most important roles that equity should play is insuring that the illiterate party to a contract fully understands all its provisions. See Edward W. Stevens, Jr., *Literacy, Law, and Social Order* (Dekalb, Ill., 1987), 8, 173–85.

90   Hyman and Wiecek, *Equal Justice under Law*, 316–34. White Southerners' violence against the newly freed slaves would have overwhelmed them were it not for federal troops stationed in their midst and the gradual imposition of federal criminal jurisdiction over crimes against them. Withal, the violence against them was part and parcel of deeply ingrained white Southern resistance to black equality of any sort. See Michael Perman, *Reunion without Compromise: The South and Reconstruction, 1865–1868* (Baton Rouge, La., 1973), 27, 29, 34ff., and Foner, *Reconstruction*, 412–59, 558–63. The use of federal troops was limited by their gradual thinning out, and the powers of federal courts were limited by their inability to obtain testimony, arrest the flight of suspects, and secure guilty verdicts from juries.

91   See generally Benedict, *Compromise*, 162ff. William Pitt Fessenden, Maine's conservative Senate majority leader, did not accuse the president of perfidy in public, but in a letter to a cousin he called up an image by then well established in the vocabulary of republican constitutionalism: Johnson had "broken faith, betrayed his trust." Fessenden to Elizabeth F. Warriner, February 25, 1866, quoted in Riddleberger, *1866*, 85. Such appeals to trusteeship did not appropriate any more than the vaguest reference to the technical rules of trusts, but they did reflect the larger ideal that government itself was a trust. That concept was alive and well in Congress.

92   Or such was the intent of the framer of the act, Lyman Trumbull, as he reported to Supreme Court Justice Noah Swayne in 1867. See Robert J. Kaczorowski, *The Politics of Judicial Interpretation: The Federal Courts, Department of Justice and Civil Rights, 1866–1876* (New York, 1985), 158. Swayne used the idea in U.S. v. Rhodes, 27 F. Cas. 786 (C.C.D. Ky. 1867); Kaczorowski, *The Nationalization of Civil Rights: Constitutional Theory and Practice in a Racist Society* (New York, 1987), 213–15.

93 Mark M. Krug, *Lyman Trumbull: Conservative Radical* (New York, 1965), 221–45; Benedict, *Compromise*, 148–49.
94 Certainly this was one of the crucial issues in the dispute about the historical precedent for antisegregation decisions. The literature of the dispute is reviewed in Robert J. Kaczorowski, "Revolutionary Constitutionalism in the Era of the Civil War and Reconstruction," 61 *New York University Law Review* 863 (1986), and Maltz, "Reconstruction without Revolution."
95 14 *U.S. Stats* 27, 28 (1866).
96 On the immunity of state officials, see Benjamin Vaughan Abbott, *A Treatise upon the United States Courts and Their Practice*, 2d. ed. (New York, 1871), 223, and William Kerr, *A Treatise on the Law and Practice of Injunctions in Equity* (New York, 1871), 599. Note that Trumbull mentioned, in passing, that the framers of the Civil Rights Act had the authority to impose civil penalties. *Congressional Globe*, 39th Cong., 1st. sess. (1866), 1759.
97 Very different accounts of the meaning and the limitations of congressional action under the amendment are given in Charles Fairman, *History of the Supreme Court of the United States*, vol. 6: *Reconstruction and Reunion, Part One* (New York, 1971), 1259ff., insisting that the framers of the Fourteenth Amendment had no intention of providing for the reordering of social domestic customs, including private discrimination on the basis of race, nor did they do so, followed by Raoul Berger, *Government by Judiciary* (Cambridge, Mass., 1977), 20ff., as against Howard Jay Graham, *Everyman's Constitution* (Madison, Wis., 1968); Jacobus tenBroek, *Equal under Law* (New York, 1965); and most recently Kaczorowski, *The Politics of Judicial Interpretation*, all of whom agree that the Fourteenth Amendment was meant and can be read as advocating the gradual end of a dual society. Every historian who has stepped onto this treacherous ground has had to deal with these polarities of interpretation.
98 16 *U.S. Stats* 433, 438 (1871); 17 *U.S. Stats* 13 (1871). The question was, did the Fourteenth Amendment's language—"no *State* shall make or enforce any law which shall abridge the privileges or immunities of citizens of the United States, nor shall any *State* deprive any person of life, liberty, or property without due process of law, nor deny to any person within its jurisdiction the equal protection of the laws" (italics added)—limit liability to state officials only? From these words the Court derived the "state action" qualification, and many in the Republican majority who passed the amendment in Congress, as well as those who supported the Ku Klux Act in 1871, either implicitly or explicitly required that the state have some part in discriminating, or the victim could not seek the aid of federal courts under the Civil Rights acts. This was according to Alfred Avins, "The Ku Klux Klan Act of 1871: Some Reflected Light on State Action and the Fourteenth Amendment," 11 *St. Louis University Law Review* 331 (1967). The argument above for "state action" based on the intentions of the framers is much weakened by the passage of the Civil Rights Act of 1875 explicitly outlawing discrimination in "public accommodations." 18 *U.S. Stats* 335, 336 (1875). Public accommodations included privately owned structures like railroad stations, theaters, and hotels.
99 In ironic counterpoint to these provisions, Governor William Sharkey of Mississippi petitioned the Supreme Court for an injunction against presidential implementation of the Reconstruction Act of 1867. The high court dismissed the petition. Mississippi v. Johnson, 68 U.S. (4 Wallace) 475 (1867). Indeed, the petition sought the wrong form of remedy (it should have asked for a writ of mandamus) and it was directed against an official, President Johnson, who had little sympathy for the Reconstruction Act. All the other southern state gover-

nors preferred to wait and see what would happen under the act. See Perman, *Reunion*, 293–95.

100   18 *U.S. Stats*, 335, but see Civil Rights Cases, 109 U.S. 3, 4 (1883) (public accommodation provisions of the Civil Rights Act of 1875 found too broad).

101   These acts remain important parts of federal civil rights law as 42 *U.S.C.* secs. 1981, 1983, and 1985. On enforcement of the Civil Rights acts in Reconstruction courts, see Kaczorowski, *Politics of Judicial Interpretation*, 81–96, and Foner, *Reconstruction*, 469–88.

102   Kaczorowski, *Politics of Judicial Enforcement*, 117ff. Until 1872, the Supreme Court allowed the lower federal courts to enforce the acts against private malefactors, though two district judges had balked at the prospect of federal invasion of a state's criminal jurisdiction. Ibid., 131. In 1872, the Supreme Court limited the scope of the acts to bar federal prosecution when state sponsorship or support of the offenders' conduct could not be proven. In such cases, prosecution was to be left to the regular state courts—a slender reed on which to base justice for former slaves. Blyew v. United States, 80 U.S. 581 (1872).

103   See, e.g., Clarke v. Board of Directors, 24 Iowa 267 (1868), *aff'd*, Smith v. Independent School District of Keokuk, 40 Iowa 518 (1875), and Coger v. The North West Union Packet, 37 Iowa 145 (1873). Kousser, *Dead End*, 5–16, provides evidence of other such cases. There was a parallel federal case of antidiscrimination and two similar southern cases: DeCuir v. Benson, 27 La. Ann. 1 (1875); United States v. Blackborn, 21 F. Cas. 1158 (C.C.D. Mo., 1874); and Donnell v. State, 48 Miss. 661 (1873). See also Railroad Co. v. Brown, 84 U.S. 445 (1873) (separate but equal does not satisfy the Federal Railroad Charter Act).

104   In 1866, Trumbull admitted "A law is good for nothing without a penalty, without a sanction to it" but told the Senate "I think it will only be necessary to go into the late slave-holding States and subject to fine and imprisonment one or two in a State, and the most prominent ones at that, to break up this whole business [of denial of freedmen and women's rights]." *Congressional Globe*, 39th Cong., 1st sess. (1866), 475. True, the Ku Klux Klan outrages had yet to erupt, but the carnage of the Civil War was still visible and the Black Codes still in force when Trumbull gave his forecast. But see Nelson, *Fourteenth Amendment*, 139, arguing that it was not a failure of will but weakness of general theory that undermined Republican efforts at constitutional revision.

105   Michael Les Benedict, "Preserving the Constitution: The Conservative Basis of Radical Reconstruction," *Journal of American History* 61 (1974): 80–81; Friedman, *History of American Law*, 177ff.; Nelson, *Roots of Bureaucracy*, 67–81.

Self-help is the assumption underlying civil litigation—if you are wronged, sue for redress. Contract, tort, property—all the traditional categories into which the common law was divided after the Civil War—begin with the private suit. Nevertheless, the chancellor intervened when litigants averred that corrupt court officers would not allow them to bring suit or powerful defendants overawed local officials. The strong arm of the chancellor's subpoena evened out the contest. Under these conditions, equity did not follow the law at all but preceded it. Without the aid of equity, the plaintiff at common law could not get a foot in the door. This is just what happened in the unreconstructed South. On the steadily declining desire of Justice Department officials to pursue the criminal sanction, see Kaczorowski, *Politics of Judicial Interpretation*, 109ff., and William Gillette, *Retreat from Reconstruction, 1869–1879* (Baton Rouge, La., 1979), 42–55.

106   Foner, *Reconstruction*, 454–59. In Minor v. Happersett, 91 U.S. (21 Wallace)

162 (1875), *aff'd*, United States v. Hiram Reece and Matthew Fourshee, 92 U.S. 214 (1876), the Supreme Court found that the Fifteenth Amendment might prohibit discrimination in voting laws on the basis of race, but it did not guarantee the vote to minority registrants when private individuals violently prevented individuals from voting. The Court concluded that the third and fourth sections of the Voting Rights Enforcement Act of 1870, which penalized such "private" actors, were overbroad.

107 Gillette, in *Retreat*, 279, concludes that the Republicans' support of the Civil Rights Act of 1875 was "empty ritualism, the results of which were more of the negative than constructive." For Sumner and many others, however, the rituals had mattered a good deal. If equality in law was their mission, the failure of enforcement was a crushing blow.

108 James M. McPherson, *The Abolitionist Legacy: From Reconstruction to the NAACP* (Princeton, N.J., 1975), 50–51; Foner, *Reconstruction*, 582–87.

109 18 *U.S. Stats* 335 (1875).

110 Edward Re, *Cases and Materials on Remedies* (Mineola, N.Y., 1982), 273.

111 See Zechariah Chafee, Jr., "Bills of Peace with Multiple Parties," 45 *Harvard Law Review* 1297 (1932), and Stephen Yeazell, "Group Litigation and Social Context: Toward a History of the Class Action," 77 *Columbia Law Review* 866, 869 (1977).

112 14 *U.S. Stats* 27, sec. 2 (1866).

113 Civil Rights Cases, 109 U.S. 3, 25 (1883).

114 Leon F. Litwack, *Been in the Storm So Long: The Aftermath of Slavery* (New York, 1979), 282–83.

115 109 U.S. at 26, 53, 61–62. Harlan, though once a slaveholder, had become a consistent defender of blacks' rights on the Court. He had, I think not coincidentally, a great chancellor's grasp of the primacy of just results. See G. Edward White, "John Marshall Harlan I: The Precursor," *American Journal of Legal History* 19 (1975): 6, 10–11.

116 According to Michael Les Benedict, this strong attachment to the generalized ideal of federalism went hand in glove with the Reconstruction program. See Benedict, "Preserving the Constitution," 80–81. The doctrine is still firmly in place. See Douglas v. City of Jeanette, 319 U.S. 157 (1943), and Younger v. Harris, 401 U.S. 37 (1971).

117 William C. Robinson, *Elements of American Jurisprudence* (Boston, 1900), 305. The more general judicial imposition of a public/private distinction is discussed in Morton Horwitz, "A History of the Public/Private Distinction," 130 *University of Pennsylvania Law Review* 1423 (1982), but see the qualifications to this thesis in Harry L. Scheiber, "Public Rights and the Rule of Law in American Legal History," 72 *California Law Review* 217 (1984).

118 Abbott, *A Treatise upon the United States Courts and Their Practice*, 223; James L. High, *A Treatise on Extraordinary Legal Remedies* (Chicago, 1874), 38. The argument that the Civil Rights Act of 1866 was framed as a criminal ordinance to avoid sovereign immunity is posed in Robert J. Kaczorowski, "The Enforcement Provisions of the Civil Rights Act of 1866: A Legislative History in Light of Runyon v. McCrary," 98 *Yale Law Journal* 565, 576–77 (1989).

119 48 U.S. (7 Howard) 1 (1849), a case in which competing governments in Rhode Island sought recognition of their legitimacy, and both wished injunctive relief. Although much eroded in fact by the voter reapportionment cases beginning with Baker v. Carr, 369 U.S. 186 (1962), the Supreme Court's aversion to purely political disputes remains strong on the grounds that such disputes are best left to the more representative branches of the government, or that parties in them fail to present a justiciable issue.

120   *In re* Sawyer, 124 U.S. 200, 213 (1888), is the traditional citation for the rule.
But see Edwin S. Mack, "The Revival of Criminal Equity," 16 *Harvard Law
Review* 389 (1903), for precedents demonstrating the renewed vitality of in-
junctions against criminal acts in the Gilded Age.

121   William Kerr, *A Treatise on the Law and Practice of Injunctions in Equity*, 3d ed.
(New York, 1891), 169. But see Thomas C. Spelling, *A Treatise on Injunctions
and Other Extraordinary Relief in Equity*, 2d ed. (Boston, 1901), 1253–58, and
Abbott, *A Treatise upon the United States Courts and Their Practice*, 223, asserting
that officials acting outside of their discretion were subject to mandatory
instructions.

122   In a representative suit, one individual or a group of individuals brought suit
for an injury or loss that was suffered by many more individuals. If the latter
class were too numerous to be joined in the suit, i.e., named and brought
before the court, the court would nevertheless proceed with the suit, but ab-
sentees were not bound by the judgment. This approach appeared first in the
Judiciary Reorganization Act of 1839, 5 *U.S. Stats* 321, and was repeated in the
Supreme Court's Equity Rule 48; 42 U.S. (1 Howard) lvi (1843). See the discussion in Yeazell, *Class Action*, 213–24, but note that Story was very much alive
when Rule 48 was promulgated, and that it derived from statutory, not judicial, initiative. By the end of the century, a new theory emerged binding absent
parties when the representative of the class spoke for a unified interest of the
class.

123   See Clyde E. Jacobs, *Law Writers and the Courts: The Influence of Thomas M.
Cooley, Christopher G. Tiedeman, and John F. Dillon upon American Constitutional
Law* (Berkeley, Calif., 1954), 687–97, and Alan R. Jones, *The Constitutional Conservatism of Thomas McIntyre Cooley: A Study in the History of Ideas* (New York,
1987), 122–65.

124   Charles A. Lofgren, *The Plessy Case: A Legal-Historical Interpretation* (New York,
1987), 95–115; Herbert Hovenkamp, "Social Science and Segregation before
Brown," 1985 *Duke Law Journal* 624.

125   This coincides with the development of the "public purpose" rule for allowing
state police power to regulate business activities. Railroads fell under the latter
category, theaters and amusement parks did not. See Charles W. McCurdy,
"Justice Field and the Jurisprudence of Business-Government Relations," *Journal of American History* 61 (1975): 970–1005.

126   Donald, *Sumner and the Rights of Man*, 382–85. In fact, segregation was well
rooted in the Reconstruction; it was so entrenched by the 1880s and 1890s that
the bilious racism of Cumming v. School Board of Richmond, Ga., 175 U.S.
528 (1899), went all but unnoticed. See Hovenkamp, "Social Science," 638–42.

PART THREE

1   Oliver Wendell Holmes, Jr., "The Path of the Law," 10 *Harvard Law Review*
457, 459 (1897).

2   14 *U.S. Stats* 517. Section 40 of the act allowed injunctive relief against the
debtor. See Friedman, *History of American Law*, 549–51.

3   These and the following figures are derived from a computation of equity
cases in the *Federal Case* records, vols. 1–30, prepared by West Company, St.
Paul, Minn., covering reports of federal district and circuit courts from their
inception to 1880. Only a portion of all cases was reported in "F. Cas.," but
there is no reason to assume that conclusions drawn from the reported cases
misrepresented the unreported cases.

4   See, e.g., Texas v. White, 74 U.S. (7 Wallace) 700 (1869), finding that, for the

purpose of settling a suit brought by the reconstructed government of Texas to recover misappropriated bonds, Texas remained a state in the Union during the Civil War though its people and government were in rebellion.

5   See Theodore Eisenberg and Stephen Yeazell, "The Ordinary and the Extraordinary in Institutional Litigation," 93 *Harvard Law Review* 465 (1980); John V. Orth, "The Virginia State Debt and the Judicial Power of the United States, 1870–1920," in David J. Bodenhamer and James W. Ely, Jr., eds., *Ambivalent Legacy: A Legal History of the South* (Jackson, Miss., 1984), 106–22; and Orth, *The Judicial Power of the United States: The Eleventh Amendment in American History* (New York, 1987), 58–120.

6   Mark W. Summers, *Railroads, Reconstruction, and the Gospel of Prosperity: Aid under the Radical Republicans, 1865–1877* (Princeton, N.J., 1984), 98–117; Foner, *Reconstruction*, 466–68.

7   83 U.S. (16 Wallace) 36 (1873). Justice Samuel F. Miller, for a five-to-four majority, restricted the rights gained through national privileges and immunities to those the newly freed slaves gained and refused to see behind the state's facial claim to exercise of its police power. For the details of the case, see Charles Fairman, *History of the Supreme Court of the United States*, vol. 6: *Reconstruction and Reunion: Part One* (New York, 1971), 1324–37. No one on the Court spent any time discussing the appropriateness of the equitable remedy. Focus on remedy and management of remedy belonged to a later age of judicial thinking.

8   Coppage v. Kansas, 236 U.S. 3, 8, 12 (1914).

9   Karl Llewellyn, *The Common Law Tradition: Deciding Appeals* (Boston, 1960), 38. Llewellyn's characterization of this style of judging was meant to condemn its reappearance in the twentieth century, but his analysis has become a staple of some modern accounts of later nineteenth-century doctrine. See, e.g., Horwitz, *Transformation*, 253–66.

10 There were elite, politically moderate lawyers and jurists who were sincerely convinced that law had lost its way in the Gilded Age. See Robert W. Gordon, "'The Ideal and the Actual in the Law': Fantasies and Practices of New York City Lawyers, 1870–1910," in Gerald W. Gawalt, ed., *The New High Priests: Lawyers in Post–Civil War America* (Westport, Conn., 1984), 51–75. Nevertheless, I am convinced that formalism almost always masked a powerful commitment to corporalist conservatism. See, e.g., Charles C. Goetsch, "The Future of Legal Formalism," *American Journal of Legal History* 24 (1980): 221–56.

11 64 Wis. 265, 272 (1885). See also, e.g., Keith v. Brewster, 114 Ga. 176 (1901) (equity does not relieve the negligent). To be sure, *Wood* was not followed by every court of equity. See, e.g., Barker v. Fitzgerald, 204 Ill. 325 (1903). Formalist courts went even the most outspoken critics of fair-price doctrine would not have trespassed fifty years before, however. Gulian Verplanck, an opponent of equitable rescission of patently unfair contracts among equals (e.g., merchants), stuck at the prospect of courts enforcing an "ignorant woman's" sale of a large bank note as a "mere curiosity" to a man who knew its value and paid her a pittance. See Verplanck, *An Essay on the Doctrine of Contracts* (New York, 1825), 6. Today, under the Uniform Commercial Code (UCC), 2.302, as interpreted in cases like Jones v. Star Credit Corp., 59 N.Y. Misc. 2d 189 (N.Y. 1969), the credit sale of a $300 freezer for over $1,400 will be deemed unconscionable, and the plaintiff who has already received over $600 from the buyer will get neither damages nor the freezer back. A court finding that a sales contract price is unconscionable may reform or rescind the contract. The UCC, it should be noted, was largely the work of Karl Llewellyn, who opposed reasoning like that in *Wood*. See Zipporah B. Wiseman, "The

Limits of Vision: Karl Llewellyn and the Merchant Rules," 100 *Harvard Law Review* 465 (1987).
12 109 U.S. 3, 17 (1883).
13 Charles E. Clark, "The Function of Law in a Democratic Society," 9 *University of Chicago Law Review* 393, 395 (1941).

CHAPTER SIX

1 The notion of a science of equitable pleading was most influentially championed by John Norton Pomeroy, a practitioner-professor at New York University and Hastings law schools. See, e.g., Pomeroy, *Remedies and Remedial Rights by Civil Action* (New York, 1876), vii, 32–33, 40, 51, 91. Pomeroy did concede that equity was in disarray, but he assayed more formalism rather than less as a remedy. Pomeroy had much support in his own day. See, e.g., George Phillips, *An Exposition of the Principles of Pleading under the Codes of Civil Procedure* (New York, 1896); Philemon Bliss, *A Treatise upon the Law of Pleading under the Codes of Civil Procedure . . .*, 2d ed. (St. Louis, Mo., 1887); and Henry Gibson, "The Philosophy of Pleading," 2 *Yale Law Journal* 181 (1893). On these "reformers," see Robert Bone, "Mapping the Boundaries of a Dispute: Conceptions of Ideal Law Suit Structure from the Field Code to the Federal Rules," 89 *Columbia Law Review* 1011 (1989).

2 Opposition to formalism in equity in the academy was led by Roscoe Pound, Walter Wheeler Cook, Wesley N. Hohfeld, and, later, Charles E. Clark. See, e.g., Pound, "Is Equity Decadent?" 5 *Columbia Law Review* 20 (1905), "Mechanical Jurisprudence," 8 *Columbia Law Review* 605 (1908), and "The End of the Law as Developed in Legal Rules and Doctrines," 27 *Harvard Law Review* 195 (1914); Cook, "The Place of Equity in Our Legal System," 3 *American Law School Review* 173 (1912), "Hohfeld's Contributions to the Science of Law," 28 *Yale Law Journal* 721 (1919), and "Statements of Fact in Pleading under the Codes," 21 *Columbia Law Review* 416 (1921); and Hohfeld, "The Relations between Equity and Law," 11 *Michigan Law Review* 537 (1913). On Clark's voluminous writings in the service of reform of equity pleading, see Burbank, "Rules Enabling Act of 1934"; Subrin, "How Equity Conquered Common Law"; and Peter Charles Hoffer and Robert Brussack, eds., *Writing the Rules: The Proceedings of the Advisory Committee for the Federal Rules of Civil Procedure, 1935–1938* (forthcoming).

3 Charles Noble Gregory, "Government by Injunction," 11 *Harvard Law Review* 487 (1898). The title itself became very popular. See, e.g., Andrew Fureseth, "Government by Injunction—The Misuses of the Equity Power," 71 *Central Law Journal* 5 (1910). In but one more irony, opponents of federal injunctive relief in civil rights cases have resuscitated these charges.

4 Charles O. Gregory and Harold A. Katz, *Labor and the Law*, 3d ed. (New York, 1979), 53–104. Union organizations were proscribed as criminal conspiracies in some state courts in the first half of the nineteenth century, but following Lemuel Shaw's opinion in Commonwealth v. Hunt, 4 Metcalf 111 (1842), many courts retreated from this position. In the later years of the nineteenth century, different state courts regarded the activities of unions differently. In New York, wide latitude was allowed organizers, picketers, and strikers. In Massachusetts, the same activities were closely scanned for evidence of criminality or civil injury. See Gregory and Katz, *Labor and the Law*, 60–82, and Charles J. Morris, *The Developing Labor Law*, 2d ed. (Washington, D.C., 1983), 3–7ff.

The long and pitched battle in the courts had opened with *In re* Dolittle, 23 F.

544 (1885), in the federal courts and Sherry v. Perkins, 147 Mass. 212 (1888), the leading state case. Injunctions against picketing, organizing, boycotts, and strikes followed regularly thereafter. The liberal attack on the practice appeared almost immediately. The arguments of the reformers were summarized with vigor in Frankfurter and Greene, *The Labor Injunction*.

5 Eugene V. Debs to a welcoming crowd at Terre Haute, Ind., May 3, 1894, quoted in Nick Salvatore, *Eugene V. Debs: Citizen and Socialist* (Urbana, Ill., 1982), 124. On the strike itself, see Almont Lindsey, *The Pullman Strike* (Chicago, 1942).

6 158 U.S. 564, 582 (1895). Brewer was a profound and vocal enemy of labor radicalism, indeed of all Progressive reform. A year before the strike, he told the New York Bar Association: "It is the unvarying law, that the wealth of a community will be in the hands of a few." Brewer, "The Nation's Safeguard," *Proceedings of the New York State Bar Association* (1893), quoted in Owen Fiss, *The Supreme Court and the Rise of the Modern State, 1888–1910*, tentative chap. 3, p. 2 (forthcoming). Such a formalist approach to injunctions abetted a biased view of labor, based in part on fears of conspiracy. See Herbert Hovenkamp, "Labor Conspiracies in American Law, 1880–1930," 66 *Texas Law Review* 919, 948–65 (1988). Such bias not only revealed the subjectivity of formalism but also undermined the equitable jurisprudence in which the injunctive power is rooted. A similar kind of formalism, masking powerful economic policies, flourished in English antilabor injunctions in the same era. See A. W. J. Thompson, "The Injunctions in Trades Disputes in Britain before 1910," 10 *Industrial and Labor Relations Review* 213 (1965).

7 158 U.S. at 564–68.

8 E.g., Adair v. United States, 208 U.S. 161 (1908), in which the Erdman Act was declared unconstitutional as an invasion of the due process rights of railroad owners and their agents; Loewe v. Lawlor (The Danbury Hatter's Case), 208 U.S. 274 (1908), finding that the Sherman Anti-Trust Act applied to unions; and United Mine Workers v. Coronado Coal Co., 259 U.S. 344 (1922), holding that disruption of commerce by union activity was liable to treble damages as well as injunctions under the Clayton Anti-Trust Act. In United States v. United Mine Workers, 330 U.S. 258 (1947), a majority of the Court found that when the federal government is an employer there is no bar to injunctions against strikes. The mine workers temporarily worked for the government under a wartime agreement, but when they sought to renegotiate their contracts with the government they were told to address their former employers, the mine owners. The union was enjoined from striking over this issue, but John L. Lewis, claiming the injunction was void because it was unlawful under the National Labor Relations Act, led a walkout. He was fined for criminal contempt and the union was fined for civil contempt. Even the dissenters on the court (and Justices Frank Murphy and Wiley Rutledge wrote powerful dissents against both of the contempt findings) did not look behind the "rules" of injunctions to weigh the plight of the miners against that of mine owners or the consumers of coal.

9 Traditionally, contempt of court for violation of an injunction was limited to the agents or conspirators of the defendant who had actual knowledge of the court's decree. See, e.g., Rigas v. Livingston, 178 N.Y. 20 (1904). Courts have construed this requirement narrowly, except in the antilabor cases. Note that third parties to an injunction are still bound by it (see, e.g., Fiss, *Civil Rights Injunction*, 16–17), but only if they are agents or confederates. See Spallone v. U.S., No. 88–854; S. Ct. 1990 West Law 794 (1990).

10 Frankfurter and Green, *The Labor Injunction*.

11 Pound to Charles McCarthy, June 23, 1915, Roscoe Pound Papers, box 156, folder 13, Harvard Law School Library.

12 Chafee, "California Justice," *New Republic*, September 19, 1923, 97–100; Chafee to Simpson, October 2, 1924, Zechariah Chafee Papers, box 83, folder 4, Harvard Law School Library.

13 Chafee, *The Inquiring Mind* (New York, 1928), 91–92, 191, 193. See also Chafee to Frankfurter, April 2, 1930, Zechariah Chafee Papers, box 89, folder 7, Harvard Law School Library.

14 154 U.S. 362, 394 (1894).

15 169 U.S. 466 (1898).

16 209 U.S. 123 (1908). A storm of protest followed, and Congress subsequently required that injunctions against state officials could be issued only by three-judge panels. See Gerald Gunther, *Cases and Materials on Constitutional Law*, 10th ed. (Mineola, N.Y., 1982), 1677.

17 A doctrine developed in Stephen J. Field's dissent in Munn v. Illinois, 94 U.S. 113 (1877), theorizing that strictly private enterprises, like the grain elevators on which Illinois imposed regulations, were not subject to state police power unless they acted outside of the law. State regulation of normal market activities was a violation of the due process clause of the Fourteenth Amendment, taking property from persons (the corporation was a legal person) without compensation. In the 1880s, an almost wholly new Court dominated by Field adopted substantive due process as its credo. See Kelly, Harbison, and Belz, *The American Constitution*, 404.

18 Gregory, "Government by Injunction," 499.

19 Kenneth L. Sokoloff, "Productivity Growth in Manufacturing during Early Industrialization: Evidence from the American Northeast, 1820–1860," in Stanley Engerman and Richard Gallman, eds., *Long Term Factors in American Economic Growth* (Chicago, 1986), 724; Jonathan Prude, *The Coming of the Industrial Order: Town and Factory Life in Rural Massachusetts, 1810–1860* (New York, 1983).

20 Though a nuisance is easily defined—an "interference with the use or enjoyment of land"—the application of the definition to actual cases is almost always a tangle of qualification. A private nuisance is actionable in the civil courts. A public nuisance, in which the injury is shared by the community rather than falling upon one individual, does not allow a private civil remedy unless the plaintiff has suffered special damage from the nuisance. Even when a private nuisance or special damage from a public nuisance is alleged in a complaint, the court must decide whether a defendant's conduct is unreasonable or unlawful; whether the interference with the petitioner's land or his personal comfort is trifling or substantial, limited in duration or likely to continue, and whether the nuisance is abatable. All these and more questions are answerable only from close examination of factual context, itself sometimes requiring expert opinions and on occasion rather sweeping predictions (a nightmare for any court) about the prospective damage of future acts to persons not represented at the bar. Added to the complexity of the threshold question—is there a nuisance?—is the bewildering variety of potential remedies. These may include conditional injunctions, permanent injunctions, and all manner of court-managed payments, easements, abatements, and buy-outs. On nuisance, see William Prosser and W. Page Keeton, *Prosser on Torts*, 5th ed. (Mineola, N.Y., 1984), 616ff.; Prosser, "Nuisance without Fault," 20 *Texas Law Review* 399 (1942); and Richard Epstein, "Nuisance Law: Corrective Justice and Its Utilitarian Constraints," 8 *Journal of Legal Studies* 49 (1979).

In early nineteenth-century England, there were a few cases of injunctive relief against nuisance. Joel F. Brenner, "Nuisance Law and the Industrial Revolution," 3 *Journal of Legal Studies* 403, 406 (1974). The standard study of early American nuisance cases finds a relative handful of injunctions in state courts in the period before the Civil War. Paul Kurtz, "Nineteenth-Century Anti-Entrepreneurial Nuisance Injunctions—Avoiding the Chancellor," 17 *William and Mary Law Review* 621 (1973).

21 As in the antilabor injunctions, formalism did not dictate the outcome of these decrees; the leading case in which the chancellor refused to countenance Balance of Equity, Hennessey v. Carmody, 50 N.J. Eq. 616 (1892), featured a formalist decree. It was crafted by Vice-Chancellor Mahlon Pitney, author of the Supreme Court opinion in *Coppage v. Kansas* twenty-two years later. In our own era of realism, the doctrine of Balance of Equity is still part of nuisance law. See *Restatement (Second) of Torts*, sec. 941 at 580, and 40 *American Law Reports* 3d 601 (1970), reporting that the injunction against a nuisance is a discretionary resort to be used when the harm to the plaintiff or plaintiffs is substantial and the inconvenience to the defendant does not greatly exceed the benefit of the injunction to the plaintiff. Modern courts' Balance of Equity is not formalist, however, for reasons discussed below.

22 57 Pa. 112, 113–14 (1868).

23 1 Cr. & Ph. 283 (Eng. Ch.), 41 Eng. Rep. 498 (1841). Neither was St. Helen's Smelting v. Tipping, 11 H.L. Cas. 642 (1854), precedent, though an injunction against industrial nuisance was here denied as well. The English courts involved merely regarded the nuisance as a trifling one. They did not balance the equities. I am grateful to Morton Horwitz for calling the latter case to my attention.

24 Bell v. Ohio and Pennsylvania R.R. Co., 25 Pa. 161 (1856). Even the court in *Richard's Appeal* was not wholly confident of its reasoning. At the end of the opinion, Thompson retreated to the old, uncontroversial doctrine that equity would not intervene when damages at common law would provide an adequate and complete remedy. 57 Pa. at 113.

25 67 U.S. (2 Black) 545, 552–53 (1862). The discretionary character of federal equitable remedies was already well established; see Holt v. Rogers, 33 U.S. (8 Peters) 420 (1834) (petitioner's delay defeats his claim), and Irwin v. Dixion, 50 U.S. (10 Howard) 10 (1850) (no equity if adequate remedy exists at law).

26 *Richard's Appeal* did have a near precedent in prior American equity. Traditional equity allowed the downstream (riparian) owner undiminished and unpolluted water flow. Increasingly, antebellum upstream industrial users claimed that the diversion was minimal, or in the alternative that the defendant's product was useful to all and should not be curbed by outdated restrictions. Chancellor Peter Vroom, in *Society for Establishing Manufacturers v. Morris Canal Company*, 1 N.J. Eq. 157 (1830), gave serious thought to resolving one such dispute by balancing the equities. In a suit for an injunction by a downstream mill owner against an upstream canal company, Vroom sought more evidence from the petitioner that the digging would actually divert significant amounts of water from the stream flow. He added, in a dictum, that he was hesitant to grant the injunction because "[the canal] is a work in which a portion of the community is deeply interested, and which, if completed and in successful operation, may be of great benefit to the State. To grant an injunction against them now, in the manner and to the extent prayed for, would be at once to prostrate their hopes, and might result in an injury which the power of the court could never repair." Id. at 192. The last sentence paraphrased the rule upon which a temporary injunction would issue—the danger that the harm would be so irreparable that no damages won at law after the fact could return

the petitioner to his previous position. Story's *Equity Jurisprudence*, 1:243, stated that preliminary injunctions were proper means of preventing irreparable damage, but at least one later scholar thinks that Story invented this rule. See William Draper Lewis to Roscoe Pound, February 3, 1914, Roscoe Pound Papers, box 225, folder 9, Harvard Law Library. By inverting the logic behind this rule to delay the issuance of this injunction, Vroom edged toward the new doctrine: balancing the prospective damage to the defendant from the injunction against the advantage the injunction would mean to the plaintiff. Chancellors had previously disavowed any power to "weigh the equities of the parties" against each other. See Seymour v. Delancey, 3 Cowen at 518. But see Walker v. Wanton, 20 F. Cas. 59 (C.C.D.C. 1807), in which Chief Judge William Cranch insisted, in dissent, that the plaintiffs were not entitled to force third-party defendants to bring their account books to court, because the "equity of [those] defendants is equal to that of the plaintiffs." In the end, Vroom drew back from this novelty. He decreed instead that he had found no evidence of irreparable harm.

27 On the reasonable use doctrine in nuisance, see Robert Bone, "Normative Theory and Legal Doctrine in American Nuisance Law, 1850 to 1920," 59 *Southern California Law Review* 1104 (1986).

28 70 Pa. 102 (1871), in which an injunction against a brickyard was denied on Balance of Equity grounds.

29 32 Mich. 494, 496 (1875).

30 61 Iowa 549, 553 (1883).

31 87 Ala. 468, 471 (1888).

32 See Horwitz, *Transformation*, 32–34, and E. P. Krauss, "The Legal Form of Liberalism: A Study of Riparian and Nuisance Law in Nineteenth-Century Ohio," 18 *Akron Law Review* 223 (1984). See also, *contra*, Gary T. Schwartz, "Tort Law and the Economy in Nineteenth-Century America: A Reinterpretation," 90 *Yale Law Journal* 1717 (1981), rejecting the subsidy theory.

33 The "locality rule" developed in England and crossed to America. The leading case here was Gilbert v. Showerman, 23 Mich. 447 (1871). The rule was not an absolute bar to an injunction when the nuisance was substantial and continuing, or when the defendant brought the nuisance onto his property and then released it onto the plaintiff's land. On the former, see Hennessey v. Carmody, 50 N.J. Eq. 616 (1892). On the latter, see Robb v. Carnegie, 145 Pa. 324 (1891).

34 See C. Vann Woodward, *The Origins of the New South*, 2d ed. (Baton Rouge, La., 1971), 107–41, and Royce Shingleton, *Richard Peters: Champion of the New South* (1985), 209–19. Southern elites remained preoccupied with the industrialization project well into the twentieth century. James Cobb, *The Selling of the South: The Southern Crusade for Industrial Development* (Baton Rouge, La., 1982). On the West, see Mansel G. Blackford, *The Politics of Business in California, 1890–1920* (Berkeley, Calif., 1977).

35 113 Tenn. 331, 339, 366, 368 (1904).

36 See Annot., 42 *American Law Reports* 3d 344 (1972). The late-coming plaintiff does not lose the suit solely on this account, but the fact that the defendant was there first was noted by courts. *Restatement (Second) of Torts*, sec. 840, comment D.

37 See, e.g., Simmons v. Mayor of Paterson, 60 N.J. Eq. 385, 393 (1900).

38 Hennessey v. Carmody, 50 N.J. Eq. 616 (1892), *aff'd*, Kroecker v. Camden Coke Co., 82 N.J. Eq. 374 (1913), and Kosich v. Poultryman's Service Corp., 136 N.J. Eq. 571 (1945).

39 60 N.J. Eq. at 393.

40 185 U.S. 93, 97 (1901). Brewer did not explicitly adopt the doctrine of Balance

of Equity. To do so might have opened his opinion in *Debs* to criticism, based as it was on an analysis of nuisance without any balancing.

41 See, e.g., Frank Coffin, *The Ways of a Judge* (Boston, 1980), 52; Harry Edwards, "The Role of a Judge in Modern Society: Some Reflections on Current Practice in Federal Appellate Jurisdiction," 32 *Cleveland State Law Review* 385, 390 (1983–84); Felix Frankfurter, "Some Reflections on the Reading of Statutes," 47 *Columbia Law Review* 527, 535 (1947); and Jon Newman, "Between Legal Realism and Neutral Principles: The Legitimacy of Institutional Values," 72 *California Law Review* 200, 205 (1984).

42 Benjamin Cardozo, *The Nature of the Judicial Process* (New Haven, Conn., 1921), 23, 117.

43 Ibid., 12.

44 Ibid., 167.

45 Richard Hofstadter, *The Age of Reform* (New York, 1956), 156–63; Jerold S. Auerbach, *Unequal Justice: Lawyers and Social Change in Modern America* (New York, 1976), 16–18.

46 U.S. Department of the Interior [Census Office], *Compendium of the Eleventh Census: 1890* (Washington, D.C., 1892), xlviii. Mourning for the lost frontier began with Frederick Jackson Turner, "The Significance of the Frontier in American History" (1893), reprinted in Turner, *The Frontier in American History* (New York, 1920), and was taken up by Turner's students. See, e.g., Frederick L. Paxson, *When the West Is Gone* (New York, 1930), and Ray Allen Billington, *Westward Expansion*, 2d ed. (New York, 1960), 754–56.

47 Jon Teaford, *The Growth of the American City* (New York, 1986); Arthur M. Schlesinger, *The Rise of the City, 1878–1898* (New York, 1933), 53–77; George M. Mowry, *The Urban Nation* (New York, 1965), 1–3; Richard Sennett, *Families against the City* (New York, 1965).

48 Loren P. Beth, *The Development of the American Constitution, 1877–1917* (New York, 1971), 95–107; Robert H. Wiebe, *The Search for Order, 1877–1920* (New York, 1967), 44–75.

49 Alfred Chandler, *The Visible Hand: The Managerial Revolution in American Business* (Cambridge, Mass., 1977), 240–84.

50 Paul L. Murphy, *The Constitution in Crisis Times, 1918–1969* (New York, 1972), 10–11, 41–67.

51 Arnold Paul, *Conservative Crisis and the Rule of Law* (New York, 1960), 20, 39–60.

52 For example, the word "sociology" first appeared in the Harvard College course catalog in 1891. So, too, the American Economic Association was chartered in 1885. See Robert L. Church, "The Economists Study Society at Harvard, 1891–1902," in Paul Buck, ed., *Social Sciences at Harvard, 1860–1920* (Cambridge, Mass., 1965), 19, 29.

53 Gerald E. Caiden, "In Search of an Apolitical Science of American Public Administration," in Jack Rabin and James S. Bowman, eds., *Politics and Administration* (New York, 1984), 55.

54 Woodrow Wilson, "The Study of Administration," *Political Science Quarterly* 2 (1887): 197, opened this field of inquiry.

55 Oliver Wendell Holmes, Jr., "The Path of the Law," 10 *Harvard Law Review* 457, 466–67 (1897).

56 James Willard Hurst, *Law and Social Processes in the United States* (Ann Arbor, Mich., 1960), 93ff.

57 See, e.g., Barbara Rosenkrantz, *Public Health and the State: Changing Views in Massachusetts, 1842–1936* (Cambridge, Mass., 1972), 97–127.

58 180 U.S. 208 (1900). Holmes was familiar with the Massachusetts State Board

of Health and its efforts to trace waterborne contagions. Rosenkrantz, *Public Health*, 111–12.

59 See, e.g., United States v. Consolidated Fisheries, 50 F. Supp. 550, 552 (1943), finding medical evidence of disease so conclusive as to make the hearing for a temporary injunction tantamount to a final hearing.

60 Samuel P. Hayes, *Conservation and the Gospel of Efficiency: The Progressive Conservation Movement* (Chicago, 1959), 27–48, 122–98.

61 Howard Mumford Jones, *The Age of Energy: Varieties of American Experience, 1865–1915* (New York, 1971), 25–26, 326–27.

62 Roderick Nash, *Wilderness and the American Mind*, 3d ed. (New York, 1982), 122–60.

63 Daniel Schaffer, *Garden Cities for America* (Philadelphia, 1982), 31–47.

64 John D. Hicks, *The Populist Revolt* (Minneapolis, 1931), 408.

65 George Mowry, *The Era of Theodore Roosevelt and the Birth of Modern America, 1900–1912* (New York, 1958), 85–105; Stephen Stagner, "The Recall of Judicial Decisions and the Due Process Debate," *American Journal of Legal History* 24 (1980): 257–65.

66 See, e.g., Beth, *American Constitution*, 190, arguing that the Supreme Court may have been conservative but its conservatism might hinder as well as aid big business, and James M. Graham, "Law's Labor Lost: Judicial Politics in the Progressive Era," 1972 *Wisconsin Law Review* 447, suggesting that conservative judges and antiprogressive elements were allies in Wisconsin but their efforts had ironic consequences.

67 In New Jersey, Hennessey v. Carmody, 50 N.J. Eq.; and in California, Hurlbut v. California Portland Cement Company, 161 Cal. 239 (1908).

68 96 Pa. 116 (1880).

69 86 Pa. 401 (1878), 94 Pa. 302 (1880), and 102 Pa. 370 (1883). In all three earlier hearings, the court refused to widen the holdings in *Richard's Appeal* and *Huckstein's Appeal* to reach riparian cases. The grip of old riparian doctrine was still tight.

70 113 Pa. 126, 149 (1886).

71 160 Pa. 209, 221 (1894).

72 See Sullivan v. Jones and Loughlin Steel, 208 Pa. 540, 554 (1904) (Thompson, J., dissenting, in the name of "progress and activity of industry" and his now repudiated opinion in *Richard's Appeal*).

73 293 Pa. 152, 159, 161 (1928).

74 63 N.Y. 568, 583 (1876).

75 164 N.Y. 303, 315, 317, 323 (1900).

76 189 N.Y. 40, 46, 50 (1907).

77 208 N.Y. 1, 3, 5 (1913).

78 The court seemed to verge on giving its judgment in favor of the creek itself, so badly damaged was it by the defendant. At the time, it would hardly have made sense to regard the creek as a litigant, but under more modern environmental consciousness such a position seems tenable. See Sierra Club v. Morton, 405 U.S. 727, 742–43 (1971) (Justice William O. Douglas, dissenting from the ruling that plaintiffs did not have sufficient interest in the property in question to bring a suit, argued instead that the wilderness had a value in itself).

79 211 N.Y. 301, 305–6 (1914).

80 Fifty years later, in *Boomer v. Atlantic Cement* (1970), the court of appeals took great pains to explain an apparent departure from its established rejection of Balance of Equity, but its exertions were needless. The polluting cement company could easily be brought under the analysis in *McCann*. In *Boomer*, the court's majority wrote: "the ground for the denial of the injunction, notwith-

standing the finding both that there is a nuisance and that plaintiffs have been damaged substantially, is the large disparity in economic consequences of the nuisance and of the injunction." Cement dust in the backyard was not a sufficient reason to close a major regional employer. The court continued, "this theory cannot, however, be sustained without overruling a doctrine which has been consistently reaffirmed in several leading cases in this court and which has never been disavowed here, namely that where a nuisance has been found and where there has been any substantial damage shown by the party complaining an injunction will be granted." The court's apology notwithstanding, *Boomer* took up where *McCann* left off, with Balance of Equity. In point of fact, the court in *Boomer* merely arranged for the defendant to pay permanent damages, which the court itself would determine, or face an injunction. 26 N.Y.2d 219, 220–21 (1970). The majority of the court also theorized that antipollution controls were best left to the legislative branch, not to the courts. Perhaps the reason for the apologetic tone of the court was that in Kennedy v. Moog Servocontrols, 21 N.Y.2d 966 (1968), the court had upheld an injunction against a sewage disposal contractor when the damages had been far less substantial than in *Boomer*. The dissent in *Boomer*, 26 N.Y.2d at 223 (Jansen, J., dissenting), reminded the court of its long-standing resistance to Balance of Equity and the particular severity of the cement dust problem. If my analysis is right, the court had long before adopted a variant of Balance of Equity. And, indeed, in *Boomer* the court arranged for a buy-out of the plaintiffs' claims.

81   18 F. 753, 806 (C.C.D. Cal. 1883).
82   53 F. 422, 423–28 (C.C.D. R.I. 1892).
83   140 F. 951, 952 (C.C.D. Utah 1904).
84   142 F. 625, 640, 642, 645 (9th Cir. 1906).
85   206 U.S. 230, 237–38 (1906).
86   164 F. 927, 936, 939–40 (C.C.D. Idaho 1908).
87   230 U.S. 46, 56 (1912).
88   44 F.2d 621, 623–24 (E.D. Mass. 1930).
89   18 F.2d 736, 737 (2d Cir. 1927). On Hand's reputation, see G. Edward White, *The American Judicial Tradition: Expanded Edition* (New York, 1988), 263–68, and Kathryn Griffith, *Judge Learned Hand and the Role of the Federal Judiciary* (Norman, Okla., 1973), 13–14.
90   304 U.S. 64 (1938), ordered federal courts to desist from fashioning a federal common law.
91   18 F.2d at 738. Hand loved the woods in his native upstate New York, it might be noted in passing.
92   289 U.S. 334, 338 (1933). With the notable exception of "dissenters" like Brandeis, the Supreme Court had lagged behind state and lower federal courts in jettisoning formalism, according to Karl Llewellyn, *The Common Law Tradition: Deciding Appeals* (Boston, 1960), 41.
93   See Horace G. Wood, *A Practical Treatise on the Law of Nuisance* (Albany, N.Y., 1875), 820–21, revised in Wood, *A Practical Treatise on the Law of Nuisances in Their Various Forms, Including Remedies Therefore at Law and in Equity*, 2d ed. (1883), sec. 555. Other writers joined in attacking Balance of Equity. See, e.g., Annot., 29 *American Law Register* (new series) 649 (1881); Note, "The 'Balance of Injury' as a Reason for Refusing an Injunction to Restrain a Nuisance," 57 *University of Pennsylvania Law Review* 396 (1909).
94   Pomeroy, *A Treatise of Equity Jurisprudence*, 3d ed. (John Norton Pomeroy, Jr., 1905), 4:904–10, repeated in Pomeroy, *Equity Jurisprudence*, 4th ed. (1918–19), 5:sec. 530. John L. Meachem, "The Peasant in His Cottage: Some Comments

on the Relative Hardship Doctrine in Equity," 28 *Southern California Law Review* 139, 142 (1955), credits Pomeroy, Sr., with popularizing the doctrine of Balance of Equity even though he derogated it.

95 George Boke, *Cases on Equity* (St. Paul, Minn., 1915), 960–68, gave a squib from *Richard's Appeal* but closed his account of the doctrine with *Hennessey* and *Hurlbut*, both of which rejected Balance of Equity root and branch. California's rejection of the doctrine may have had an influence on Boke.

96 Thomas C. Spelling and James H. Lewis, *A Treatise on the Law Governing Injunctions* (St. Louis, Mo., 1926), 109–10.

97 Chafee, "Teaching Diary for Equity III," November 17, 1917, Zechariah Chafee Papers, box 40, folder 13, Harvard Law School Library.

98 Chafee, "Progress of the Law, 1919–1920—Equitable Relief against Torts," 34 *Harvard Law Review* 388, 390 (1921); Chafee, *Cases on Equitable Relief against Torts* (Cambridge, Mass., 1924), 288; Chafee and Pound, *Cases on Equitable Relief against Torts* (Cambridge, Mass., 1933), 304. Chafee's earliest treatment of Balance of Equity seems to rely on the views of his teacher at Harvard, James Barr Ames, compiler of *A Selection of Cases on Equitable Jurisdiction* (Cambridge, Mass., 1904), 574. Ames would have opposed the doctrine in its earliest form on moral grounds. See Ames, "Law and Morals," 22 *Harvard Law Review* 97 (1909).

99 William Walsh, "Equitable Relief against Nuisance," 7 *New York University Law Review* 352, 361 (1929).

100 Comment, "Injunction—Nuisance—Balance of Convenience," 37 *Yale Law Journal* 96 (1927).

101 The fear of activist judging, so often expressed during the Warren Court years, has a long history and is not limited to political conservatives. Reformers launched an all-out attack on the activism of the Fuller Court when the Court declared some state regulations on safety and health unconstitutional using an expansive reading of the due process clause of the Fourteenth Amendment. The assault was led, among others, by Louis Brandeis. See Thomas McCraw, *Prophets of Regulation* (Cambridge, Mass., 1984), 80–142. Within the Court Holmes pleaded for judicial restraint. Beth, *American Constitution*, 187–88.

102 Henry L. McClintock, "Discretion to Deny Injunctions against Trespass and Nuisance," 12 *Minnesota Law Review* 565, 573 (1928); McClintock, *Handbook of Equity* (St. Paul, Minn., 1936), 247–48; *Handbook of the Principles of Equity*, 2d ed. (St. Paul, Minn., 1948), 382–83.

103 Annot., 61 *American Law Reports* 924, 927 (1929).

104 [W. Keeton and C. Morris], Note, "Balancing the Equities," 18 *Texas Law Review* 412, 416 (1940).

105 Thurman Arnold to Felix Frankfurter, June 11, 1934, in Gene M. Gressley, ed., *Voltaire and the Cowboy: The Letters of Thurman Arnold* (Boulder, Colo., 1977), 202. Arnold later admitted that one reason he left the federal bench was that "I was impatient with legal precedents that seemed to me to reach an unjust result." Arnold, *Fair Fights and Foul: A Dissenting Lawyer's Life* (New York, 1965), 159. See also the discussion of Jerome Frank's judicial writings in Robert Jerome Glennon, *The Iconoclast as Reformer: Jerome Frank's Impact on American Law* (Ithaca, N.Y., 1985), 102–63, and Charles Clark, "The Function of Law in a Democratic Society," 9 *University of Chicago Law Review* 393 (1941). On the Realists as a movement, see Laura Kalman, *Legal Realism at Yale, 1920–1960* (Chapel Hill, N.C., 1985).

106 See, e.g., Roy v. Chevrolet, 262 Mich. 663, 666 (1933).

107 See, e.g., Roger Traynor, "La Rude Vida, La Dolce Giustanza, or Hard Cases

Can Make Good Law," 29 *Chicago Law Review* 223, 229–30, 232 (1962); Charles Wyzanski, *A Trial Judge's Freedom and Responsibility* (New York, 1952), 21; Coffin, *Ways of a Judge*, 56.

108   On the Progressives and facts, see Thomas Bender, *New York Intellect: A History of Intellectual Life in New York City from 1750 to the Beginnings of Our Own Time* (Baltimore, 1987), 302–8. The Federal Rules of Civil Procedure (1938) were a triumph of equity over formalism. On the Federal Rules and managerial judging, see Abram Chayes, "The Role of the Judge in Public Law Litigation," 89 *Harvard Law Review* 1281 (1976), and Peter Charles Hoffer, Introduction to Hoffer and Brussack, eds., *Writing the Rules* (forthcoming).

109   Edward Corwin, "The Basic Doctrine of American Constitutional Law," 12 *Michigan Law Review* 247 (1914); James L. Kainen, "Nineteenth-Century Interpretations of the Contract Clause," 31 *Buffalo Law Review* 381 (1982). I am grateful to Terry Fisher for calling my attention to these citations.

110   By the end of the 1940s, Lord Chancellor Eldon's dictum in *Gee v. Pritchard*, 2 Swans. 402 (1818), that the chancellor could only protect property rights had been greatly broadened to include rights to religious worship and personal privacy. These rights are collected in *Restatement (Second) of Torts*, sec. 937 (1977). They include feelings, good name, honor, and constitutional rights to liberty and privacy.

111   The equitable discretion folded into Balance of Equity is still the core of antipollution injunctions. See Daniel A. Farber, "Equitable Discretion, Legal Duties, and Environmental Injunctions," 45 *University of Pittsburgh Law Review* 513 (1984).

112   Roscoe Pound, "Interests of Personality," 28 *Harvard Law Review* 343, 349 (1915). Compare Pound with James Madison, *Federalist* No. 51, and Alexander Hamilton, *Federalist* No. 60, in *Federalist*, 323–24, 367. The confrontation of special "interests" and the public interest in eighteenth-century American political ideology is traced in Richard N. Bushman, *King and People in Provincial Massachusetts* (Chapel Hill, N.C., 1985), 88–132.

113   Harlan F. Stone, "The Common Law in the United States," 50 *Harvard Law Review* 4, 10, 20 (1936).

114   Roscoe Pound, "Mechanical Jurisprudence," 8 *Columbia Law Review* 605 (1908). The incident is reported in Alpheus T. Mason, *Harlan Fiske Stone: Pillar of the Law* (New York, 1956), 436.

115   See, e.g., David B. Truman, *The Government Process*, 2d ed. (New York, 1971).

116   See, e.g., Abrams v. United States, 250 U.S. 616 (1919): seditious speech measured by a balancing test; Near v. Minnesota, 283 U.S. 697 (1931): legality of state injunction barring speech measured by a balancing test; and Branzburg v. Hayes, 408 U.S. 665 (1972): refusal by reporter to surrender notes in grand jury hearing weighed under balancing test.

117   Jerry L. Mashaw, *Due Process in the Administrative State* (New Haven, Conn., 1985), 46–47. Balancing tests are employed in other than purely public-law or constitutional settings. See, e.g., Jay M. Feinman, "Promissory Estoppel and Judicial Method," 97 *Harvard Law Review* 678, 710–11 (1984).

118   Bernard Schwartz, *Administrative Law* (Boston, 1976), 18.

119   In a seminal article, Frankfurter claimed that administrative law was wholly alien to law scholars though it was already a central part of American governance by 1927; see Felix Frankfurter, "The Task of Administrative Law," 75 *University of Pennsylvania Law Review* 614 (1927). A decade later, James M. Landis, one of the foremost interpreters of administrative law within the academy and the federal bureaucracy, and a protégé of Frankfurter, agreed that administrative law had no real theoretical origin. It was based on the

"exigencies of governance." Landis, *The Administrative Process* (New Haven, Conn., 1938), 1.

120   On the roots of the antitrust campaign, see Martin J. Sklar, *The Corporate Reconstruction of American Capitalism, 1890–1916* (Cambridge, Mass., 1988), 86–145.

121   Wabash, St. Louis, and Pacific Railway Company v. Illinois, 118 U.S. 557 (1886).

122   Interstate Commerce Commission Act, 24 *U.S. Stats* 379 (1887). Kelly, Harbison, and Belz, *The American Constitution*, 384–86, describes the travails of the ICC.

123   26 *U.S. Stats* 209 (1890). On the purposes of the act, see David Millon, "The Sherman Act and the Balance of Power," 61 *University of Southern California Law Review* 1219 (1988).

124   A. D. Neale and D. G. Goyder, *The Antitrust Laws of the United States of America*, 3d ed. (Cambridge, Mass., 1980), 1–33.

125   See, e.g., Central Ohio Salt v. Guthrie, 35 Ohio 666 (1880), holding that an agreement among salt producers to regulate supply and prices was not enforceable against a salt producer who reneged on his promise to cooperate.

126   See, e.g., Northern Securities Co. v. United States, 193 U.S. 197, 331 (1904), and Standard Oil of New Jersey v. United States, 221 U.S. 96 (1911).

127   United States v. Standard Oil of New Jersey, 173 F. 177, 192 (E.D. Mo. 1909).

128   For example, in the lead case of antitrust in the 1940s, Paramount Pictures v. United States, 70 F. Supp. 53, 76 (S.D. N.Y. 1946), the trial court found Paramount's control over the distribution and display of its product to be an unfair restraint of trade. Judge Augustus Hand ordered Paramount to allow competitive bidding for the right to show its movies. The Supreme Court, on appeal by Paramount, 334 U.S. 131 (1948), sent the case back to the lower court with orders to supervise divestiture of Paramount's interests in the movie theaters.

129   Landis, *The Administrative Process*, 2, 24–26. On the FTC in the doldrums of the 1920s, see McCraw, *Prophets of Regulation*, 149–52.

130   See, e.g., Peter H. Irons, *The New Deal Lawyers* (Princeton, N.J., 1982), 6–7, 20–21, 118–22ff.

131   Martin Shapiro, *Who Guards the Guardians? Judicial Control of Administration* (Athens, Ga., 1988), 62–77. Capture is rarely complete, however, for the agencies are not independent of political influence, public opinion, the careerist ambitions of their staff, and other external forces. See James Q. Wilson, "The Politics of Regulation," in Wilson, ed., *The Politics of Regulation* (New York, 1980), 383–90.

132   See, e.g., George David Smith, *From Monopoly to Competition: The Transformations of Alcoa, 1888–1986* (Cambridge, Mass., 1989), 201–14.

133   Schwartz, *Administrative Law*, 608.

134   The Administrative Procedure Act of 1946 is still in effect; 5 *U.S.C.* 551.

135   Richard B. Stewart, "The Reformation of American Administrative Law," 88 *Harvard Law Review* 1669 (1975).

136   Landis, *The Administrative Process*, 17. But see Edwin W. Patterson, "The Place of Equity in the Law School Curriculum," 8 *American Law School Review* 385, 390 (1936), and Thurman Arnold, "Apologia for Jurisprudence," 44 *Yale Law Journal* 729, 743 (1935), arguing for the comparison.

137   " 'Balancing of Interests' remains with no indication of how to tell an interest when you see one, much less with any study of how they are or should be balanced." Karl N. Llewellyn, "A Realistic Jurisprudence—The Next Step," *Columbia Law Review* 431, 433 n. 3 (1930). Llewellyn's target was Roscoe Pound's

interest balancing (see n. 112 above), but Llewellyn's point had and still has far broader application.

CHAPTER SEVEN

1   Civil rights litigation should not be divorced from the broader campaign for racial justice. See, e.g., Robert Korstad and Nelson Lichtenstein, "Opportunities Found and Lost: Labor, Radicals, and the Early Civil Rights Movement," *Journal of American History* 75 (1988): 786–811, a sharply argued reminder of the role of black union leaders in civil rights agitation, and Adam Fairclough, *To Redeem the Soul of America: The Southern Christian Leadership Conference and Martin Luther King, Jr.* (Athens, Ga., 1987), 57–192, a treatise on the crucial role of the Southern Christian Leadership Conference in initiating litigation.

2   Simple facts: on the Eastern Shore of Delaware, in the farm hamlet of Hockessin, there were two schoolhouses. One was a pretty new building on a hill. It was reserved for white children. Two miles away, a one-room schoolhouse served all the black children of the area. To Sarah Bulah and a handful of other parents determined to get fair treatment from the Department of Public Instruction, something had to be done. Why should their children ride a bus to a school far away when there was one at their door? They turned to the NAACP, one of whose gifted young lawyers, Louis Redding, brought the case before the federal courts. To it he joined a similar suit against the segregated high schools of Wilmington and its suburb of Clayton on behalf of Ethel Louise Belton and her children. The state, the defendant, pleaded that the case ought to come first before the state's own equity court, since the petitioners wanted injunctive relief against the state's segregation laws. Redding agreed to refile in the state's court of chancery. *Belton v. Gebhart* and *Bulah v. Gebhart* came before Chancellor Collins J. Seitz in the fall of 1951. Testimony took three days, but the chancellor was not satisfied with passive recitation of evidence by counsel. He wanted to see for himself what the schoolhouses looked like. Was separate but equal truly equal? Could it be? He visited the elementary schools and the high schools in question and was appalled. In an interview years later, Seitz recalled, "I found it inexcusable that the state would lend its support to dividing its citizens this way." Seitz quoted in Kluger, *Simple Justice* (New York, 1976), 447. The account of Hockessin is taken from ibid., 425–50.

Louise Belton and the other petitioners alleged that the state denied them equal protection of the law under the Fourteenth Amendment; state courts were competent triers of such federal constitutional questions whose decisions could be appealed through the federal courts. Belton v. Gebhart, 32 Del. Ch. Repts. 343, 345 (1952). If the state upheld the federal constitutional claim against the state's own laws, the state (defendant) might appeal against its own court's decision through a writ of certiorari. The federal courts need not hear the case, however. Should the state rule against the federal constitutional claim, the loser had an appeal of right which must be taken up by the federal courts (though, of course, they might agree with the state court's view of the Constitution and summarily dismiss the appeal). *Belton* would come to the U.S. Supreme Court on certiorari after the state had lost all its motions for reversal because the Court wanted to join the Delaware case with the three other state cases and the District of Columbia case on segregation.

The relief sought was an equitable one—an injunction—and Seitz found no trouble stating that the blacks' schools were inferior to the whites' schools in physical plant, student-teacher ratio, curriculum, and even the time that it took students to get to school. Most striking for him, a model of the indifference (or worse, antagonism) of the state to the interest of its black schoolchildren, was that no buses were provided for black children despite the fact that they had to travel much farther to their schools than did white children to theirs. Such inequality could not be tolerated. Seitz would not accept the state's promise to equalize facilities in the future, for promises of future remedy did not aid the petitioners in the court before him. His decree enjoining the defendant from segregating the schools wedded the moral vision of the chancellor with his authority in court to remedy injustice. It brought together trusteeship, equality, and reality. But would Seitz's opinion be sustained? The state supreme court upheld the order of the chancellor but qualified his reasoning. The state supreme court refused to find that separate but equal was inherently unequal and permitted the state to reapply for dissolution of the injunction (in effect, to reestablish a segregated system) if and when it could prove that such a system could offer equal educational opportunities to black students. 33 Del. Ch. Repts. 144, 172 (1952).

3   Compare Felix Frankfurter and James M. Landis, *The Business of the Supreme Court* (New York, 1928), 300, finding that the Court was absorbed by "cases [that] center about the interplay of government, and economic enterprise," with the figures on civil rights suits in Arthur D. Hellman, "The Business of the Supreme Court under the Judiciary Act of 1925: The Plenary Docket in the 1970s," 91 *Harvard Law Review* 1709 (1978), and Richard D. Posner, *The Federal Courts: Crisis and Reform* (Cambridge, Mass., 1985), 82.

4   Briefs and position papers on these cases are preserved in Legal File, 1940–55, NAACP Papers, boxes 138–40, Library of Congress. On the early education cases, see Kluger, *Simple Justice*, and Tushnet, *NAACP's Legal Strategy*. The original dispute over antisegregation tactics within the NAACP—Nathan Margold's proposal for a constitutional challenge to segregation muted by Charles Houston's counter that separate but equal could be attacked as a sham—continued in various forms throughout this formative period. See Genna Rae McNeil, *Groundwork: Charles Hamilton Houston and the Struggle for Civil Rights* (Philadelphia, 1983), 114–18, and Tushnet, *NAACP's Legal Strategy*. The same questions can still be raised. See Derrick Bell, *And We Are Not Saved: The Elusive Quest for Racial Justice* (New York, 1987), 102–22.

5   Indeed, I believe that it is only because *Brown* I postponed enforcement, refusing to spell out the means of desegregation, that some scholars favor it and still find ways to question *Brown* II. See, e.g., Alexander Bickel, *The Least Dangerous Branch* (New York, 1962), 244–72; Philip Kurland, *Politics, the Constitution, and the Warren Court* (Chicago, 1970), 98–169; Lino Graglia, *Disaster by Decree* (Ithaca, N.Y., 1976), 31–32; and Robert Bork, *The Tempting of America: The Political Seduction of the Law* (New York, 1989), 69–128. Nevertheless, getting "right" with *Brown* has a powerful effect on legal scholarship as well as federal jurisprudence. See, e.g., Fiss, *Civil Rights Injunction*, 5.

6   Brief for the Appellants on Questions Number Four and Five, December 1952, Kurland and Casper, eds., *Landmark Briefs*, 49:704.

7   Brief by the Attorney General of the State of Florida, December 1954, Kurland and Casper, eds., *Landmark Briefs*, 49A:942.

8   Paul Gewirtz, in "Remedies and Resistance," 92 *Yale Law Journal* 587 (1983), measures the claims of "Rights Maximizers," who argue that remedies must provide the fullest measure of relief possible, against "Interest Balancers," who wish to avoid great costs for little gains and so trim the scope of the remedy. He regards *Brown* as an "Interest Balancing" decree. As I have suggested in

Chapter 6, Balance of Equity is not quite the same as balancing interests, and the distinction goes to the heart of the problem civil rights advocates have with *Brown* II.

9 See Kluger, *Simple Justice*, 582ff.

10 Frankfurter, "Memorandum for the Conference," June 4, 1953, Felix Frankfurter Papers, box 72, folder 9, Harvard Law School Library. Elman's recollections of his role and the impact of the amicus brief for the United States, which he wrote, appear in 100 *Harvard Law Review* 817 (1987). On his relations with Frankfurter, see ibid., 827. The Elman-authored brief for the United States as amicus appears in Kurland and Casper, eds., *Landmark Briefs*, 49:113. One should also see Randall Kennedy, "A Reply to Philip Elman," 100 *Harvard Law Review* 1938 (1987), noting that NAACP counsel, not the United States as amicus, framed the issues for the court and persuaded the court to strike down segregation in the elementary schools. The text of the questions appears, among other places, in Brown v. Board of Education, 98 L. Ed. 881 (1954).

11 The cases on enforcement that Elman cited in his brief were Eccles v. Peoples Bank, 333 U.S. 426, holding that the chancellor has discretion to refuse or to tailor a remedy to do justice to all parties; and Radio Station WOW v. Johnson, 326 U.S. 120; Standard Oil Co. v. United States, 221 U.S. 1; United States v. Aluminum Co., 148 F.2d 416; United States v. National Lead, 332 U.S. 319; and United States v. Paramount Pictures, 70 F. Supp. 53—all finding that remedies in antitrust proceedings could be tempered by equitable discretion, including delay to gain good-faith compliance from the defendant. These did not, however, fully develop Balance of Equity; they were closer to balance of interests.

12 Kurland and Casper, eds., *Landmark Briefs*, 49:144.

13 Ibid., 49A:538.

14 See David Pinsky's memo on Question Four, Legal File, 1940–55, NAACP Papers, box 141, Library of Congress. Pinsky prepared the memo for a conference on September 25, 1953, bringing together leading lawyers, scholars, and social scientists to aid the LDF. "Seminar #4," Legal File, 1940–55, box 138, ibid. The many cases Pinsky cited were examples of discretionary refusals to give equitable remedies. None illustrated the managerial style. I am grateful to Mark Tushnet for calling this reference to my attention.

15 Ervin to Warren, June 3, 1955, Segregation Cases File, Earl Warren Papers, box 574, Library of Congress.

16 See, e.g., William Chafe, *Civilities and Civil Rights: Greensboro, North Carolina, and the Black Struggle for Freedom* (New York, 1980), 42–70, on local elites' reaction. On Ervin, see David R. Colburn, "Florida's Governors Confront the *Brown* Decision: A Case Study of the Constitutional Politics of School Desegregation, 1954–1970," in Kermit L. Hall and James W. Ely, Jr., eds., *An Uncertain Tradition: Constitutionalism and the History of the South* (Athens, Ga., 1989), 328–31.

17 Frankfurter to Warren, May 17, 1955, Segregation Cases File, Earl Warren Papers, box 574, Library of Congress. See also Kluger, *Simple Justice*, 600, and Bickel, *Least Dangerous Branch*, 249–54.

18 Frankfurter to the Conference, memo dated January 15, 1954, "Draft I," Felix Frankfurter Papers, box 72, Harvard Law School Library. Frankfurter's reverence for facts was often demonstrated throughout his career. As a traveling troubleshooter for the Wilson administration, he had gathered facts on the mistreatment of industrial laborers. As a protégé of Brandeis, Frankfurter had supplied facts on social issues. In his attack on the labor injunction, in his

brilliant articles on the business of the Supreme Court, and in his service to the New Deal, Frankfurter proved that facts can change minds when arguments fail. On Frankfurter's fact-gathering activities, see John W. Johnson, *American Legal Culture, 1908–1940* (Westport, Conn., 1981), 36, 108–10.

19   Frankfurter to Warren, July 5, 1954, Segregation Cases File, Earl Warren Papers, box 574, Library of Congress.

20   Schwartz, *Unpublished Opinions*, 447.

21   349 U.S. at 298.

22   349 U.S. at 299–300. The argument that *Brown* II was a balancing case is hotly contested by Alexander Aleinikoff, "Constitutional Law in the Age of Balancing," 96 *Yale Law Journal* 943, 998 (1987), even though Aleinikoff finds that the Court was fully adept at such balancing in constitutional cases—e.g., free speech, right to counsel—by the late 1940s. Aleinikoff is not alone in his condemnation of an interest-balancing view of the rights question. See, e.g., Derrick Bell, *Race, Racism, and American Law*, 2d ed. (Boston, 1980), 381–84.

23   349 U.S. at 301.

24   Frankfurter to Warren, May 24, 1955, Segregation Cases File, Earl Warren Papers, box 574, Library of Congress. See also Kluger, *Simple Justice*, 742–43.

25   The mistake may not have made any difference. *Brown* II was needlessly unclear—its guidelines were indecently vague—but the political repercussions would likely have been the same whether the opinion said "earliest possible date," Warren's initial phrasing, or "all deliberate speed." What is more, the problem of enforcement remained. District courts would still have borne the burden of monitoring compliance, as in fact they had to do under "all deliberate speed."

26   349 U.S. at 300. Brownell wanted the defendants ordered to present desegregation plans within ninety days. See Interview with Herbert Brownell, October 17, 1979, in Jack Bass, *Unlikely Heroes* (New York, 1981), 151.

27   Schwartz, *Unpublished Opinions*, 466. Douglas said that he had worked closely with Warren on the first *Brown* opinion. See Douglas, "Memorandum for the File, May 17, 1954," in Melvin I. Urofsky, ed., *The Douglas Letters* (Bethesda, Md., 1987), 167. Justice Black "was not fond of class action suits" and preferred to treat the cases on a one-by-one basis. Justice Harold H. Burton's Conference Notes, April 16, 1955, quoted in Tinsley E. Yarbrough, *Mr. Justice Black and His Critics* (Durham, N.C., 1988), 239.

28   Schwartz, *Unpublished Opinions*, 465.

29   Brown v. Board of Education, 84 F.R.D. 383 (D. Kans. 1979), is once again a class action.

30   Fed. R. Civ. P. 23(b)2. See Fiss, *Civil Rights Injunction*, 15, and Yeazell, *Class Action*, 240–49. Yeazell mentions the difficulty that this oblique aid to civil rights suits creates for the formulation of a unified theory of class action; indeed, he argues that the rule undercuts the otherwise sound notion of permitting class actions only because the named plaintiff represents the best interests of the absent class members.

31   For examples of this scholarship, see Jack W. Peltason, *Fifty-Eight Lonely Men: Southern Federal Judges and School Desegregation* (New York, 1961), 18; Dennis J. Hutchinson, "Unanimity and Desegregation: Decisionmaking in the Supreme Court, 1948–1958," 68 *Georgetown Law Journal* 1, 56 (1979); and Kenneth L. Karst, "All Deliberate Speed," in *Encyclopedia of the American Constitution* (New York, 1986), 1:44. But could the Court take jurisdiction from the state courts when the subject matter—here, education—was hedged around by voluminous state codes? Some very learned scholars at the time had obvious doubts. See Henry M. Hart, Jr., "The Power of Congress to Limit the Jurisdiction of Fed-

eral Courts: An Exercise in Dialectic," 66 *Harvard Law Review* 1362, 1401 (1953).

32   Abe Fortas, "Chief Justice Warren: The Enigma of Leadership," 84 *Yale Law Journal* 405, 411 (1975).

33   Walter Huxman to Warren, November 1, 1955, and Warren to Huxman, November 14, 1955, Segregation Cases File, Earl Warren Papers, box 574, Library of Congress. Huxman wrote the opinion for the three-judge panel in *Brown* when it was remanded for rehearing under the *Brown* II guidelines. Huxman left the Buchanan School District schools wholly black, refusing to equate desegregation with integration. A copy of his order, dated October 28, 1955, can be found in Legal File, 1940–55, NAACP Papers, box 139, Library of Congress. The LDF appealed. On Topeka, see Mary L. Dudziak, "The Limits of Good Faith: Desegregation in Topeka, Kansas, 1950–1956," *Law and History Review* 5 (1987): 351–91.

34   On Frankfurter's caution, see, e.g., Hurd v. Hodge, 334 U.S. 24, 36 (1948). Frankfurter concurred with the Court's striking down of restrictive housing covenants in the District of Columbia but based his concurrence on the discretion of a chancellor *not* to issue an injunction.

35   Hand to Frankfurter, April 6, 1953, Felix Frankfurter Papers, box 199, folder 9, Harvard Law School Library.

36   Chafee, "The Disintegration of Integration," December 19, 1956, Zechariah Chafee Papers, box 86, folder 1, Harvard Law School Library. Oddly, Chafee did not add that the cases ought properly to have remained class actions.

37   Stephen E. Ambrose, *Eisenhower*, vol. 2: *The President* (New York, 1984), 189–92. The president refused to fully honor his commitment to uphold the Court's decision as well. Ibid., 143, 498.

38   Frankfurter to Bickel, December 27, 1956, Felix Frankfurter Papers, box 183, folder 12, Harvard Law School Library. This was a turnabout of sorts, for Professor Frankfurter had on earlier occasions chided Chafee for being too cautious about advocacy of the cause of the weak. See Donald L. Smith, *Zechariah Chafee, Jr.: Defender of Liberty and Law* (Cambridge, Mass., 1986), 130–32.

39   Bickel to Frankfurter, January 5, 1957, Felix Frankfurter Papers, box 183, folder 12, Harvard Law School Library.

40   See, e.g., the response in Nashville described in Richard A. Pride and J. David Woodard, *The Burden of Busing: The Politics of Desegregation in Nashville, Tennessee* (Knoxville, Tenn., 1985), 54–58. See also Frank T. Read and Lucy S. McGough, *Let Them Be Judged: The Judicial Integration of the Deep South* (Metuchin, N.J., 1978), 1–168.

41   Briggs v. Elliott, 132 F. Supp. 776 (E.D. S.C. 1955). The opinion was written by Circuit Court Judge John J. Parker, sitting on the three-man court. The "Briggs doctrine" became one of the most common ways to evade full-scale desegregation.

42   See, e.g., Bell v. Rippy, 133 F. Supp. 811 (N.D. Tex. 1955). The district court found that Dallas' school board was in compliance with *Brown* if segregated facilities were equal. The Fifth Circuit reversed and remanded, 233 F.2d 796 (1956), but later adopted the "Briggs doctrine" that *Brown* had ordered the end of state-directed segregation, not the beginning of court-supervised integration. See Avery v. Wichita Falls Independent School System, 241 F.2d 230 (1957).

43   Peltason, *Fifty-Eight Lonely Men*, 7–9, 22–23, 93–134; Leon Friedman, "The Federal Courts of the South: Judge Bryan Simpson and His Reluctant Brethren," in Leon Friedman, ed., *Southern Justice* (Cleveland, 1965), 187–213.

44   Harold W. Horowitz and Kenneth L. Karst, *Law, Lawyers, and Social Change*

(Indianapolis, 1969), 239–40; Alexander Bickel, *Politics and the Warren Court* (New York, 1965), 14–15.

45 Robert L. Carter, "The Warren Court and Desegregation," 67 *Michigan Law Review* 237 (1968); J. Skelly Wright, "Public School Desegregation: Legal Remedies for De Facto Segregation," 40 *New York University Law Review* 285 (1965). It should be noted that Carter was a key member of the NAACP team and later sat on the federal bench himself, and that Wright dismantled *de facto* segregation in the District of Columbia. The Eisenhower Republicans on the Fifth Circuit—Rives, Tuttle, Wisdom, and Brown—had begun their campaign to enforce *Brown*.

46 In Green v. New Kent County School Board, 391 U.S. 430 (1968), Justice William Brennan, for a unanimous court, wrote the first detailed opinion on remedies, holding that "freedom-of-choice" plans were unacceptable and that local school boards must bring forward plans that would truly desegregate the schools immediately. It should be noted that Brennan tracked the language of the Fifth Circuit's liberals.

47 Paul Brest, "Race Discrimination," in Vincent Blasi, ed., *The Burger Court: The Counter Revolution that Wasn't* (New Haven, Conn., 1983), 115–16.

48 402 U.S. 43 (1971).

49 James B. McMillan, "Social Science and the District Court: The Observations of a Journeyman Trial Judge," in Betsy Levin and Willis D. Hawley, eds., *The Courts, Social Science, and School Desegregation* (New Brunswick, N.J., 1977), 160.

50 Bernard Schwartz, *Swann's Way* (New York, 1986), 13–15, 16–24, 48–50, 52–53, 56–57, 102, 114–15, 117, 119–20, 124–26, 128, 132–33, 146–47, 186, 228–30, 235, 239. The Finger plan for busing the students is reproduced in Brief for the Appellant, Petitioner, October Term, 1970, Kurland and Casper, eds., *Landmark Briefs*, 70:127–223.

51 Harvey C. Couch, *A History of the Fifth Circuit, 1891–1981* (Washington, D.C., 1984), 105–39; Bass, *Unlikely Heroes*, 23–55, 213–47, 297–310. Another refrain of judges opposed to equitable enforcement of desegregation was that courts were ill-designed to alter deep-seated social folkways. This was the contention of judges like Ben F. Cameron of the Fifth Circuit and Judge Dozier A. DeVane of the Northern District of Florida in the early 1960s. See Deborah J. Barrow and Thomas G. Walker, *A Court Divided: The Fifth Circuit Court of Appeals and the Politics of Judicial Reform* (New Haven, Conn., 1989), 43–44, 47.

52 Bell, *Racism*, 389–415.

53 Brinkman v. Dayton Board of Education, 503 F.2d 684 (1974); Penick v. Columbus Board of Education, 429 F. Supp. 229 (1977); Evans v. Buchanan, 393 F. Supp. 428 (1975); Bradley v. Milliken, 388 F. Supp. 582 (1971); Bradley v. Milliken, 411 F. Supp. 943 (1975). Every one of these cases, like those in Denver, Norfolk, Nashville, and Greensboro, was appealed, remanded, rewritten, and revised between 1971 and the present. On the judges, see Phillip J. Cooper, *Hard Judicial Choices: Federal District Court Judges and State and Local Officials* (New York, 1988), 85–135, and Paul R. Dimond, *Beyond Busing: Inside the Challenge to Urban Segregation* (Ann Arbor, Mich., 1985).

54 Milliken v. Bradley, 418 U.S. 717 (1974); Missouri v. Jenkins 88–1150 (1990).

55 379 F. Supp. 410, 417, 425–27, 480, 482 (D. Mass. 1974), *aff'd, sub nom* Morgan v. Kerrigan, 509 F.2d 580 (1st Cir. 1974), *cert. denied*, 421 U.S. 963 (1975).

56 George R. Metcalf, *From Little Rock to Boston: The History of School Desegregation* (Westport, Conn., 1983), 197–220; J. Harvie Wilkinson III, *From Brown to Bakke: The Supreme Court and School Integration* (New York, 1979), 203–14; J. Brian Sheehan, *The Boston School Integration Dispute: Social Change and Legal Maneuvers* (New York, 1984), 91ff.

57   See, e.g., Derrick A. Bell, Jr., "Serving Two Masters: Integration Ideals and Client Interests in School Desegregation Litigation," 85 *Yale Law Journal* 470 (1976), and Jacqueline Fleming, *Blacks in College* (San Francisco, 1984). But see, in defense of the intervention of the courts, Kimberle M. Crenshaw, "Race Reforms and Retrenchment: Transformation and Legitimation in Anti-Discrimination Law," 101 *Harvard Law Review* 1331, 1382 (1988).

58   Malloy, *Southie Won't Go: A Teacher's Diary of South Boston High School* (Urbana, Ill., 1986); but see Sheehan, *Boston School Integration*, 97–138, arguing that federal supervision had "modernized" and improved the school system. In all fairness, it should be noted that Sheehan's overall thesis, an attack on "elite" Afro-Americans and Brahmins using the integration issue to divide and conquer working-class families, is far closer to Malloy's views than to Judge Garrity's position.

59   Federal judges facing years of discovery and pre-trial motions commonly resort to a jawboning style in their chambers. Under rules for each appellate district agreed upon by the district and appellate judges in it, litigants may be given all sorts of incentives to resolve their differences short of trial, or to abbreviate the trial itself. This style of judicial conduct has become common in many complex equity cases, particularly copyright and patent infringement suits and antitrust cases, which otherwise would consume a judge's entire career on the bench. See Steven Flanders, "Blind Umpires—A Response to Professor Resnik," 35 *Hastings Law Journal* 505, 512: "Most federal judges regard their primary role in the settlement process as that of an indirect facilitator." See also Robert F. Peckham, "A Judicial Response to the Cost of Litigation: Case Management, Two-Stage Discovery Planning, and Alternative Dispute Resolution," 37 *Rutgers Law Review* 253, 254 (1985); E. Donald Elliott, "Managerial Judging and the Evolution of Procedure," 53 *University of Chicago Law Review* 306, 307–8 (1986); and Marc Galanter, "The Emergence of the Judge as a Mediator in Civil Cases," 69 *Judicature* 257 (1986). In 1983, Rule 16 of the Federal Rules of Civil Procedure was amended to authorize judicial management of pre-trial conferences. Ironically, as the lower federal courts extended their discretionary powers to settle private disputes, the Supreme Court seemed increasingly disinclined to allow lower federal courts to extend their managerial powers into new areas of civil rights. See, e.g., Rizzo v. Goode, 423 U.S. 362 (1976), holding that federal courts cannot act as receivers of local police departments when the latter fail to provide adequate civilian complaint review procedures, because plaintiffs lack standing to bring the suit.

60   Michal R. Belknap, *Federal Law and Southern Order: Racial Violence and Constitutional Conflict in the Post-Brown South* (Athens, Ga., 1987), 229–51; Abigail Thernstrom, *Whose Votes Count? Affirmative Action and Minority Voting Rights* (Cambridge, Mass., 1987), 11–30.

61   Wyatt v. Stickney, 325 F. Supp. 781 (M.D. Ala. 1971). Johnson gave the state every opportunity to clean up the mental hospitals before he acted, and he made Fob James, the governor of Alabama, the receiver. Nonetheless, a receiver is supervised by the court. See Cooper, *Hard Judicial Choices*, 163–204, and Tinsley E. Yarbrough, *Judge Frank Johnson and Human Rights in Alabama* (University, Ala., 1981), 182–217. Johnson had to threaten the same fate to the prison system to obtain any significant improvements in it. See Larry W. Yackle, *Reform and Regret: The Story of Federal Judicial Involvement in the Alabama Prison System* (New York, 1989), 79ff.

62   Frank Johnson, "The Role of the Federal Courts in Institutional Litigation," 32 *Alabama Law Review* 271, 273–74 (1981).

63   See Charles L. Black, Jr., *Structure and Relationship in Constitutional Law* (Baton

Rouge, La., 1969), 22–23, 25–26, 53–60; Lawrence L. Tribe, "Structural Due Process," 10 *Harvard Civil Rights–Civil Liberties Review* 269 (1975); Paul Brest, "In Defense of the Anti-Discrimination Principle," 90 *Harvard Law Review* 1 (1977); and John Hart Ely, *Democracy and Distrust* (Cambridge, Mass., 1985), 150.

64   Bickel, *Politics and the Warren Court*, 15.

65   The maxim is "he who wishes equity must do equity." On busing, see Wolters, *The Burden of Brown*. Wolters demonstrates that even those black petitioners who sought integration did not always approve of busing as a remedy, but he also provides one example, from his follow-up studies of the five school districts joined in the *Brown* opinion, of integration that did work—in Prince Edward County, Va. That district, which had been among the most militant in segregation, integrated its schools when leading white families joined with leading black families in a good-faith effort to improve all public education. When good faith was demonstrated, Balance of Equity worked—but then, all equity begins with good faith.

66   Robert A. Merhige, Interview, April 3, 1987, quoted in Robert A. Pratt, "School Desegregation in Richmond, Virginia, 1954–1984: A Study of Race and Class in a Southern City" (Ph.D. diss., University of Virginia, 1987), 146. The important point is that such discretion is principled because it captures the reality—the real harm—remedied by the chancellor. As Judge J. Skelly Wright told an interviewer, "But if you don't take it to extremes, I think that it's good to come out with a fair and just result and then look for law to support it." Interview with Jack Bass, January 15, 1979, quoted in Bass, *Unlikely Heroes*, 116. Judge Wright is less constrained by *legal* rules than by *equitable* principles; he seeks mutual fairness, making the world whole.

EPILOGUE

1   See, e.g., Manning Marable, *Race, Reform and Rebellion: The Second Reconstruction in Black America, 1945–1982* (Jackson, Miss., 1984), 168–212. But see Herman Schwartz, "The 1986 and 1987 Affirmative Action Cases: It's All Over but the Shouting," 86 *Michigan Law Review* 524 (1987), for a much more optimistic forecast.

2   See Randall Kennedy, "Persuasion and Distrust: A Comment on the Affirmative Action Debate," 99 *Harvard Law Review* 1327, 1338 (1986), finding subtle racism behind the criticism of affirmative action plans. Nevertheless, when the state of Alabama acted in bad faith, refusing to implement court-ordered plans to remedy the state's own prior discriminatory policy, the Court did not hesitate to order promotion of one black state trooper for every white state trooper promoted. United States v. Paradise, 480 U.S. 149 (1987). In *Paradise*, the Court was willing to wield its equitable powers to the fullest. This is not the same as reading the Constitution in an equitable way.

3   *Brief of Columbia University, Harvard University, Stanford University, and the University of Pennsylvania as Amici Curiae*, Supreme Court of the United States, October Term, 1976, in The Regents of the University of California v. Allan Bakke, 11–16; Andrew Hacker, "Affirmative Action: The New Look," *New York Review of Books*, October 12, 1989, 63.

4   *Brief of Columbia University*, 16–18.

5   See, e.g., DeFunis v. Odegaard, 416 U.S. 312 (1974), a challenge to affirmative action in professional education which was mooted by the time the Court came to hear it.

6   Bernard Schwartz, *Behind Bakke: Affirmative Action and the Supreme Court* (New York, 1988), 1–10.
7   Ibid., 11–26.
8   Smith v. Allwright, 321 U.S. 649 (1944).
9   Colgrove v. Green, 328 U.S. 549 (1946).
10 See Runyon v. McCrary, 427 U.S. 160 (1976), for the limits of the quasi-public exemption. But see Patterson v. McLean Credit Union, 105 L. Ed. 2d 132 (1989), —— U.S. —— (1989), narrowing the reach of the equal protection clause into private discrimination.
11 Schwartz, *Behind Bakke*, 45–46.
12 Chief Justice Warren Burger, Memo of October 21, 1977, 6, 5, reproduced in Schwartz, *Behind Bakke*, Appendix A, 172, 171. See the distinction between "fair shakers," who want the elimination of all racial categorization, and "social engineers," who call for continued reparation, that appears in Morris B. Abrams, "Affirmative Action: Fair Shakers and Social Engineers," 99 *Harvard Law Review* 1312 (1986).
13 Justice William Rehnquist, Memo of November 10–11, 1977, 2, 4, 8, 10, 14, 16–17, reproduced in Schwartz, *Behind Bakke*, Appendix B, 177, 179, 183, 185, 189, 191–92.
14 438 U.S. 265, 309–11, 315–16 (1978). Powell, a practicing lawyer for much of his career, always stayed close to the facts in the particular case before the Court. See Richard H. Fallon, Jr., "Tribute to Lewis F. Powell, Jr.," 101 *Harvard Law Review* 399, 401–3 (1987).
15 448 U.S. 448 (1980).
16 448 U.S. at 463, 472, 483, 485, 489.
17 448 U.S. at 498, 501, 508, 514.
18 448 U.S. at 552.
19 448 U.S. at 548, 554. Justice Stevens has developed his own tests for the constitutionality of these programs. See Note, "Justice Stevens' Equal Protection Jurisprudence," 100 *Harvard Law Review* 1146 (1987).
20 476 U.S. 267 (1986).
21 476 U.S. at 275, 278.
22 City of Richmond v. J. A. Croson Company, 102 L. Ed. 2d 854 (1989), —— U.S. —— (1989).
23 102 L. Ed. 2d at 893.
24 My account of the Minority Business Enterprise set-aside program and the arguments at the trial stage is taken from the Opinion of the Court, 102 L. Ed. 2d 859 et seq.
25 102 L. Ed. 2d 885, 890, 886. In 1977, the first black mayor of Richmond, Henry L. Marsh III, had been more optimistic. At his inaugural, he promised: "Here in Richmond, where free government had its foundations, we should make our city a place where racial justice abounds." Richmond *Times-Dispatch*, March 9, 1977.
26 102 L. Ed. 2d 893 (Stevens, J.), 897 (Kennedy, J.), 899 (Scalia, J.).
27 Justice William Brennan, Memo of November 23, 1977, 2, 5–7, reproduced in Schwartz, *Behind Bakke*, 228, 231–33.
28 Justice Harry Blackmun, Memo of May 1, 1978, 5, 2, 9, 11, reproduced in Schwartz, *Behind Bakke*, 251, 248, 255, 257.
29 Schwartz, *Behind Bakke*, 112.
30 476 U.S. at 298–300, 307. There is a striking continuity between Marshall's dissent in *Wygant* and the Court's decision in *Brown*. The linkage runs through Fifth Circuit Judge John Minor Wisdom's opinion in Local 189 v. United States, 416 F.2d 980 (1969), *cert. denied*, 397 U.S. 919 (1970), holding that a

seniority system of retention that discriminated against minorities violated the Constitution.

31 476 U.S. at 295.

32 476 U.S. at 315, 317–19.

33 Richmond was a target of earlier civil rights cases. See Bradley v. School Board of the City of Richmond, 462 F.2d 1058 (1972), aff'd, 412 U.S. 92 (1973); Richmond v. United States, 422 U.S. 358 (1975), both cited by Marshall, 102 L. Ed. 2d 910.

34 102 L. Ed. 2d 905, 910.

35 102 L. Ed. 2d 910, 922.

36 102 L. Ed. 2d 926. Richmond had the feel of a declaratory judgment, a pronouncement of rights without an enforcement decree. Indeed, the offending city ordinance was no longer in effect when the opinion in Richmond came down. True, a declaratory judgment under Fed. R. Civ. P. Rule 57 and the Declaratory Judgment Act of 1934 must refer to a "case or controversy"; 28 U.S.C.A. 2201, notes 14, 126, 132. There was no longer a case or controversy in Richmond, though there was rumor that the city intended to reenact the ordinance. Croson could have been asking the Court to declare his rights so that he could bring suit against the city for damages, but the city could arguably have asserted its sovereign immunity from such a suit. The Court's opinion did strike at other city affirmative action plans, but Croson was not applying for contracts from these cities, so the Court was not declaring his rights against them or their duties to him. In fact, the Court did not style its opinion a declaratory judgment at all. In the end, the Court might just as well have dismissed the appeal for mootness. Nevertheless, the disassembly of local affirmative action plans is well under way, as state courts endeavor to apply Richmond to their own cities and counties. In Georgia and Wisconsin, the weight of Richmond has brought down set-asides, and more are under scrutiny. See American Subcontractors Association, Georgia Chapter, Inc. v. Atlanta, 259 Ga. 14 (1989), and Milwaukee County Pavers Association v. Fiedler, W.D. Wis., No. 89-C-0177-C, February 27, 1989.

37 Croson and Wygant nonetheless appear to be the harbingers of a retreat of broad proportions from affirmative action. See, e.g., Wards Cove Packing Company, Inc. v. Frank Antonio et al., 104 L. Ed. 2d 733 (1989), —— U.S. —— (1989), and Patterson. I do not believe that we can read the majority opinions in such cases as qualified affirmations of minority set-asides, nor do I agree that "The Supreme Court has rejected the notions that race-conscious affirmative action measures adopted by a local government or other body must as a constitutional matter be limited to redressing the effects of that government's or body's own past discrimination, or to making whole the actual victims of identified incidents of past discrimination" (italics added). Joint Statement, "Constitutional Scholars' Statement on Affirmative Action after City of Richmond v. J. A. Croson Co.," 98 Yale Law Journal 1711, 1713 (1989).

38 Here the historian waits upon the legal academic. In the course of his attempt to harmonize the constitutional principles of equality and liberty, Ronald Dworkin argued "that any appealing defense of the morally important liberties must proceed . . . not by insisting that liberty is more important than equality, but by showing that these [privileged] liberties must be protected according to the best view of what distribution of property treats each citizen with equal concern." For Dworkin that concern is metered by "equality of resources," a phrase that recalls the older and still resonant "equality of opportunity." Dworkin's language aspires to the higher equity, a communal justice captured in his notion of a "fair share of resources available to all." Dworkin also recog-

nizes that the allotment of such shares can only proceed in a "community of equal concern," based on "true costs" and "authentic" estimates of human need and human desire. Above all, the law must treat everyone "with equal concern." Dworkin, "What Is Equality? Part B: The Place of Liberty," 73 *Iowa Law Review* 1, 2–3 (1987).

The critical insight in Dworkin's account is neither his ideal of redistributive equality (that is as old as *epieikeia* itself), nor his enumeration of privileged liberties (constitutional jurists have been preparing such lists throughout our republican experience), but the concept Dworkin uses to align liberty and equality: "equal concern." When working courts are asked to issue decrees in equity—injunctions barring operation of affirmative action programs, for example—equal concern implicates strict scrutiny of a deeper and broader nature than "equal protection"—a fairness-rooted historical context, rich in social sensitivity. An equitable "equal concern" allows a bigger piece of social and economic reality to come into the Court's calculations. Equal protection is a constitutional requirement; equal concern is the equitable maxim nestled within the constitutional mandate.

I am indebted for the phrase "bigger piece of social reality" and for much more on this subject to Lewis Sargentish, "Complex Enforcement," ms. in author's possession. In his *Belonging to America: Equal Citizenship and the Constitution* (New Haven, Conn., 1989), 12, Kenneth L. Karst suggests that a constitutional adjudication that fully deployed "equal citizenship" would begin by judges "widen[ing] their inquiries to include more in the way of social and historical context." Here, "equal citizenship," like Dworkin's "equal concern," is inherently equitable in tenor.

No student of equity—surely not the critics of court-mandated integration at any rate—can deny that the chancellor can always refuse to intervene when a "sound discretion" counsels restraint. See, e.g., Hurd v. Hodge, 334 U.S. 24, 36 (1948) (Frankfurter, J., concurring). He may send the claimants to law for a complete and adequate remedy. He may give them a little time and encourage them to work out their differences. He may prod other branches of government to take a "second look" at the evil, believing that more effective relief may come from these sources than from him. He may not, in good conscience, close his eyes to palpable harms. He may not deny reality. Equal protection can be read as a formal mandate to ignore race, including the fact of past racial degradation and discrimination, and its harms. Prudential—judicially originated—doctrines of "state action" and "privacy" may trigger such formalistic visions of equal protection. The limits on equal concern are never formalist, because equal concern is rooted in equitable fairness. Instead, equal concern marries the two equities, using technical powers of the chancellor in the service of the higher equity of mutual fairness, trusteeship, equality, and reality.

INDEX